e

EXPERIENCING SERIES

EXPERIENCING CIVIL PROCEDURE

■

James Moliterno

Vincent Bradford Professor of Law
Washington & Lee University

WEST®

MAT#41185054

© 2013 LEG, Inc. d/b/a West Academic Publishing

610 Opperman Drive
St. Paul, MN 55123
1-800-313-9378

Printed in the United States of America

ISBN: 978-0-314-27777-0

To all Legal Education reform fellow travelers.

Table of Contents

Table of Cases

The principal cases are in bold type. Cases cited or discussed in the text are in roman type. References are to pages. Cases cited in principal cases and within other quoted materials are not included.

Table of Statutes,
Rules and Constitutional Provisions

Preface

THIS BOOK IS THE FIRST in a new series designed to blend traditional materials and teaching styles with experiential education materials and teaching styles. The books in the series will cover the mainstream courses in legal education. The books are not supplements but instead are meant to cover full courses.

This book, *Experiencing Civil Procedure*, includes the core civil procedure cases, excerpted as they are in traditional casebooks. It includes the necessary statutes and rules and obviates the need for students to purchase an additional statutory/rule supplement. These materials are meant to support teaching the substance of civil procedure law in traditional modes. Much of the course supported by this book will be indistinguishable from traditional Civil Procedure courses.

But this book then departs from tradition by including fewer notes and additional readings from law reviews and treatises. Those materials are generally available and may be accessed by those who wish to read them. Instead of those materials, the book includes scenarios and experiential assignments. These scenarios and experiential assignments are meant to place the student in the role of lawyer, doing civil procedure work done by beginning lawyers.

Students learn from traditional teaching methods, but they gain greater insights into the meaning, the theory, and the function of the law when they must use the law. Many students say that they learned law when they later used it in clinics, externships, or summer work experiences. Of course they did learn during the traditional course, but in a way they did not realize the gain in knowledge until they later used the law they learned in their courses. In this book's design, students learn the substance of the law and immediately use is. Closing the time between acquisition of knowledge and its use further solidifies the gains students can make in their advance toward becoming professionals.

— James Moliterno
March 2013

EXPERIENCING CIVIL PROCEDURE

CHAPTER 1

An Overview of the Litigation Process and This Book

THIS BOOK IS MEANT to support a course in Civil Procedure in which students are active, engaged participants, doing basic civil procedure work of lawyers along the way.

There are three main types of materials covered in the Civil Procedure course. First and most prominent, much of the Civil Procedure course is rule-bound. The Federal Rules of Civil Procedure, first adopted in 1938, govern most of what happens in civil litigation in federal courts. Nearly all the states have procedure codes modeled on the federal rules. They are the basis of chapters 4, 5, 6, 7, 8, and 9 of this book. Rules can be tedious and difficult to read, but there is no substitute for carefully parsing the words of the FRCP. Most of the answers to civil procedure questions are found in the language of the rules themselves. Second, the U.S. Constitution and statutes form the basis for some topics in the Civil Procedure course. Mainly, they govern the fundamental concepts of jurisdiction (chapter 2), the delicate federalism topic of the use of state law in federal courts (chapter 3), and the basis for the rules material governing the jury trial right (the 7th amendment in chapter 9). Always, the due process clauses of the 5th and 14th amendments are a backdrop for the fairness of process across the range of Civil Procedure topics. Third, some general legal principles, mostly from the common law, have developed that make the civil dispute resolution process work. The doctrine of preclusion is the best example (chapter 10).

But so, too, are the concepts relating to burdens of proof and presumptions (chapter 8). When constitutional and statutory authorities are the main focus, the Civil Procedure course sometimes feels like a Constitutional Law course. When the general legal principles are being studied, it feels like a common law course such as Property or Torts. And when, as is true for the vast majority of the course, the rules are at the center of discussion, it feels like nothing else, except perhaps the parts of the Criminal Law course in which the Model Penal Code is being studied or parts of the Contracts course in which the Uniform Commercial Code is being studied. Noticing what part of this course you happen to be in can be quite helpful to your studies.

A. How a Civil Action Works

Rule Materials

Rule 1: Scope and Purpose

These rules govern the procedure in all civil actions and proceedings in the United States district courts, except as stated in Rule 81. They should be construed and administered to secure the just, speedy, and inexpensive determination of every action and proceeding.

Rule 2: One Form of Action

There is one form of action—the civil action.

1. Some Design Questions: If you were designing a civil dispute resolution system, how would you answer the following questions?

1. Should the plaintiff get to choose among alternative courts to hear case?

2. What should start the process?

3. Should defendant be notified? How?

4. Should defendant ever have a say in where a case is brought?

5. What should happen after the matter begins?

6. How, if at all, should information be formally gathered and exchanged?

7. Should all cases go to trial?

8. If not, which ones should go to a trial? How should other cases be resolved?

9. At trial, what should happen when the evidence seems like a tie?

10. What about juries? Yes or no, always or sometimes? Should a jury decision have to be unanimous or should majority be enough?

11. How should "judgments"/ results work? What should happen after a party wins?

12. What if a related claim is brought later?

13. What if a similar case has been decided elsewhere?

2. A Checklist: In the U.S. model of civil litigation, no two cases proceed in exactly the same way. But it is possible to form a general chronology of events of civil litigation understanding that there are many exceptions that cause the general order to be different. Here is a sort of checklist of the steps of a civil action with the relevant Federal Rules of Civil Procedure listed in parentheses. Use it to form a sense of where the law and this course will lead you.

STEPS	FEDERAL RULE
• Complaint	(7, 8, 9, 10)
• Service of Summons and Complaint	(4)
• Default	(55)
• Answer and Counterclaim	(same as complaint)
• Joinder Issues	(14, 19, 20, 21, 22, 24)
• Answer to Counterclaims, Cross-Claims, Third-Party Claims, if any	(same as complaint)
• Mandatory, Initial Discovery Exchange	(26)
• Scheduling Order	(16)
• Amendments to Pleadings	(15)
• Motion to Dismiss	(12)

STEPS	FEDERAL RULE
• Interrogatories	(33)
• Depositions	(30)
• Requests for Admissions and Production of Documents	(36, 34)
• Discovery Sanctions	(37)
• Various Non-Dispositive Motions	(7)
• Motion for Summary Judgment	(7, 56)
• Pretrial Order	(16)
• Judgment as a Matter Of Law	(50)
• Proposed Findings of Fact and Conclusions of Law/ Jury Instructions	(51, 52)
• Verdict	(49)
• Judgment Order	(54)
• Post-Trial Motions	(59, 60)
• Notice of Appeal	(Federal Rule of Appellate Procedure 3)

3. Basic Court Structure: This simple chart (opposite) indicates the basic court structure in the United States and the lines of direct appeal. The names of courts vary from state to state, but in generic terms, most state court systems follow the pattern on this chart. A few states have no intermediate court of appeals. Notice that the direct appeal from the state court of last resort is to the U.S. Supreme Court, not to the federal district court.

Figure 1-1: Basic United States Court Structure

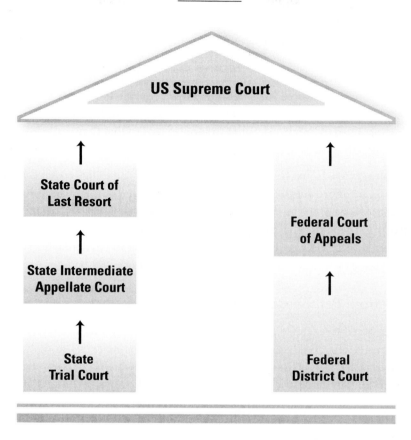

There is at least one federal district court (the federal trial court) that sits in each state (for example, The United States District Court for the District of North Dakota). Many states have two or more that are set up with geographical coverage of a portion of a state (for example, The United States District Court for the Southern District of Ohio). There are 11 federal courts of appeal (for example, The United States Court of Appeals for the Sixth Circuit), each of which has jurisdiction over appeals from the federal district courts that sit in a specified group of states. There is also a court of appeals for the District of Columbia (The United States Court of Appeals for the District of Columbia Circuit) and a special one for certain kinds of federal cases (The Federal Circuit). Appeals from the federal courts of appeal, sometimes referred to in shorthand as the "federal circuit courts," go to the U.S. Supreme Court. You can find a map of the federal court system at *http://lawschool. westlaw.com/federalcourt/federalcourt.asp*

B. A Civil Procedure Overview

Civil Procedure is the road map for litigated matters. This summary will use the federal model as its focus. Most states have modeled their civil procedure systems on the Federal Rules of Civil Procedure. Some questions, notably subject matter jurisdiction, arise almost exclusively in federal court, because the federal courts are courts of limited jurisdiction, while state courts (at least the full system of any state's courts) are courts of general jurisdiction. Needless to say, even nonlitigators need to know procedure to some extent so that they can predict the consequences of choices made in transactional documents and such.

This overview is just that. You will study each of the topics covered in this overview in far more depth in the chapters to come, and you will get the opportunity to use some of the knowledge along the way as well. For now, this overview will give you the lay of the civil procedure land as if you were viewing it from 30,000 feet above. You may find it helpful to refer back to particular sections of this overview as you study the specific chapters to come.

Jurisdiction: Personal and Subject Matter

To proceed to exercise power, courts must have both jurisdiction over the subject matter of a civil action and jurisdiction over the parties to that action. A related topic, venue, sets parameters for determining which courts among those having jurisdiction must be chosen as the geographic location of the civil matter's filing. 28 U.S.C. 1391.

Subject Matter Jurisdiction

Subject matter jurisdiction represents the court's power over the type of matter that is the subject of a civil action. The court raises the issue of subject matter at any time. The parties have no power to agree to ignore a flaw in the court's subject matter jurisdiction. See FRCP 12(b)(1); 12(h)(3).

Personal Jurisdiction

Personal jurisdiction is a court's power over the parties to the litigation. Unlike subject matter jurisdiction, personal jurisdiction may be waived by a party who voluntarily appears in court or fails to object to the court's personal jurisdiction in a timely way. FRCP 12(b)(2). Personal jurisdiction is an issue in every federal and state court matter. States have statutes granting their courts personal jurisdiction. Some of these are called "long-arm" statutes and they seek to define the instances when a court has personal jurisdiction over a defendant, for example, when the defendant has committed a tort within the jurisdiction. Other jurisdiction-granting statutes give the state's courts all the personal jurisdiction power that is permissible under the due process clause of the federal constitution. The due process clause effectively defines the outer limit of personal jurisdiction. A court's exercise of too much such power is simply unfair to a defendant and offends the federal due process clause.

To issue orders that are binding on parties, a court must have jurisdiction over them. Plaintiffs voluntarily submit to the court in which they file a complaint, so the court always has personal jurisdiction over plaintiffs. But defendants are being ordered to appear and answer, and there must be a determination of the court's power over them.

If a defendant is served with a summons and complaint while physically in the state where the court sits, the court has jurisdiction. This is sometimes referred to as "gotcha jurisdiction" because it would apply to even an entirely transient presence in the state by a defendant who had no other contacts with the state.

When a defendant has committed a tort or entered a contract with a state and that is the matter in controversy, the state's courts may exercise personal jurisdiction over that defendant.

When neither of the preceding circumstances is present, the question is whether the defendant has "minimum contacts" with the forum state, thereby allowing that state's courts to exercise personal jurisdiction over the defendant. *International Shoe v. Washington*, 326 U.S. 310 (1945); *World-Wide Volkswagon v. Woodson*, 444 U.S. 286 (1980)[1] There is no quick and dirty rule for satisfying the minimum contacts test. If a defendant has availed itself of the benefits of doing business in a state, then the test will likely be met.

Removal

When an action is filed in state court, but could have supported federal subject matter jurisdiction, a defendant may usually remove the action to the federal court that sits in that state and district. 28 U.S.C. 1441. (Defendants may not remove when the action was filed in the defendant's home state courts and the federal subject matter jurisdiction would have been based on diversity of citizenship.)

---

1 One might think that the defendants in these two cases could have chosen more jurisdictionally narrow names for their companies if they were going to contest state court personal jurisdiction, essentially contesting whether they were "present" outside their home state.

Defendants often find removal to be a litigation advantage, especially when the defendant's lawyers are unaccustomed to litigating in the particular state's courts or when the federal court has a reputation for being less "plaintiff-friendly" than the particular state court in question.

The Litigation Process

Beyond questions of jurisdiction and federalism, litigators need to understand the civil procedure concepts involved in the litigation process. Every court paper mentioned in this summary begins with a caption. See FRCP Form 1. For every possible document, look first for a form in the appendix to the Federal Rules of Civil Procedure. They are excellent starting places for creating your own documents.

Pleadings

Pleadings begin the litigation process by giving notice to the defendant of the plaintiff's claim, and by joining fact issues when the defendant responds to the plaintiff's allegation. Further, the pleadings allow defendants to assert affirmative defenses, state counterclaims against the plaintiffs, assert cross-claims against codefendants, and join additional parties pursuant to third party claims. The level of factual material necessary in the claim of any kind is undergoing fairly dramatic revision. *Bell Atlantic v. Twombly*, 550 U.S. 544 (2007); *Ashcroft v. Iqbal*, 129 S. Ct. 1937 (2009). More on this issue under the "motion to dismiss" heading.

In theory, pleadings need only make a "short and plain statement" showing that the pleader is entitled to relief. FRCP 8. The federal rules of civil procedure effected a change of previous fact-intensive pleading to "notice pleading." The *Twombly* and *Iqbal* cases are causing plaintiffs to be more fact-descriptive than the rules themselves appear to require.

A complaint states the plaintiff's claims against the defendant. It must recite the basis of the court's subject matter and personal jurisdiction over the action. See FRCP Form 7. A complaint should recite facts that, if true, entitle the plaintiff to relief. It should recite allegations one fact at a time, numbered paragraph by numbered paragraph. When multiple claims are being made, the complaint should be divided into separate sections for each claim. It is appropriate to incorporate by reference any allegations, once made in the complaint, that are necessary for a subsequent claim.

A complaint must also recite the facts necessary to evaluate the plaintiff's damages or other relief sought. It must conclude with a "request for relief" in which the plaintiff asks the court for the relief the plaintiff believes she is entitled to.

An answer may include counterclaims against the plaintiff, cross-claims against codefendants, and third party claims against defendants the defendant seeks to join in the action. FRCP 8, 13, 14. It should address each numbered paragraph in the plaintiff's complaint. For each, the answer must do one of three things: admit the allegation; deny the allegation; or state that the defendant lacks sufficient knowledge to admit or deny. An admission operates to conclude that fact matter in the case in the plaintiff's favor. A denial or a "lack of information" response places the plaintiff's allegation in issue. This narrowing of fact issues begins the process of focusing the court's attention on what will be necessary to resolve the action.

When the defendant states a counterclaim in the answer, the plaintiff files a reply, which operates as an answer to the defendant's counterclaim and follows the rules for admitting and denying allegations that apply to answers. When a defendant states a cross-claim or a third party claim, the cross-defendant or the third party defendant answers by the same rules that apply to an answer.

To state a third party claim and join that third party, a defendant must comply with the standards articulated in FRCP 14 for third party complaints. In short, the claim must not be a claim that suggests that the third party defendant is liable to the plaintiff instead of the defendant; rather, the claim must state that the third party defendant is liable to the defendant for amounts that the defendant may be liable to the plaintiff. The typical scenario is an indemnity claim in which the third party defendant has by contract agreed to stand in the defendant's shoes for purposes of certain liabilities the defendant may have to the plaintiff. Such agreements are common in construction or parts- supply contracts. The subcontractor or parts supplier may agree in their contract to reimburse the manufacturer or the general contractor for any damages that result from failures by the parts supplier or subcontractor.

Additionally, the defendant needs to satisfy subject matter and personal jurisdiction requirements with respect to a third party claim. It is as if the defendant were filing his own civil action in the court. The court must have subject matter and personal jurisdiction over the claim and third party defendant to proceed.

Every pleading, and other court papers requiring a lawyer's signature, implicates the certification requirements of FRCP 11. FRCP 11 requires the signing lawyer to certify that she has engaged a reasonable factual investigation and that the pleading is fairly supported by facts and legal theories so that the paper is not frivolous and is not being filed for an improper purpose. A party may be liable for money and other sanctions for violating FRCP 11. A party requesting FRCP 11 sanctions must give the recipient 21 days notice prior to filing the motion for sanctions. During that period, the recipient party may amend their paper to remedy the issue being raised regarding the flaw in their paper. The use of FRCP 11 is a popular litigation strategy. It disrupts the recipient of a sanctions motion. It must be remembered that signing a motion for sanctions under FRCP 11 *itself* implicates the duties imposed by FRCP 11.

Pleadings may be amended under certain circumstances. FRCP 15. A party may, once, amend a pleading within 21 days after serving it or within 21 days after the opponent has served a responsive pleading or a motion under FRCP 12 (b, e, or f). This one-time amendment may be done "no-questions-asked." If the pleader has missed these deadlines for freely amending, then she may amend with the written consent of the opponent or with leave of court. Leave of court should be freely given when justice so requires. Importantly, amendments most commonly only relate back in time so as to be treated as if filed when the pleading being amended was filed when the amendment asserts a claim that arose from the same conduct or transaction from which the original pleading arose. This "relation-back" concept can be critically important when the statute of limitations has run during the time between the initial filing and the amendment. FRCP 15(c).

Motions to Dismiss

A motion to dismiss may be filed for any of the listed reasons in FRCP 12(b). The most common are based on the court's lack of subject matter jurisdiction (FRCP 12(b)(1)), personal jurisdiction over the defendant (FRCP12(b)(2)), and the plaintiff's failure to state a claim upon which relief may be granted (FRCP 12(b)(6)). Any of these, if successful, ends the action at the pleadings stage when in all likelihood no discovery has occurred. Each of these operates on the pleadings in isolation. In other words, on the face of the plaintiff's complaint, the court lacks jurisdiction or the law provides no relief for the sum of the plaintiff's allegations, even if all are true.

Timing of these motions matters. FRCP 12(g) and (h). A motion claiming that the court lacks subject matter jurisdiction can be made at any time and can-not be waived by any action of the defendant or plaintiff. A motion contesting personal jurisdiction must be made before the defendant submits to the personal power of the court by entering a formal appearance and contesting the allegations in the plaintiff's complaint. The motion for failure to state a claim may be made before an answer, in conjunction with an answer, or later if cast as a motion for judgment under FRCP 12(c).

The motion to dismiss for failure to state a claim may have more likelihood of success since the *Twombly* and *Iqbal* cases. In each of these, the Court made clear that a Complaint must include more than mere allegations that the plaintiff can satisfy the elements of the cause of action. Since *Iqbal*, it is clear that these requirements apply to all kinds of civil actions. The requirement now is that the allegations in a plaintiff's complaint make it "plausible" that the facts will satisfy the elements of the cause of action. Lower federal courts have been dismissing claims that in the past would have passed on to the next phase of litigation and entered discovery.

When a motion to dismiss is being considered by the court, the facts must be viewed as if all allegations in the plaintiff's complaint are true and reasonable inferences have been drawn in the plaintiff's favor. In other words, a motion to dismiss asks whether the law provides relief for a plaintiff when what the plaintiff says is true. If a law student were horribly offended that his Civil Procedure professor wore blue jeans and a T-shirt rather than dress slacks, a coat, and tie to class, the student might attempt to state that as a claim in the local court, demanding significant damages for the student's offended sensibilities about professorial formality. The professor would no doubt file a motion to dismiss for failure to state a claim upon which relief may be granted, asserting that even if what the plaintiff-student said is all true, the law does not provide relief for such a perceived harm. The motion would be granted.

When there is a flaw in the plaintiff's theory of recovery, a motion to dismiss is an appropriate vehicle to challenge the claim. If successful, the litigation has been ended at the earliest possible stage.

Discovery

Despite courts' significant efforts to rein in the length, cost, and complexities in the discovery process, discovery remains the chief expense and time-consumption of most litigated matters. The US form of discovery is a major distinction between our litigation process and that of civil law systems in most of the rest of the world. Foreign lawyers and parties blanch at the length and intensity of US discovery.

The major devices for discovery are well known: depositions, written and oral; interrogatories; requests for admission; and inspection and production of documents. There are others for specialized circumstances. This summary will discuss formal discovery, but informal forms of discovery should never be ignored. Informal witness interviews, public records searches, Internet searches, visual inspections of places and things, social network information-mining, and more, all provide invaluable information to the litigator.

The threshold standard for the scope of discovery is "any nonprivileged matter that is relevant to any party's claim or defense." FRCP 26(b). The court may expand the scope to include any matter relevant to the *subject matter* of the action. To be discoverable, material need not be admissible as evidence as long as it is reasonably calculated to lead to admissible evidence. The scope of discovery is very broad.

Many pieces of information are subject to mandatory, automatic disclosure, very early in the litigation. FRCP 26(a). These mandatory disclosures come in two main phases, initial disclosures and pretrial disclosures. They include contact information on people who are likely to have relevant information about the action, calculations of plaintiff's damages, copies of documents that the disclosing party is likely to use to support her claims or defenses, and more. Much of this material would be discovered by use of interrogatories and requests for production of documents if it was not subject to the relatively new mandatory disclosure requirements.

Parties must disclose the name of experts they expect to call as a witness at trial, and those persons must produce a written report summarizing their findings. FRCP 26(a)(2).

Beyond the various mandatory disclosures, an initial conference will be held at which the court will order volume and time limits for discovery. An end date for all discovery, and limits on the number of interrogatories, depositions and requests for admission and production of documents will typically be ordered at this conference.

From here, the parties will proceed mostly without court supervision to pose interrogatories, requests for admission and production of documents, and take depositions within the terms of the court's order. The terms on which each device may be used can be found by reading the appropriate specific discovery rule. FRCP 27-36. Local court rules will also include such limitations. They may be found on court websites. No good litigator fails to search the local court rules. When disputes occur, parties may file motions for a protective order or motions to compel discovery. FRCP 26(c). Sanctions may be imposed by the court against particularly belligerent or recalcitrant parties for their abuses of the discovery process. FRCP 37. The sanctions can range from repeated orders to cooperate to money sanctions to dismissal of claims or defenses.

Motion Practice Generally

In every motion, a party asks the court to do something. In response, the court issues an order, granting or denying the request in whole or in part. We are very familiar with many standard motions that are filed frequently: motions to dismiss; motions for summary judgment; motions to quash a discovery request; motions for sanctions; motions to exclude or admit evidence. But motions can run the spectrum from these very common ones all the way to whatever request of a court the party might have occasion to make. Some unusual ones filed in actual cases include the very poorly received "Motion to Kiss My Ass," one litigant's effort to require a opponent to sit down and consider a settlement proposal, "Motion for Lunch," and one lawyer's effort to enhance everyone's courtroom experience, "Motion for Better Coffee."

There is really no limit to the range of possible motions. After an opportunity for the nonmoving party to respond and possibly a hearing, a court will enter an order to respond to the motion's request. Remember that motions and orders are partners in this sense. For every motion, there should be an order.

Motions for Summary Judgment

The motion for summary judgment is a key, pretrial stage for ending litigation. FRCP 56. At this stage, most if not all discovery has been completed but there has been no trial, so the facts can come into play to some extent but not completely. A party is entitled to summary judgment, ending the litigation before trial, when there are no genuine issues of material fact and the moving party is entitled to judgment as a matter of law. FRCP 56. A summary judgment motion may be partially granted, ending one or more pending claims but not the entire action.

There are no genuine issues of material fact when either of two basic circumstances pertain. First, the parties may essentially agree on the facts of the matter, in which case, there is no genuine dispute. Second, the plaintiff may have been unable through the discovery process to generate any evidence that would be admissible at trial on one or more of the elements of his claim. When this happens, the moving party is essentially saying that the plaintiff cannot meet his burden of production when trial comes. That is, he cannot produce evidence sufficient to support a jury finding on every element of his claim. If this is the case, there is no "genuine" dispute about the facts plaintiff lacks, and the court can proceed to evaluate the legal merits of what remains, often granting summary judgment for the defendant.

In cases that rest on scientific or technical evidence, a motion will typically occur at which the admissibility of the plaintiff's scientific or technical evidence will be evaluated. In federal court and many state courts, this motion is called a *Daubert* motion. If the defendant is successful at the *Daubert* motion, then a summary judgment motion is soon to follow. It will argue that the plaintiff now lacks admissible evidence on the issue his scientific evidence would have addressed.

Less commonly, the situation can be flipped, with the plaintiff moving for summary judgment and sometimes based on the court's rejection of the defendant's scientific evidence. Successful summary judgment motions for plaintiffs are much less common.

Once it is determined that there is no genuine issue of material fact, the court can simply evaluate the legal merit of the set of facts that pertains. If there is no need to conduct a trial because there are no fact issues to be resolved, considerable cost savings will occur.

Judgments After Trial

Trials have become rare events. More than 90% of disputes are resolved without resort to litigation. Of those in which a complaint is filed, the vast majority are resolved by negotiation during litigation, motions to dismiss or for summary judgment.

Once in trial, judgment can result from a jury verdict (or in a bench trial, the court's findings of fact and conclusions of law, FRCP 52) or from a motion for judgment. FRCP 50. Motions for judgment may be made at the close of the plaintiff's case, at the close of all evidence submission, and they may be renewed even after the jury verdict is announced. New trial motions and motions for relief from a judgment may also be filed within strictly followed time limits and circumstances. FRCP 59, 60.

Aside from the jury verdict or a court's findings and conclusions, the chief form of judgment during trial results from motions for judgment. A motion for judgment should be granted when the party bearing the burden of production (usually the plaintiff) has failed to meet that burden. In other words, a plaintiff has failed to offer admissible evidence sufficient to support a finding in its favor. A court may grant such a motion in whole or in part, precluding jury consideration of one or more issues or the entire matter.

Preclusion Doctrine

Any system of dispute resolution needs a way of limiting repeat presentation of the same claims. The old names for these doctrines were *res judicata* and *collateral estoppel.* These names are still commonly used. The more modern terms are *claim preclusion* and *issue preclusion,* respectively.

In the simplest situation, a plaintiff who has made a claim in litigation and had judgment entered against her cannot bring the same claim again. This is the simplest form of claim preclusion. Expanding slightly, when a plaintiff brings a claim and fails to bring a very closely related claim in a first litigation, the plaintiff cannot later bring the closely related claim, no matter what the outcome of the first litigation was. In the classic example, a plaintiff crashed her motorcycle as a result of a pothole in a city-maintained street. Initially, she brought a claim against the city for damage to the motorcycle. After winning on that claim, she brought a claim for her personal injuries that had resulted from the same crash. The court said she was precluded from doing so because she had failed to bring the two closely related claims in the first litigation. All of these closely related claims are said to have "merged" into the first judgment, precluding further litigation of the same claims.

Issue preclusion affects a single issue in a case rather than the entire claim, although often enough, that single issue determines the entire outcome of the matter. When an issue has been fully litigated and a party has lost on that issue, the losing party cannot relitigate the same issue against the same or an analogously situated party in later litigation. Let's say that a law student has brought a claim against a bar review course provider for fraud in its advertisements, and the law student wins that claim after fully litigating the issues. In a later action brought by a different law student against the same bar review provider claiming the same frauds in the same advertisements, the bar review provider will be precluded from contesting the already-decided fraud issue. Thus, issue preclusion.

The form of issue preclusion described in the preceding paragraph would not have been permitted until the Supreme Court decision in *Parklane Hosiery v. Shore*, 439 U.S. 322 (1979). Prior to that decision, and still in a few states, there can be no use of issue preclusion without "mutuality." In other words, a party wishing to use issue preclusion doctrine cannot do so unless she would have been precluded by an opposite decision in the initial litigation. The second law student, who was not a party to the first litigation described in the preceding paragraph, would not have been precluded had the first law student lost the fraud issue. In federal court and in most states, mutuality is no longer a bar to the use of issue preclusion in most instances.

Preclusion doctrine often comes into play in mass tort actions, where 20 injured passengers in a bus crash sue the bus company for negligence, 4000 residents of a community claim injury from a contaminated water supply, 10,000 miners claim diseases have resulted from exposure to chemicals or dust, or 100,000 customers of a credit card company claim damages attributable to unlawful credit practices, and then the various claimants state claims in sequential litigation.

Once a defendant loses an issue in one such litigation, he will likely be precluded from relitigating that same issue in subsequent litigation against analogous claimants.

C. Example Documents

Examples of documents are provided in this book. Some are forms from the Federal Rules of Civil Procedure Appendix of Forms. Some are documents drawn from the dockets of actual cases. Most of these are from a case called *Two Old Hippies LLC v. Catch the Bus LLC*. This case is somewhat more complicated than the hypothetical ones you will be working on, but seeing an actual document can be very useful in forming a mental framework for producing your own work. The example documents are not exemplars. In other words, they are not presented as perfect. Your professor is likely to have preferences that are not met by the examples. So do not use them as if they were a model to be followed in every detail. Rather, use them as examples of actual documents prepared by lawyers and filed in an actual case.

D. Basic Materials for Scenarios

Throughout this book, you will be asked to perform various lawyer activities that illustrate the civil procedure concepts under study. Most of those activities will arise from work to be done on one of the following three cases. Additional facts may be added as later assignments require them. For purposes of these exercises, "year 0" is the first year of the academic year during which you are using this book. So, if you were using this book in the fall semester of 2013, year 0 would be 2013. Likewise if you were using this book in spring semester 2014 (academic year 2013-14), year 0 would still be 2013. Other years are indicated with plus and minus years from year 0. So, in this example, in either of the two semesters, year –3 would be 2010.

EXPERIENTIAL ASSIGNMENTS

1. Tort case

On July 16, year 0, Carlene Frensch was walking down the outdoor/picnic supplies aisle of the local Nickel n Dime store in Cary, Ohio. As she leaned over to select a package of plastic plates, she slipped and fell. Her already ailing back slammed to the hard floor and she could not get up. A customer called an ambulance and she was taken to the emergency room. After a day of tests, doctors determined that surgery was needed. Carlene was hospitalized for two weeks and returned home with a back brace, a walker, and major medical debt. The combined hospital, doctor and medical equipment bills owed shortly after her hospital release was $139,476.

Nickel 'n Dime is a chain of retail stores selling low-priced household goods. It is incorporated in Delaware and has its principal offices in Pittsburgh, Pennsylvania. It operates 127 stores in 17 states, including 12 Ohio stores.

Carlene does not know with certainty what she slipped on. She remembers seeing a can of lighter fluid on the floor just up the aisle on which she was shopping when she fell. She believes that the can may have been leaking and she may have stepped in some of the fluid a dozen steps or so before she slipped and fell. As she lay on the floor in pain, she remembers hearing a store employee say, "I told Joey to clean that up!"

For purposes of work on this scenario, assume that the general law of torts applies, including the basic elements of a negligence action: duty, breach, causation, and damage.

2. Contract case

Cari Pearsall is a young artist in Wisconsin who makes beaded bracelets and necklaces. She had often attended craft fairs and her products were wellreceived. She decided to start a small business, selling her wares on-line. She designed a simple website (Carisbeads.com) and orders started to roll in. Cari's birthdate is August 8, year-18.

Becky Cash loves beaded jewelry and owns a small shop on the beach in Duck, North Carolina. While visiting her daughter in Lynchburg, Virginia, Becky, sitting at her daughter's computer and playing on the Internet, encountered Carisbeads.com. Becky fell in love with Cari's products and on May 16, year 0, Becky ordered 100 pieces for a total cost of $2500.

Cari had never sold 100 pieces in a single order and was not capable of producing enough product to fill the order without expansion. She hired four workers, trained them in her production techniques and filled the order, all from her own home in Eau Claire, Wisconsin.

Back in North Carolina, Becky displayed Cari's products and sold them out within a month at a retail total value of $5200. Becky was thrilled and saw Cari's products as a gold mine.

Becky rented additional space near her current shop under a two year lease at a rent of $700 per month, and devoted it to beaded jewelry, calling the new shop Becky's Beads by Cari. Now, on July 15, year 0, once again on one of her regular visits to her daughter's home in Virginia, Becky took a bold step and ordered 4000 pieces from Carisbeads.com. She paid Cari $82,000 and prints the simple Internet receipt.

Cari was a bit overwhelmed. Although her business had been advertised over the Internet, she had received only 184 orders for jewelry, mostly one or two pieces at a time. Becky's was the only major order, and none of her orders had come from North Carolina. Cari accepted Becky's order, deposited the payment and bought $47,000 worth of beads from a supplier of beads in Wisconsin, Wiscbeads, also a sole-proprietorship. Cari paid down her credit card debt with the remaining money from Becky's order.

Two weeks into her effort to fill the order, on August 14, year 0, Cari fell ill and was hospitalized. She contacted Becky and delivered the regrettable news that she would not be able to fill the order and had no money with which to repay Becky.

For purposes of work on this problem, assume that the general law of contracts applies.

3. Advanced, blended case

Terry Williams is a footloose young person searching for a purpose, with an affinity for environmental causes (Terry joined Greenpeace two months ago) as well as a good fight against what Terry perceives to be "Big Business against the Little Guy". One of his favorite songs is an old Creedence Clearwater hit, "Lodi."

In the song, the character is repeatedly "stuck in Lodi," because he has enough money to get to the town, but can never seem to earn enough to get out. After bumming around for five years, Terry has taken a liking to Emporia, Virginia and the recreational sports the area offers. Consequently, Emporia, Virginia, has been Terry's home for one year, longer than anywhere else he has lived since high school. Terry was hired by the owner of FastGas, Gerry Mancini, upon Terry's arrival in Emporia in May, year-1. There was no written contract. Terry indicated a predisposition to wanderlust and was quite agreeable to a handshake deal, starting at an hourly rate of $7.25/hour (or the current minimum wage).

Gerry Mancini has owned FastGas since year-8, ever since Mancini moved to Emporia. Mancini owned a gas station in Oklahoma before moving to Emporia. Rumors that Mancini had problems in Oklahoma and moved quickly out of town before any charges were brought against him have circulated through Emporia. Mancini ingratiated himself with the leaders of Emporia from the time of his arrival. Billy Rossland, the town mayor, became a particularly good friend of Mancini's.

Terry claims the pump used to transfer the gas is defective and places Terry (when Terry has to operate the pump) and any customers in the vicinity in danger whenever it is used. Terry says he complained about the leaky pump to Mancini and when nothing was done he placed a note to the same effect on Mancini's cluttered office desk. When still nothing happened to repair the pump, Terry contacted the state regulatory commission whose job it is to inspect facilities of various kinds for safety. The commission sent an inspector, and concluded there was no safety violation. The inspection occurred on May 23, year 0; Terry was fired by Mancini on May 25, year 0.

Terry wants to sue Mancini, insisting that Terry was a good worker and was fired only because Terry exposed Mancini's dangerous pumping method. Mancini will deny Terry's claim, insisting that Terry knew that the job was temporary, and that Terry had been driving customers away with long speeches on the harmfulness and greed of the gasoline industry. The market has dropped, and since Mancini had to cut back on employees to keep the station's profit margins up, Terry was a logical choice to be let go.

Williams filed a complaint about the firing with the Virginia Department of Labor and received the following communication in response, satisfying the requirement that he exhaust administrative remedies before filing a civil action.

Figure 1-2: Blended Case, Right to Sue Letter

VIRGINIA DEPARTMENT OF LABOR AND INDUSTRY

Notice of Right to Sue (Issued on Request)

To: Terry Williams
555 Greentree Lane
Emporia, Virginia 29999

From:Virginia Department
of Labor and Industry
Emporia Area Office
123 Mail Street, Room 456
Emporia, Virginia 29999

Complaint No. 8251997-AMT AMT   Telephone No. 804-555-1212

NOTICE TO THE PERSON AGGRIEVED:

This is your Notice of Right to Sue, issued under Virginia Code §40.1-51.2:2, based on the above-numbered complaint. It has been issued at your request. Your suit under Virginia Code §40.1-51.2:2 must be filed in the federal or state court <u>WITHIN 180 DAYS</u> of your receipt of this Notice. Otherwise, your right to sue based on the above-numbered complaint will be lost.

[ ]   More than 180 days have passed since the filing of this complaint.

[x]   Less than 180 days have passed since the filing of this complaint, but I have determined that it is unlikely that the VDOL will be able to complete its administrative processing within 180 days from the filing of the complaint.

[ ]   The VDOL is terminating its processing of this complaint.

[ ]   The VDOL will continue to process this complaint.

If you file suit based this complaint, please send a copy of your court complaint to this office.

On behalf of the Commission

Enclosure(s)
Copy of Complaint

<u>   A. B. Smith   </u>
A. B. Smith, Area Director

<u> August 20, year 0 </u>
(Date Mailed)

Figure 1-3: Diagram of FastGas Location

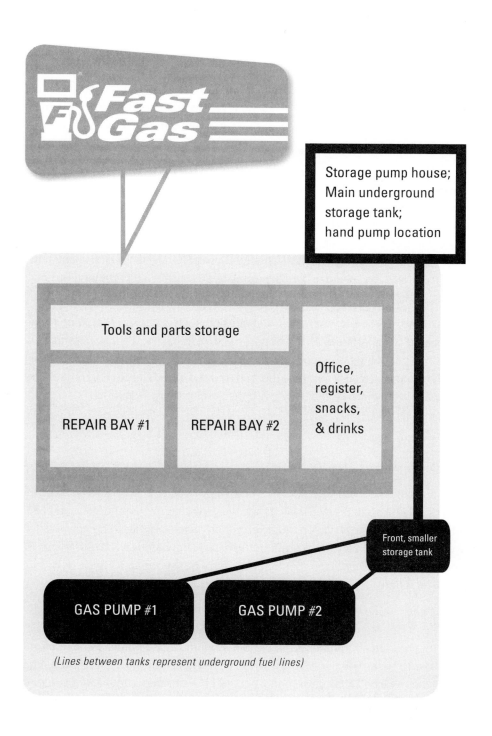

(Lines between tanks represent underground fuel lines)

Here is some information about people who have information regarding the dispute between Williams and Mancini.

■ Billy Rossland

I am the mayor of Emporia, Billy Rossland. I have known Gerry Mancini ever since Gerry moved to Emporia in year-8 and opened up FastGas. It distresses me to know that Gerry could be involved in something illegal like maintaining a dangerous work place with this complaint thing; however, the charges have not been proved.

One of the reasons I like Gerry is the way Gerry is willing to give anybody a chance. This Terry Williams is one of those chances. Terry came to town a year ago looking like a gypsy with everything Terry owned packed into a minivan. I am as open as the next person, but I'm a little leery of vagrant-type people in my town. Gerry, however, gave Terry a job right away. I guess things worked out well because Gerry kept this Williams for a year. Gerry has told me many times that Terry was extra help and was hired with the understanding that if business drops, there wouldn't be a place for Terry on the staff of FastGas.

I really don't know why Terry is causing such a stink about being let go. Gerry told me that Terry is a wanderer and didn't want a formal contract so Terry could leave when the mood struck. Since his gas station wasn't making much of a profit, Gerry felt that the belt needed to be tightened somewhere, and that somewhere would begin with the surplus staff. This move is only good business sense.

■ Stacy Duvall

Emporia Gas has been in my family for 40 years, and I have run it for the last 10. My name is Stacy Duvall. I met Terry Williams when the minivan pulled into town a year ago. I couldn't hire Terry then, since in order to be competitive, we operate with a very small staff, but I shared a few stories with Terry and we became friends. Ever since that first day, Terry has dropped by once or twice a week for lunch.

I have wondered for some time how Gerry Mancini was able to do so well with FastGas. Mancini has offered many bennies to the public, like full service at self-serve prices, rebates for a certain amount of gas purchases in a month and others. These are great business ideas, if you can afford them. At the time, gas prices weren't that strong and I couldn't understand how Mancini did it.

I couldn't understand, that is, until Terry realized that Mancini was cutting so many corners that things were dangerous over there. No one but Mancini has used those old pumps for years. Boy was I mad! Not nearly as mad as Mancini, it seems, since right after Mancini's dangerous practices were disclosed by Terry, Terry was fired. I suppose I could have reacted in a similar fashion if one of my employees had turned me in for wrongdoing, but Terry was a good worker. I sure would have hired Terry if I could have afforded it. Terry has always demonstrated a conscientious, honest nature. I have never heard that Terry has missed scheduled work or has violated any rules of employee behavior.

■ Frankie Fortunato

I own Frankie's, a local watering hole in Emporia. I know Williams by reputation and Mancini as a regular customer. Mancini is in a couple times a week, minimum. On Fridays, he is in with the Mayor, and usually with some of the officials at the state regulatory commission. I recall Mancini complaining about this new employee (Williams) who was pestering customers with whining about environmental stuff. Eventually, Mancini did say he was going to fire Williams. Fortunato remembers saying, "It's about time." The day Mancini said he was going to fire Williams was early to mid-May, year 0.

Mancini wasn't the only one who ever came into Fortunato's place talking about Williams. Once when Mancini was in, a local guy named Taylor started a rant about Williams. Taylor said he was sick and tired of having Williams hack on him at the station about safety and environmental things. Taylor told Mancini that he would take his gas purchasing and small car repairs elsewhere to get away from having to listen to Williams. I remember a few others muttering about Williams and his environmental causes.

■ Louise Cos

Louise Cos is a massage therapist in Emporia. She dated Peter Bargman of the State Regulatory Commission. She recalls a time when Peter was assigned to check out a complaint filed against FastGas about some gas pump issue.

She thinks well of Peter's honesty. Regarding the investigation of FastGas, Peter told her that it could be a problem because Gerry Mancini, the owner of FastGas, is wellconnected. The mayor is some good friend of Mancini and through the mayor, Mancini knows some state officials in Peter's office. Peter said to her that he was worried about the results if he found Mancini in violation of the state safety code.

■ Martin Fletcher

Martin Fletcher used to work at Mancini's gas station in Norman, Oklahoma, for several years until year-9. Fletcher will testify that Mancini would cut any corner to keep his costs down.

He will also testify that there was a fire at the station in which one of the employees was burned. Fletcher isn't sure what happened after that, but he heard rumors that Mancini settled with the employee out of court.

Fletcher left the station soon after and now lives in Miami, where he delivers flowers. He has not seen Mancini since year-9 and doesn't know anything about his current business.

CHAPTER 2

Jurisdiction and Venue

FOR A LITIGATED MATTER to proceed, a court must have both Subject Matter Jurisdiction over the controversy and Personal Jurisdiction over the parties.

A. Subject Matter Jurisdiction

Subject matter jurisdiction is the court's power over the particular kind of case. State courts are courts of *general* jurisdiction and with a few exceptions, some court within every state's system has subject matter jurisdiction over any particular action. The few exceptions are topics over which Congress has declared that federal courts have exclusive jurisdiction, such as certain patent matters.

Federal courts are courts of *limited* subject matter jurisdiction. They have subject matter jurisdiction over only such matters as the federal constitution and Congress have given them jurisdiction. The major grants of federal subject matter jurisdiction are over federal questions (28 U.S.C. 1331), actions between citizens of different states, called diversity of citizenship jurisdiction (28 U.S.C. 1332), and supplemental jurisdiction (28 U.S.C. 1367) over state law matters that are connected in certain ways to actions over which federal courts have jurisdiction by some other grant, most often federal question or diversity of citizenship. If federal courts have not been granted jurisdiction, they lack it and have no power to proceed in the matter.

On the following page is a "map" showing the universe of civil actions that could be filed in the United States. *Everything* in the "State Courts' General Jurisdiction Sea," including the islands of "Federal Question Jurisdiction,"

"Diversity of Citizenship Jurisdiction" and "Other Nonexclusive Grants of Jurisdiction to Federal Courts," is within the general subject matter jurisdiction of state courts. Only the small, shoreline, rocky outcropping called "Exclusive Federal Court Jurisdictional Grants" is outside the subject matter jurisdiction of the state courts. Federal courts have subject matter jurisdiction *only* over the outcropping and the three islands.

Figure 2-1 Map of Civil Actions in Federal and State Courts

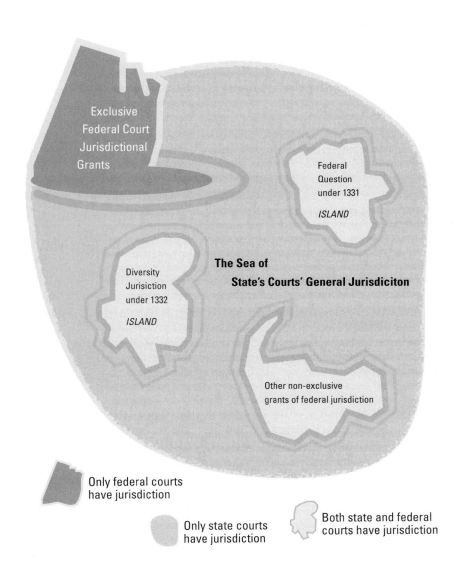

■ Constitutional Material

Article III

Section 1. The judicial power of the United States, shall be vested in one Supreme Court, and in such inferior courts as the Congress may from time to time ordain and establish. The judges, both of the supreme and inferior courts, shall hold their offices during good behaviour, and shall, at stated times, receive for their services, a compensation, which shall not be diminished during their continuance in office.

Section 2. The judicial power shall extend to all cases, in law and equity, arising under this Constitution, the laws of the United States, and treaties made or which shall be made, under their authority;—to all cases affecting ambassadors, other public ministers and consuls;—to all cases of admiralty and maritime jurisdiction;—to controversies to which the United States shall be a party;—to controversies between two or more states;—*between a state and citizens of another state*;—between citizens of different states;—between citizens of the same state claiming lands under grants of different states, and between a state, or the citizens thereof, and foreign states, citizens or subjects.

1. Federal Question Jurisdiction

■ Statutory Material
28 USC 1331

The district courts shall have original jurisdiction of all civil actions arising under the Constitution, laws, or treaties of the United States.

Louisville & N. R. Co. v. Mottley

211 U.S. 149 (1908)

The appellees (husband and wife), being residents and citizens of Kentucky, brought this suit in equity in the circuit court of the United States for the western district of Kentucky against the appellant, a railroad company and a citizen of the same state. The object of the suit was to compel the specific performance of the following contract:

Louisville, Ky., Oct. 2d, 1871

The Louisville & Nashville Railroad Company, in consideration that E. L. Mottley and wife, Annie E. Mottley, have this day released company from all damages or claims for damages for injuries received by them on the 7th of September, 1871, in consequence of a collision of trains on the railroad of said company at Randolph's Station, Jefferson County, Kentucky, hereby agrees to issue free passes on said railroad and branches now existing or to exist, to said E. L. & Annie E. Mottley for the remainder of the present year, and thereafter to renew said passes annually during the lives of said Mottley and wife or either of them.

The bill alleged that in September, 1871, plaintiffs, while passengers upon the defendant railroad, were injured by the defendant's negligence, and released their respective claims for damages in consideration of the agreement for transportation during their lives, expressed in the contract. It is alleged that the contract was performed by the defendant up to January 1, 1907, when the defendant declined to renew the passes. The bill then alleges that the refusal to comply with the contract was based solely upon that part of the act of Congress of June 29, 1906, which forbids the giving of free passes or free transportation. The bill further alleges: First, that the act of Congress referred to does not prohibit the giving of passes under the circumstances of this case; and, second, that, if the law is to be construed as prohibiting such passes, it is in conflict with the 5th Amendment of the Constitution, because it deprives the plaintiffs of their property without due process of law. The defendant demurred to the bill. The judge of the circuit court overruled the demurrer, entered a decree for the relief prayed for, and the defendant appealed directly to this court.

Mr. Justice Moody, after making the foregoing statement, delivered the opinion of the court:

Two questions of law were raised by the demurrer to the bill, were brought here by appeal, and have been argued before us. They are, first, whether that part of the act of Congress of June 29, 1906, which forbids the giving of free passes or the collection of any different compensation for transportation of passengers than that specified in the tariff filed, makes it unlawful to perform a contract for transportation of persons who, in good faith, before the passage of the act, had accepted such contract in satisfaction of a valid cause of action against the railroad; and, second, whether the statute, if it should be construed to render such a contract unlawful, is in violation of the 5th Amendment of the Constitution of the United States. We do not deem it necessary, however, to consider either of these questions, because, in our opinion, the court below was without jurisdiction of the cause. Neither party has questioned that jurisdiction, but it is the duty of this court to see to it that the jurisdiction of the circuit court, which is defined and limited by statute, is not exceeded.

There was no diversity of citizenship, and it is not and cannot be suggested that there was any ground of jurisdiction, except that the case was 'suit . . . arising under the Constitution or laws of the United States.' It is the settled interpretation of these words, as used in this statute, conferring jurisdiction, that a suit arises under the Constitution and laws of the United States only when the plaintiff's statement of his own cause of action shows that it is based upon those laws or that Constitution. It is not enough that the plaintiff alleges some anticipated defense to his cause of action, and asserts that the defense is invalidated by some provision of the Constitution of the United States. Although such allegations show that very likely, in the course of the litigation, a question under the Constitution would arise, they do not show that the suit, that is, the plaintiff's original cause of action, arises under the Constitution. In *Tennessee v. Union & Planters' Bank*, 152 U.S. 454, 38 L. ed. 511, 14 Sup. Ct. Rep. 654, the plaintiff, the state of Tennessee, brought suit in the circuit court of the United States to recover from the defendant certain taxes alleged to be due under the laws of the state. The plaintiff alleged that the defendant claimed an immunity from the taxation by virtue of its charter, and that therefore the tax was void, because in violation of the provision of the Constitution of the United States, which forbids any state from passing a law impairing the obligation of contracts. The cause was held to be beyond the jurisdiction of the circuit court, the court saying, by Mr. Justice Gray: 'A suggestion of one party, that the other will or may set up a claim under the Constitution or laws of the United States, does not make the suit one arising under that Constitution or those laws.' Again, in *Boston & M. Consol. Copper & S. Min. Co. v. Montana Ore Purchasing Co.* 188 U.S. 632 , 47 L. ed. 626, 23 Sup. Ct. Rep. 434, the plaintiff brought suit in the circuit court of the United States for the conversion of copper ore and for an injunction against its continuance. The plaintiff then alleged, for the purpose of showing jurisdiction, in substance, that the defendant would set up in defense certain laws of the United States. The cause was held to be beyond the jurisdiction of the circuit court, the court saying, by Mr. Justice Peckham (pp. 638, 639):

> 'It would be wholly unnecessary and improper, in order to prove complainant's cause of action, to go into any matters of defense which the defendants might possibly set up, and then attempt to reply to such defense, and thus, if possible, to show that a Federal question might or probably would arise in the course of the trial of the case. To allege such defense and then make an answer to it before

the defendant has the opportunity to itself plead or prove its own defense is inconsistent with any known rule of pleading, so far as we are aware, and is improper.

'The rule is a reasonable and just one that the complainant in the first instance shall be confined to a statement of its cause of action, leaving to the defendant to set up in his answer what his defense is, and, if anything more than a denial of complainant's cause of action, imposing upon the defendant the burden of proving such defense.

'Conforming itself to that rule, the complainant would not, in the assertion or proof of its cause of action, bring up a single Federal question. The presentation of its cause of action would not show that it was one arising under the Constitution or laws of the United States. 'The only way in which it might be claimed that a Federal question was presented would be in the complainant's statement of what the defense of defendants would be, and complainant's answer to such defense. Under these circumstances the case is brought within the rule laid down in *Tennessee v. Union & Planters' Bank, supra*. That case has been cited and approved many times since.'

The application of this rule to the case at bar is decisive against the jurisdiction of the circuit court.

It is ordered that the judgment be reversed and the case remitted to the circuit court with instructions to dismiss the suit for want of jurisdiction.

Grable & Sons Metal Products, Inc. v. Darue Engineering & Manufacturing

545 U.S. 308, 125 S.Ct. 2363 (2005)

Justice SOUTER delivered the opinion of the Court.

The question is whether want of a federal cause of action to try claims of title to land obtained at a federal tax sale precludes removal to federal court of a state action with nondiverse parties raising a disputed issue of federal title law. We answer no, and hold that the national interest in providing a federal forum for federal tax litigation is sufficiently substantial to support the exercise of federal-question jurisdiction over the disputed issue on removal, which would not distort any division of labor between the state and federal courts, provided or assumed by Congress.

I

In 1994, the Internal Revenue Service seized Michigan real property belonging to petitioner Grable & Sons Metal Products, Inc., to satisfy Grable's federal tax delinquency. Title 26 U.S.C. § 6335 required the IRS to give notice of the seizure, and there is no dispute that Grable received actual notice by certified mail before the IRS sold the property to respondent Darue Engineering & Manufacturing. Although Grable also received notice of the sale itself, it did not exercise its statutory right to redeem the property within 180 days of the sale, § 6337(b)(1), and after that period had passed, the Government gave Darue a quitclaim deed, § 6339.

Five years later, Grable brought a quiet title action in state court, claiming that Darue's record title was invalid because the IRS had failed to notify Grable of its seizure of the property in the exact manner required by § 6335(a), which provides that written notice must be "given by the Secretary to the owner of the property [or] left at his usual place of abode or business." Grable said that the statute required personal service, not service by certified mail.

Darue removed the case to Federal District Court as presenting a federal question, because the claim of title depended on the interpretation of the notice statute in the federal tax law. The District Court declined to remand the case at Grable's behest after finding that the "claim does pose a 'significant question of federal law,'" and ruling that Grable's lack of a federal right of action to enforce its claim against Darue did not bar the exercise of federal jurisdiction. On the merits, the court granted summary judgment to Darue, holding that although § 6335 by its terms required personal service, substantial compliance with the statute was enough.

The Court of Appeals for the Sixth Circuit affirmed. On the jurisdictional question, the panel thought it sufficed that the title claim raised an issue of federal law that had to be resolved, and implicated a substantial federal interest (in construing federal tax law). The court went on to affirm the District Court's judgment on the merits. We granted certiorari on the jurisdictional question alone, to resolve a split within the Courts of Appeals on whether *Merrell Dow Pharmaceuticals Inc. v. Thompson*, 478 U.S. 804, 106 S.Ct. 3229, 92 L.Ed.2d 650 (1986), always requires a federal cause of action as a condition for exercising federal-question jurisdiction. We now affirm.

II

Darue was entitled to remove the quiet title action if Grable could have brought it in federal district court originally, 28 U.S.C. § 1441(a), as a civil action "arising under the Constitution, laws, or treaties of the United States," § 1331.

This provision for federal-question jurisdiction is invoked by and large by plaintiffs pleading a cause of action created by federal law (*e.g.*, claims under 42 U.S.C. § 1983). There is, however, another longstanding, if less frequently encountered, variety of federal "arising under" jurisdiction, this Court having recognized for nearly 100 years that in certain cases federal-question jurisdiction will lie over state-law claims that implicate significant federal issues. The doctrine captures the commonsense notion that a federal court ought to be able to hear claims recognized under state law that nonetheless turn on substantial questions of federal law, and thus justify resort to the experience, solicitude, and hope of uniformity that a federal forum offers on federal issues.

The classic example is *Smith v. Kansas City Title & Trust Co.*, 255 U.S. 180, 41 S.Ct. 243, 65 L.Ed. 577 (1921), a suit by a shareholder claiming that the defendant corporation could not lawfully buy certain bonds of the National Government because their issuance was unconstitutional. Although Missouri law provided the cause of action, the Court recognized federal-question jurisdiction because the principal issue in the case was the federal constitutionality of the bond issue. *Smith* thus held, in a somewhat generous statement of the scope of the doctrine, that a state-law claim could give rise to federal-question jurisdiction so long as it "appears from the [complaint] that the right to relief depends upon the construction or application of [federal law]." *Id.*, at 199, 41 S.Ct. 243.

The *Smith* statement has been subject to some trimming to fit earlier and later cases recognizing the vitality of the basic doctrine, but shying away from the expansive view that mere need to apply federal law in a state-law claim will suffice to open the "arising under" door. As early as 1912, this Court had confined federal-question jurisdiction over state-law claims to those that "really and substantially involv[e] a dispute or controversy respecting the validity, construction or effect of [federal] law." *Shulthis v. McDougal*, 225 U.S. 561, 569, 32 S.Ct. 704, 56 L.Ed. 1205. This limitation was the ancestor of Justice Cardozo's later explanation that a request to exercise federal-question jurisdiction over a state action calls for a "common-sense accommodation of judgment to [the] kaleidoscopic situations" that present a federal issue, in "a selective process which picks the substantial causes out of the web and lays the other ones aside." *Gully v. First Nat. Bank in Meridian*, 299 U.S. 109, 117-118, 57 S.Ct. 96, 81 L.Ed. 70 (1936). It has in fact become a constant refrain in such cases that federal jurisdiction demands not only a contested federal issue, but a substantial one, indicating a serious federal interest in claiming the advantages thought to be inherent in a federal forum.

But even when the state action discloses a contested and substantial federal question, the exercise of federal jurisdiction is subject to a possible veto. For the federal issue will ultimately qualify for a federal forum only if federal juris-diction is consistent with congressional judgment about the sound division of labor between state and federal courts governing the application of § 1331. Thus, *Franchise Tax Bd.* explained that the appropriateness of a federal forum to hear an embedded issue could be evaluated only after considering the "welter of issues regarding the interrelation of federal and state authority and the proper management of the federal judicial system." *Id.,* at 8, 103 S.Ct. 2841. Because arising-under jurisdiction to hear a state-law claim always raises the possibility of upsetting the state-federal line drawn (or at least assumed) by Congress, the presence of a disputed federal issue and the ostensible importance of a federal forum are never necessarily dispositive; there must always be an assessment of any disruptive portent in exercising federal jurisdiction.

These considerations have kept us from stating a "single, precise, all-embracing" test for jurisdiction over federal issues embedded in state-law claims between nondiverse parties. We have not kept them out simply because they appeared in state raiment, as Justice Holmes would have done, but neither have we treated "federal issue" as a password opening federal courts to any state action embracing a point of federal law. Instead, the question is, does a state-law claim necessarily raise a stated federal issue, actually disputed and substantial, which a federal forum may entertain without disturbing any congressionally approved balance of federal and state judicial responsibilities.

III

A

This case warrants federal jurisdiction. Grable's state complaint must specify "the facts establishing the superiority of [its] claim," and Grable has pre-mised its superior title claim on a failure by the IRS to give it adequate notice, as defined by federal law. Whether Grable was given notice within the meaning of the federal statute is thus an essential element of its quiet title claim, and the meaning of the federal statute is actually in dispute; it appears to be the only legal or factual issue contested in the case. The meaning of the federal tax provision is an important issue of federal law that sensibly belongs in a federal court. The Government has a strong interest in the "prompt and certain collec-tion of delinquent taxes," *United States v. Rodgers*, 461 U.S. 677, 709, 103 S.Ct. 2132, 76 L.Ed.2d 236 (1983), and the ability of the IRS to satisfy its claims from the property of delinquents requires clear terms of notice to allow buyers like Darue to satisfy themselves that the Service has touched the bases necessary for good title. The Government thus has a direct interest in the availability of a federal forum to vindicate its own administrative action, and buyers (as well as tax delinquents) may find it valuable to come before judges used to federal tax matters. Finally, because it will be the rare state title case that raises a contested matter of federal law, federal jurisdiction to resolve genuine disagreement over federal tax title provisions will portend only a microscopic effect on the federal-state division of labor.

B

Merrell Dow Pharmaceuticals Inc. v. Thompson, 478 U.S. 804, 106 S.Ct. 3229, 92 L.Ed.2d 650 (1986), on which Grable rests its position, is not to the contrary. *Merrell Dow* considered a state tort claim resting in part on the allegation that the defendant drug company had violated a federal misbranding prohibition, and was thus presumptively negligent under Ohio law. The Court assumed that federal law would have to be applied to resolve the claim, but after closely examining the strength of the federal interest at stake and the implications of opening the federal forum, held federal jurisdiction unavailable. Congress had not provided a private federal cause of action for violation of the federal branding requirement, and the Court found "it would . . . flout, or at least undermine, congressional intent to conclude that federal courts might nevertheless exercise federal-question jurisdiction and provide remedies for violations of that federal statute solely because the violation . . . is said to be a . . . 'proximate cause' under state law." *Id.,* at 812, 106 S.Ct. 3229.

Because federal law provides for no quiet title action that could be brought against Darue, Grable argues that there can be no federal jurisdiction here, stressing some broad language in *Merrell Dow* (including the passage just quoted) that on its face supports Grable's position. But an opinion is to be read as a whole, and *Merrell Dow* cannot be read whole as overturning decades of precedent, as it would have done by effectively adopting the Holmes dissent in *Smith,* and converting a federal cause of action from a sufficient condition for federal-question jurisdiction[1] into a necessary one.

In the first place, *Merrell Dow* disclaimed the adoption of any bright-line rule, as when the Court reiterated that "in exploring the outer reaches of § 1331, determinations about federal jurisdiction require sensitive judgments about congressional intent, judicial power, and the federal system."

Accordingly, *Merrell Dow* should be read in its entirety as treating the absence of a federal private right of action as evidence relevant to, but not dispositive of, the "sensitive judgments about congressional intent" that § 1331

---

1 For an extremely rare exception to the sufficiency of a federal right of action, see *Shoshone Mining Co. v. Rutter,* 177 U.S. 505, 507, 20 S.Ct. 726, 44 L.Ed. 864 (1900).

requires. The absence of any federal cause of action affected *Merrell Dow's* result two ways. The Court saw the fact as worth some consideration in the assessment of substantiality. But its primary importance emerged when the Court treated the combination of no federal cause of action and no preemption of state remedies for misbranding as an important clue to Congress's conception of the scope of jurisdiction to be exercised under § 1331. The Court saw the missing cause of action not as a missing federal door key, always required, but as a missing welcome mat, required in the circumstances, when exercising federal jurisdiction over a state misbranding action would have attracted a horde of original filings and removal cases raising other state claims with embedded federal issues. For if the federal labeling standard without a federal cause of action could get a state claim into federal court, so could any other federal standard without a federal cause of action. And that would have meant a tremendous number of cases.

As already indicated, however, a comparable analysis yields a different jurisdictional conclusion in this case. Although Congress also indicated ambivalence in this case by providing no private right of action to Grable, it is the rare state quiet title action that involves contested issues of federal law. Consequently, jurisdiction over actions like Grable's would not materially affect, or threaten to affect, the normal currents of litigation. Given the absence of threatening structural consequences and the clear interest the Government, its buyers, and its delinquents have in the availability of a federal forum, there is no good reason to shirk from federal jurisdiction over the dispositive and contested federal issue at the heart of the state-law title claim.[2]

IV

The judgment of the Court of Appeals, upholding federal jurisdiction over Grable's quiet title action, is affirmed.

It is so ordered.

[A concurring opinion by Justice THOMAS is omitted.]

---

2 At oral argument Grable's counsel espoused the position that after Merrell Dow, federal-question jurisdiction over state-law claims absent a federal right of action could be recognized only where a constitutional issue was at stake. There is, however, no reason in text or otherwise to draw such a rough line. As Merrell Dow itself suggested, constitutional questions may be the more likely ones to reach the level of substantiality that can justify federal jurisdiction. But a flat ban on statutory questions would mechanically exclude significant questions of federal law like the one this case presents.

NOTE

Empire Healthchoice Assur., Inc. v. McVeigh, 126 S.Ct. 2121 (2006) marks a very useful opposite pole of analysis from *Grable*. In *Empire Health*, an Insurer had a contract with the federal government to provide medical insurance coverage to federal employees. Insured was a federal employee covered by this policy. Insured was injured by Tortfeasor. Insurer paid Insured's medical bills resulting from these injuries. Insured sued Tortfeasor and collected substantial damages. Insurer sued Insured to recover under the insurance policy (subrogation), and claimed that the statute that governed Insured's relationship with federal government, pursuant to which the policy was written, made this a section 1331 claim.

First, there was no private right of action under the statute that would have triggered *Merrill Dow's* provision of federal question jurisdiction for this fundamentally state law claim.

Second, although perhaps some federal questions could come up in the litigation, they are far from substantial ones.

Unsurprisingly, the Court ruled that the measure of federal question present in the state law claim was too modest to support the intrusion of federal courts into state matters.

2. Diversity of Citizenship

■ Statutory Material
28 USC 1332

(a) The district courts shall have original jurisdiction of all civil actions where the matter in controversy exceeds the sum or value of $75,000, exclusive of interest and costs, and is between—

(1) citizens of different States;

(2) citizens of a State and citizens or subjects of a foreign state, except that the district courts shall not have original jurisdiction under this subsection of an action between citizens of a State and citizens or subjects of a foreign state who are lawfully admitted for permanent residence in the United States and are domiciled in the same State;

(3) citizens of different States and in which citizens or subjects of a foreign state are additional parties; a

(4) a foreign state, defined in section 1603(a) of this title, as plaintiff and citizens of a State or of different States.

(b) Except when express provision therefor is otherwise made in a statute of the United States, where the plaintiff who files the case originally in the Federal courts is finally adjudged to be entitled to recover less than the sum or value of $75,000, computed without regard to any setoff or counterclaim to which the defendant may be adjudged to be entitled, and exclusive of interest and costs, the district court may deny costs to the plaintiff and, in addition, may impose costs on the plaintiff

(c) For the purposes of this section and section 1441 of this title—

(1) a corporation shall be deemed to be a citizen of every State and foreign state by which it has been incorporated and of the State or foreign state where it has its principal place of business, except that in any direct action against the insurer of a policy or contract of liability insurance, whether incorporated or unincorporated, to which action the insured is not joined as a party-defendant, such insurer shall be deemed a citizen of—

(A) every State and foreign state of which the insured is a citizen;

(B) every State and foreign state by which the insurer has been incorporated; and

(C) the State or foreign state where the insurer has its principal place of business; and

(2) the legal representative of the estate of a decedent shall be deemed to be a citizen only of the same State as the decedent, and the legal representative of an infant or incompetent shall be deemed to be a citizen only of the same State as the infant or incompetent.

(d) *[class action rules omitted—ed.]*

(e) The word "States", as used in this section, includes the Territories, the District of Columbia, and the Commonwealth of Puerto Rico.

Strawbridge et al. v. Curtiss et al.

3 Cranch 267, 7 U.S. 267 (1806)

This was an appeal from a decree of the circuit court, for the district of Massachusetts, which dismissed the complainants' bill in chancery, for want of jurisdiction.

Some of the complainants were alleged to be citizens of the state of Massachusetts. The defendants were also stated to be citizens of the same state, excepting Curtiss, who was averred to be a citizen of the state of Vermont, and upon whom the subpoena was served in that state.

MARSHALL, Ch. J. delivered the opinion of the court.

The court has considered this case, and is of opinion that the jurisdiction cannot be supported.

The words of the act of congress are, 'where an alien is a party; or the suit is between a citizen of a state where the suit is brought, and a citizen of another state.'

The court understands these expressions to mean that each distinct interest should be represented by persons, all of whom are entitled to sue, or may be sued, in the federal courts. That is, that where the interest is joint, each of the persons concerned in that interest must be competent to sue, or liable to be sued, in those courts.

Decree affirmed.

NOTES

1. Although *Strawbridge* is still good law with respect to the requirement of complete diversity under 28 USC 1332, Congress has the power to create other "diversity" statutes granting jurisdiction for specific kinds of cases with less than "complete diversity." For example, the Class Action Fairness Act of 2005 (CAFA) allows claims with large numbers of plaintiffs to be brought with "minimal diversity." The class action is not specifically covered in this book, but CAFA was Congress' attempt to funnel class actions into federal courts through the use of removal jurisdiction, where the rules for certification of classes are more stringent. The hoped-for result was a reduction in the number of successful class actions.

2. Where does a party have domicile for diversity purposes? It can be an easy mistake to confuse domicile for diversity jurisdiction purposes with the kind of presence in a jurisdiction that would support a court's exercise of personal jurisdiction over a party. You will learn about minimum contacts with a state for personal jurisdiction purposes later in this chapter. Consider *Sheehan v. Gustafson*, 967 F.2d 1214 (8th Cir. 1992). Sheehan was a citizen of Nevada who sued Gustafson. Sheehan based his assertion of federal court subject matter jurisdiction on section 1332, claiming that Gustafson was a citizen of Minnesota. The court applied the proper two-part test asking where the party has a "presence" and an "intention to remain." Gustafson had some presence in multiple states. For example, he had homes in Nevada and Minnesota and bank accounts in several states. He had managed the Tropicana Hotel in Las Vegas, which he had purchased in 1972, but was convicted of misappropriation of bank funds in Minnesota. He used a Minnesota address for reports to his probation officer and had his physician and dentist there as well. In Nevada, Gustafson held a driver's license and owned Nevada-registered vehicles. He was a registered voter in Nevada and his passport showed a Nevada address. As of the date of filing Plaintiff's Complaint (the date that matters for analysis of citizenship under 1332), he was constructing a new house in Nevada. On that same date, he owned significant corporate interests in Minnesota.

The court of appeals upheld the district court's finding that Gustafson was a citizen of Nevada for 1332 purposes, but because the standard of review is a relaxed one ("clearly erroneous"), the court of appeals would almost surely have upheld the district court had it found that Gustafson was a citizen of Minnesota. Close calls that are reviewed under relaxed standards of review are in fact decided by the district judge because they are so rarely overturned by courts of appeal.

Compare back to this case once you have the minimum contacts knowledge. For diversity of citizenship purposes, a person can have but one state of citizenship (but check the statute for the status of corporations). But surely, Gustafson would be found to have had contacts adequate to justify personal jurisdiction in multiple states.

3. Creedance Clearwater, "Stuck in Lodi Again". Read the lyrics (or better still listen) to Lodi by Creedance Clearwater Revival. *http://www.creedence-online.net/lyrics/lodi.php*

Assume that Lodi is in California (it is). And assume the character in the song was born and raised in Louisiana (he wasn't). If he left his Louisiana home at age 22 and has roamed around since, repeatedly being "stuck in Lodi again," where is his citizenship for section 1332 purposes? (Many thanks to former student and Teaching Assistant Kyle Bahr for bringing the lyrics to my attention.)

3. Removal Jurisdiction

■ Statutory Material
28 USC 1441

(a) **Generally.**— Except as otherwise expressly provided by Act of Congress, any civil action brought in a State court of which the district courts of the United States have original jurisdiction, may be removed by the defendant or the defendants, to the district court of the United States for the district and division embracing the place where such action is pending.

(b) **Removal Based on Diversity of Citizenship.**—

(1) In determining whether a civil action is removable on the basis of the jurisdiction under section 1332(a) of this title, the citizenship of defendants sued under fictitious names shall be disregarded.

(2) A civil action otherwise removable solely on the basis of the jurisdiction under section 1332(a) of this title may not be removed if any of the parties in interest properly joined and served as defendants is a citizen of the State in which such action is brought.

(c) **Joinder of Federal Law Claims and State Law Claims.**—

(1) If a civil action includes—

(A) a claim arising under the Constitution, laws, or treaties of the United States (within the meaning of section 1331 of this title), and

(B) a claim not within the original or supplemental jurisdiction of the district court or a claim that has been made nonremovable by statute, the entire action may be removed if the action would be removable without the inclusion of the claim described in subparagraph (B).

(2) Upon removal of an action described in paragraph (1), the district court shall sever from the action all claims described in paragraph (1)(B) and shall remand the severed claims to the State court from which the action was removed. Only defendants against whom a claim described in paragraph (1)(A) has been asserted are required to join in or consent to the removal under paragraph (1).

. . .

28 USC 1446

(a) Generally.— A defendant or defendants desiring to remove any civil action from a State court shall file in the district court of the United States for the district and division within which such action is pending a notice of removal signed pursuant to Rule 11 of the Federal Rules of Civil Procedure and containing a short and plain statement of the grounds for removal, together with a copy of all process, pleadings, and orders served upon such defendant or defendants in such action.

(b) Requirements; Generally.—

(1) The notice of removal of a civil action or proceeding shall be filed within 30 days after the receipt by the defendant, through service or otherwise, of a copy of the initial pleading setting forth the claim for relief upon which such action or proceeding is based, or within 30 days after the service of summons upon the defendant if such initial pleading has then been filed in court and is not required to be served on the defendant, whichever period is shorter.

(2)

(A) When a civil action is removed solely under section 1441(a), all defendants who have been properly joined and served must join in or consent to the removal of the action.

(B) Each defendant shall have 30 days after receipt by or service on that defendant of the initial pleading or summons described in paragraph (1) to file the notice of removal.

(C) If defendants are served at different times, and a later-served defendant files a notice of removal, any earlier-served defendant may consent to the removal even though that earlier-served defendant did not previously initiate or consent to removal.

(3) Except as provided in subsection (c), if the case stated by the initial pleading is not removable, a notice of removal may be filed within thirty days after receipt by the defendant, through service or otherwise, of a copy of an amended pleading, motion, order or other paper from which it may first be ascertained that the case is one which is or has become removable.

(c) Requirements; Removal Based on Diversity of Citizenship.—

(1) A case may not be removed under subsection (b)(3) on the basis of jurisdiction conferred by section 1332 more than 1 year after commencement of the action, unless the district court finds that the plaintiff has acted in bad faith in order to prevent a defendant from removing the action.

(2) If removal of a civil action is sought on the basis of the jurisdiction conferred by section 1332(a), the sum demanded in good faith in the initial pleading shall be deemed to be the amount in controversy, except that—

(A) the notice of removal may assert the amount in controversy if the initial pleading seeks—

(i) nonmonetary relief; or

(ii) a money judgment, but the State practice either does not permit demand for a specific sum or permits recovery of damages in excess of the amount demanded; and

(B) removal of the action is proper on the basis of an amount in controversy asserted under subparagraph (A) if the district court finds, by the preponderance of the evidence, that the amount in controversy exceeds the amount specified in section 1332(a).

(3)

(A) If the case stated by the initial pleading is not removable solely because the amount in controversy does not exceed the amount specified in section 1332(a), information relating to the amount in controversy in the record of the State proceeding, or in responses to discovery, shall be treated as an "other paper" under subsection (b)(3).

(B) If the notice of removal is filed more than 1 year after commencement of the action and the district court finds that the plaintiff deliberately failed to disclose the actual amount in controversy to prevent removal, that finding shall be deemed bad faith under paragraph (1).

(d) Notice to Adverse Parties and State Court.— Promptly after the filing of such notice of removal of a civil action the defendant or defendants shall give written notice thereof to all adverse parties and shall file a copy of the notice with the clerk of such State court, which shall effect the removal and the State court shall proceed no further unless and until the case is remanded.

. . .

Example Document

Here is a sample Notice of Removal.

IN THE UNITED STATES DISTRICT COURT FOR THE WESTERN DISTRICT OF VIRGINIA, LYNCHBURG DIVISION

HOLLY BRANHAM,	)	
	)	
Plaintiff,	)	
v.	)	C.A. No.
	)	
DOLGENCORP, INC., etc.,	)	
Defendant.)		

DOLGENCORP, INC.'S NOTICE OF REMOVAL

The defendant, Dolgencorp, Inc. ("Dolgencorp"), by counsel, hereby provides Notice of Removal of this action from the Circuit Court of Amherst County, Virginia, where the action is now pending. This Notice of Removal is filed under Title 28, sections 1441 and 1446 of the United States Code. This removal is based upon the following:

1. This action was filed against Dolgencorp on or about June 8, 2009, in the Circuit Court for Amherst County, Virginia, styled *Holly Branham v. Dolgen Com, Inc.* , C.A. No. 09007449 (the "State Court Action"), by Holly Branham. A copy of the Summons and Complaint is attached.

2. On or about June 17, 2009, legal service in the above-styled case was made upon Dolgencorp's registered agent, Corporation Service Company, in Richmond, Virginia.

3. To the best of Dolgencorp's knowledge, no other proceedings, process, pleadings, orders, or other papers have been filed or served in the State Court Action.

4. Dolgencorp files this Notice of Removal within thirty (30) days of the receipt by Dolgencorp of the Summons and Complaint in the State Court Action.

5. Dolgencorp is a citizen of Kentucky and Tennessee, as it is a limited liability company (formerly a corporation)[3] organized and existing under the laws of the Commonwealth of Kentucky, with its principal place of business in Goodlettsville, Tennessee. None of Dolgencorp's members resides in Virginia.

6. Upon information and belief, Branham is a citizen of Virginia.

7. The amount in controversy exceeds $75,000.00, exclusive of interest and costs.

8. This matter is removable to federal court under Title 28, section 1332 of the United States Code, as there is complete diversity of citizenship between the parties, and the amount in controversy exceeds $75,000.

9. Branham commenced this action in a state court that is within this district and division.

10. Dolgencorp will file this Notice of Removal with the Circuit Court of the County of Amherst, Virginia, and also will serve a copy of this Notice of Removal on Branham.

WHEREFORE, Dolgencorp prays that the State Court Action be removed from the Circuit Court of Amherst County, Virginia, to this Court.

Done this 29th day of June, 2009.

DOLGENCORP, INC.

By: MIDKIFF, MUNCIE & ROSS, P.C.

Of Counsel

James G. Muncie, Jr. (VSB No. 28660)
Kevin T. Streit (VSB No. 45024)

Midkiff, Muncie & Ross, P.C. | 300 Arboretum Place, Suite 420
Richmond, Virginia 23236 | (804) 560-9600 (804) 560-5997 (facsimile)
jmuncie@midkifflaw.com kstreit@midkifflaw.com *Counsel for Dolgencorp, Inc.*

---

3 Dolgencorp converted from a corporation to a limited liability company on or about November 6, 2008. Its correct name is Dolgencorp, LLC.

EXPERIENTIAL ASSIGNMENTS

Gun violence has taken a serious toll in many cities. Mayors of Pittsburgh, Cleveland and Detroit combined forces to try to tackle one aspect of the problem.

These mayors believed that significant numbers of handguns sold in Virginia were being used in crimes in their cities. One technique they believed was used at Virginia gun dealers involved substitute buyers. In this technique, a gun buyer would choose the gun he wanted to buy and have someone else, someone without a criminal background, fill out the various federal forms and background check documents, to facilitate the gun purchase. The mayors believed that gun dealers in Virginia knowingly allowed this scam and sold guns to such phony buyers.

The mayors enlisted the aid of investigators who were Virginia corporations to venture into Virginia gun shops to play out the phony buyer scenario. As expected, the gun dealers knowingly sold to false buyers who filled out the federal forms necessary to make the purchases.

At a joint press conference announcing the results of their investigation, the mayors made the following statements:

- "–and most are sold by a small [group] of rogue gun dealers who refuse to obey federal laws."

- "caught them. . . breaking the Federal laws regulating gun sales."

- "group of bad apples who routinely ignore federal regulations."

- "stop your illegal conduct or you too will face this kind of penalty"; and

- ". . . holding gun dealers who break the law accountable. . . ."

One of the gun dealers involved filed a state law defamation action in Virginia state court in Richmond. The Defendants removed the action to federal district court. The Plaintiff is contesting the federal court's subject matter jurisdiction.

As assigned by your professor, fashion a two-page argument supporting the removal, a two-page argument opposing the removal, or both.

4. Supplemental Jurisdiction

Plaintiffs may join more than one claim in a Complaint, as we will see in chapter 4. What should happen when a federal court would have jurisdiction over one of the claims but not others? Supplemental jurisdiction defines those circumstances in which a federal court may exercise subject matter jurisdiction over additional claims over which it would not otherwise have subject matter jurisdiction. The older terms for this concept are *pendent jurisdiction* and *ancillary jurisdiction*. Both of these terms have now been merged into the single term, *supplemental jurisdiction*.

For now, consider the basic thrust of section 1367: often but not always, when a federal court has subject matter jurisdiction of a claim under either 1331 or 1332, it will also have subject matter jurisdiction over related state law claims brought in the same civil action. We will return to consider supplemental jurisdiction in chapter 4 when we consider joinder of parties and claims. At that time, we will consider some rather confusing wrinkles in 1367(b).

■ Statutory Material
28 USC 1367

(a) Except as provided in subsections (b) and (c) or as expressly provided otherwise by Federal statute, in any civil action of which the district courts have original jurisdiction, the district courts shall have supplemental jurisdiction over all other claims that are so related to claims in the action within such original jurisdiction that they form part of the same case or controversy under Article III of the United States Constitution. Such supplemental jurisdiction shall include claims that involve the joinder or intervention of additional parties.

(b) In any civil action of which the district courts have original jurisdiction founded solely on section 1332 of this title, the district courts shall not have supplemental jurisdiction under subsection (a) over claims by plaintiffs against persons made parties under Rule 14, 19, 20, or 24 of the Federal Rules of Civil Procedure, or over claims by persons proposed to be joined as plaintiffs under Rule 19 of such rules, or seeking to intervene as plaintiffs under Rule 24 of such rules, when exercising supplemental jurisdiction over such claims would be inconsistent with the jurisdictional requirements of section 1332.

(c) The district courts may decline to exercise supplemental jurisdiction over a claim under subsection (a) if—

(1) the claim raises a novel or complex issue of State law,

(2) the claim substantially predominates over the claim or claims over which the district court has original jurisdiction,

(3) the district court has dismissed all claims over which it has original jurisdiction, or

(4) in exceptional circumstances, there are other compelling reasons for declining jurisdiction.

(d) The period of limitations for any claim asserted under subsection (a), and for any other claim in the same action that is voluntarily dismissed at the same time as or after the dismissal of the claim under subsection (a), shall be tolled while the claim is pending and for a period of 30 days after it is dismissed unless State law provides for a longer tolling period.

(e) As used in this section, the term "State" includes the District of Columbia, the Commonwealth of Puerto Rico, and any territory or possession of the United States.

EXPERIENTIAL ASSIGNMENTS

1. Draft federal Subject Matter Jurisdictional Allegations for the Cash and Frensch cases as assigned by your professor. 2. Assume that the Frensch and Cash cases have been filed in state court (Ohio and North Carolina respectively). Draft the Notice of Removal to the correct federal court in the Frensch or Cash case, as assigned by your professor.

B. Personal Jurisdiction

A court always has personal jurisdiction over the plaintiff because the plaintiff has subjected him (her)(it)self to the personal jurisdiction of the court by filing a complaint in that court. But a defendant has not agreed to personal jurisdiction and a court must find that it has personal jurisdiction over the defendant to have the power to proceed.

A court may have personal jurisdiction over the defendant by one of several means. First, a defendant may consent to jurisdiction, intentionally or otherwise. A defendant's explicit consent confers personal jurisdiction. But a defendant may also consent by appearing and filing documents in the matter without challenging personal jurisdiction. Second, owning property in a state may provide that state's courts with personal jurisdiction over the property's owner under certain circumstances (see *Shaffer v. Heitner*, 433 U.S. 186 (1977)). Third, a court has personal jurisdiction over a defendant who happens to be present in a state even for a short time and be served with the Complaint and Summons during that time. This is often called "gotcha" personal jurisdiction.

Most importantly, personal jurisdiction may exist when the defendant has "minimum contacts" with the forum state. How much contact with the state is determined by "traditional notions of fair play and substantial justice (TNOFPASJ). The level of contact necessary to confer personal jurisdiction by this means varies according to whether the claim is (specific jurisdiction) or is not (general jurisdiction) about the contacts of the defendant with the jurisdiction.

In any event, personal jurisdiction must be accompanied by proper notice to the defendant of the civil action.

Further, for a state's courts to assert personal jurisdiction over absent defendants, the state must have adopted statutory authority for the court to do so. These statutes, called "long-arm statutes," come essentially in two forms. One form lists the types of cases over which the state's courts may assert jurisdiction, for instance, torts committed within the state or contracts made within the state. The other form asserts the maximum amount of personal jurisdiction possible, as much as the federal due process clause would allow. In either event, the state's courts may not assert personal jurisdiction beyond what the due process clause allows.

■ Constitutional Material

Fifth Amendment

No person shall. . . be deprived of life, liberty, or property, without due process of law.

Fourteenth Amendment

No state shall. . . deprive any person of life, liberty, or property, without due process of law.

■ Statutory Material

Here are two examples of state long-arm statutes:

Arizona Long-Arm Statute

AZ ST RCP R 4.2 (2003)

Rule 4.2. Service of process outside the state.
(a) Extraterritorial jurisdiction; personal service out of state.

A court of this state may exercise personal jurisdiction over parties, whether found within or outside the state, to the maximum extent permitted by the Constitution of this state and the Constitution of the United States.

Ohio Long-Arm Statute

Ohio Rev. Code Ann. § 2307.382

§ 2307.382. Personal jurisdiction

(A) A court may exercise personal jurisdiction over a person who acts directly or by an agent, as to a cause of action arising from the person's:

(1) Transacting any business in this state;

(2) Contracting to supply services or goods in this state;

(3) Causing tortious injury by an act or omission in this state;

(4) Causing tortious injury in this state by an act or omission outside this state if he regularly does or solicits business, or engages in any other persistent course of conduct, or derives substantial revenue from goods used or consumed or services rendered in this state;

(5) Causing injury in this state to any person by breach of warranty expressly or impliedly made in the sale of goods outside this state when he might reasonably have expected such person to use, consume, or be affected by the goods in this state, provided that he also regularly does or solicits business, or engages in any other persistent course of conduct, or derives substantial revenue from goods used or consumed or services rendered in this state;

(6) Causing tortious injury in this state to any person by an act outside this state committed with the purpose of injuring persons, when he might reasonably have expected that some person would be injured thereby in this state;

(7) Causing tortious injury to any person by a criminal act, any element of which takes place in this state, which he commits or in the commission of which he is guilty of complicity.

(8) Having an interest in, using, or possessing real property in this state;

(9) Contracting to insure any person, property, or risk located within this state at the time of contracting.

(B) For purposes of this section, a person who enters into an agreement, as a principal, with a sales representative for the solicitation of orders in this state is transacting business in this state. As used in this division, "principal" and "sales representative" have the same meanings as in section 1335.11 of the Revised Code.

(C) When jurisdiction over a person is based solely upon this section, only a cause of action arising from acts enumerated in this section may be asserted against him.

Rule Material

Rule 4 Summons

(a) Contents; Amendments.

(1) *Contents.* A summons must:

(A) name the court and the parties;

(B) be directed to the defendant;

(C) state the name and address of the plaintiff's attorney or—if unrepresented—of the plaintiff;

(D) state the time within which the defendant must appear and defend;

(E) notify the defendant that a failure to appear and defend will result in a default judgment against the defendant for the relief demanded in the complaint;

(F) be signed by the clerk; and

(G) bear the court's seal.

(2) *Amendments.* The court may permit a summons to be amended.

(b) Issuance. On or after filing the complaint, the plaintiff may present a summons to the clerk for signature and seal. If the summons is properly completed, the clerk must sign, seal, and issue it to the plaintiff for service on the defendant. A summons—or a copy of a summons that is addressed to multiple defendants—must be issued for each defendant to be served.

(c) Service.

(1) *In General.* A summons must be served with a copy of the complaint. The plaintiff is responsible for having the summons and complaint served within the time allowed by Rule 4(m) and must furnish the necessary copies to the person who makes service.

(2) *By Whom.* Any person who is at least 18 years old and not a party may serve a summons and complaint.

(3) *By a Marshal or Someone Specially Appointed.* At the plaintiff's request, the court may order that service be made by a United States marshal or deputy marshal or by a person specially appointed by the court. The court must so order if the plaintiff is authorized to proceed in forma pauperis under 28 U.S.C. §1915 or as a seaman under 28 U.S.C. §1916.

(d) Waiving Service.

(1) *Requesting a Waiver.* An individual, corporation, or association that is subject to service under Rule 4(e), (f), or (h) has a duty to avoid unnecessary expenses of serving the summons. The plaintiff may notify such a defendant that an action has been commenced and request that the defendant waive service of a summons. The notice and request must:

(A) be in writing and be addressed:

(i) to the individual defendant; or

(ii) for a defendant subject to service under Rule 4(h), to an officer, a managing or general agent, or any other agent authorized by appointment or by law to receive service of process;

(B) name the court where the complaint was filed;

(C) be accompanied by a copy of the complaint, 2 copies of a waiver form, and a prepaid means for returning the form;

(D) inform the defendant, using text prescribed in Form 5, of the consequences of waiving and not waiving service;

(E) state the date when the request is sent;

(F) give the defendant a reasonable time of at least 30 days after the request was sent—or at least 60 days if sent to the defendant outside any judicial district of the United States—to return the waiver; and

(G) be sent by first-class mail or other reliable means.

(2) *Failure to Waive.* If a defendant located within the United States fails, without good cause, to sign and return a waiver requested by a plaintiff located within the United States, the court must impose on the defendant:

(A) the expenses later incurred in making service; and

(B) the reasonable expenses, including attorney's fees, of any motion required to collect those service expenses.

(3) *Time to Answer After a Waiver.* A defendant who, before being served with process, timely returns a waiver need not serve an answer to the complaint until 60 days after the request was sent—or until 90 days after it was sent to the defendant outside any judicial district of the United States.

(4) *Results of Filing a Waiver.* When the plaintiff files a waiver, proof of service is not required and these rules apply as if a summons and complaint had been served at the time of filing the waiver.

(5) *Jurisdiction and Venue Not Waived.* Waiving service of a summons does not waive any objection to personal jurisdiction or to venue.

(e) Serving an Individual Within a Judicial District of the United States. Unless federal law provides otherwise, an individual—other than a minor, an incompetent person, or a person whose waiver has been filed—may be served in a judicial district of the United States by:

(1) following state law for serving a summons in an action brought in courts of general jurisdiction in the state where the district court is located or where service is made; or

(2) doing any of the following:

(A) delivering a copy of the summons and of the complaint to the individual personally;

(B) leaving a copy of each at the individual's dwelling or usual place of abode with someone of suitable age and discretion who resides there; or

(C) delivering a copy of each to an agent authorized by appointment or by law to receive service of process.

. . .

(h) Serving a Corporation, Partnership, or Association. Unless federal law provides otherwise or the defendant's waiver has been filed, a domestic or foreign corporation, or a partnership or other unincorporated association that is subject to suit under a common name, must be served:

(1) in a judicial district of the United States:

(A) in the manner prescribed by Rule 4(e)(1) for serving an individual; or

(B) by delivering a copy of the summons and of the complaint to an officer, a managing or general agent, or any other agent authorized by appointment or by law to receive service of process and—if the agent is one authorized by statute and the statute so requires—by also mailing a copy of each to the defendant; or

(2) at a place not within any judicial district of the United States, in any manner prescribed by Rule 4(f) for serving an individual, except personal delivery under (f)(2)(C)(i).

. . .

(k) Territorial Limits of Effective Service.

(1) In General. Serving a summons or filing a waiver of service establishes personal jurisdiction over a defendant:

(A) who is subject to the jurisdiction of a court of general jurisdiction in the state where the district court is located;

(B) who is a party joined under Rule 14 or 19 and is served within a judicial district of the United States and not more than 100 miles from where the summons was issued; or

(C) when authorized by a federal statute.

(2) Federal Claim Outside State-Court Jurisdiction. For a claim that arises under federal law, serving a summons or filing a waiver of service establishes personal jurisdiction over a defendant if:

(A) the defendant is not subject to jurisdiction in any state's courts of general jurisdiction; and

(B) exercising jurisdiction is consistent with the United States Constitution and laws.

(l) Proving Service.

(1) *Affidavit Required.* Unless service is waived, proof of service must be made to the court.

. . .

(m) Time Limit for Service. If a defendant is not served within 120 days after the complaint is filed, the court—on motion or on its own after notice to the plaintiff—must dismiss the action without prejudice against that defendant or order that service be made within a specified time. But if the plaintiff shows good cause for the failure, the court must extend the time for service for an appropriate period. This subdivision (m) does not apply to service in a foreign country under Rule 4(f) or 4(j)(1).

(n) Asserting Jurisdiction over Property or Assets.

(1) *Federal Law.* The court may assert jurisdiction over property if authorized by a federal statute. Notice to claimants of the property must be given as provided in the statute or by serving a summons under this rule.

(2) *State Law.* On a showing that personal jurisdiction over a defendant cannot be obtained in the district where the action is brought by reasonable efforts to serve a summons under this rule, the court may assert jurisdiction over the defendant's assets found in the district. Jurisdiction is acquired by seizing the assets under the circumstances and in the manner provided by state law in that district.

Pennoyer v. Neff

95 U.S. 714, 1877 WL 18188 (1877)

MR. JUSTICE FIELD delivered the opinion of the court.

This is an action to recover the possession of a tract of land, of the alleged value of $15,000, situated in the State of Oregon. The plaintiff asserts title to the premises by a patent of the United States issued to him in 1866. The defendant claims to have acquired the premises under a sheriff's deed, made upon a sale of the property on execution issued upon a judgment recovered against the plaintiff in one of the circuit courts of the State. The case turns upon the validity of this judgment.

[T]he judgment was rendered in February, 1866, in favor of J. H. Mitchell, for less than $300, including costs, in an action brought by him upon a demand for services as an attorney. [A]t the time the action was commenced and the judgment rendered, the defendant [in the original action who is] the plaintiff here, was a non-resident of the State. [H]e was not personally served with process, and did not appear [in the original action] [The] judgment was entered upon his default in not answering the complaint, upon a constructive service of summons by publication.

The Code of Oregon provides for such service when an action is brought against a non-resident and absent defendant, who has property within the State. It also provides, where the action is for the recovery of money or damages, for the attachment of the property of the non-resident. And it also declares that no natural person is subject to the jurisdiction of a court of the State, 'unless he appear in the court, or be found within the State, or be a resident thereof, or have property therein; and, in the last case, only to the extent of such property at the time the jurisdiction attached.' Construing this latter provision to mean, that, in an action for money or damages where a defendant does not appear in the court, and is not found within the State, and is not a resident thereof, but has property therein, the jurisdiction of the court extends only over such property, the declaration expresses a principle of general, if not universal, law. The authority of every tribunal is necessarily restricted by the territorial limits of the State in which it is established. Any attempt to exercise authority beyond those limits would be deemed in every other forum, as has been said by this court, in illegitimate assumption of power, and be resisted as mere abuse. In the case against the plaintiff, the property here in controversy sold under the judgment rendered was not attached, nor in any way brought under the jurisdiction of the court. Its first connection with the case was caused by a levy of the execution. It was not, therefore, disposed of pursuant to any adjudication, but only in enforcement of a personal judgment, having no relation to the property, rendered against a non-resident without service of process upon him in the action, or his appearance therein. The court below did not consider that an attachment of the property was essential to its jurisdiction or to the validity of the sale, but held that the judgment was invalid from defects in the affidavit upon which the order of publication was obtained, and in the affidavit by which the publication was proved.

If, therefore, we were confined to the rulings of the court below upon the defects in the affidavits mentioned, we should be unable to uphold its decision. But it was also contended in that court, and is insisted upon here, that the judgment in the State court against the plaintiff was void for want of personal service of process on him, or of his appearance in the action in which it was rendered and that the premises in controversy could not be subjected to the payment of the demand of a resident creditor except by a proceeding *in rem;* that is, by a direct proceeding against the property for that purpose. If these positions are sound, the ruling of the Circuit Court as to the invalidity of that judgment must be sustained, notwithstanding our dissent from the reasons upon which it was made. And that they are sound would seem to follow from two well-established principles of public law respecting the jurisdiction of an independent State over persons and property. The several States of the Union are not, it is true, in every respect independent, many of the rights and powers which originally belonged to them being now vested in the government created by the Constitution. But, except as restrained and limited by that instrument, they possess and exercise the authority of independent States, and the principles of public law to which we have referred are applicable to them. One of these principles is that every State possesses exclusive jurisdiction and sovereignty over persons and property within its territory. As a consequence, every State has the power to determine for itself the civil *status* and capacities of its inhabitants; to prescribe the subjects upon which they may contract, the forms and solemnities with which their contracts shall be executed, the rights and obligations arising from them, and the mode in which their validity shall be determined and their obligations enforced; and also to regulate the manner and conditions upon which property situated within such territory, both personal and real, may be acquired, enjoyed, and transferred. The other principle of public law referred to follows from the one mentioned; that is, that no State can exercise direct jurisdiction and authority over persons or property without its territory. Story, Confl. Laws, c. 2; Wheat. Int. Law, pt. 2, c. 2. The several States are of equal dignity and authority, and the independence of one implies the exclusion of power from all others. And so it is laid down by jurists, as an elementary principle, that the laws of one State have no operation outside of its territory, except so far as is allowed by comity; and that no tribunal established by it can extend its process beyond that territory so as to subject either persons or property to its decisions. 'Any exertion of authority of this sort beyond this limit,' says Story, 'is a mere nullity, and incapable of binding such persons or property in any other tribunals.' Story, Confl. Laws, sect. 539.

But as property may be held by non-residents, the exercise of the jurisdiction which every State is admitted to possess over persons and property within its own territory will often affect persons and property without it. To any influence exerted in this way by a State affecting persons resident or property situated elsewhere, no objection can be justly taken; whilst any direct exertion of authority upon them, in an attempt to give ex-territorial operation to its laws, or to enforce an ex-territorial jurisdiction by its tribunals, would be deemed an encroachment upon the independence of the State in which the persons are domiciled or the property is situated, and be resisted as usurpation.

Thus the State, through its tribunals, may compel persons domiciled within its limits to execute, in pursuance of their contracts respecting property elsewhere situated, instruments in such form and with such solemnities as to transfer the title, so far as such formalities can be complied with; and the exercise of this jurisdiction in no manner interferes with the supreme control over the property by the State within which it is situated. *Penn* v. *Lord Baltimore*, 1 Ves. 444; *Massie v. Watts*, 6 Cranch, 148; *Watkins v. Holman*, 16 Pet. *Corbett v. Nutt*, 10 Wall. 464.

So the State, through its tribunals, may subject property situated within its limits owned by non-residents to the payment of the demand of its own citizens against them; and the exercise of this jurisdiction in no respect infringes upon the sovereignty of the State where the owners are domiciled. Every State owes protection to its own citizens; and, when non-residents deal with them, it is a legitimate and just exercise of authority to hold and appropriate any property owned by such non-residents to satisfy the claims of its citizens. It is in virtue of the State's jurisdiction over the property of the non-resident situated within its limits that its tribunals can inquire into that non-resident's obligations to its own citizens, and the inquiry can then be carried only to the extent necessary to control the disposition of the property. If the non-resident have no property in the State, there is nothing upon which the tribunals can adjudicate.

These views are not new. They have been frequently expressed, with more or less distinctness, in opinions of eminent judges, and have been carried into adjudications in numerous cases.

If, without personal service, judgments *in personam*, obtained *ex parte* against non-residents and absent parties, upon mere publication of process, which, in the great majority of cases, would never be seen by the parties interested, could be upheld and enforced, they would be the constant instruments of fraud and oppression. Judgments for all sorts of claims upon contracts and for torts, real or pretended, would be thus obtained, under which property would be seized, when the evidence of the transactions upon which they were founded, if they ever had any existence, had perished.

Substituted service by publication, or in any other authorized form, may be sufficient to inform parties of the object of proceedings taken where property is once brought under the control of the court by seizure or some equivalent act. The law assumes that property is always in the possession of its owner, in person or by agent; and it proceeds upon the theory that its seizure will inform him, not only that it is taken into the custody of the court, but that he must look to any proceedings authorized by law upon such seizure for its condemnation and sale. Such service may also be sufficient in cases where the object of the action is to reach and dispose of property in the State, or of some interest therein, by enforcing a contract or a lien respecting the same, or to partition it among different owners, or, when the public is a party, to condemn and appropriate it for a public purpose. In other words, such service may answer in all actions which are substantially proceedings *in rem*. But where the entire object of the action is to determine the personal rights and obligations of the defendants, that is, where the suit is merely *in personam*, constructive service in this form upon a non-resident is ineffectual for any purpose. Process from the tribunals of one State cannot run into another State, and summon parties there domiciled to leave its territory and respond to proceedings against them. Publication of process or notice within the State where the tribunal sits cannot create any greater obligation upon the non-resident to appear. Process sent to him out of the State, and process published within it, are equally unavailing in proceedings to establish his personal liability.

The want of authority of the tribunals of a State to adjudicate upon the obligations of non-residents, where they have no property within its limits, is not denied by the court below: but the position is assumed, that, where they have property within the State, it is immaterial whether the property is in the first instance brought under the control of the court by attachment or some other equivalent act, and afterwards applied by its judgment to the satisfaction of demands against its owner; or such demands be first established in a personal action, and the property of the non-resident be afterwards seized and sold on execution. But the answer to this position has already been given in the statement, that the jurisdiction of the court to inquire into and determine his obligations at all is only incidental to its jurisdiction over the property. Its jurisdiction in that respect cannot be made to depend upon facts to be ascertained after it has tried the cause and rendered the judgment. If the judgment be previously void, it will not become valid by the subsequent discovery of property of the defendant, or by his subsequent acquisition of it. The judgment, if void when rendered, will always remain void: it cannot occupy the doubtful position of being valid if property be found, and void if there be none. Even if the position assumed were confined to cases where the non-resident defendant possessed property in the State at the commencement of the action, it would still make the validity of the proceedings and judgment depend upon the question whether, before the levy of the execution, the defendant had or had not disposed of the property. If before the levy the property should be sold, then, according to this position, the judgment would not be binding. This doctrine would introduce a new element of uncertainty in judicial proceedings. The contrary is the law: the validity of every judgment depends upon the jurisdiction of the court before it is rendered, not upon what may occur subsequently.

The force and effect of judgments rendered against non-residents without personal service of process upon them, or their voluntary appearance, have been the subject of frequent consideration in the courts of the United States and of the several States, as attempts have been made to enforce such judgments in States other than those in which they were rendered, under the provision of the Constitution requiring that 'full faith and credit shall be given in each State to the public acts, records, and judicial proceedings of every other State;' and the act of Congress providing for the mode of authenticating such acts, records, and proceedings, and declaring that, when thus authenticated, 'they shall have such faith and credit given to them in every court within the United States as they have by law or usage in the courts of the State from which they are or shall or taken.' In the earlier cases, it was supposed that the act gave to all judgments the same effect in other States which they had by law in the State where rendered. But this view was afterwards qualified so as to make the act applicable only when the court rendering the judgment had jurisdiction of the parties and of the subject-matter, and not to preclude an inquiry into the jurisdiction of the court in which the judgment was rendered, or the right of the State itself to exercise authority over the person or the subject-matter.

In several cases, the decision has been accompanied with the observation that a personal judgment thus recovered has no binding force without the State in which it is rendered, implying that in such State it may be valid and binding. But if the court has no jurisdiction over the person of the defendant by reason of his nonresidence, and, consequently, no authority to pass upon his personal rights and obligations; if the whole proceeding, without service upon him or his appearance, is *coram non judice* and void; if to hold a defendant bound by such a judgment is contrary to the first principles of justice,-it is difficult to see how the judgment can legitimately have any force within the State. The language used can be justified only on the ground that there was no mode of directly reviewing such judgment or impeaching its validity within the State where rendered; and that, therefore, it could be called in question only when its enforcement was elsewhere attempted. In later cases, this language is repeated with less frequency than formerly, it beginning to be considered, as it always ought to have been, that a judgment which can be treated in any State of this Union as contrary to the first principles of justice, and as an absolute nullity, because rendered without any jurisdiction of the tribunal over the party, is not entitled to any respect in the State where rendered.

Be that as it may, the courts of the United States are not required to give effect to judgments of this character when any right is claimed under them. Whilst they are not foreign tribunals in their relations to the State courts, they are tribunals of a different sovereignty, exercising a distinct and independent jurisdiction, and are bound to give to the judgments of the State courts only the same faith and credit which the courts of another State are bound to give to them.

Since the adoption of the Fourteenth Amendment to the Federal Constitution, the validity of such judgments may be directly questioned, and their enforcement in the State resisted, on the ground that proceedings in a court of justice to deter mine the personal rights and obligations of parties over whom that court has no jurisdiction do not constitute due process of law. Whatever difficulty may be experienced in giving to those terms a definition which will embrace every permissible exertion of power affecting private rights, and exclude such as is forbidden, there can be no doubt of their meaning when applied to judicial proceedings. They then mean a course of legal proceedings according to those rules and principles which have been established in our systems of jurisprudence for the protection and enforcement of private rights. To give such proceedings any validity, there must be a tribunal competent by its constitution-that is, by the law of its creation-to pass upon the subject-matter of the suit; and, if that involves merely a determination of the personal liability of the defendant, he must be brought within its jurisdiction by service of process within the State, or his voluntary appearance.

Except in cases affecting the personal *status* of the plaintiff, and cases in which that mode of service may be considered to have been assented to in advance, as hereinafter mentioned, the substituted service of process by publication, allowed by the law of Oregon and by similar laws in other States, where actions are brought against non-residents, is effectual only where, in connection with process against the person for commencing the action, property in the State is brought under the control of the court, and subjected to its disposition by process adapted to that purpose, or where the judgment is sought as a means of reaching such property or affecting some interest therein; in other words, where the action is in the nature of a proceeding *in rem*. As stated by Cooley in his Treatise on Constitutional Limitations, 405, for any other purpose than to subject the property of a non-resident to valid claims against him in the State, 'due process of law would require appearance or personal service before the defendant could be personally bound by any judgment rendered.'

It is true that, in a strict sense, a proceeding *in rem* is one taken directly against property, and has for its object the disposition of the property, without reference to the title of individual claimants; but, in a larger and more general sense, the terms are applied to actions between parties, where the direct object is to reach and dispose of property owned by them, or of some interest therein. Such are cases commenced by attachment against the property of debtors, or instituted to partition real estate, foreclose a mortgage, or enforce a lien. So far as they affect property in the State, they are substantially proceedings *in rem* in the broader sense which we have mentioned.

It is hardly necessary to observe, that in all we have said we have had reference to proceedings in courts of first instance, and to their jurisdiction, and not to proceedings in an appellate tribunal to review the action of such courts. The latter may be taken upon such notice, personal or constructive, as the State creating the tribunal may provide. They are considered as rather a continuation of the original litigation than the commencement of a new action. *Nations et al. v. Johnson et al.*, 24 How. 195.

It follows from the views expressed that the personal judgment recovered in the State court of Oregon against the plaintiff herein, then a non-resident of the State, was without any validity, and did not authorize a sale of the property in controversy.

To prevent any misapplication of the views expressed in this opinion, it is proper to observe that we do not mean to assert, by any thing we have said, that a State may not authorize proceedings to determine the *status* of one of its citizens towards a non-resident, which would be binding within the State, though made without service of process or personal notice to the non-resident. The jurisdiction which every State possesses to determine the civil *status* and capacities of all its inhabitants involves authority to prescribe the conditions on which proceedings affecting them may be commenced and carried on within its territory. The State, for example, has absolute right to prescribe the conditions upon which the marriage relation between its own citizens shall be created, and the causes for which it may be dissolved. One of the parties guilty of acts for which, by the law of the State, a dissolution may be granted, may have removed to a State where no dissolution is permitted. The complaining party would, therefore, fail if a divorce were sought in the State of the defendant; and if application could not be made to the tribunals of the complainant's domicile in such case, and proceedings be there instituted without personal service of process or personal notice to the offending party, the injured citizen would be without redress.

Neither do we mean to assert that a State may not require a non-resident entering into a partnership or association within its limits, or making contracts enforceable there, to appoint an agent or representative in the State to receive service of process and notice in legal proceedings instituted with respect to such partnership, association, or contracts, or to designate a place where such service may be made and notice given, and provide, upon their failure, to make such appointment or to designate such place that service may be made upon a public officer designated for that purpose, or in some other prescribed way, and that judgments rendered upon such service may not be binding upon the non-residents both within and without the State. Nor do we doubt that a State, on creating corporations or other institutions for pecuniary or charitable purposes, may provide a mode in which their conduct may be investigated, their obligations enforced, or their charters revoked, which shall require other than personal service upon their officers or members. Parties becoming members of such corporations or institutions would hold their interest subject to the conditions prescribed by law.

In the present case, there is no feature of this kind, and, consequently, no consideration of what would be the effect of such legislation in enforcing the contract of a non-resident can arise. The question here respects only the validity of a money judgment rendered in one State, in an action upon a simple contract against the resident of another, without service of process upon him, or his appearance therein.

Judgment affirmed.

World-Wide Volkswagen Corporation et al., v. Woodson

444 U.S. 286, 100 S.Ct. 559 (1980)

Mr. Justice WHITE delivered the opinion of the Court.

The issue before us is whether, consistently with the Due Process Clause of the Fourteenth Amendment, an Oklahoma court may exercise *in personam* jurisdiction over a nonresident automobile retailer and its wholesale distributor in a products-liability action, when the defendants' only connection with Oklahoma is the fact that an automobile sold in New York to New York residents became involved in an accident in Oklahoma.

I

Respondents Harry and Kay Robinson purchased a new Audi automobile from petitioner Seaway Volkswagen, Inc. (Seaway), in Massena, N. Y., in 1976. The following year the Robinson family, who resided in New York, left that State for a new home in Arizona. As they passed through the State of Oklahoma, another car struck their Audi in the rear, causing a fire which severely burned Kay Robinson and her two children.

The Robinsons subsequently brought a products-liability action in the District Court for Creek County, Okla., claiming that their injuries resulted from defective design and placement of the Audi's gas tank and fuel system. They joined as defendants the automobile's manufacturer, Audi NSU Auto Union Aktiengesellschaft (Audi); its importer Volkswagen of America, Inc. (Volkswagen); its regional distributor, petitioner World-Wide Volkswagen Corp. (World-Wide); and its retail dealer, petitioner Seaway. Seaway and World-Wide entered special appearances,[4] claiming that Oklahoma's exercise of jurisdiction over them would offend the limitations on the State's jurisdiction imposed by the Due Process Clause of the Fourteenth Amendment.

World-Wide is incorporated and has its business office in New York. It distributes vehicles, parts, and accessories, under contract with Volkswagen, to retail dealers in New York, New Jersey, and Connecticut. Seaway, one of these retail dealers, is incorporated and has its place of business in New York. Insofar as the record reveals, Seaway and World-Wide are fully independent corporations whose relations with each other and with Volkswagen and Audi are contractual only. Respondents adduced no evidence that either World-Wide or Seaway does any business in Oklahoma, ships or sells any products to or in that State, has an agent to receive process there, or purchases advertisements in any media calculated to reach Oklahoma. In fact, as respondents' counsel conceded at oral argument, there was no showing that any automobile sold by World-Wide or Seaway has ever entered Oklahoma with the single exception of the vehicle involved in the present case.

Despite the apparent paucity of contacts between petitioners and Oklahoma, the District Court rejected their constitutional claim and reaffirmed that ruling in denying petitioners' motion for reconsideration. Petitioners then sought a writ of prohibition in the Supreme Court of Oklahoma to restrain the District Judge, respondent Charles S. Woodson, from exercising *in personam* jurisdiction over them. They renewed their contention that, because they had no "minimal contacts," with the State of Oklahoma, the actions of the District Judge were in violation of their rights under the Due Process Clause.

The Supreme Court of Oklahoma denied the writ, holding that personal jurisdiction over petitioners was authorized by Oklahoma's "long-arm" stat-

---

4 Volkswagen also entered a special appearance in the District Court, but unlike World-Wide and Seaway did not seek review in the Supreme Court of Oklahoma and is not a petitioner here. Both Volkswagen and Audi remain as defendants in the litigation pending before the District Court in Oklahoma.

ute.[5] Although the court noted that the proper approach was to test jurisdiction against both statutory and constitutional standards, its analysis did not distinguish these questions, probably because § 1701.03(a)(4) has been interpreted as conferring jurisdiction to the limits permitted by the United States Constitution. The court's rationale was contained in the following paragraph:

> "In the case before us, the product being sold and distributed by the petitioners is by its very design and purpose so mobile that petitioners can foresee its possible use in Oklahoma. This is especially true of the distributor, who has the exclusive right to distribute such automobile in New York, New Jersey and Connecticut. The evidence presented below demonstrated that goods sold and distributed by the petitioners were used in the State of Oklahoma, and under the facts we believe it reasonable to infer, given the retail value of the automobile, that the petitioners derive substantial income from automobiles which from time to time are used in the State of Oklahoma. This being the case, we hold that under the facts presented, the trial court was justified in concluding that the petitioners derive substantial revenue from goods used or consumed in this State."

We granted certiorari to consider an important constitutional question with respect to state-court jurisdiction and to resolve a conflict between the Supreme Court of Oklahoma and the highest courts of at least four other States.

We reverse.

II

The Due Process Clause of the Fourteenth Amendment limits the power of a state court to render a valid personal judgment against a nonresident defendant. *Kulko v. California Superior Court*, 436 U.S. 84, 91, 98 S.Ct. 1690, 1696, 56 L.Ed.2d 132 (1978). A judgment rendered in violation of due process is void in the rendering State and is not entitled to full faith and credit elsewhere. *Pennoyer v. Neff*, 95 U.S. 714, 732-733, 24 L.Ed. 565 (1878). Due process requires that the

---

5 This subsection provides:

"A court may exercise personal jurisdiction over a person, who acts directly or by an agent, as to a cause of action or claim for relief arising from the person's. . . causing tortious injury in this state by an act or omission outside this state if he regularly does or solicits business or engages in any other persistent course of conduct, or derives substantial revenue from goods used or consumed or services rendered, in this state. . . ."

The State Supreme Court rejected jurisdiction based on § 1701.03(a)(3), which authorizes jurisdiction over any person "causing tortious injury in this state by an act or omission in this state." Something in addition to the infliction of tortious injury was required.

defendant be given adequate notice of the suit, *Mullane v. Central Hanover Trust Co.*, 339 U.S. 306, 313-314, 70 S.Ct. 652, 657, 94 L.Ed. 865 (1950), and be subject to the personal jurisdiction of the court, *International Shoe Co. v. Washington*, 326 U.S. 310, 66 S.Ct. 154, 90 L.Ed. 95 (1945). In the present case, it is not contended that notice was inadequate; the only question is whether these particular petitioners were subject to the jurisdiction of the Oklahoma courts.

As has long been settled, and as we reaffirm today, a state court may exercise personal jurisdiction over a nonresident defendant only so long as there exist "minimum contacts" between the defendant and the forum State. *International Shoe Co. v. Washington, supra,* at 316, 66 S.Ct., at 158. The concept of minimum contacts, in turn, can be seen to perform two related, but distinguishable, functions. It protects the defendant against the burdens of litigating in a distant or inconvenient forum. And it acts to ensure that the States through their courts, do not reach out beyond the limits imposed on them by their status as coequal sovereigns in a federal system.

The protection against inconvenient litigation is typically described in terms of "reasonableness" or "fairness." We have said that the defendant's contacts with the forum State must be such that maintenance of the suit "does not offend 'traditional notions of fair play and substantial justice.' " *International Shoe Co. v. Washington, supra,* at 316, 66 S.Ct., at 158, quoting *Milliken v. Meyer,* 311 U.S. 457, 463, 61 S.Ct. 339, 342, 85 L.Ed. 278 (1940). The relationship between the defendant and the forum must be such that it is "reasonable. . . to require the corporation to defend the particular suit which is brought there." 326 U.S., at 317, 66 S.Ct., at 158. Implicit in this emphasis on reasonableness is the understanding that the burden on the defendant, while always a primary concern, will in an appropriate case be considered in light of other relevant factors, including the forum State's interest in adjudicating the dispute; the plaintiff's interest in obtaining convenient and effective relief, at least when that interest is not adequately protected by the plaintiff's power to choose the forum; the interstate judicial system's interest in obtaining the most efficient resolution of controversies; and the shared interest of the several States in furthering fundamental substantive social policies.

The limits imposed on state jurisdiction by the Due Process Clause, in its role as a guarantor against inconvenient litigation, have been substantially relaxed over the years.[T]his trend is largely attributable to a fundamental transformation in the American economy:

"Today many commercial transactions touch two or more States and may involve parties separated by the full continent. With this increasing nationalization of commerce has come a great increase in the amount of business conducted by mail across state lines. At the same time modern transportation and communication have made it much less burdensome for a party sued to defend himself in a State where he engages in economic activity."

Nevertheless, we have never accepted the proposition that state lines are irrelevant for jurisdictional purposes, nor could we, and remain faithful to the principles of interstate federalism embodied in the Constitution. The economic interdependence of the States was foreseen and desired by the Framers. In the Commerce Clause, they provided that the Nation was to be a common market, a "free trade unit" in which the States are debarred from acting as separable economic entities. But the Framers also intended that the States retain many essential attributes of sovereignty, including, in particular, the sovereign power to try causes in their courts. The sovereignty of each State, in turn, implied a limitation on the sovereignty of all of its sister States-a limitation express or implicit in both the original scheme of the Constitution and the Fourteenth Amendment.

Hence, even while abandoning the shibboleth that "[t]he authority of every tribunal is necessarily restricted by the territorial limits of the State in which it is established," *Pennoyer v. Neff, supra*, 95 U.S., at 720, we emphasized that the reasonableness of asserting jurisdiction over the defendant must be assessed "in the context of our federal system of government," *International Shoe Co. v. Washington*, 326 U.S., at 317, 66 S.Ct., at 158.

Thus, the Due Process Clause "does not contemplate that a state may make binding a judgment *in personam* against an individual or corporate defendant with which the state has no contacts, ties, or relations." *International Shoe Co. v. Washington*, 326 U.S., at 319, 66 S.Ct., at 159. Even if the defendant would suffer minimal or no inconvenience from being forced to litigate before the tribunals of another State; even if the forum State has a strong interest in applying its law to the controversy; even if the forum State is the most convenient location for litigation, the Due Process Clause, acting as an instrument of interstate federalism, may sometimes act to divest the State of its power to render a valid judgment. *Hanson v. Denckla, supra*, 357 U.S., at 251, 254, 78 S.Ct., at 1238, 1240.

III

Applying these principles to the case at hand,[6] we find in the record before us a total absence of those affiliating circumstances that are a necessary predi-

---

6 Respondents argue, as a threshold matter, that petitioners waived any objections to personal jurisdiction by (1) joining with their special appearances a challenge to the District Court's subject-matter jurisdiction, see n. 4, *supra*, and (2) taking depositions on the merits of the case in Oklahoma. The trial court, however, characterized the appearances as "special," and the Oklahoma Supreme Court, rather than finding jurisdiction waived, reached and decided the statutory and constitutional questions.

cate to any exercise of state-court jurisdiction. Petitioners carry on no activity whatsoever in Oklahoma. They close no sales and perform no services there. They avail themselves of none of the privileges and benefits of Oklahoma law. They solicit no business there either through salespersons or through advertising reasonably calculated to reach the State. Nor does the record show that they regularly sell cars at wholesale or retail to Oklahoma customers or residents or that they indirectly, through others, serve or seek to serve the Oklahoma market. In short, respondents seek to base jurisdiction on one, isolated occurrence and whatever inferences can be drawn therefrom: the fortuitous circumstance that a single Audi automobile, sold in New York to New York residents, happened to suffer an accident while passing through Oklahoma.

It is argued, however, that because an automobile is mobile by its very design and purpose it was "foreseeable" that the Robinsons' Audi would cause injury in Oklahoma. Yet "foreseeability" alone has never been a sufficient benchmark for personal jurisdiction under the Due Process Clause.

If foreseeability were the criterion, a local California tire retailer could be forced to defend in Pennsylvania when a blowout occurs there; a Wisconsin seller of a defective automobile jack could be haled before a distant court for damage caused in New Jersey; or a Florida soft-drink concessionaire could be summoned to Alaska to account for injuries happening there. Every seller of chattels would in effect appoint the chattel his agent for service of process. His amenability to suit would travel with the chattel.

This is not to say, of course, that foreseeability is wholly irrelevant. But the foreseeability that is critical to due process analysis is not the mere likelihood that a product will find its way into the forum State. Rather, it is that the defendant's conduct and connection with the forum State are such that he should reasonably anticipate being haled into court there.

When a corporation "purposefully avails itself of the privilege of conducting activities within the forum State," *Hanson v. Denckla*, 357 U.S., at 253, 78 S.Ct., at 1240, it has clear notice that it is subject to suit there, and can act to alleviate the risk of burdensome litigation by procuring insurance, passing the expected costs on to customers, or, if the risks are too great, severing its connection with the State. Hence if the sale of a product of a manufacturer or distributor such as Audi or Volkswagen is not simply an isolated occurrence, but arises from the efforts of the manufacturer or distributor to serve directly or indirectly, the market for its product in other States, it is not unreasonable to subject it to suit in one of those States if its allegedly defective merchandise has there been the source of injury to its owner or to others. The forum State does not exceed its powers under the Due Process Clause if it asserts personal jurisdiction over a corporation that delivers its products into the stream of commerce with the expectation that they will be purchased by consumers in the forum State.

But there is no such or similar basis for Oklahoma jurisdiction over World-Wide or Seaway in this case. Seaway's sales are made in Massena, N. Y. World-Wide's market, although substantially larger, is limited to dealers in New York, New Jersey, and Connecticut. There is no evidence of record that any automobiles distributed by World-Wide are sold to retail customers outside this tristate area. It is foreseeable that the purchasers of automobiles sold by World-Wide and Seaway may take them to Oklahoma. But the mere "unilateral activity of those who claim some relationship with a nonresident defendant cannot satisfy the requirement of contact with the forum State." *Hanson v. Denckla, supra,* at 253, 78 S.Ct., at 1239-1240.

Because we find that petitioners have no "contacts, ties, or relations" with the State of Oklahoma, *International Shoe Co. v. Washington, supra,* 326 U.S., at 319, 66 S.Ct., at 159, the judgment of the Supreme Court of Oklahoma is

Reversed.

Mr. Justice MARSHALL, with whom Mr. Justice BLACKMUN joins, dissenting.

This is a difficult case, and reasonable minds may differ as to whether respondents have alleged a sufficient "relationship among the defendant[s], the forum, and the litigation," *Shaffer v. Heitner,* 433 U.S. 186, 204, 97 S.Ct. 2569, 2580, 53 L.Ed.2d 683 (1977), to satisfy the requirements of *International Shoe.* I am concerned, however, that the majority has reached its result by taking an unnecessarily narrow view of petitioners' forum-related conduct. The majority asserts that "respondents seek to base jurisdiction on one, isolated occurrence and whatever inferences can be drawn therefrom: the fortuitous circumstance that a single Audi automobile, sold in New York to New York residents, happened to suffer an accident while passing through Oklahoma." If that were the case, I would readily agree that the minimum contacts necessary to sustain jurisdiction are not present. But the basis for the assertion of jurisdiction is not the happenstance that an individual over whom petitioner had no control made a unilateral decision to take a chattel with him to a distant State. Rather, jurisdiction is premised on the deliberate and purposeful actions of the defendants themselves in choosing to become part of a nationwide, indeed a global, network for marketing and servicing automobiles.

Petitioners are sellers of a product whose utility derives from its mobility. The unique importance of the automobile in today's society needs no further elaboration. Petitioners know that their customers buy cars not only to make short trips, but also to travel long distances. In fact, the nationwide service network with which they are affiliated was designed to facilitate and encourage such travel. Seaway would be unlikely to sell many cars if authorized service were available only in Massena, N. Y. Moreover, local dealers normally derive a substantial portion of their revenues from their service operations and thereby obtain a further economic benefit from the opportunity to service cars which were sold in other States. It is apparent that petitioners have not attempted to minimize the chance that their activities will have effects in other States; on the contrary, they have chosen to do business in a way that increases that chance, because it is to their economic advantage to do so.

To be sure, petitioners could not know in advance that this particular automobile would be driven to Oklahoma. They must have anticipated, however, that a substantial portion of the cars they sold would travel out of New York. Seaway, a local dealer in the second most populous State, and World-Wide, one of only seven regional Audi distributors in the entire country, would scarcely have been surprised to learn that a car sold by them had been driven in Oklahoma on Interstate 44, a heavily traveled transcontinental highway. In the case of the distributor, in particular, the probability that some of the cars it sells will be driven in every one of the contiguous States must amount to a virtual certainty. This knowledge should alert a reasonable businessman to the likelihood that a defect in the product might manifest itself in the forum State-not because of some unpredictable, aberrant, unilateral action by a single buyer, but in the normal course of the operation of the vehicles for their intended purpose.

It is misleading for the majority to characterize the argument in favor of jurisdiction as one of "'foreseeability' alone." As economic entities petitioners reach out from New York, knowingly causing effects in other States and receiving economic advantage both from the ability to cause such effects themselves and from the activities of dealers and distributors in other States. While they did not receive revenue from making direct sales in Oklahoma, they intentionally became part of an interstate economic network, which included dealerships in Oklahoma, for pecuniary gain. In light of this purposeful conduct I do not believe it can be said that petitioners "had no reason to expect to be haled before a[n Oklahoma] court." *Shaffer v. Heitner, supra*, 433 U.S., at 216, 97 S.Ct., at 2586.

Of course, the Constitution forbids the exercise of jurisdiction if the defendant had no judicially cognizable contacts with the forum. But as the majority acknowledges, if such contacts are present the jurisdictional inquiry requires a balancing of various interests and policies. I believe such contacts are to be found here and that, considering all of the interests and policies at stake, requiring petitioners to defend this action in Oklahoma is not beyond the bounds of the Constitution. Accordingly, I dissent.

Mr. Justice BLACKMUN, dissenting.

I confess that I am somewhat puzzled why the plaintiffs in this litigation are so insistent that the regional distributor and the retail dealer, the petitioners here, who handled the ill-fated Audi automobile involved in this litigation, be named defendants. It would appear that the manufacturer and the importer, whose subjectability to Oklahoma jurisdiction is not challenged before this Court, ought not to be judgment-proof. It may, of course, ultimately amount to a contest between insurance companies that, once begun, is not easily brought to a termination. Having made this much of an observation, I pursue it no further.

Asahi Metal Industry Co., Ltd., Petitioner v. Superior Court Of California, Solano County (Cheng Shin Rubber Industrial Co., Ltd., Real Party In Interest)

107 S.Ct. 1026 (1987)

Justice O'CONNOR announced the judgment of the Court and delivered the unanimous opinion of the Court with respect to Part I, the opinion of the Court with respect to Part II-B, in which THE CHIEF JUSTICE, Justice BRENNAN, Justice WHITE, Justice MARSHALL, Justice BLACKMUN, Justice POWELL, and Justice STEVENS join, and an opinion with respect to Parts II-A and III, in which THE CHIEF JUSTICE, Justice POWELL, and Justice SCALIA join.

This case presents the question whether the mere awareness on the part of a foreign defendant that the components it manufactured, sold, and delivered outside the United States would reach the forum State in the stream of commerce constitutes "minimum contacts" between the defendant and the forum State such that the exercise of jurisdiction "does not offend 'traditional notions of fair play and substantial justice.' " *International Shoe Co. v. Washington*, 326 U.S. 310, 316, 66 S.Ct. 154, 158, 90 L.Ed. 95 (1945), quoting *Milliken v. Meyer*, 311 U.S. 457, 463, 61 S.Ct. 339, 342, 85 L.Ed. 278 (1940).

I

On September 23, 1978, on Interstate Highway 80 in Solano County, California, Gary Zurcher lost control of his Honda motorcycle and collided with a tractor. Zurcher was severely injured, and his passenger and wife, Ruth Ann Moreno, was killed. In September 1979, Zurcher filed a product liability action in the Superior Court of the State of California in and for the County of Solano. Zurcher alleged that the 1978 accident was caused by a sudden loss of air and an explosion in the rear tire of the motorcycle, and alleged that the motorcycle tire, tube, and sealant were defective. Zurcher's complaint named, *inter alia,* Cheng Shin Rubber Industrial Co., Ltd. (Cheng Shin), the Taiwanese manufacturer of the tube. Cheng Shin in turn filed a cross-complaint seeking indemnification from its codefendants and from petitioner, Asahi Metal Industry Co., Ltd. (Asahi), the manufacturer of the tube's valve assembly. Zurcher's claims against Cheng Shin and the other defendants were eventually settled and dismissed, leaving only Cheng Shin's indemnity action against Asahi.

California's long-arm statute authorizes the exercise of jurisdiction "on any basis not inconsistent with the Constitution of this state or of the United States." Cal.Civ.Proc.Code Ann. § 410.10 (West 1973). Asahi moved to quash Cheng Shin's service of summons, arguing the State could not exert jurisdiction over it consistent with the Due Process Clause of the Fourteenth Amendment.

In relation to the motion, the following information was submitted by Asahi and Cheng Shin. Asahi is a Japanese corporation. It manufactures tire valve assemblies in Japan and sells the assemblies to Cheng Shin, and to several other tire manufacturers, for use as components in finished tire tubes. Asahi's sales to Cheng Shin took place in Taiwan. The shipments from Asahi to Cheng Shin were sent from Japan to Taiwan. Cheng Shin bought and incorporated into its tire tubes 150,000 Asahi valve assemblies in 1978; 500,000 in 1979; 500,000 in 1980; 100,000 in 1981; and 100,000 in 1982. Sales to Cheng Shin accounted for 1.24 percent of Asahi's income in 1981 and 0.44 percent in 1982. Cheng Shin alleged that approximately 20 percent of its sales in the United States are in California. Cheng Shin purchases valve assemblies from other suppliers as well, and sells finished tubes throughout the world.

In 1983 an attorney for Cheng Shin conducted an informal examination of the valve stems of the tire tubes sold in one cycle store in Solano County. The attorney declared that of the approximately 115 tire tubes in the store, 97 were purportedly manufactured in Japan or Taiwan, and of those 97, 21 valve stems were marked with the circled letter "A", apparently Asahi's trademark. Of the 21 Asahi valve stems, 12 were incorporated into Cheng Shin tire tubes. The store contained 41 other Cheng Shin tubes that incorporated the valve assemblies of other manufacturers. Declaration of Kenneth B. Shepard in Opposition to Motion to Quash Subpoena, App. to Brief for Respondent 5-6. An affidavit of a manager of Cheng Shin whose duties included the purchasing of component parts stated: "In discussions with Asahi regarding the purchase of valve stem assemblies the fact that my Company sells tubes throughout the world and specifically the United States has been discussed. I am informed and believe that Asahi was fully aware that valve stem assemblies sold to my Company and to others would end up throughout the United States and in California." An affidavit of the president of Asahi, on the other hand, declared that Asahi "has never contemplated that its limited sales of tire valves to Cheng Shin in Taiwan would subject it to lawsuits in California." The record does not include any contract between Cheng Shin and Asahi.

Primarily on the basis of the above information, the Superior Court denied the motion to quash summons, stating: "Asahi obviously does business on an international scale. It is not unreasonable that they defend claims of defect in their product on an international scale." Order Denying Motion to Quash Summons, *Zurcher v. Dunlop Tire & Rubber Co.*, No. 76180 (Super.Ct., Solano County, Cal., Apr. 20, 1983).

The Court of Appeal of the State of California [reversed] conclude[ing] that "it would be unreasonable to require Asahi to respond in California solely on the basis of ultimately realized foreseeability that the product into which its component was embodied would be sold all over the world including California."

The Supreme Court of the State of California reversed and discharged the writ issued by the Court of Appeal. 39 Cal.3d 35, 216 Cal.Rptr. 385, 702 P.2d 543 (1985). The court observed: "Asahi has no offices, property or agents in California. It solicits no business in California and has made no direct sales [in California]." *Id.*, at 48, 216 Cal.Rptr., at 392, n. 4, 702 P.2d, at 549. Moreover, "Asahi did not design or control the system of distribution that carried its valve assemblies into California." *Id.*, at 49, 216 Cal.Rptr., at 392, 702 P.2d, at 549. Nevertheless, the court found the exercise of jurisdiction over Asahi to be consistent with the Due Process Clause. It concluded that Asahi knew that some of the valve assemblies sold to Cheng Shin would be incorporated into tire tubes sold in California, and that Asahi benefited indirectly from the sale in California of products incorporating its components. The court considered Asahi's intentional act of placing its components into the stream of commerce-that is, by delivering the components to Cheng Shin in Taiwan-coupled with Asahi's awareness that some of the components would eventually find their way into California, sufficient to form the basis for state court jurisdiction under the Due Process Clause.

We granted certiorari, and now reverse.

II
[a four-Justice plurality. Ed.]

The Due Process Clause of the Fourteenth Amendment limits the power of a state court to exert personal jurisdiction over a nonresident defendant. "[T]he constitutional touchstone" of the determination whether an exercise of personal jurisdiction comports with due process "remains whether the defendant purposefully established 'minimum contacts' in the forum State." *Burger King Corp. v. Rudzewicz,* 471 U.S. 462, 474, 105 S.Ct. 2174, 2183, 85 L.Ed.2d 528 (1985), quoting *International Shoe Co. v. Washington,* 326 U.S., at 316, 66 S.Ct., at 158. Most recently we have reaffirmed the oft-quoted reasoning of *Hanson v. Denckla,* 357 U.S. 235, 253, 78 S.Ct. 1228, 1239, 2 L.Ed.2d 1283 (1958), that minimum contacts must have a basis in "some act by which the defendant purposefully avails itself of the privilege of conducting activities within the forum State, thus invoking the benefits and protections of its laws." *Burger King,* 471 U.S., at 475, 105 S.Ct., at 2183. "Jurisdiction is proper . . . where the contacts proximately result from actions by the defendant *himself* that create a 'substantial connection' with the forum State." (emphasis in original).

Applying the principle that minimum contacts must be based on an act of the defendant, the Court in *World-Wide Volkswagen Corp. v. Woodson,* 444 U.S. 286, 100 S.Ct. 559, 62 L.Ed.2d 490 (1980), rejected the assertion that a *consumer's* unilateral act of bringing the defendant's product into the forum State was a sufficient constitutional basis for personal jurisdiction over the defendant. It had been argued in *World-Wide Volkswagen* that because an automobile retailer and its wholesale distributor sold a product mobile by design and purpose, they could foresee being haled into court in the distant States into which their customers might drive. The Court rejected this concept of foreseeability as an insufficient basis for jurisdiction under the Due Process Clause. *Id.,* at 295-296, 100 S.Ct., at 566. The Court disclaimed, however, the idea that "foreseeability is wholly irrelevant" to personal jurisdiction, concluding that "[t]he forum State does not exceed its powers under the Due Process Clause if it asserts personal jurisdiction over a corporation that delivers its products into the stream of commerce with the expectation that they will be purchased by consumers in the forum State." *Id.,* at 297-298, 100 S.Ct., at 567 (citation omitted). The Court reasoned:

> "When a corporation 'purposefully avails itself of the privilege of conducting activities within the forum State,' *Hanson v. Denckla,* 357 U.S. [235,] 253 [78 S.Ct. 1228, 1239, 2 L.Ed.2d 1283 (1958)], it has clear notice that it is subject to suit there, and can act to alleviate the risk of burdensome litigation by procuring insurance, passing the expected costs on to customers, or, if the risks are too great, severing its connection with the State. Hence if the sale of a product of a manufacturer or distributor . . . is not simply an isolated occurrence, but arises from the efforts of the manufacturer or distributor to serve, directly or indirectly, the market for its product in other States, it is not unreasonable to subject it to suit in one of those States if its allegedly defective merchandise has there been the source of injury to its owners or to others." *Id.,* at 297, 100 S.Ct., at 567.

In *World-Wide Volkswagen* itself, the state court sought to base jurisdiction not on any act of the defendant, but on the foreseeable unilateral actions of the consumer. Since *World-Wide Volkswagen,* lower courts have been confronted with cases in which the defendant acted by placing a product in the stream of commerce, and the stream eventually swept defendant's product into the forum State, but the defendant did nothing else to purposefully avail itself of the market in the forum State. Some courts have understood the Due Process Clause, as interpreted in *World-Wide Volkswagen,* to allow an exercise of personal jurisdiction to be based on no more than the defendant's act of placing the product in the stream of commerce. Other courts have understood the Due Process Clause and the above-quoted language in *World-Wide Volkswagen* to require the action of the defendant to be more purposefully directed at the forum State than the mere act of placing a product in the stream of commerce.

The reasoning of the Supreme Court of California in the present case illustrates the former interpretation of *World-Wide Volkswagen.* The Supreme Court of California held that, because the stream of commerce eventually brought some valves Asahi sold Cheng Shin into California, Asahi's awareness that its valves would be sold in California was sufficient to permit California to exercise jurisdiction over Asahi consistent with the requirements of the Due Process Clause. The Supreme Court of California's position was consistent with those courts that have held that mere foreseeability or awareness was a constitutionally sufficient basis for personal jurisdiction if the defendant's product made its way into the forum State while still in the stream of commerce.

Other courts, however, have understood the Due Process Clause to require something more than that the defendant was aware of its product's entry into the forum State through the stream of commerce in order for the State to exert jurisdiction over the defendant. In the present case, for example, the State Court of Appeal did not read the Due Process Clause, as interpreted by *World-Wide Volkswagen,* to allow "mere foreseeability that the product will enter the forum state [to] be enough by itself to establish jurisdiction over the distributor and retailer." App. to Pet. for Cert. B5. In *Humble v. Toyota Motor Co.,* 727 F.2d 709 (CA8 1984), an injured car passenger brought suit against Arakawa Auto Body Company, a Japanese corporation that manufactured car seats for Toyota. Arakawa did no business in the United States; it had no office, affiliate, subsidiary, or agent in the United States; it manufactured its component parts outside the United States and delivered them to Toyota Motor Company in Japan. The Court of Appeals, adopting the reasoning of the District Court in that case, noted that although it "does not doubt that Arakawa could have foreseen that its product would find its way into the United States," it would be "manifestly unjust" to require Arakawa to defend itself in the United States.

We now find this latter position to be consonant with the requirements of due process. The "substantial connection," *Burger King,* 471 U.S., at 475, 105 S.Ct., at 2184; *McGee,* 355 U.S., at 223, 78 S.Ct., at 201, between the defendant and the forum State necessary for a finding of minimum contacts must come about by *an action of the defendant purposefully directed toward the forum State. Burger King, supra,* 471 U.S., at 476, 105 S.Ct., at 2184; *Keeton v. Hustler Magazine, Inc.,* 465 U.S. 770, 774, 104 S.Ct. 1473, 1478, 79 L.Ed.2d 790 (1984). The placement of a product into the stream of commerce, without more, is not an act of the defendant purposefully directed toward the forum State. Additional conduct of the defendant may indicate an intent or purpose to serve the market in the forum State, for example, designing the product for the market in the forum State, advertising in the forum State, establishing channels for providing regular advice to customers in the forum State, or marketing the product through a distributor who has agreed to serve as the sales agent in the forum State. But a defendant's awareness that the stream of commerce may or will sweep the product into the forum State does not convert the mere act of placing the product into the stream into an act purposefully directed toward the forum State.

Assuming, *arguendo,* that respondents have established Asahi's awareness that some of the valves sold to Cheng Shin would be incorporated into tire tubes sold in California, respondents have not demonstrated any action by Asahi to purposefully avail itself of the California market. Asahi does not do business in California. It has no office, agents, employees, or property in California. It does not advertise or otherwise solicit business in California. It did not create, control, or employ the distribution system that brought its valves to California. There is no evidence that Asahi designed its product in anticipation of sales in California. On the basis of these facts, the exertion of personal jurisdiction over Asahi by the Superior Court of California[7] exceeds the limits of due process.

B

The strictures of the Due Process Clause forbid a state court to exercise personal jurisdiction over Asahi under circumstances that would offend " 'traditional notions of fair play and substantial justice.' " *International Shoe Co. v.*

---

7 We have no occasion here to determine whether Congress could, consistent with the Due Process Clause of the Fifth Amendment, authorize federal court personal jurisdiction over alien defendants based on the aggregate of national contacts, rather than on the contacts between the defendant and the State in which the federal court sits.

Washington, 326 U.S., at 316, 66 S.Ct., at 158; quoting *Milliken v. Meyer,* 311 U.S., at 463, 61 S.Ct., at 342.

We have previously explained that the determination of the reasonableness of the exercise of jurisdiction in each case will depend on an evaluation of several factors. A court must consider the burden on the defendant, the interests of the forum State, and the plaintiff's interest in obtaining relief. It must also weigh in its determination "the interstate judicial system's interest in obtaining the most efficient resolution of controversies; and the shared interest of the several States in furthering fundamental substantive social policies." *World-Wide Volkswagen,* 444 U.S., at 292, 100 S.Ct., at 564 (citations omitted).

A consideration of these factors in the present case clearly reveals the unreasonableness of the assertion of jurisdiction over Asahi, even apart from the question of the placement of goods in the stream of commerce.

Certainly the burden on the defendant in this case is severe. Asahi has been commanded by the Supreme Court of California not only to traverse the distance between Asahi's headquarters in Japan and the Superior Court of California in and for the County of Solano, but also to submit its dispute with Cheng Shin to a foreign nation's judicial system. The unique burdens placed upon one who must defend oneself in a foreign legal system should have significant weight in assessing the reasonableness of stretching the long arm of personal jurisdiction over national borders.

When minimum contacts have been established, often the interests of the plaintiff and the forum in the exercise of jurisdiction will justify even the serious burdens placed on the alien defendant. In the present case, however, the interests of the plaintiff and the forum in California's assertion of jurisdiction over Asahi are slight. All that remains is a claim for indemnification asserted by Cheng Shin, a Taiwanese corporation, against Asahi. The transaction on which the indemnification claim is based took place in Taiwan; Asahi's components were shipped from Japan to Taiwan. Cheng Shin has not demonstrated that it is more convenient for it to litigate its indemnification claim against Asahi in California rather than in Taiwan or Japan.

Because the plaintiff is not a California resident, California's legitimate interests in the dispute have considerably diminished. The Supreme Court of California argued that the State had an interest in "protecting its consumers by ensuring that foreign manufacturers comply with the state's safety standards." The State Supreme Court's definition of California's interest, however, was overly broad. The dispute between Cheng Shin and Asahi is primarily about indemnification rather than safety standards. Moreover, it is not at all clear at this point that California law should govern the question whether a Japanese corporation should indemnify a Taiwanese corporation on the basis of a sale made in Taiwan and a shipment of goods from Japan to Taiwan. The possibility of being haled into a California court as a result of an accident involving Asahi's components undoubtedly creates an additional deterrent to the manufacture of unsafe components; however, similar pressures will be placed on Asahi by the purchasers of its components as long as those who use Asahi components in their final products, and sell those products in California, are subject to the application of California tort law.

Considering the international context, the heavy burden on the alien defendant, and the slight interests of the plaintiff and the forum State, the exercise of personal jurisdiction by a California court over Asahi in this instance would be unreasonable and unfair.

III
[a four-Justice plurality. Ed.]

Because the facts of this case do not establish minimum contacts such that the exercise of personal jurisdiction is consistent with fair play and substantial justice, the judgment of the Supreme Court of California is reversed, and the case is remanded for further proceedings not inconsistent with this opinion.

It is so ordered.

Justice BRENNAN, with whom Justice WHITE, Justice MARSHALL, and Justice BLACKMUN join, concurring in part and concurring in the judgment.

I do not agree with the interpretation in Part II-A of the stream-of-commerce theory, nor with the conclusion that Asahi did not "purposely avail itself of the California market." *Ante,* at 1034. I do agree, however, with the Court's conclusion in Part II-B that the exercise of personal jurisdiction over Asahi in this case would not comport with "fair play and substantial justice," *International Shoe Co. v. Washington,* 326 U.S. 310, 320, 66 S.Ct. 154, 160, 90 L.Ed. 95 (1945). This is one of those rare cases in which "minimum requirements inherent in the concept of 'fair play and substantial justice' . . . defeat the reasonableness of jurisdiction even [though] the defendant has purposefully engaged in forum activities." *Burger King Corp. v. Rudzewicz,* 471 U.S. 462, 477-478, 105 S.Ct. 2174, 2184-2185, 85 L.Ed.2d 528 (1985). I therefore join Parts I and II-B of the Court's opinion, and write separately to explain my disagreement with Part II-A.

Part II-A states that "a defendant's awareness that the stream of commerce may or will sweep the product into the forum State does not convert the mere act of placing the product into the stream into an act purposefully directed toward the forum State." *Ante,* at 1033. Under this view, a plaintiff would be required to show "[a]dditional conduct" directed toward the forum before finding the exercise of jurisdiction over the defendant to be consistent with the Due Process Clause. *Ibid.* I see no need for such a showing, however. The stream of commerce refers not to unpredictable currents or eddies, but to the regular and anticipated flow of products from manufacture to distribution to retail sale. As long as a participant in this process is aware that the final product is being marketed in the forum State, the possibility of a lawsuit there cannot come as a surprise. Nor will the litigation present a burden for which there is no corresponding benefit. A defendant who has placed goods in the stream of commerce benefits economically from the retail sale of the final product in the forum State, and indirectly benefits from the State's laws that regulate and facilitate commercial activity. These benefits accrue regardless of whether that participant directly conducts business in the forum State, or engages in additional conduct directed toward that State. Accordingly, most courts and commentators have found that jurisdiction premised on the placement of a product into the stream of commerce is consistent with the Due Process Clause, and have not required a showing of additional conduct.

The endorsement in Part II-A of what appears to be the minority view among Federal Courts of Appeals represents a marked retreat from the analysis in *World-Wide Volkswagen v. Woodson,* 444 U.S. 286, 100 S.Ct. 559, 62 L.Ed.2d 490 (1980).

Justice STEVENS, with whom Justice WHITE and Justice BLACKMUN join, concurring in part and concurring in the judgment.

The judgment of the Supreme Court of California should be reversed for the reasons stated in Part II-B of the Court's opinion. While I join Parts I and II-B, I do not join Part II-A for two reasons. First, it is not necessary to the Court's decision. An examination of minimum contacts is not always necessary to determine whether a state court's assertion of personal jurisdiction is constitutional. See *Burger King Corp. v. Rudzewicz,* 471 U.S. 462, 476-478, 105 S.Ct. 2174, 2184-2185, 85 L.Ed.2d 528 (1985). Part II-B establishes, after considering the factors set forth in *World-Wide Volkswagen Corp. v. Woodson,* 444 U.S. 286, 292, 100 S.Ct. 559, 564, 62 L.Ed.2d 490 (1980), that California's exercise of jurisdiction over Asahi in this case would be "unreasonable and unfair." *Ante,* at 1035. This finding alone requires reversal; this case fits within the rule that "minimum requirements inherent in the concept of 'fair play and substantial justice' may defeat the reasonableness of jurisdiction even if the defendant has purposefully engaged in forum activities." *Burger King,* 471 U.S., at 477-478, 105 S.Ct., at

2184-2185 (quoting *International Shoe Co. v. Washington*, 326 U.S. 310, 320, 66 S.Ct. 154, 160, 90 L.Ed. 95 (1945)). Accordingly, I see no reason in this case for the plurality to articulate "purposeful direction" or any other test as the nexus between an act of a defendant and the forum State that is necessary to establish minimum contacts.

Second, even assuming that the test ought to be formulated here, Part II-A misapplies it to the facts of this case. The plurality seems to assume that an unwavering line can be drawn between "mere awareness" that a component will find its way into the forum State and "purposeful availment" of the forum's market. *Ante*, at 1033. Over the course of its dealings with Cheng Shin, Asahi has arguably engaged in a higher quantum of conduct than "[t]he placement of a product into the stream of commerce, without more. . .." *Ibid*. Whether or not this conduct rises to the level of purposeful availment requires a constitutional determination that is affected by the volume, the value, and the hazardous character of the components. In most circumstances I would be inclined to conclude that a regular course of dealing that results in deliveries of over 100,000 units annually over a period of several years would constitute "purposeful availment" even though the item delivered to the forum State was a standard product marketed throughout the world.

Rio Properties, Inc. v. Rio International Interlink

284 F.3d 1007 (2002)

Before: GOODWIN, SNEED, and TROTT, Circuit Judges.

TROTT, Circuit Judge.

Las Vegas hotel and casino operator Rio Properties, Inc. ("RIO") sued Rio International Interlink ("RII"), a foreign Internet business entity, asserting various statutory and common law trademark infringement claims. The district court entered default judgment against RII for failing to comply with the court's discovery orders. RII now appeals the sufficiency of the service of process, effected via email and regular mail pursuant to Federal Rule of Civil Procedure 4(f)(3), the district court's exercise of personal jurisdiction, and ultimately, the entry of default judgment. We have jurisdiction and we affirm the district court's decision.

BACKGROUND

RIO owns the RIO All Suite Casino Resort. In addition to its elegant hotel, RIO's gambling empire consists of the Rio Race & Sports Book, which allows customers to wager on professional sports. To protect its exclusive rights in the "RIO" name, RIO registered numerous trademarks with the United States Patent and Trademark Office. When RIO sought to expand its presence onto the Internet, it registered the domain name, www.playrio.com. At that address, RIO operates a website that informs prospective customers about its hotel and allows those enticed by Lady Luck to make reservations.

RII is a Costa Rican entity that participates in an Internet sports gambling operation. RII enables its customers to wager on sporting events online or via a 1-800 telephone number. Far from a penny ante operation, RII grosses an estimated $3 million annually.

RIO became aware of RII's existence by virtue of RII's advertisement in the Foot-ball Betting Guide '98 Preview. RIO later discovered, in the Nevada edition of the Daily Racing Form, another RII advertisement which invited customers to visit RII's website, www.riosports.com.

Upon learning of RII, RIO fired off an epistle demanding that RII cease and desist from operating the www.riosports.com website. Although RII did not formally respond, it promptly disabled the objectionable website. Apparently not ready to cash in its chips, RII soon activated the URL http:// www.betrio. com to host an identical sports gambling operation. Perturbed, RIO filed the present action alleging various trademark infringement claims and seeking to enjoin RII from the continued use of the name "RIO."

To initiate suit, RIO attempted to locate RII in the United States for service of process. RIO discovered that RII claimed an address in Miami, Florida when it registered the allegedly infringing domain names. As it turned out, however, that address housed only RII's international courier, IEC, which was not authorized to accept service on RII's behalf. Nevertheless, IEC agreed to forward the summons and complaint to RII's Costa Rican courier.

After sending a copy of the summons and complaint through IEC, RIO received a telephone call from Los Angeles attorney John Carpenter ("Carpenter") inquiring about the lawsuit. Apparently, RII received the summons and complaint from IEC and subsequently consulted Carpenter about how to respond. Carpenter indicated that RII provided him with a partially illegible copy of the complaint and asked RIO to send him a complete copy. RIO agreed to resend the complaint and, in addition, asked Carpenter to accept service for RII; Carpenter politely declined. Carpenter did, however, request that RIO notify him upon successful completion of service of process on RII.

Thus thwarted in its attempt to serve RII in the United States, RIO investigated the possibility of serving RII in Costa Rica. Toward this end, RIO searched international directory databases looking for RII's address in Costa Rica. These efforts proved fruitless however; the investigator learned only that RII preferred communication through its email address, email@betrio.com, and received snail mail, including payment for its services, at the IEC address in Florida.

Unable to serve RII by conventional means, RIO filed an emergency motion for alternate service of process. RII opted not to respond to RIO's motion. The district court granted RIO's motion, and pursuant to Federal Rules of Civil Procedure 4(h)(2) and 4(f)(3), ordered service of process on RII through the mail to Carpenter and IEC and via RII's email address, email@betrio.com.

Court order in hand, RIO served RII by these court-sanctioned methods. RII filed a motion to dismiss for insufficient service of process and lack of personal jurisdiction. The parties fully briefed the issues, and the district court denied RII's motion without a hearing. RII then filed its answer, denying RIO's allegations and asserting twenty-two affirmative defenses.

[Once underway, discovery disputes arose. T]he district court granted RIO's motion for [discovery] sanctions and entered default judgment against RII.

RII now appeals the sufficiency of the court-ordered service of process, [and] the district court's exercise of personal jurisdiction. . . .

DISCUSSION

I. ALTERNATIVE SERVICE OF PROCESS

A. Applicability of Rule 4(f)(3)

We review for an abuse of discretion the district court's decision regarding the sufficiency of service of process. Federal Rule of Civil Procedure 4(h)(2) authorizes service of process on a foreign business entity in the manner prescribed by Rule 4(f) for individuals. The subsection of Rule 4(f) relevant to our decision, Rule 4(f)(3), permits service in a place not within any judicial district of the United States "by . . . means not prohibited by international agreement as may be directed by the court."

As obvious from its plain language, service under Rule 4(f)(3) must be (1) directed by the court; and (2) not prohibited by international agreement. No other limitations are evident from the text. In fact, as long as court-directed and not prohibited by an international agreement, service of process ordered under Rule 4(f)(3) may be accomplished in contravention of the laws of the foreign country.

RII argues that Rule 4(f) should be read to create a hierarchy of preferred methods of service of process. RII's interpretation would require that a party attempt service of process by those methods enumerated in Rule 4(f)(2), including by diplomatic channels and letters rogatory, before petitioning the court for alternative relief under Rule 4(f)(3). We find no support for RII's position. No such requirement is found in the Rule's text, implied by its structure, or even hinted at in the advisory committee notes.

By all indications, court-directed service under Rule 4(f)(3) is as favored as service available under Rule 4(f)(1) or Rule 4(f)(2). Indeed, Rule 4(f)(3) is one of three separately numbered subsections in Rule 4(f), and each subsection is separated from the one previous merely by the simple conjunction "or." Rule 4(f)(3) is not subsumed within or in any way dominated by Rule 4(f)'s other subsections; it stands independently, on equal footing. Moreover, no language in Rules 4(f)(1) or 4(f)(2) indicates their primacy, and certainly Rule 4(f)(3) includes no qualifiers or limitations which indicate its availability only after attempting service of process by other means.

The advisory committee notes ("advisory notes") bolster our analysis. Beyond stating that service ordered under Rule 4(f)(3) must comport with constitutional notions of due process and must not be prohibited by international agreement, the advisory notes indicate the availability of alternate service of process under Rule 4(f)(3) without first attempting service by other means. Specifically, the advisory notes suggest that in cases of "urgency," Rule 4(f)(3) may allow the district court to order a "special method of service," even if other methods of service remain incomplete or unattempted.

Thus, examining the language and structure of Rule 4(f) and the accompanying advisory committee notes, we are left with the inevitable conclusion that service of process under Rule 4(f)(3) is neither a "last resort" nor "extraordinary relief." It is merely one means among several which enables service of process on an international defendant.

. . .

Contrary to RII's assertions, RIO need not have attempted every permissible means of service of process before petitioning the court for alternative relief. Instead, RIO needed only to demonstrate that the facts and circumstances of the present case necessitated the district court's intervention. Thus, when RIO presented the district court with its inability to serve an elusive international defendant, striving to evade service of process, the district court properly exercised its discretionary powers to craft alternate means of service. We expressly agree with the district court's handling of this case and its use of Rule 4(f)(3) to ensure the smooth functioning of our courts of law.

B. Reasonableness of the Court Ordered Methods of Service

Even if facially permitted by Rule 4(f)(3), a method of service of process must also comport with constitutional notions of due process. To meet this requirement, the method of service crafted by the district court must be "reasonably calculated, under all the circumstances, to apprise interested parties of the pendency of the action and afford them an opportunity to present their objections." *Mullane v. Cent. Hanover Bank & Trust Co.*, 339 U.S. 306, 314, 70 S.Ct. 652, 94 L.Ed. 865 (1950) (Jackson, J.).

Without hesitation, we conclude that each alternative method of service of process ordered by the district court was constitutionally acceptable. In our view, each method of service was reasonably calculated, under these circumstances, to apprise RII of the pendency of the action and afford it an opportunity to respond.

In particular, service through IEC was appropriate because RII listed IEC's address as its own when registering the allegedly infringing domain name. The record also reflects that RII directed its customers to remit payment to IEC's address. Moreover, when RIO sent a copy of the summons and complaint to RII through IEC, RII received it. All told, this evidence indicates that RII relied heavily upon IEC to operate its business in the United States and that IEC could effectively pass information to RII in Costa Rica.

Service upon Carpenter was also appropriate because he had been specifically consulted by RII regarding this lawsuit. He knew of RII's legal positions, and it seems clear that he was in contact with RII in Costa Rica. Accordingly, service to Carpenter was also reasonably calculated in these circumstances to apprise RII of the pendency of the present action.

Finally, we turn to the district court's order authorizing service of process on RII by email at email@betrio.com. We acknowledge that we tread upon untrodden ground. The parties cite no authority condoning service of process over the Internet or via email, and our own investigation has unearthed no decisions by the United States Courts of Appeals dealing with service of process by email and only one case anywhere in the federal courts. Despite this dearth of authority, however, we do not labor long in reaching our decision. Considering the facts presented by this case, we conclude not only that service of process by email was proper-that is, reasonably calculated to apprise RII of the pendency of the action and afford it an opportunity to respond-but in this case, it was the method of service most likely to reach RII.

To be sure, the Constitution does not require any particular means of service of process, only that the method selected be reasonably calculated to provide notice and an opportunity to respond. See Mullane, 339 U.S. at 314, 70 S.Ct. 652. In proper circumstances, this broad constitutional principle unshackles the federal courts from anachronistic methods of service and permits them entry into the technological renaissance.

Courts . . . cannot be blind to changes and advances in technology. No longer do we live in a world where communications are conducted solely by mail carried by fast sailing clipper . . . ships. Electronic communication via satellite can and does provide instantaneous transmission of notice and information. No longer must process be mailed to a defendant's door when he can receive complete notice at an electronic terminal inside his very office, even when the door is steel and bolted shut.

Although communication via email and over the Internet is comparatively new, such communication has been zealously embraced within the business community. RII particularly has embraced the modern e-business model and profited immensely from it. In fact, RII structured its business such that it could be contacted only via its email address. RII listed no easily discoverable street address in the United States or in Costa Rica. Rather, on its website and print media, RII designated its email address as its preferred contact information.

If any method of communication is reasonably calculated to provide RII with notice, surely it is email-the method of communication which RII utilizes and prefers. In addition, email was the only court-ordered method of service aimed directly and instantly at RII, as opposed to methods of service effected through intermediaries like IEC and Carpenter. Indeed, when faced with an international e-business scofflaw, playing hide-and-seek with the federal court, email may be the only means of effecting service of process. Certainly in this case, it was a means reasonably calculated to apprise RII of the pendency of the lawsuit, and the Constitution requires nothing more.

. . .

Although RII is correct that a plaintiff may not generally resort to email service on his own initiative, in this case, email service was properly ordered by the district court using its discretion under Rule 4(f)(3).

In our case, the district court performed the balancing test admirably, crafting methods of service reasonably calculated under the circumstances to apprise RII of the pendency of the action.

II. JURISDICTION

The district court's determination that personal jurisdiction can be exercised is a question of law reviewed de novo. Although the defendant is the moving party on a motion to dismiss, the plaintiff bears the burden of establishing that jurisdiction exists. Where, as here, the district court receives only written submissions, the plaintiff need only make a prima facie showing of jurisdiction to avoid the defendant's motion to dismiss. In determining whether RIO has met this burden, uncontroverted allegations in RIO's complaint must be taken as true, and conflicts between the facts contained in the parties' affidavits must be resolved in RIO's favor.

To establish that personal jurisdiction over RII is proper, RIO must show that (1) Nevada's long-arm statute confers personal jurisdiction over RII; and (2) that the exercise of jurisdiction comports with the constitutional principles of due process. Nevada's long-arm statute permits the exercise of jurisdiction to the same extent as the Constitution. Hence, we consider only the constitutional principles of due process which require that RII have minimum contacts with Nevada "such that the maintenance of the suit does not offend traditional notions of fair play and substantial justice." *Int'l Shoe Co. v. Washington*, 326 U.S. 310, 316, 66 S.Ct. 154, 90 L.Ed. 95 (1945).

General jurisdiction is not at issue on appeal; we consider only whether the district court properly exercised specific jurisdiction over RII. A three-part test dictates whether specific jurisdiction can be exercised over the defendant: (1) RII must have performed some act or consummated some transaction with the forum by which it purposefully availed itself of the privilege of conducting business in Nevada; (2) RIO's claims must arise out of or result from RII's forum-related activities; and (3) the exercise of jurisdiction must be reasonable.

A. Purposeful Availment

The purposeful availment requirement ensures that a non-resident defendant will not be haled into court based upon random, fortuitous, or attenuated contacts with the forum state. A non-resident defendant purposefully avails itself of the forum if its contacts with the forum are attributable to (1) intentional acts; (2) expressly aimed at the forum; (3) causing harm, the brunt of which is suffered—and which the defendant knows is likely to be suffered—in the forum.

In *Cybersell, Inc. v. Cybersell, Inc.*, 130 F.3d 414, 418-20 (9th Cir.1997), we considered the exercise of specific jurisdiction over a website advertiser. The website advertiser had done nothing other than register a domain name and post an essentially passive website. Certainly, it had done nothing to encourage residents of the forum state to access its site. We held that these acts were insufficient to confer jurisdiction over a non-resident defendant. The objectionable webpage "simply was not aimed intentionally at [the forum state] knowing that harm was likely to be caused there." Under the effects doctrine, "something more" was required to indicate that the defendant purposefully directed its activity in a substantial way to the forum state.

RIO alleged that RII operated a website that "allows customers throughout the United States and the world to place wagers on sporting events." RII responded that merely operating an Internet advertisement or a passive website cannot confer personal jurisdiction. While RII's assertion may be true, operating even a passive website in conjunction with "something more"-conduct directly targeting the forum- is sufficient to confer personal jurisdiction.

Here, RIO sufficiently alleged that RII engaged in "something more" than the operation of a passive website. In its complaint, RIO alleged that RII "specifically targeted consumers" in Nevada "by running radio and print advertisements in Las Vegas." In particular, RIO alleged that RII advertised in the Football Betting Guide '98 Preview and the Daily Racing Form. In fact, RIO attached to its complaint a copy of RII's print advertisement from the Nevada edition of the Daily Racing Form. Clearly, RII knowingly injured RIO in Nevada-its principal place of business and the capital of the gambling industry. All told, RII's actions in Nevada, including its radio and print advertisements, demonstrate an insistent marketing campaign directed toward Nevada. Therefore, we have no problem finding that under the effects doctrine, the purposeful availment requirement for the exercise of personal jurisdiction is satisfied.

B. RII's Forum Related Activities

The second requirement for specific jurisdiction is that RIO's claim arise out of RII's Nevada-related activities. This requirement is satisfied if RIO would not have been injured "but for" RII's conduct in Nevada.

Here, RII's maintenance and promotion of a gambling website injured RIO in Nevada, its principal place of business and the capital of the gambling industry. In addition, RII specifically competed with RIO in Nevada by targeting Nevada consumers in radio and print media. But for RII's activities in Nevada, RIO's injury would not have occurred. Thus, under the effects doctrine, the second requirement for the exercise of personal jurisdiction is satisfied.

C. Reasonableness

The exercise of jurisdiction is reasonable if it comports with traditional notions of fair play and substantial justice. In determining reasonableness, seven factors are considered: (1) the extent of a defendant's purposeful interjection; (2) the burden on the defendant in defending in the forum; (3) the extent of conflict with the sovereignty of the defendant's state; (4) the forum state's interest in adjudicating the dispute; (5) the most efficient judicial resolution of the controversy; (6) the importance of the forum to the plaintiff's interest in convenient and effective relief; and (7) the existence of an alternative forum. As no single factor is dispositive, a court must balance all seven.

RII has purposefully interjected itself into Nevada, and although RII may be burdened by defending in Nevada, it would be so burdened defending in any judicial district in the United States. RII addresses no germane conflict that exists between the United States and Costa Rica. Moreover, as the gambling center of the United States and home of RIO, Nevada asserts a strong interest in adjudicating RIO's claims, and with its expertise resolving disputes involving gambling entities, Nevada can most efficiently resolve the dispute. It is also convenient for RIO to litigate in Nevada, its principal place of business and the location of many pertinent documents. Finally, we note that RII suggests no alternative forum, nor can we conceive of one. In sum, the factors weigh overwhelmingly in favor of the reasonable exercise of personal jurisdiction over RII.

. . .

CONCLUSION

For the reasons delineated above, we affirm the district court's decision in all respects.

AFFIRMED.

NOTE

If a company hopes to avoid being subject to the personal jurisdiction of states outside its home, it might do well to choose a name other than "World-Wide Volkswagon" or "International Shoe." Just a thought if you are ever asked by a client to prepare incorporation documents.

C

Draft Allegations for Minimum Contacts personal jurisdiction in the Frensch (as if being filed in a federal district court in Ohio) or Cash (as if being filed in a federal district court in North Carolina) cases, as assigned.

C. Venue

■ Statutory material
28 USC 1391

(a) Applicability of Section.— Except as otherwise provided by law—

(1) this section shall govern the venue of all civil actions brought in district courts of the United States; and

(2) the proper venue for a civil action shall be determined without regard to whether the action is local or transitory in nature.

(b) Venue in General.— A civil action may be brought in—

(1) a judicial district in which any defendant resides, if all defendants are residents of the State in which the district is located;

(2) a judicial district in which a substantial part of the events or omissions giving rise to the claim occurred, or a substantial part of property that is the subject of the action is situated; or

(3) if there is no district in which an action may otherwise be brought as provided in this section, any judicial district in which any defendant is subject to the court's personal jurisdiction with respect to such action.

(c) Residency.— For all venue purposes—

(1) a natural person, including an alien lawfully admitted for permanent residence in the United States, shall be deemed to reside in the judicial district in which that person is domiciled;

(2) an entity with the capacity to sue and be sued in its common name under applicable law, whether or not incorporated, shall be deemed to reside, if a defendant, in any judicial district in which such defendant is subject to the court's personal jurisdiction with respect to the civil action in question and, if a plaintiff, only in the judicial district in which it maintains its principal place of business; and

(3) a defendant not resident in the United States may be sued in any judicial district, and the joinder of such a defendant shall be disregarded in determining where the action may be brought with respect to other defendants.

(d) Residency of Corporations in States With Multiple Districts.— For purposes of venue under this chapter, in a State which has more than one judicial district and in which a defendant that is a corporation is subject to personal jurisdiction at the time an action is commenced, such corporation shall be deemed to reside in any district in that State within which its contacts would be sufficient to subject it to personal jurisdiction if that district were a separate State, and, if there is no such district, the corporation shall be deemed to reside in the district within which it has the most significant contacts.

. . .

28 USC 1404

(a) For the convenience of parties and witnesses, in the interest of justice, a district court may transfer any civil action to any other district or division where it might have been brought or to any district or division to which all parties have consented.

(b) Upon motion, consent or stipulation of all parties, any action, suit or proceeding of a civil nature or any motion or hearing thereof, may be transferred, in the discretion of the court, from the division in which pending to any other division in the same district. Transfer of proceedings in rem brought by or on behalf of the United States may be transferred under this section without the consent of the United States where all other parties request transfer.

(c) A district court may order any civil action to be tried at any place within the division in which it is pending.

. . .

Piper Aircraft Company v. Reyno

454 U.S. 235 (1981)

Justice MARSHALL delivered the opinion of the Court.

These cases arise out of an air crash that took place in Scotland. Respondent, acting as representative of the estates of several Scottish citizens killed in the accident, brought wrongful-death actions against petitioners that were ultimately transferred to the United States District Court for the Middle District of Pennsylvania. Petitioners moved to dismiss on the ground of forum non conveniens. After noting that an alternative forum existed in Scotland, the District Court granted their motions. The United States Court of Appeals for the Third Circuit reversed. The Court of Appeals based its decision, at least in part, on the ground that dismissal is automatically barred where the law of the alternative forum is less favorable to the plaintiff than the law of the forum chosen by the plaintiff. Because we conclude that the possibility of an unfavorable change in law should not, by itself, bar dismissal, and because we conclude that the District Court did not otherwise abuse its discretion, we reverse.

I

A

In July 1976, a small commercial aircraft crashed in the Scottish highlands during the course of a charter flight from Blackpool to Perth. The pilot and five passengers were killed instantly. The decedents were all Scottish subjects and residents, as are their heirs and next of kin. There were no eyewitnesses to the accident. At the time of the crash the plane was subject to Scottish air traffic control.

The aircraft, a twin-engine Piper Aztec, was manufactured in Pennsylvania by petitioner Piper Aircraft Co. (Piper). The propellers were manufactured in Ohio by petitioner Hartzell Propeller, Inc. (Hartzell). At the time of the crash the aircraft was registered in Great Britain and was owned and maintained by Air Navigation and Trading Co., Ltd. (Air Navigation). It was operated by McDonald Aviation, Ltd. (McDonald), a Scottish air taxi service. Both Air Navigation and McDonald were organized in the United Kingdom. The wreckage of the plane is now in a hangar in Farnsborough, England.

The British Department of Trade investigated the accident shortly after it occurred. A preliminary report found that the plane crashed after developing a spin, and suggested that mechanical failure in the plane or the propeller was responsible.

In July 1977, a California probate court appointed respondent Gaynell Reyno administratrix of the estates of the five passengers. Reyno is not related to and does not know any of the decedents or their survivors; she was a legal secretary to the attorney who filed this lawsuit. Several days after her appointment, Reyno commenced separate wrongful-death actions against Piper and Hartzell in the Superior Court of California, claiming negligence and strict liability. Air Navigation, McDonald, and the estate of the pilot are not parties to this litigation. The survivors of the five passengers whose estates are represented by Reyno filed a separate action in the United Kingdom against Air Navigation, McDonald, and the pilot's estate. Reyno candidly admits that the action against Piper and Hartzell was filed in the United States because its laws regarding liability, capacity to sue, and damages are more favorable to her position than are those of Scotland. Scottish law does not recognize strict liability in tort. Moreover, it permits wrongful-death actions only when brought by a decedent's relatives. The relatives may sue only for "loss of support and society."

On petitioners' motion, the suit was removed to the United States District Court for the Central District of California. Piper then moved for transfer to the United States District Court for the Middle District of Pennsylvania, pursuant to 28 U.S.C. § 1404(a). Hartzell moved to dismiss for lack of personal jurisdiction, or in the alternative, to transfer. In December 1977, the District Court quashed service on Hartzell and transferred the case to the Middle District of Pennsylvania. Respondent then properly served process on Hartzell.

B

In May 1978, after the suit had been transferred, both Hartzell and Piper moved to dismiss the action on the ground of forum non conveniens. The District Court granted these motions in October 1979. It relied on the balancing test set forth by this Court in *Gulf Oil Corp. v. Gilbert*, 330 U.S. 501, 67 S.Ct. 839, 91 L.Ed. 1055 (1947), and its companion case, *Koster v. Lumbermens Mut. Cas. Co.*, 330 U.S. 518, 67 S.Ct. 828, 91 L.Ed. 1067 (1947). In those decisions, the Court stated that a plaintiff's choice of forum should rarely be disturbed. However, when an alternative forum has jurisdiction to hear the case, and when trial in the chosen forum would "establish . . . oppressiveness and vexation to a defendant . . . out of all proportion to plaintiff's convenience," or when the "chosen forum [is] inappropriate because of considerations affecting the court's own administrative and legal problems," the court may, in the exercise of its sound discretion, dismiss the case. To guide trial court discretion, the Court provided a list of "private interest factors" affecting the convenience of the litigants, and a list of "public interest factors" affecting the convenience of the forum.[8]

. . .

C

On appeal, the United States Court of Appeals for the Third Circuit reversed and remanded for trial.

II

The Court of Appeals erred in holding that plaintiffs may defeat a motion to dismiss on the ground of forum non conveniens merely by showing that the substantive law that would be applied in the alternative forum is less favorable to the plaintiffs than that of the present forum. The possibility of a change in substantive law should ordinarily not be given conclusive or even substantial weight in the forum non conveniens inquiry.

[B]y holding that the central focus of the forum non conveniens inquiry is convenience, Gilbert implicitly recognized that dismissal may not be barred solely because of the possibility of an unfavorable change in law. Under Gilbert, dismissal will ordinarily be appropriate where trial in the plaintiff's chosen forum imposes a heavy burden on the defendant or the court, and where the plaintiff is unable to offer any specific reasons of convenience supporting his choice. If substantial weight were given to the possibility of an unfavorable change in law, however, dismissal might be barred even where trial in the chosen forum was plainly inconvenient.

. . .

The Court of Appeals' decision is inconsistent with this Court's earlier forum non conveniens decisions in another respect. Those decisions have repeatedly emphasized the need to retain flexibility. In Gilbert, the Court refused to identify specific circumstances "which will justify or require either grant or denial of remedy." Similarly, in Koster, the Court rejected the contention that where a trial would involve inquiry into the internal affairs of a foreign corporation, dismissal was always appropriate. "That is one, but only one,

---

8 The factors pertaining to the private interests of the litigants included the "relative ease of access to sources of proof; availability of compulsory process for attendance of unwilling, and the cost of obtaining attendance of willing, witnesses; possibility of view of premises, if view would be appropriate to the action; and all other practical problems that make trial of a case easy, expeditious and inexpensive." The public factors bearing on the question included the administrative difficulties flowing from court congestion; the "local interest in having localized controversies decided at home"; the interest in having the trial of a diversity case in a forum that is at home with the law that must govern the action; the avoidance of unnecessary problems in conflict of laws, or in the application of foreign law; and the unfairness of burdening citizens in an unrelated forum with jury duty.

factor which may show convenience." "Each case turns on its facts." If central emphasis were placed on any one factor, the forum non conveniens doctrine would lose much of the very flexibility that makes it so valuable.

In fact, if conclusive or substantial weight were given to the possibility of a change in law, the forum non conveniens doctrine would become virtually useless. Jurisdiction and venue requirements are often easily satisfied. As a result, many plaintiffs are able to choose from among several forums. Ordinarily, these plaintiffs will select that forum whose choice-of-law rules are most advantageous. Thus, if the possibility of an unfavorable change in substantive law is given substantial weight in the forum non conveniens inquiry, dismissal would rarely be proper.

The Court of Appeals' approach is not only inconsistent with the purpose of the forum non conveniens doctrine, but also poses substantial practical problems. If the possibility of a change in law were given substantial weight, deciding motions to dismiss on the ground of forum non conveniens would become quite difficult. Choice-of-law analysis would become extremely important, and the courts would frequently be required to interpret the law of foreign jurisdictions. First, the trial court would have to determine what law would apply if the case were tried in the chosen forum, and what law would apply if the case were tried in the alternative forum. It would then have to compare the rights, remedies, and procedures available under the law that would be applied in each forum. Dismissal would be appropriate only if the court concluded that the law applied by the alternative forum is as favorable to the plaintiff as that of the chosen forum. The doctrine of forum non conveniens, however, is designed in part to help courts avoid conducting complex exercises in comparative law. As we stated in Gilbert, the public interest factors point towards dismissal where the court would be required to "untangle problems in conflict of laws, and in law foreign to itself."

Upholding the decision of the Court of Appeals would result in other practical problems. At least where the foreign plaintiff named an American manufacturer as defendant, a court could not dismiss the case on grounds of forum non conveniens where dismissal might lead to an unfavorable change in law. The American courts, which are already extremely attractive to foreign plaintiffs, would become even more attractive. The flow of litigation into the United States would increase and further congest already crowded courts.

The Court of Appeals based its decision, at least in part, on an analogy between dismissals on grounds of forum non conveniens and transfers between federal courts pursuant to § 1404(a). In *Van Dusen v. Barrack*, 376 U.S. 612, 84

S.Ct. 805, 11 L.Ed.2d 945 (1964), this Court ruled that a § 1404(a) transfer should not result in a change in the applicable law. Relying on dictum in an earlier Third Circuit opinion interpreting Van Dusen, the court below held that that principle is also applicable to a dismissal on forum non conveniens grounds. However, § 1404(a) transfers are different than dismissals on the ground of forum non conveniens.

Congress enacted § 1404(a) to permit change of venue between federal courts. Although the statute was drafted in accordance with the doctrine of forum non conveniens, it was intended to be a revision rather than a codification of the common law. District courts were given more discretion to transfer under § 1404(a) than they had to dismiss on grounds of forum non conveniens.

The reasoning employed in *Van Dusen v. Barrack* is simply inapplicable to dismissals on grounds of forum non conveniens. That case did not discuss the common-law doctrine. Rather, it focused on "the construction and application" of § 1404(a). Emphasizing the remedial purpose of the statute, Barrack concluded that Congress could not have intended a transfer to be accompanied by a change in law. The statute was designed as a "federal housekeeping measure," allowing easy change of venue within a unified federal system. The Court feared that if a change in venue were accompanied by a change in law, forum-shopping parties would take unfair advantage of the relaxed standards for transfer. The rule was necessary to ensure the just and efficient operation of the statute.

We do not hold that the possibility of an unfavorable change in law should never be a relevant consideration in a forum non conveniens inquiry. Of course, if the remedy provided by the alternative forum is so clearly inadequate or unsatisfactory that it is no remedy at all, the unfavorable change in law may be given substantial weight; the district court may conclude that dismissal would not be in the interests of justice.[9] In these cases, however, the remedies that would be provided by the Scottish courts do not fall within this category. Although the relatives of the decedents may not be able to rely on a strict liability theory, and although their potential damages award may be smaller, there is no danger that they will be deprived of any remedy or treated unfairly.

---

9 At the outset of any forum non conveniens inquiry, the court must determine whether there exists an alternative forum. Ordinarily, this requirement will be satisfied when the defendant is "amenable to process" in the other jurisdiction. In rare circumstances, however, where the remedy offered by the other forum is clearly unsatisfactory, the other forum may not be an adequate alternative, and the initial requirement may not be satisfied. Thus, for example, dismissal would not be appropriate where the alternative forum does not permit litigation of the subject matter of the dispute.

III

The Court of Appeals also erred in rejecting the District Court's Gilbert analysis. The Court of Appeals stated that more weight should have been given to the plaintiff's choice of forum, and criticized the District Court's analysis of the private and public interests. However, the District Court's decision regarding the deference due plaintiff's choice of forum was appropriate. Furthermore, we do not believe that the District Court abused its discretion in weighing the private and public interests.

A

The District Court acknowledged that there is ordinarily a strong presumption in favor of the plaintiff's choice of forum, which may be overcome only when the private and public interest factors clearly point towards trial in the alternative forum. It held, however, that the presumption applies with less force when the plaintiff or real parties in interest are foreign.

The District Court's distinction between resident or citizen plaintiffs and foreign plaintiffs is fully justified. In Koster, the Court indicated that a plaintiff's choice of forum is entitled to greater deference when the plaintiff has chosen the home forum. When the home forum has been chosen, it is reasonable to assume that this choice is convenient. When the plaintiff is foreign, however, this assumption is much less reasonable. Because the central purpose of any forum non conveniens inquiry is to ensure that the trial is convenient, a foreign plaintiff's choice deserves less deference.

In analyzing the private interest factors, the District Court stated that the connections with Scotland are "overwhelming." This characterization may be somewhat exaggerated. Particularly with respect to the question of relative ease of access to sources of proof, the private interests point in both directions. As respondent emphasizes, records concerning the design, manufacture, and testing of the propeller and plane are located in the United States. She would have greater access to sources of proof relevant to her strict liability and negligence theories if trial were held here. However, the District Court did not act unreasonably in concluding that fewer evidentiary problems would be posed if the trial were held in Scotland. A large proportion of the relevant evidence is located in Great Britain.

The District Court's review of the factors relating to the public interest was also reasonable. On the basis of its choice-of-law analysis, it concluded that if the case were tried in the Middle District of Pennsylvania, Pennsylvania law would apply to Piper and Scottish law to Hartzell. It stated that a trial involving two sets of laws would be confusing to the jury. It also noted its own lack of familiarity with Scottish law. Consideration of these problems was clearly appropriate under Gilbert; in that case we explicitly held that the need to apply foreign law pointed towards dismissal. The Court of Appeals found that the District Court's choice-of-law analysis was incorrect, and that American law would apply to both Hartzell and Piper. Thus, lack of familiarity with foreign law would not be a problem. Even if the Court of Appeals' conclusion is correct, however, all other public interest factors favored trial in Scotland.

Scotland has a very strong interest in this litigation. The accident occurred in its airspace. All of the decedents were Scottish. Apart from Piper and Hartzell, all potential plaintiffs and defendants are either Scottish or English. As we stated in Gilbert, there is "a local interest in having localized controversies decided at home." Respondent argues that American citizens have an interest in ensuring that American manufacturers are deterred from producing defective products, and that additional deterrence might be obtained if Piper and Hartzell were tried in the United States, where they could be sued on the basis of both negligence and strict liability. However, the incremental deterrence that would be gained if this trial were held in an American court is likely to be insignificant. The American interest in this accident is simply not sufficient to justify the enormous commitment of judicial time and resources that would inevitably be required if the case were to be tried here.

IV

The Court of Appeals erred in holding that the possibility of an unfavorable change in law bars dismissal on the ground of forum non conveniens. It also erred in rejecting the District Court's Gilbert analysis. The District Court properly decided that the presumption in favor of the respondent's forum choice applied with less than maximum force because the real parties in interest are foreign. It did not act unreasonably in deciding that the private interests pointed towards trial in Scotland. Nor did it act unreasonably in deciding that the public interests favored trial in Scotland. Thus, the judgment of the Court of Appeals is

Reversed.

Justice POWELL took no part in the decision of these cases.

Justice O'CONNOR took no part in the consideration or decision of these cases.

Justice WHITE, concurring in part and dissenting in part.

[A dissenting opinion by Justice STEVENS, with whom Justice BRENNAN joins, is omitted.]

C

EXPERIENTIAL ASSIGNMENTS

Advise your partner on proper federal venue choices for filing a Complaint in the Frensch and Cash cases, as assigned by your professor.

CHAPTER 3

State Law in Federal Court

SOMETIMES AN ACTION that is pending in federal court, or some aspects of it, should be governed by state law. That requires a federal judge to learn and apply state law rather than federal law. The circumstances under which this phenomenon should occur have been highly controversial and complex.

Since 1789, federal law has commanded federal courts to apply state law in certain circumstances. (See 28 U.S.C. 1652.) In *Swift v. Tyson*, the scope of that obligation was significantly limited. Although the statutory language had not changed, the limitations of Swift were lifted in *Erie RR v. Tompkins* in 1938, shortly after the adoption of the Federal Rules of Civil Procedure.

■ Statutory Material
28 USC 1652 (The Rules of Decision Act)

The laws of the several states, except where the Constitution or treaties of the United States or Acts of Congress otherwise require or provide, shall be regarded as rules of decision in civil actions in the courts of the United States, in cases where they apply.

Swift v. Tyson

41 U.S. 1, 1842 WL 5662 (1842)

[Tyson gave a "bill of exchange" (a negotiable instrument functionally like a modern bank check) to a third party to pay for a piece of land. In fact, the third party did not own the land he claimed to be selling to Tyson. The third party endorsed the check over to Swift to pay off an existing debt owed to Swift. When Swift tried to collect the money that the check represented, Tyson claimed that since he had been defrauded by the third party, the check had no value. New York courts had held that such underlying fraud had the effect on the check claimed by Tyson. They held that one who took such a check in payment of a pre-existing debt was not a *bona fide* holder in due course. Many other courts held that someone who took such a check in payment of a preexisting debt, like Swift, was a bona fide holder in due course of such a check and could recover from the maker of the check, here Tyson. This case was being decided in federal court with subject matter jurisdiction based on diversity of citizenship. The Court had to decide whether New York's rule should govern, or the by-now-more-common rule of the "general commercial law."]

STORY, Justice, delivered the opinion of the court.

There is no doubt, that a *bonâ fide* holder of a negotiable instrument, for a valuable consideration, without any notice of facts which impeach its validity, as between the antecedent parties, if he takes it under an indorsement made before the same becomes due, holds the title unaffected by these facts, and may recover thereon, although, as between the antecedent parties, the transaction may be without any legal validity. This is a doctrine so long and so well established, and so essential to the security of negotiable paper, that it is laid up among the fundamentals of the law, and requires no authority or reasoning to be now brought in its support.

In the present case, the plaintiff is a *bonâ fide* holder, without notice, for what the law deems a good and valid consideration, that is, for a preexisting debt; and the only real question in the cause is, whether, under the circumstances of the present case, such a pre-existing debt constitutes a valuable consideration, in the sense of the general rule applicable to negotiable instruments. We say, under the circumstances of the present case, for the acceptance having been made in New York, the argument on behalf of the defendant is, that the contract is to be treated as a New York contract, and therefore, to be governed by the laws of New York, as expounded by its courts, as well upon general principles, as by the express provisions of the [Rules of Decision Act]. And then it is further contended, that by the law of New York, as thus expounded by its courts, a pre-existing debt does not constitute, in the sense of the general rule, a valuable consideration applicable to negotiable instruments.

But, admitting the doctrine to be fully settled in New York, it remains to be considered, whether it is obligatory upon this court, if it differs from the principles established in the general commercial law. It is observable, that the courts of New York do not found their decisions upon this point, upon any local statute, or positive, fixed or ancient local usage; but they deduce the doctrine from the general principles of commercial law. It is, however, contended, that the [Rules of Decision Act] furnishes a rule obligatory upon this court to follow the decisions of the state tribunals in all cases to which they apply. That section provides 'that the laws of the several states, except where the constitution, treaties or statutes of the United States shall otherwise require or provide, shall be regarded as rules of decision, in trials at common law, in the courts of the United States, in cases where they apply.' In order to maintain the argument, it is essential, therefore, to hold, that the word 'laws,' in this section, includes within the scope of its meaning, the decisions of the local tribunals. In the ordinary use of language, it will hardly be contended, that the decisions of courts constitute laws. They are, at most, only evidence of what the laws are, and are not, of themselves, laws. They are often re-examined, reversed and qualified by the courts themselves, whenever they are found to be either defective, or ill-founded, or otherwise incorrect. The laws of a state are more usually understood to mean the rules and enactments promulgated by the legislative authority thereof, or long-established local customs having the force of laws. In all the various cases, which have hitherto come before us for decision, this court have uniformly supposed, that the true interpretation of the [Rules of Decision Act] limited its application to state laws, strictly local, that is to say, to the positive statutes of the state, and the construction thereof adopted by the local tribunals, and to rights and titles to things having a permanent locality, such as the rights and titles to real estate, and other matters immovable and intra-territorial in their nature and character. It never has been supposed by us, that the section did apply, or was designed to apply, to questions of a more general nature, not at all dependent upon local statutes or local usages of a fixed and permanent operation, as, for example, to the construction of ordinary contracts or other written instruments, and especially to questions of general commercial law, where the state tribunals are called upon to perform the like functions as ourselves, that is, to ascertain, upon general reasoning and legal analogies, what is the true exposition of the contract or instrument, or what is the just rule furnished by the principles of commercial law to govern the case. And we have not now the slightest difficulty in holding, that this section, upon its true intendment and construction, is strictly limited to local statutes and local usages of the character before stated, and does not extend to contracts and other instruments of a commercial nature, the true interpretation and effect whereof are to be sought, not in the decisions of the local tribunals, but in the general principles and doctrines of commercial jurisprudence. Undoubtedly, the decisions of the local tribunals upon such subjects are entitled to, and will receive, the most deliberate attention and respect of this court; but they cannot furnish positive rules, or conclusive authority, by which our own judgments are to be bound up and governed. The law respecting negotiable instruments may be truly declared in the languages of Cicero, adopted by Lord MANSFIELD in *Luke v. Lyde*, 2 Burr. 883, 887, to be in a great measure, not the law of a single country only, but of the commercial world. *Non erit alia lex Romae, alia Athenis; alia nunc, alia posthac; sed et apud omnes gentes, et omni tempore una eademque lex obtinebit.*

It becomes necessary for us, therefore, upon the present occasion, to express our own opinion of the true result of the commercial law upon the question now before us. And we have no hesitation in saying, that a pre-existing debt does constitute a valuable consideration, in the sense of the general rule already stated, as applicable to negotiable instruments. Assuming it to be true (which, however, may well admit of some doubt from the generality of the language), that the holder of a negotiable instrument is unaffected with the equities between the antecedent parties, of which he has no notice, only where he receives it in the usual course of trade and business, for a valuable consideration, before it becomes due; we are prepared to say, that receiving it in payment of, or as security for, a pre-existing debt, is according to the known usual course of trade and business. . . . But establish the opposite conclusion, that negotiable paper cannot be applied in payment of, or as security for, pre-existing debts, without letting in all the equities between the original and antecedent parties, and the value and circulation of such securities must be essentially diminished, and the debtor driven to the embarrassment of making a sale thereof, often at a ruinous discount, to some third person, and then, by circuity, to apply the proceeds to the payment of his debts. What, indeed, upon such a doctrine, would become of that large class of cases, where new notes are given by the same or by other parties, by way of renewal or security to banks, in lieu of old securities discounted by them, which have arrived at maturity? Probably, more than one-half of all bank transactions in our country, as well as those of other countries, are of this nature. The doctrine would strike a fatal blow at all discounts of negotiable securities for pre-existing debts.

In the American courts, so far as we have been able to trace the decisions, the same doctrine seems generally, but not universally, to prevail. In *Brush v. Scribner*, 11 Conn. 388, the supreme court of Connecticut, after an elaborate review of the English and New York adjudications, held, upon general principles of commercial law, that a pre-existing debt was a valuable consideration, sufficient to convey a valid title to a *bonâ fide* holder against all the antecedent parties to a negotiable note. There is no reason to doubt, that the same rule has been adopted and constantly adhered to in Massachusetts; and certainly, there is no trace to be found to the contrary. In truth, in the silence of any adjudications upon the subject, in a case of such frequent and almost daily occurrence in the commercial states, it may fairly be presumed, that whatever constitutes a valid and valuable consideration, in other cases of contract, to support titles of the most solemn nature, is held à fortiori to be sufficient in cases of negotiable instruments, as indispensable to the security of holders, and the facility and safety of their circulation. Be this as it may, we entertain no doubt, that a *bonâ fide* holder, for a pre-existing debt, of a negotiable instrument, is not affected by any equities between the antecedent parties, where he has received the same, before it became due, without notice of any such equities. We are all, therefore, of opinion, that the question on this point, propounded by the circuit court for our consideration, ought to be answered in the negative; and we shall, accordingly, direct it so to be certified to the circuit court.

[A concurring opinion by Justice CATRON is omitted.]

Erie R. Co. v. Tompkins

304 U.S. 64, 58 S.Ct. 817 (1938)

On Certiorari to the United States Circuit Court of Appeals for the Second Circuit.

Mr. Justice BRANDEIS delivered the opinion of the Court.

The question for decision is whether the oft-challenged doctrine of *Swift v. Tyson* shall now be disapproved.

Tompkins, a citizen of Pennsylvania, was injured on a dark night by a passing freight train of the Erie Railroad Company while walking along its right of way at Hughestown in that state. He claimed that the accident occurred through negligence in the operation, or maintenance, of the train; that he was rightfully on the premises as licensee because on a commonly used beaten footpath which ran for a short distance alongside the tracks; and that he was struck by something which looked like a door projecting from one of the moving cars. To enforce that claim he brought an action in the federal court for Southern New

York, which had jurisdiction because the company is a corporation of that state. It denied liability; and the case was tried by a jury.

The Erie insisted that its duty to Tompkins was no greater than that owed to a trespasser. It contended, among other things, that its duty to Tompkins, and hence its liability, should be determined in accordance with the Pennsylvania law; that under the law of Pennsylvania, as declared by its highest court, persons who use pathways along the railroad right of way-that is, a longitudinal pathway as distinguished from a crossing-are to be deemed trespassers; and that the railroad is not liable for injuries to undiscovered trespassers resulting from its negligence, unless it be wanton or willful. Tompkins . . . contended that, since there was no statute of the state on the subject, the railroad's duty and liability is to be determined in federal courts as a matter of general law.

The trial judge refused to rule that the applicable law precluded recovery. The jury brought in a verdict of $30,000; and the judgment entered thereon was affirmed by the Circuit Court of Appeals, which held that it was unnecessary to consider whether the law of Pennsylvania was as contended, because the question was one not of local, but of general, law, and that 'upon questions of general law the federal courts are free, in absence of a local statute, to exercise their independent judgment as to what the law is; and it is well settled that the question of the responsibility of a railroad for injuries caused by its servants is one of general law. * * * Where the public has made open and notorious use of a railroad right of way for a long period of time and without objection, the company owes to persons on such permissive pathway a duty of care in the operation of its trains. * * * It is likewise generally recognized law that a jury may find that negligence exists toward a pedestrian using a permissive path on the railroad right of way if he is hit by some object projecting from the side of the train.'

The Erie had contended that application of the Pennsylvania rule was required, among other things, by [the Rules of Decision Act] which provides: 'The laws of the several States, except where the Constitution, treaties, or statutes of the United States otherwise require or provide, shall be regarded as rules of decision in trials at common law, in the courts of the United States, in cases where they apply.'

Because of the importance of the question whether the federal court was free to disregard the alleged rule of the Pennsylvania common law, we granted certiorari.

First. *Swift v. Tyson* held that federal courts exercising jurisdiction on the ground of diversity of citizenship need not, in matters of general jurisprudence, apply the unwritten law of the state as declared by its highest court; that they are free to exercise an independent judgment as to what the common law of the state is-or should be; and that, as there stated by Mr. Justice Story, 'the true interpretation of the [Rules of Decision Act] limited its application to state laws, strictly local, that is to say, to the positive statutes of the state, and the construction thereof adopted by the local tribunals, and to rights and titles to things having a permanent locality, such as the rights and titles to real estate, and other matters immovable and intra-territorial in their nature and character. It never has been supposed by us, that the section did apply, or was designed to apply, to questions of a more general nature, not at all dependent upon local statutes or local usages of a fixed and permanent operation, as, for example, to the construction of ordinary contracts or other written instruments, and especially to questions of general commercial law, where the state tribunals are called upon to perform the like functions as ourselves, that is, to ascertain, upon general reasoning and legal analogies, what is the true exposition of the contract or instrument, or what is the just rule furnished by the principles of commercial law to govern the case.'

But it was the more recent research of a competent scholar, who examined the original document, which established that the construction given to it by the Court was erroneous; and that the purpose of the section was merely to make certain that, in all matters except those in which some federal law is controlling, the federal courts exercising jurisdiction in diversity of citizenship cases would apply as their rules of decision the law of the state, unwritten as well as written.[1]

Criticism of the doctrine became widespread after the decision of *Black & White Taxicab & Transfer Co. v. Brown & Yellow Taxicab & Transfer Co.*, 276 U.S. 518, 48 S.Ct. 404, 72 L.Ed. 681, 57 A.L.R. 426. There, Brown &Yellow, a Kentucky corporation owned by Kentuckians, and the Louisville & Nashville Railroad, also a Kentucky corporation, wished that the former should have the exclusive privilege of soliciting passenger and baggage transportation at the Bowling Green, Ky., Railroad station; and that the Black & White, a competing Kentucky corporation, should be prevented from interfering with that privilege. Knowing that such a contract would be void under the common law of Kentucky, it was arranged that the Brown & Yellow reincorporate under the law of Tennessee, and that the contract with the railroad should be executed there. The suit was then brought by the Tennessee corporation in the federal court for Western Kentucky to enjoin competition by the Black & White; an injunction issued by the District Court was sustained by the Court of Appeals; and this Court, citing many decisions in which the doctrine of Swift & Tyson had been applied, affirmed the decree.

---

1 Charles Warren, New Light on the History of the Federal Judiciary Act of 1789 (1923) 37 *Harv.L.Rev.* 49, 51-52, 81-88, 108.

Second. Experience in applying the doctrine of *Swift v. Tyson*, had revealed its defects, political and social; and the benefits expected to flow from the rule did not accrue. Persistence of state courts in their own opinions on questions of common law prevented uniformity; and the impossibility of discovering a satisfactory line of demarcation between the province of general law and that of local law developed a new well of uncertainties.

On the other hand, the mischievous results of the doctrine had become apparent. Diversity of citizenship jurisdiction was conferred in order to prevent apprehended discrimination in state courts against those not citizens of the state. *Swift v. Tyson* introduced grave discrimination by noncitizens against citizens. It made rights enjoyed under the unwritten 'general law' vary according to whether enforcement was sought in the state or in the federal court; and the privilege of selecting the court in which the right should be determined was conferred upon the noncitizen.[2] Thus, the doctrine rendered impossible equal protection of the law. In attempting to promote uniformity of law throughout the United States, the doctrine had prevented uniformity in the administration of the law of the state.

In part the discrimination resulted from the wide range of persons held entitled to avail themselves of the federal rule by resort to the diversity of citizenship jurisdiction. Through this jurisdiction individual citizens willing to remove from their own state and become citizens of another might avail themselves of the federal rule. And, without even change of residence, a corporate citizen of the state could avail itself of the federal rule by reincorporating under the laws of another state, as was done in the Taxicab Case.

The injustice and confusion incident to the doctrine of *Swift v. Tyson* have been repeatedly urged as reasons for abolishing or limiting diversity of citizenship jurisdiction. Other legislative relief has been proposed. If only a question of statutory construction were involved, we should not be prepared to abandon a doctrine so widely applied throughout nearly a century. But the unconstitutionality of the course pursued has now been made clear, and compels us to do so.

Third. Except in matters governed by the Federal Constitution or by acts of Congress, the law to be applied in any case is the law of the state. And whether the law of the state shall be declared by its Legislature in a statute or by its highest court in a decision is not a matter of federal concern. There is no federal general common law. Congress has no power to declare substantive rules of common law applicable in a state whether they be local in their nature or 'general,' be they

---

2 It was even possible for a nonresident plaintiff defeated on a point of law in the highest court of a State nevertheless to win out by taking a nonsuit and renewing the controversy in the federal court.

commercial law or a part of the law of torts. And no clause in the Constitution purports to confer such a power upon the federal courts.

The fallacy underlying the rule declared in *Swift v. Tyson* is made clear by Mr. Justice Holmes. The doctrine rests upon the assumption that there is 'a transcendental body of law outside of any particular State but obligatory within it unless and until changed by statute,' that federal courts have the power to use their judgment as to what the rules of common law are; and that in the federal courts 'the parties are entitled to an independent judgment on matters of general law':

'But law in the sense in which courts speak of it today does not exist without some definite authority behind it. The common law so far as it is enforced in a State, whether called common law or not, is not the common law generally but the law of that State existing by the authority of that State without regard to what it may have been in England or anywhere else. * * *

'The authority and only authority is the State, and if that be so, the voice adopted by the State as its own (whether it be of its Legislature or of its Supreme Court) should utter the last word.'

Thus the doctrine of *Swift v. Tyson* is, as Mr. Justice Holmes said, 'an unconstitutional assumption of powers by the Courts of the United States which no lapse of time or respectable array of opinion should make us hesitate to correct.' In disapproving that doctrine we do not hold unconstitutional [The Rules of Decision Act]. We merely declare that in applying the doctrine this Court and the lower courts have invaded rights which in our opinion are reserved by the Constitution to the several states.

Fourth. The defendant contended that by the common law of Pennsylvania as declared by its highest court in *Falchetti v. Pennsylvania R. Co.*, 307 Pa. 203, 160 A. 859, the only duty owed to the plaintiff was to refrain from willful or wanton injury. The plaintiff denied that such is the Pennsylvania law. In support of their respective contentions the parties discussed and cited many decisions of the Supreme Court of the state. The Circuit Court of Appeals ruled that the question of liability is one of general law; and on that ground declined to decide the issue of state law. As we hold this was error, the judgment is reversed and the case remanded to it for further proceedings in conformity with our opinion.

Reversed.

Mr. Justice CARDOZO took no part in the consideration or decision of this case.

Mr. Justice BUTLER (dissenting).

Mr. Justice McREYNOLDS, concurs in this opinion.

Mr. Justice REED (concurring in part).

I concur in the conclusion reached in this case, in the disapproval of the doctrine of *Swift v. Tyson*, and in the reasoning of the majority opinion, except in so far as it relies upon the unconstitutionality of the 'course pursued' by the federal courts.

The 'doctrine of Swift v. Tyson,' as I understand it, is that the words 'the laws,' as used in [the Rules of Decision Act], do not include in their meaning 'the decisions of the local tribunals.' Mr. Justice Story, in deciding that point, said, 16 Pet. 1, 19, 10 L.Ed. 865: 'Undoubtedly, the decisions of the local tribunals upon such subjects are entitled to, and will receive, the most deliberate attention and respect of this court; but they cannot furnish positive rules, or conclusive authority, by which our own judgments are to be bound up and governed.'

To decide the case now before us and to 'disapprove' the doctrine of *Swift v. Tyson* requires only that we say that the words 'the laws' include in their meaning the decisions of the local tribunals. As the majority opinion shows, by its reference to Mr. Warren's researches and the first quotation from Mr. Justice Holmes, that this Court is now of the view that 'laws' includes 'decisions,' it is unnecessary to go further and declare that the 'course pursued' was 'unconstitutional,' instead of merely erroneous.

The 'unconstitutional' course referred to in the majority opinion is apparently the ruling in *Swift v. Tyson* that the supposed omission of Congress to legislate as to the effect of decisions leaves federal courts free to interpret general law for themselves. I am not at all sure whether, in the absence of federal statutory direction, federal courts would be compelled to follow state decisions. There was sufficient doubt about the matter in 1789 to induce the first Congress to legislate. No former opinions of this Court have passed upon it. Mr. Justice Holmes evidently saw nothing 'unconstitutional' which required the overruling of *Swift v. Tyson*, for he said in the very opinion quoted by the majority, 'I should leave *Swift v. Tyson* undisturbed, as I indicated in *Kuhn v. Fairmont Coal Co.*, but I would not allow it to spread the assumed dominion into new fields.' *Black & White Taxicab Co. v. Brown & Yellow Taxicab Co.*, 276 U.S. 518, 535, 48 S.Ct. 404, 409, 72 L.Ed. 681, 57 A.L.R. 426. If the opinion commits this Court to the position that the Congress is without power to declare what rules of substantive law shall govern the federal courts, that conclusion also seems questionable. The line between procedural and substantive law is hazy, but no one doubts federal power over procedure. *Wayman v. Southard*, 10 Wheat. 1, 6 L.Ed. 253. The Judiciary Article, 3, and the 'necessary and proper' clause of article 1, s 8, may fully authorize legislation, such as this section of the Judiciary Act.

NOTES

1. Some interesting *Erie* facts. At the trial court, Tompkins won a verdict for $30,000. On appeal, the railroad offered him $7,500, still serious money in the 1930s. Had Tompkins accepted, there would have been no *Erie v. Tompkins* Supreme Court decision. Overturning *Swift v. Tyson* would have had to wait for another day and case. Tompkins was interested in the railroad's offer and may have wanted to accept it. But his lawyer, so excited by the prospect of appearing in the United States Supreme Court, dissuaded him from accepting and had Tompkins live in the lawyer's house in New York, during which time the railroad withdrew the offer to settle. Unfortunately for Tompkins, the result in the Supreme Court and subsequent proceedings meant he recovered nothing. There is no evidence that his lawyer was ever disciplined for this act of misconduct.

2. Although *Erie* tells the tale of the expansion of state law use in federal cases, particularly those supported by diversity of citizenship jurisdiction, many subsequent cases have added nuance to the basic Erie outline. The basic Erie lesson, use state law for substance and federal law for procedure, is a useful rule of thumb, but one that like all such simple statements, hides an iceberg of confusion under the waterline.

The Erie doctrine rests on two themes: federalism and litigant equality. Maintaining a respectful balance between federal and state law and courts is one target of the doctrine. Under *Swift v. Tyson,* there was a federal court superiority complex that extended beyond the Supremacy Clause. Federal courts just seemed to think they knew better and if only state courts would come into line with the "general common law," then the law would become consistent through the United States. In fact, what happened was quite different, with states going in different directions on many points of law and the better views emerging from state experimentation. In other words, law development occurred from the states up rather than the federal courts down. Of course, only the federal courts seemed to think that the direction from federal courts to state courts was "down."

The reinterpretation of the Rules of Decision Act was critical to the result in *Erie*. The language of the statute had not changed between *Swift* and *Erie*. The key reinterpretive moment was the focus on the word "*laws.*" Legal philosophy had developed from full-bore formalism to legal realism by the time of the *Erie* decision. In the earlier time, the word "*laws*" connoted statutes adopted by the legislature. But legal realism recognized that the common law was not some amorphous cloud always existent and discovered by courts. Instead, legal realists said, judges made law when they decided disputes. Courts were by this time seen as an authoritative, public body with power to make law with the predictive power of their resolution of live disputes. In other words, by the time of *Erie*, court decisions were "laws," too.

To be sure, courts make law in a way far different from legislatures. Legislatures create expressly prospective statements of law. They can decide what social ills to conquer and create from scratch whatever they wish, within constitutional bounds. Courts by contrast must wait for disputes to be brought. And when a common law court announces and explains its resolution of a dispute, it creates law with the predictive value of the decision. Lawyers and people generally learn the likely legal result of conduct by reading court decisions. In this way, people's conduct is governed by court decisions, and those court decisions, by virtue of their effect on conduct, are seen as law. But by one means or another, court decisions in common law jurisdictions are law. The *Erie* court determined that they are laws within the meaning of the Rules of Decision Act.

And the other change between *Swift* and *Erie* was the adoption of the Federal Rules of Civil Procedure. The time was ripe for reform of procedure and the Rules' adoption swept the change from *Swift* to *Erie* along.

Choice of Law. Consider choice of law, both horizontal and vertical. If multiple courts have jurisdiction over a particular matter, a plaintiff, at least initially, gets to choose in which court to file her complaint. In "horizontal" terms, that means that if courts in several states, let's say Ohio, New York and Texas, would all have personal jurisdiction over the defendant, the plaintiff could choose among them. Each state is one of 51 jurisdictions that are at the same level in a court organizational chart, so this choice is a horizontal one. The Erie doctrine has nothing to do with a plaintiff choosing Texas over

Ohio because the plaintiff thinks that Texas law is more favorable to her case.

The Erie doctrine is about vertical choice of law. Within any given state, if the federal court would have subject matter jurisdiction (typically under either 1331 or 1332), the plaintiff again has a choice of where to file. But this time the choice is between federal and state court. This time, on an organizational chart, the choice is vertical and not between courts of entirely distinct equal political bodies like Ohio and Texas.

If the court chosen is the federal one, the next question to ask is what law applies. If jurisdiction is based on a federal question, federal law will govern the decision. A state court would also apply federal law to decide the same federal question. So when the question is one of federal law, the rule of decision will be the same whether the plaintiff chooses federal or state court.

But when the question is one of state law, as typically happens in diversity of citizenship cases, the Erie doctrine comes into play. In the absence of a controlling state statute, the state court would apply state common law. The federal court, however, under *Swift v. Tyson,* would apply the "general common law" without regard to whether it produced the same result as the specific state's common law. As a result, before *Erie,* there were two different rules governing a person's conduct within the same state. A person could not know whether their conduct would be later challenged in a state or federal court and therefore could not know how to safely behave. This disruption, in part, led the Court to the decision in *Erie.*

The Taxicab Case, cited in *Erie,* was a prime example of the abuse that *Swift* fostered. Brown and Yellow Taxicab and a railroad company that operated a station in Kentucky wanted to enter into an exclusive contract that would allow only Brown and Yellow taxis to take passengers at the station. The contract was illegal under Kentucky law. Both Brown and Yellow and their competitor, Black and White Taxi companies, were Kentucky corporations. Brown and Yellow and the railroad knew that if they entered the contract and were sued in Kentucky courts, the contract would be ruled void. So Brown and Yellow, despite having no relationship with Tennessee, dissolved and reformed as a Tennessee corporation, apparently for the sole reason of getting into federal courts under diversity jurisdiction. The ploy worked because Swift required the federal court sitting in Kentucky to apply the general common law, upholding the contract. All of the actions under the contract took place in Kentucky, where such a contract was illegal.

Substance vs. Procedure. When the rule being applied is purely procedural, it is not a "rule of decision." It merely allows the civil action to proceed in an orderly and predictable way so that the substantive decisions can be made. But knowing what is substance and what is procedure bedeviled courts after *Erie* and continues to do so. Some things are known, however.

Choice of law rules, such as would determine whether Texas or Ohio law applies to some dispute, are substantive and therefore governed by state and not federal law.

The statute of limitations is substantive and therefore state and not federal law applies.

For a time, the test hinged solely on whether the rule at issue was "outcome determinative." If it was, it was substantive and state law would apply; if not, it was procedural and federal rules would apply. But this test was ill conceived. Let's say, as was common, that under a state's court rules, court filings had to be on 8½ x 14 inch paper, while in federal court, filings had to be on 8½ x 11 inch paper. If the federal court clerk would refuse to accept the 8½ x 14 inch papers for filing, then the outcome would be determined by the paper-size rule and it would be deemed substantive, and governed by state law. Such results were a bit ludicrous, not to mention the irritation of federal court clerks who would have to start accepting 8½ x 14 inch paper, causing no end to their filing cabinet difficulties. The outcome-determinative test was doomed from the start.

A series of cases pushed too far toward the use of state law in borderline situations between substance and procedure. In the mid-1960s the *Byrd* and *Hanna* cases reversed this trend and allowed federal courts to use their own procedural systems when enforcing state rights, even if sometimes the result might be affected by the procedural rule.

The *Gasperini* case that follows is the latest in the line of cases searching for the proper federalism balance.

Applying the choice of law rules, including the Erie doctrine, is a complex task. This flowchart is a good summary, but as you will see in *Gasperini*, the analysis continues to evolve.

1. Is there a clear, federal directive on point?

a. If yes, apply it, the Supremacy Clause demands.

b. If there is no clear, federal directive on point, then apply the Rules of Decision Act/Erie analysis.

2. Rules of Decision/Erie analysis. Is the rule under consideration clear substance, in essence, an element of the law governing the claim?

a. If so, state law applies.

b. If the rule is not clear substance, but rather deals with the "form and mode" of application of the clear substance, is the rule outcome determinative?

i. If not, the federal court may ignore the state law without offending federalism concerns.

ii. If so, then the federal court should apply state law unless there is a good reason, such as the federal courts' systematic interest in allocating responsibility between judge and jury (*Byrd*) or between trial and appellate courts (*Gasperini*).

Gasperini v. Center For Humanities, Inc.

518 U.S. 415, 116 S.Ct. 2211(1996)

Justice GINSBURG delivered the opinion of the Court.

Under the law of New York, appellate courts are empowered to review the size of jury verdicts and to order new trials when the jury's award "deviates materially from what would be reasonable compensation." N.Y. Civ. Prac. Law and Rules (CPLR) § 5501(c) (McKinney 1995). Under the Seventh Amendment, which governs proceedings in federal court, but not in state court, "the right of trial by jury shall be preserved, and no fact tried by a jury, shall be otherwise re-examined in any Court of the United States, than according to the rules of the common law." U.S. Const., Amdt. 7. The compatibility of these provisions, in an action based on New York law but tried in federal court by reason of the parties' diverse citizenship, is the issue we confront in this case. We hold that New York's law controlling compensation awards for excessiveness or inadequacy can be given effect, without detriment to the Seventh Amendment, if the review standard set out in CPLR § 5501(c) is applied by the federal trial court judge, with appellate control of the trial court's ruling limited to review for "abuse of discretion."

I

Petitioner William Gasperini, a journalist for CBS News and the Christian Science Monitor, began reporting on events in Central America in 1984. He earned his living primarily in radio and print media and only occasionally sold his photographic work. During the course of his seven-year stint in Central America, Gasperini took over 5,000 slide transparencies, depicting active war zones, political leaders, and scenes from daily life. In 1990, Gasperini agreed to supply his original color transparencies to The Center for Humanities, Inc. (Center) for use in an educational videotape, Conflict in Central America. Gasperini selected 300 of his slides for the Center; its videotape included 110 of them. The Center agreed to return the original transparencies, but upon the completion of the project, it could not find them.

Gasperini commenced suit in the United States District Court for the Southern District of New York, invoking the court's diversity jurisdiction pursuant to 28 U.S.C. § 1332. He alleged several state-law claims for relief, including breach of contract, conversion, and negligence. The Center conceded liability for the lost transparencies and the issue of damages was tried before a jury.

At trial, Gasperini's expert witness testified that the "industry standard" within the photographic publishing community valued a lost transparency at $1,500. Gasperini estimated that his earnings from photography totaled just over $10,000 for the period from 1984 through 1993. He also testified that he intended to produce a book containing his best photographs from Central America.

[T]he jury awarded Gasperini $450,000 in compensatory damages. This sum, the jury foreperson announced, "is [$]1500 each, for 300 slides." Moving for a new trial under Federal Rule of Civil Procedure 59, the Center attacked the verdict on various grounds, including excessiveness. Without comment, the District Court denied the motion.

The Court of Appeals for the Second Circuit vacated the judgment entered on the jury's verdict. Mindful that New York law governed the controversy, the Court of Appeals endeavored to apply CPLR § 5501(c), which instructs that, when a jury returns an itemized verdict, as the jury did in this case, the New York Appellate Division "shall determine that an award is excessive or inadequate if it deviates materially from what would be reasonable compensation." Surveying Appellate Division decisions that reviewed damage awards for lost transparencies, the Second Circuit concluded that testimony on industry standard alone was insufficient to justify a verdict; prime among other factors warranting consideration were the uniqueness of the slides' subject matter and the photographer's earning level.

Guided by Appellate Division rulings, the Second Circuit held that the $450,000 verdict "materially deviates from what is reasonable compensation." [T]he Second Circuit set aside the $450,000 verdict and ordered a new trial, unless Gasperini agreed to an award of $100,000.

This case presents an important question regarding the standard a federal court uses to measure the alleged excessiveness of a jury's verdict in an action for damages based on state law. We therefore granted certiorari.

II

Before 1986, state and federal courts in New York generally invoked the same judge-made formulation in responding to excessiveness attacks on jury verdicts: courts would not disturb an award unless the amount was so exorbitant that it "shocked the conscience of the court."

In both state and federal courts, trial judges made the excessiveness assessment in the first instance, and appellate judges ordinarily deferred to the trial court's judgment.

In 1986, as part of a series of tort reform measures, New York codified a standard for judicial review of the size of jury awards. Placed in CPLR § 5501(c), the prescription reads:

> In reviewing a money judgment . . . in which it is contended that the award is excessive or inadequate and that a new trial should have been granted unless a stipulation is entered to a different award, the appellate division shall determine that an award is excessive or inadequate if it deviates materially from what would be reasonable compensation.

As stated in Legislative Findings and Declarations accompanying New York's adoption of the "deviates materially" formulation, the lawmakers found the "shock the conscience" test an insufficient check on damage awards; the legislature therefore installed a standard "invit[ing] more careful appellate scrutiny."

New York state-court opinions confirm that § 5501(c)'s "deviates materially" standard calls for closer surveillance than "shock the conscience" oversight.

To determine whether an award "deviates materially from what would be reasonable compensation," New York state courts look to awards approved in similar cases. Under New York's former "shock the conscience" test, courts also referred to analogous cases. The "deviates materially" standard, however, in design and operation, influences outcomes by tightening the range of tolerable awards.

III

In cases like Gasperini's, in which New York law governs the claims for relief, does New York law also supply the test for federal-court review of the size of the verdict? The Center answers yes. The "deviates materially" standard, it argues, is a substantive standard that must be applied by federal appellate courts in diversity cases. The Second Circuit agreed.

As the parties' arguments suggest, CPLR § 5501(c), appraised under *Erie R. Co. v. Tompkins,* and decisions in Erie's path, is both "substantive" and "procedural": "substantive" in that § 5501(c)'s "deviates materially" standard controls how much a plaintiff can be awarded; "procedural" in that § 5501(c) assigns decisionmaking authority to New York's Appellate Division. Parallel application of § 5501(c) at the federal appellate level would be out of sync with the federal system's division of trial and appellate court functions, an allocation weighted by the Seventh Amendment. The dispositive question, therefore, is whether federal courts can give effect to the substantive thrust of § 5501(c) without untoward alteration of the federal scheme for the trial and decision of civil cases.

A

Federal diversity jurisdiction provides an alternative forum for the adjudication of state-created rights, but it does not carry with it generation of rules of substantive law. As *Erie* read the Rules of Decision Act: "Except in matters governed by the Federal Constitution or by Acts of Congress, the law to be applied in any case is the law of the State." Under the Erie doctrine, federal courts sitting in diversity apply state substantive law and federal procedural law.

Classification of a law as "substantive" or "procedural" for *Erie* purposes is sometimes a challenging endeavor. *Guaranty Trust Co. v. York*, 326 U.S. 99, 65 S.Ct. 1464, 89 L.Ed. 2079 (1945), an early interpretation of *Erie*, propounded an "outcome-determination" test: "[D]oes it significantly affect the result of a litigation for a federal court to disregard a law of a State that would be controlling in an action upon the same claim by the same parties in a State court?" Ordering application of a state statute of limitations to an equity proceeding in federal court, the Court said in Guaranty Trust: "[W]here a federal court is exercising jurisdiction solely because of the diversity of citizenship of the parties, the outcome of the litigation in the federal court should be substantially the same, so far as legal rules determine the outcome of a litigation, as it would be if tried in a State court." A later pathmarking case, qualifying *Guaranty Trust*, explained that the "outcome-determination" test must not be applied mechanically to sweep in all manner of variations; instead, its application must be guided by "the twin aims of the *Erie* rule: discouragement of forum-shopping and avoidance of inequitable administration of the laws." *Hanna v. Plumer*, 380 U.S. 460, 468, 85 S.Ct. 1136, 1142, 14 L.Ed.2d 8 (1965).

Informed by these decisions, we address the question whether New York's "deviates materially" standard, codified in CPLR § 5501(c), is outcome affective in this sense: Would "application of the [standard] . . . have so important an effect upon the fortunes of one or both of the litigants that failure to [apply] it would [unfairly discriminate against citizens of the forum State, or] be likely to cause a plaintiff to choose the federal court"?

We start from a point the parties do not debate. Gasperini acknowledges that a statutory cap on damages would supply substantive law for *Erie* purposes. Although CPLR § 5501(c) is less readily classified, it was designed to provide an analogous control.

New York's Legislature codified in § 5501(c) a new standard, one that requires closer court review than the common-law "shock the conscience" test. We think it a fair conclusion that CPLR § 5501(c) differs from a statutory cap principally "in that the maximum amount recoverable is not set forth by statute, but rather is determined by case law." In sum, § 5501(c) contains a procedural instruction, but the State's objective is manifestly substantive.

It thus appears that if federal courts ignore the change in the New York standard and persist in applying the "shock the conscience" test to damage awards on claims governed by New York law, " 'substantial' variations between state and federal [money judgments]" may be expected. We therefore agree with the Second Circuit that New York's check on excessive damages implicates what we have called *Erie's* "twin aims." Just as the *Erie* principle precludes a federal court from giving a state-created claim "longer life . . . than [the claim] would have had in the state court," so *Erie* precludes a recovery in federal court significantly larger than the recovery that would have been tolerated in state court.

B

CPLR § 5501(c) is phrased as a direction to the New York Appellate Division. Acting essentially as a surrogate for a New York appellate forum, the Court of Appeals reviewed Gasperini's award to determine if it "deviate[d] materially" from damage awards the Appellate Division permitted in similar circumstances. The Court of Appeals performed this task without benefit of an opinion from the District Court, which had denied "without comment" the Center's Rule 59 motion. Concentrating on the authority § 5501(c) gives to the Appellate Division, Gasperini urges that the provision shifts fact-finding responsibility from the jury and the trial judge to the appellate court. Assigning such responsibility to an appellate court, he maintains, is incompatible with the Seventh Amendment's Reexamination Clause, and therefore, Gasperini concludes, § 5501(c) cannot be given effect in federal court. Although we reach a different conclusion than Gasperini, we agree that the Second Circuit did not attend to "[a]n essential characteristic of [the federal court] system," *Byrd v. Blue Ridge Rural Elec. Cooperative, Inc.*, 356 U.S. 525, 537, 78 S.Ct. 893, 901, 2 L.Ed.2d 953 (1958), when it used § 5501(c) as "the standard for [federal] appellate review."

That "essential characteristic" was described in *Byrd*, a diversity suit for negligence in which a pivotal issue of fact would have been tried by a judge were the case in state court. The *Byrd* Court held that, despite the state practice, the plaintiff was entitled to a jury trial in federal court. In so ruling, the Court said that the Guaranty Trust "outcome-determination" test was an insufficient guide in cases presenting countervailing federal interests. The Court described the countervailing federal interests present in *Byrd* this way:

> The federal system is an independent system for administering justice to litigants who properly invoke its jurisdiction. An essential characteristic of that system is the manner in which, in civil common-law actions, it distributes trial functions between judge and jury and, under the influence—if not the command—of the Seventh Amendment, assigns the decisions of disputed questions of fact to the jury.

The Seventh Amendment, which governs proceedings in federal court, but not in state court, bears not only on the allocation of trial functions between judge and jury, the issue in *Byrd*; it also controls the allocation of authority to review verdicts, the issue of concern here. The Amendment reads:

> "In Suits at common law, where the value in controversy shall exceed twenty dollars, the right of trial by jury shall be preserved, and no fact tried by a jury, shall be otherwise re-examined in any Court of the United States, than according to the rules of the common law." U.S. Const., Amdt. 7.

Byrd involved the first Clause of the Amendment, the "trial by jury" Clause. This case involves the second, the "Reexamination" Clause. In keeping with the historic understanding, the Reexamination Clause does not inhibit the authority of trial judges to grant new trials "for any of the reasons for which new trials have heretofore been granted in actions at law in the courts of the United States." Fed. Rule Civ. Proc. 59(a). That authority is large.

In contrast, appellate review of a federal trial court's denial of a motion to set aside a jury's verdict as excessive is a relatively late, and less secure, development. Such review was once deemed inconsonant with the Seventh Amendment's Reexamination Clause. We subsequently recognized that, even in cases in which the Erie doctrine was not in play—cases arising wholly under federal law—the question was not settled; we twice granted certiorari to decide the unsettled issue, but ultimately resolved the cases on other grounds.

Before today, we have not "expressly [held] that the Seventh Amendment allows appellate review of a district court's denial of a motion to set aside an award as excessive." *Browning-Ferris Industries of Vt., Inc. v. Kelco Disposal, Inc.*, 492 U.S. 257, 279, n. 25, 109 S.Ct. 2909, 2922, n. 25, 106 L.Ed.2d 219 (1989). But in successive reminders that the question was worthy of this Court's attention, we noted, without disapproval, that courts of appeals engage in review of district court excessiveness determinations, applying "abuse of discretion" as their standard:

> "[T]he role of the district court is to determine whether the jury's verdict is within the confines set by state law, and to determine, by reference to federal standards developed under Rule 59, whether a new trial or remittitur should be ordered. The court of appeals should then review the district court's determination under an abuse-of-discretion standard."

As the Second Circuit explained, appellate review for abuse of discretion is reconcilable with the Seventh Amendment as a control necessary and proper to the fair administration of justice: "We must give the benefit of every doubt to the judgment of the trial judge; but surely there must be an upper limit, and whether that has been surpassed is not a question of fact with respect to which reasonable men may differ, but a question of law." We now approve this line of decisions, and thus make explicit what Justice Stewart thought implicit in our *Grunenthal* disposition: "[N]othing in the Seventh Amendment . . . precludes appellate review of the trial judge's denial of a motion to set aside [a jury verdict] as excessive." 393 U.S., at 164, 89 S.Ct., at 336 (Stewart, J., dissenting).

C

In *Byrd*, the Court faced a one-or-the-other choice: trial by judge as in state court, or trial by jury according to the federal practice. In the case before us, a choice of that order is not required, for the principal state and federal interests can be accommodated. The Second Circuit correctly recognized that when New York substantive law governs a claim for relief, New York law and decisions guide the allowable damages. But that court did not take into account the characteristic of the federal court system that caused us to reaffirm: "The proper role of the trial and appellate courts in the federal system in reviewing the size of jury verdicts is . . . a matter of federal law."

New York's dominant interest can be respected, without disrupting the federal system, once it is recognized that the federal district court is capable of performing the checking function, i.e., that court can apply the State's "deviates materially" standard in line with New York case law evolving under CPLR § 5501(c).[3] We recall, in this regard, that the "deviates materially" standard serves as the guide to be applied in trial as well as appellate courts in New York.

Within the federal system, practical reasons combine with Seventh Amendment constraints to lodge in the district court, not the court of appeals, primary responsibility for application of § 5501(c)'s "deviates materially" check. Trial judges have the "unique opportunity to consider the evidence in the living courtroom context," while appellate judges see only the "cold paper record."

District court applications of the "deviates materially" standard would be subject to appellate review under the standard the Circuits now employ when inadequacy or excessiveness is asserted on appeal: abuse of discretion. In light of *Erie*'s doctrine, the federal appeals court must be guided by the damage-control standard state law supplies, but as the Second Circuit itself has said: "If we reverse, it must be because of an abuse of discretion. . . . The very nature of the problem counsels restraint. . . . We must give the benefit of every doubt to the judgment of the trial judge." *Dagnello*, 289 F.2d, at 806.

---

3 Justice SCALIA finds in Federal Rule of Civil Procedure 59 a "federal standard" for new trial motions in " 'direct collision' " with, and " 'leaving no room for the operation of,' " a state law like CPLR § 5501(c). The relevant prescription, Rule 59(a), has remained unchanged since the adoption of the Federal Rules by this Court in 1937. Rule 59(a) is as encompassing as it is uncontroversial. It is indeed "Hornbook" law that a most usual ground for a Rule 59 motion is that "the damages are excessive." Whether damages are excessive for the claim-in-suit must be governed by *some* law. And there is no candidate for that governance other than the law that gives rise to the claim for relief—here, the law of New York.

IV

It does not appear that the District Court checked the jury's verdict against the relevant New York decisions demanding more than "industry standard" testimony to support an award of the size the jury returned in this case. As the Court of Appeals recognized, see 66 F.3d, at 429, the uniqueness of the photographs and the plaintiff's earnings as photographer—past and reasonably projected—are factors relevant to appraisal of the award. Accordingly, we vacate the judgment of the Court of Appeals and instruct that court to remand the case to the District Court so that the trial judge, revisiting his ruling on the new trial motion, may test the jury's verdict against CPLR § 5501(c)'s "deviates materially" standard.

It is so ordered.

[A dissenting opinion of Justice STEVENS is omitted.]

Justice SCALIA, with whom the CHIEF JUSTICE and Justice THOMAS join, dissenting.

The Court holds today that a state practice that relates to the division of duties between state judges and juries must be followed by federal courts in diversity cases.

As I would reverse the judgment of the Court of Appeals, I respectfully dissent.

. . .

II

. . .

The Court acknowledges that state procedural rules cannot, as a general matter, be permitted to interfere with the allocation of functions in the federal court system. Indeed, it is at least partly for this reason that the Court rejects direct application of § 5501(c) at the appellate level as inconsistent with an " 'essential characteristic' " of the federal court system—by which the Court presumably means abuse-of-discretion review of denials of motions for new trials. But the scope of the Court's concern is oddly circumscribed. The "essential characteristic" of the federal jury, and, more specifically, the role of the federal trial court in reviewing jury judgments, apparently counts for little. The Court approves the "accommodat[ion]" achieved by having district courts review jury verdicts under the " deviates materially" standard, because it regards that as a means of giving effect to the State's purposes "without disrupting the federal system." But changing the standard by which trial judges review jury verdicts does disrupt the federal system, and is plainly inconsistent with the "strong federal policy against allowing state rules to disrupt the judge-jury relationship in federal court." *Byrd v. Blue Ridge Rural Elec. Cooperative, Inc.*, 356 U.S. 525, 538, 78 S.Ct. 893, 901, 2 L.Ed.2d 953 (1958). The Court's opinion does not even acknowledge, let alone address, this dislocation.

We discussed precisely the point at issue here in *Browning-Ferris Industries of Vt., Inc. v. Kelco Disposal, Inc.*, 492 U.S. 257, 109 S.Ct. 2909, 106 L.Ed.2d 219 (1989), and gave an answer altogether contrary to the one provided today. Browning-Ferris rejected a request to fashion a federal common-law rule limiting the size of punitive damages awards in federal courts, reaffirming the principle of *Erie R. Co. v. Tompkins*, 304 U.S. 64, 58 S.Ct. 817, 82 L.Ed. 1188 (1938), that "[i]n a diversity action, or in any other lawsuit where state law provides the basis of decision, the propriety of an award of punitive damages . . ., and the factors the jury may consider in determining their amount, are questions of state law." But the opinion expressly stated that "[f]ederal law . . . will control on those issues involving the proper review of the jury award by a federal district court and court of appeals." "In reviewing an award of punitive damages," it said, "the role of the district court is to determine whether the jury's verdict is within the confines set by state law, and to determine, by reference to federal standards developed under Rule 59, whether a new trial or remittitur should be ordered." The same distinction necessarily applies where the judgment under review is for compensatory damages: State substantive law controls what injuries are compensable and in what amount; but federal standards determine whether the award exceeds what is lawful to such degree that it may be set aside by order for new trial or remittitur.

The Court does not disavow those statements in Browning-Ferris (indeed, it does not even discuss them), but it presumably overrules them, at least where the state rule that governs "whether a new trial or remittitur should be ordered" is characterized as "substantive" in nature. That, at any rate, is the reason the Court asserts for giving § 5501(c) dispositive effect. The objective of that provision, the Court states, "is manifestly substantive," since it operates to "contro[l] how much a plaintiff can be awarded" by "tightening the range of tolerable awards." Although "less readily classified" as substantive than "a statutory cap on damages," it nonetheless "was designed to provide an analogous control," by making a new trial mandatory when the award "deviat[es] materially" from what is reasonable.

I do not see how this can be so. It seems to me quite wrong to regard this provision as a "substantive" rule for *Erie* purposes. The "analog[y]" to "a statutory cap on damages" fails utterly. There is an absolutely fundamental distinction between a *rule of law* such as that, which would ordinarily be imposed upon the jury in the trial court's instructions, and a *rule of review*, which simply determines how closely the jury verdict will be scrutinized for compliance with the instructions. A tighter standard for reviewing jury determinations can no more plausibly be called a "substantive" disposition than can a tighter appellate standard for reviewing trial-court determinations. The one, like the other, provides additional assurance that *the law has been complied with*; but the other, like the one, *leaves the law unchanged.*

The Court commits the classic *Erie* mistake of regarding whatever changes the outcome as substantive. That is not the only factor to be considered. See *Byrd, supra,* at 537, 78 S.Ct., at 900 ("[W]ere 'outcome' the only consideration, a strong case might appear for saying that the federal court should follow the state practice. But there are affirmative countervailing considerations at work here"). Outcome determination "was never intended to serve as a talisman," *Hanna v. Plumer,* 380 U.S. 460, 466-467, 85 S.Ct. 1136, 1141, 14 L.Ed.2d 8 (1965), and does not have the power to convert the most classic elements of the *process* of assuring that the law is observed into the substantive law itself. The right to have a jury make the findings of fact, for example, is generally thought to favor plaintiffs, and that advantage is often thought significant enough to be the basis for forum selection. But no one would argue that *Erie* confers a right to a jury in federal court wherever state courts would provide it; or that, were it not for the Seventh Amendment, *Erie* would require federal courts to dispense with the jury whenever state courts do so.

The foregoing describes why I think the Court's *Erie* analysis is flawed. But in my view, one does not even reach the *Erie* question in this case. The standard to be applied by a district court in ruling on a motion for a new trial is set forth in Rule 59 of the Federal Rules of Civil Procedure, which provides that "[a] new trial may be granted . . . for any of the reasons for which new trials have heretofore been granted in actions at law *in the courts of the United States.*" (Emphasis added.) That is undeniably a federal standard. Federal District Courts in the Second Circuit have interpreted that standard to permit the granting of new trials where " 'it is quite clear that the jury has reached a seriously erroneous result' " and letting the verdict stand would result in a " 'miscarriage of justice.'" *Koerner v. Club Mediterranee, S.A., supra,* at 331 (quoting *Bevevino v. Saydjari,* 574 F.2d 676, 684 (C.A.2 1978)). Assuming (as we have no reason to question) that this is a correct interpretation of what Rule 59 requires, it is undeniable that the Federal Rule is " 'sufficiently broad' to cause a 'direct collision' with the state law or, implicitly, to 'control the issue' before the court, thereby leaving no room for the operation of that law." *Burlington Northern R. Co. v. Woods,* 480 U.S. 1, 4-5, 107 S.Ct. 967, 969, 94 L.Ed.2d 1 (1987). It is simply not possible to give controlling effect both to the federal standard and the state standard in reviewing the jury's award. That being so, the court has no choice but to apply the Federal Rule, which is an exercise of what we have called Congress's "power to regulate matters which, though falling within the uncertain area between substance and procedure, are rationally capable of classification as either."

There is no small irony in the Court's declaration today that appellate review of refusals to grant new trials for error of fact is "a control necessary and proper to the fair administration of justice." It is objection to precisely that sort of "control" by federal appellate judges that gave birth to the Reexamination Clause of the Seventh Amendment. Alas, those who drew the Amendment, and the citizens who approved it, did not envision an age in which the Constitution means whatever this Court thinks it ought to mean—or indeed, whatever the courts of appeals have recently thought it ought to mean.

When there is added to the revision of the Seventh Amendment the Court's precedent-setting disregard of Congress's instructions in Rule 59, one must conclude that this is a bad day for the Constitution's distinctive Article III courts in general, and for the role of the jury in those courts in particular. I respectfully dissent.

EXPERIENTIAL ASSIGNMENTS

Your partner stops you in the hallway and says she is preparing to file a Complaint in the Frensch, Cash and Williams cases. She asks if it will make any difference in the governing law if she files in state or federal court. Choose a classmate to play the role of your partner and explain your answer.

CHAPTER 4

Pleadings and Parties

THERE ARE NO CIVIL ACTIONS without pleadings and parties. At the very least, there must be a Complaint, a plaintiff and a defendant. Typically, the defendant will file an Answer, a Motion to Dismiss, or both. When available, a defendant may also file a Counterclaim, in which case the plaintiff will file an Answer to the Counterclaim. Beyond these basic pleadings and motions, other parties and claims may be joined as permitted, generating additional pleadings.

The Federal Rules of Civil Procedure provide forms with the promise that they will be adequate to satisfy clerks as United States courthouses. Use them. *http://www.uscourts.gov/RulesAndPolicies/FederalRulemaking/RulesAndForms/ IllustrativeCivilRulesForms.aspx*

You may also wish to use other available forms, but do so judiciously. In any event, you as the pleader, are responsible for ensuring that you have complied with the federal pleading rules and have satisfied substantive law requirements for the claims you intend to state.

The very closely related topic of Motions to Dismiss will be dealt with in chapter 5.

FRCP Forms 1 and 2 provide a format for a caption, the first part of any pleading or motion, and the signature lines.

UNITED STATES DISTRICT COURT

for the

<_____> DISTRICT OF <_____>

<Name(s) of plaintiff(s)>,	)
Plaintiff(s)	)
v.	)
<Name(s) of defendant(s)>,	)
Defendant(s)	)
v.　<Use if needed>	)
<Name(s) of third-party defendant(s)>,	)
Third-Party Defendant(s)	

Civil Action No. <Number>

<NAME OF DOCUMENT>

Body of Document

Date: <Date>

<Signature of the attorney or unrepresented party>

_____

<Printed name>

<Address>

<E-mail address>

<Telephone number>

A. The Pleading Rules: Stating a Claim

Rule Material

Rule 7 Pleadings Allowed; Form of Motions and Other Papers

(a) Pleadings. Only these pleadings are allowed:

(1) a complaint;

(2) an answer to a complaint;

(3) an answer to a counterclaim designated as a counterclaim;

(4) an answer to a cross-claim;

(5) a third-party complaint;

(6) an answer to a third-party complaint; and

(7) if the court orders one, a reply to an answer.

(b) Motions and Other Papers.

(1) *In General.* A request for a court order must be made by motion. The motion must:

(A) be in writing unless made during a hearing or trial;

(B) state with particularity the grounds for seeking the order; and

(C) state the relief sought.

(2) *Form.* The rules governing captions and other matters of form in pleadings apply to motions and other papers.

Rule 8 General Rules of Pleading

(a) Claim for Relief. A pleading that states a claim for relief must contain:

(1) a short and plain statement of the grounds for the court's jurisdiction, unless the court already has jurisdiction and the claim needs no new jurisdictional support;

(2) a short and plain statement of the claim showing that the pleader is entitled to relief; and

(3) a demand for the relief sought, which may include relief in the alternative or different types of relief.

(b) Defenses; Admissions and Denials.

(1) *In General.* In responding to a pleading, a party must:

(A) state in short and plain terms its defenses to each claim asserted against it; and

(B) admit or deny the allegations asserted against it by an opposing party.

(2) *Denials—Responding to the Substance.* A denial must fairly respond to the substance of the allegation.

(3) *General and Specific Denials.* A party that intends in good faith to deny all the allegations of a pleading—including the jurisdictional grounds—may do so by a general denial. A party that does not intend to deny all the allegations must either specifically deny designated allegations or generally deny all except those specifically admitted.

(4) *Denying Part of an Allegation.* A party that intends in good faith to deny only part of an allegation must admit the part that is true and deny the rest.

(5) *Lacking Knowledge or Information.* A party that lacks knowledge or information sufficient to form a belief about the truth of an allegation must so state, and the statement has the effect of a denial.

(6) *Effect of Failing to Deny.* An allegation—other than one relating to the amount of damages—is admitted if a responsive pleading is required and the allegation is not denied. If a responsive pleading is not required, an allegation is considered denied or avoided.

(c) Affirmative Defenses.

(1) *In General.* In responding to a pleading, a party must affirmatively state any avoidance or affirmative defense, including:

- accord and satisfaction;
- arbitration and award;
- assumption of risk;
- contributory negligence;
- duress;
- estoppel;
- failure of consideration;
- fraud;

- illegality;

- injury by fellow servant;

- laches;

- license;

- payment;

- release;

- res judicata;

- statute of frauds;

- statute of limitations; and

- waiver.

(2) *Mistaken Designation.* If a party mistakenly designates a defense as a counterclaim, or a counterclaim as a defense, the court must, if justice requires, treat the pleading as though it were correctly designated, and may impose terms for doing so.

(d) Pleading to Be Concise and Direct; Alternative Statements; Inconsistency.

(1) *In General.* Each allegation must be simple, concise, and direct. No technical form is required.

(2) *Alternative Statements of a Claim or Defense.* A party may set out two or more statements of a claim or defense alternatively or hypothetically, either in a single count or defense or in separate ones. If a party makes alternative statements, the pleading is sufficient if any one of them is sufficient.

(3) *Inconsistent Claims or Defenses.* A party may state as many separate claims or defenses as it has, regardless of consistency.

(e) Construing Pleadings. Pleadings must be construed so as to do justice.

Rule 9 Pleading Special Matters

(a) Capacity or Authority to Sue; Legal Existence.

(1) *In General.* Except when required to show that the court has jurisdiction, a pleading need not allege:

(A) a party's capacity to sue or be sued;

(B) a party's authority to sue or be sued in a representative capacity; or

(C) the legal existence of an organized association of persons that is made a party.

(2) *Raising Those Issues.* To raise any of those issues, a party must do so by a specific denial, which must state any supporting facts that are peculiarly within the party's knowledge.

(b) Fraud or Mistake; Conditions of Mind. In alleging fraud or mistake, a party must state with particularity the circumstances constituting fraud or mistake. Malice, intent, knowledge, and other conditions of a person's mind may be alleged generally.

(c) Conditions Precedent. In pleading conditions precedent, it suffices to allege generally that all conditions precedent have occurred or been performed. But when denying that a condition precedent has occurred or been performed, a party must do so with particularity.

(d) Official Document or Act. In pleading an official document or official act, it suffices to allege that the document was legally issued or the act legally done.

(e) Judgment. In pleading a judgment or decision of a domestic or foreign court, a judicial or quasi-judicial tribunal, or a board or officer, it suffices to plead the judgment or decision without showing jurisdiction to render it.

(f) Time and Place. An allegation of time or place is material when testing the sufficiency of a pleading.

(g) Special Damages. If an item of special damage is claimed, it must be specifically stated.

.   .   .

Rule 10 Form of Pleadings

(a) Caption; Names of Parties. Every pleading must have a caption with the court's name, a title, a file number, and a Rule 7(a) designation. The title of the complaint must name all the parties; the title of other pleadings, after naming the first party on each side, may refer generally to other parties.

(b) Paragraphs; Separate Statements. A party must state its claims or defenses in numbered paragraphs, each limited as far as practicable to a single set of circumstances. A later pleading may refer by number to a paragraph in an earlier pleading. If doing so would promote clarity, each claim founded on a separate transaction or occurrence—and each defense other than a denial— must be stated in a separate count or defense.

(c) Adoption by Reference; Exhibits. A statement in a pleading may be adopted by reference elsewhere in the same pleading or in any other pleading or motion. A copy of a written instrument that is an exhibit to a pleading is a part of the pleading for all purposes.

Rule 11 *Signing Pleadings, Motions, and Other Papers; Representations to the Court; Sanctions*

(a) Signature. Every pleading, written motion, and other paper must be signed by at least one attorney of record in the attorney's name—or by a party personally if the party is unrepresented. The paper must state the signer's address, e-mail address, and telephone number. Unless a rule or statute specifically states otherwise, a pleading need not be verified or accompanied by an affidavit. The court must strike an unsigned paper unless the omission is promptly corrected after being called to the attorney's or party's attention.

(b) Representations to the Court. By presenting to the court a pleading, written motion, or other paper—whether by signing, filing, submitting, or later advocating it—an attorney or unrepresented party certifies that to the best of the person's knowledge, information, and belief, formed after an inquiry reasonable under the circumstances:

(1) it is not being presented for any improper purpose, such as to harass, cause unnecessary delay, or needlessly increase the cost of litigation;

(2) the claims, defenses, and other legal contentions are warranted by existing law or by a nonfrivolous argument for extending, modifying, or reversing existing law or for establishing new law;

(3) the factual contentions have evidentiary support or, if specifically so identified, will likely have evidentiary support after a reasonable opportunity for further investigation or discovery; and

(4) the denials of factual contentions are warranted on the evidence or, if specifically so identified, are reasonably based on belief or a lack of information.

(c) Sanctions.

(1) *In General.* If, after notice and a reasonable opportunity to respond, the court determines that Rule 11(b) has been violated, the court may impose an appropriate sanction on any attorney, law firm, or party that violated the rule or is responsible for the violation. Absent exceptional circumstances, a law firm must be held jointly responsible for a violation committed by its partner, associate, or employee.

(2) *Motion for Sanctions.* A motion for sanctions must be made separately from any other motion and must describe the specific conduct that allegedly violates Rule 11(b). The motion must be served under Rule 5, but it must not be filed or be presented to the court if the challenged paper, claim, defense, contention, or denial is withdrawn or appropriately corrected within 21 days after service or within another time the court sets. If warranted, the court may award to the prevailing party the reasonable expenses, including attorney's fees, incurred for the motion.

(3) *On the Court's Initiative.* On its own, the court may order an attorney, law firm, or party to show cause why conduct specifically described in the order has not violated Rule 11(b).

(4) *Nature of a Sanction.* A sanction imposed under this rule must be limited to what suffices to deter repetition of the conduct or comparable conduct by others similarly situated. The sanction may include nonmonetary directives; an order to pay a penalty into court; or, if imposed on motion and warranted for effective deterrence, an order directing payment to the movant of part or all of the reasonable attorney's fees and other expenses directly resulting from the violation.

(5) *Limitations on Monetary Sanctions.* The court must not impose a monetary sanction:

> (A) against a represented party for violating Rule 11(b)(2); or

> (B) on its own, unless it issued the show-cause order under Rule 11(c)(3) before voluntary dismissal or settlement of the claims made by or against the party that is, or whose attorneys are, to be sanctioned.

(6) *Requirements for an Order.* An order imposing a sanction must describe the sanctioned conduct and explain the basis for the sanction.

(d) Inapplicability to Discovery. This rule does not apply to disclosures and discovery requests, responses, objections, and motions under Rules 26 through 37.

Rule 13 Counterclaim and Cross-claim

(a) Compulsory Counterclaim.

(1) *In General.* A pleading must state as a counterclaim any claim that—at the time of its service—the pleader has against an opposing party if the claim:

(A) arises out of the transaction or occurrence that is the subject matter of the opposing party's claim; and

(B) does not require adding another party over whom the court cannot acquire jurisdiction.

(2) *Exceptions.* The pleader need not state the claim if:

(A) when the action was commenced, the claim was the subject of another pending action; or

(B) the opposing party sued on its claim by attachment or other process that did not establish personal jurisdiction over the pleader on that claim, and the pleader does not assert any counterclaim under this rule.

(b) Permissive Counterclaim. A pleading may state as a counterclaim against an opposing party any claim that is not compulsory.

(c) Relief Sought in a Counterclaim. A counterclaim need not diminish or defeat the recovery sought by the opposing party. It may request relief that exceeds in amount or differs in kind from the relief sought by the opposing party.

. . .

(g) Crossclaim Against a Coparty. A pleading may state as a cross-claim any claim by one party against a coparty if the claim arises out of the transaction or occurrence that is the subject matter of the original action or of a counterclaim, or if the claim relates to any property that is the subject matter of the original action. The cross-claim may include a claim that the coparty is or may be liable to the cross-claimant for all or part of a claim asserted in the action against the cross-claimant.

(h) Joining Additional Parties. Rules 19 and 20 govern the addition of a person as a party to a counterclaim or cross-claim.

. . .

Rule 15 Amended and Supplemental Pleadings

(a) Amendments Before Trial.

(1) *Amending as a Matter of Course.* A party may amend its pleading once as a matter of course within:

(A) 21 days after serving it, or

(B) if the pleading is one to which a responsive pleading is required, 21 days after service of a responsive pleading or 21 days after service of a motion under Rule 12(b), (e), or (f), whichever is earlier.

(2) Other Amendments. In all other cases, a party may amend its pleading only with the opposing party's written consent or the court's leave. The court should freely give leave when justice so requires.

(3) Time to Respond. Unless the court orders otherwise, any required response to an amended pleading must be made within the time remaining to respond to the original pleading or within 14 days after service of the amended pleading, whichever is later.

(b) Amendments During and After Trial.

(1) Based on an Objection at Trial. If, at trial, a party objects that evidence is not within the issues raised in the pleadings, the court may permit the pleadings to be amended. The court should freely permit an amendment when doing so will aid in presenting the merits and the objecting party fails to satisfy the court that the evidence would prejudice that party's action or defense on the merits. The court may grant a continuance to enable the objecting party to meet the evidence.

. . .

(c) Relation Back of Amendments.

(1) *When an Amendment Relates Back.* An amendment to a pleading relates back to the date of the original pleading when:

(A) the law that provides the applicable statute of limitations allows relation back;

(B) the amendment asserts a claim or defense that arose out of the conduct, transaction, or occurrence set out—or attempted to be set out—in the original pleading; or

(C) the amendment changes the party or the naming of the party against whom a claim is asserted, if Rule 15(c)(1)(B) is satisfied and if, within the period provided by Rule 4(m) for serving the summons and complaint, the party to be brought in by amendment:

(i) received such notice of the action that it will not be prejudiced in defending on the merits; and

(ii) knew or should have known that the action would have been brought against it, but for a mistake concerning the proper party's identity.

. . .

Rule 55 Default Judgments

(a) Entering a Default. When a party against whom a judgment for affirmative relief is sought has failed to plead or otherwise defend, and that failure is shown by affidavit or otherwise, the clerk must enter the party's default.

(b) Entering a Default Judgment.

(1) *By the Clerk.* If the plaintiff's claim is for a sum certain or a sum that can be made certain by computation, the clerk—on the plaintiff's request, with an affidavit showing the amount due—must enter judgment for that amount and costs against a defendant who has been defaulted for not appearing and who is neither a minor nor an incompetent person.

(2) *By the Court.* In all other cases, the party must apply to the court for a default judgment. .   .   .

(c) Setting Aside a Default or a Default Judgment. The court may set aside an entry of default for good cause, and it may set aside a default judgment under Rule 60(b).

. . .

NOTES

1. The Rule 11 story. In 1983, to combat the perception that more frivolous claims were being filed, Congress amended Federal Rule of Civil Procedure 11 to make judges more likely to impose sanctions on lawyers who file frivolous claims or motions. The goal was to "discourage dilatory or abusive tactics and to streamline the litigation process by lessening the amount of frivolous matters brought before the federal courts."[1] Most states followed with their own versions of the same. The trouble with the new Rule 11 was that it was used. Now, with its encouragement for judges to impose sanctions, more and more lawyers filed motions under the newly amended rule asking judges to sanction opposing counsel.

Called the most controversial civil procedure amendment ever[2] the 1983 version became a lightning rod, with many claiming that it chilled the civil rights and employment law plaintiff and the plaintiff with a novel claim.[3] The pre-1983 version of Rule 11 was ineffective because it was largely ignored, but the 1983 rule generated a tremendous amount of satellite litigation, defeating its own purpose. Because determinations under Rule 11 are largely fact-based, judges found themselves engaged in ancillary litigation over the application of Rule 11 itself.[4] So great was the added burden imposed by the 1983 amendment that by 1993, Congress amended the rule once again, this time to encourage private settlement of Rule 11 disputes by adding a "safe-harbor" provision. Under the 1993 version, a party seeking Rule 11 sanctions must first give notice to the alleged Rule 11

---

1 Fed. R. Civ. P. 11 advisory committee's note (1983).

2 Carl Tobias, *Reconsidering Rule 11*, 46 U. MIAMI L. REV. 855, 856-57 (1992).

3 *See* Stephen B. Burbank, *The Transformation of American Civil Procedure: The Example of Rule 11*, 137 U. PA. L. REV. 1925, 1925 (1989); Carl Tobias, *Rule 11 and Civil Rights Litigation*, 37 BUFF. L. REV. 485, 485 (1988-89); Georgene M. Vairo, *Rule 11: A Critical Analysis*, 118 F.R.D. 189, 197 (1988).

4 *See* Georgene M. Vairo, *Rule 11: A Critical Analysis*, 118 F.R.D. 189, 197 (1988). In 1991, Professor Vairo reported that over 3,000 cases dealing with Rule 11 had been reported, which one can assume are just a fraction of the number of cases in which sanctions were imposed (or refused) under the rule. *See* Georgene M. Vairo, *Rule 11: Where We Are and Where We Are Going*, 60 FORDHAM L. REV. 475, 480 (1991); *see also* Lawrence C. Marshall, et al., *The Use and Impact of Rule 11*, 86 NW. U. L. REV. 943, 952 (1992) (finding that in the twelve months before a survey conducted by the authors: 24.3 percent of attorneys surveyed reported involvement in a case in which formal Rule 11 motions were made but no sanctions imposed; 7.6 percent were involved in cases in which Rule 11 sanctions were imposed; 24.5 percent of attorneys surveyed had experience with in-court reference to Rule 11, with no formal motion or request for sanctions; and 30.3 percent had experienced references to Rule 11 out of court).

transgressor, allowing 21 days to correct statements or allegations in a pleading to conform to Rule 11 before a court would get involved.

2. The states have adopted their own "Rule 11's" for the functioning of pleadings and papers filed in state courts. In general, it seems that the states' significant departures from Federal Rule of Civil Procedure occur with regards to the length of the safe harbor provision, if one is included in the state statute, as well as with whether a claim may be made on the basis that it may be found to have evidentiary support after further investigation. Additionally, it appears that many states have embraced the 1993 amendments to federal rule 11, and for the most part, it seemed that the states which did imitate the current provisions of rule 11 tended to adopt them in their entirety.

3. What should happen when a defendant fails to answer a complaint? What if the complaint includes a claim that has no merit?

4. Pleadings must be amended from time to time. Parse FRCP 15 and make a flowchart for when a party is permitted to amend. A critical issue sometimes arises about the "relation back" of an amendment. When a statute of limitations has passed between the time of filing the initial Complaint and a plaintiff's amendment of that Complaint, failure to satisfy FRCP 15(c) means that the plaintiff's Amended Complaint will be dismissed for violating the statute of limitations.

5. Don't be late, even by a minute. Here is an excerpt from an opinion denying a motion for lateness, costing the lawyer's client about $1,000,000. Of course, that really means the one-minute of lateness cost the law firm $1,000,000.

UNITED STATES DISTRICT COURT
CENTRAL DISTRICT OF CALIFORNIA
SOUTHERN DIVISION

TOSHIBA AMERICA INFORMATION SYSTEMS, INC.,	Case No.: SACV 05-00955-
Plaintiff,	
vs.	
NEW ENGLAND TECHNOLOGY, INC., et al.	ORDER DENYING PLAINTIFF'S MOTION FOR ATTORNEYS' FEES [filed 10/11/07]
Defendant,	

INTRODUCTION

On September 26, 2007, this Court entered a judgment in favor of Plaintiff Toshiba America Information Systems, Inc. ("TAIS") in the amount of $482,430.00, plus interest, costs and attorneys' fees to be resolved by way of motion filed with the Court. TAIS filed a motion for attorneys' fees on October II, 2007, seeking to recover $996,865.83 in attorneys' fees. Defendant New England Technology, Inc. ("NETI") asserts that the motion for fees should be denied because it was not timely filed, it improperly seeks fees in relation to the litigation of NETI's counterclaim, and because TAIS has not submitted sufficient evidence to justify such a large award of fees. Because the Court agrees that the motion was not timely filed and that TAIS has not submitted sufficient evidence to justify an award of fees, TAIS' motion is DENIED.

ANALYSIS

NETI argues that TAIS' motion must be denied because it was not filed within fourteen days of the entry of judgment, in violation of Fed. R. Civ. P. 54(n)(2)(B) and Central District L.R. 54-12. The Court finds that TAIS' motion was untimely because the Court entered judgment on September 26, 2007, and TAIS' motion was not filed until October 11, 2007, 15 days later. The 14 day deadline under Rule 54(d)(2)(B) includes Saturdays, Sundays, and legal holidays. Failure to file a motion for attorneys' fees within the prescribed time period waives a party's right to request fees. . . . Fed. R. Civ. P. 6(B), however, permits a court to enlarge the period of time within which a party must file a motion for attorneys' fees "where the failure to act was the result of excusable neglect..." Unfortunately for TAIS, its one day delay in filing its motion was not the result of "excusable neglect."

. . .

Here, TAIS' purported reason for its delay is that its courier was caught in traffic a 3:30 in the afternoon in Santa Ana, California. Mr. Mersel, attorney for TAIS, asserts that he waited until 3:14 p.m. on the last day of the filing period to deliver the motion to Morrison & Foerster's regular courier service. (Mersel Decl., 2.) Mr. Mersel asserts that although he was aware that the filing deadline was 4:00p.m., he had "never had a problem with getting papers filed by 4:00p.m. when delivering them to the attorney service" 45 minutes in advance. The courier, Mr. Moskus, swiftly responded to Mr. Mersel's request, leaving on his motorcycle for the courthouse at approximately 3:30p.m. (Moskus Decl., 3.) Unfortunately, Mr. Moskus encountered "unusually heavy traffic" and had to "wait at the railroad crossing on Grand Avenue for a long train to pass." (Moskus Decl., 3.) Consequently, Mr. Moskus arrived at the Courthouse after the office had closed and Mr. Mersel was unable to file the motion until the following day, on October 11, 2007. (Mersel Decl., 7.)

These circumstances, however regrettable, do not meet the standard for "excusable neglect." Although the delay was not lengthy and it does not appear that NETI was prejudiced by it, the reason for the delay was entirely within TAIS' control and TAIS has not offered a good faith reason for the delay. Given that the Ninth Circuit has held that a good faith misunderstanding of local rules is not sufficient to rise to the standard of "excusable neglect," the entirely foreseeable obstacle of traffic in Southern California in the late afternoon also cannot justify an enlargement of time. Unlike the parties in Yost and Kyle, Mr. Mersel is not even arguing that he had a good faith reason to believe that he had extra time to file the motion for fees. Instead, Mr. Mersel asserts that he has a practice of waiting until 45 minutes prior to the filing deadline before passing off a motion to his courier, and because that plan has worked in the past, it should have been sufficient on this occasion. Although this pattern of conduct may have previously worked for Mr. Mersel, it is not a good faith reason for the delay. Unlike the circumstances discussed in Yost that would constitute legitimate reasons for delay, such as the illness of counsel or destruction of his law office, the reason for delay in this case was entirely foreseeable and avoidable. Mr. Mersel knew since at least September 10, 2007, the date of this Court's Tentative Order Granting TAIS' Motions for Summary Judgment, that he would need to prepare a motion for attorneys' fees. He waited a month later, until 3:14 p.m. on October 10, to attempt to file the motion. Because Mr. Mersel made a conscious decision to wait until the final hour to file his motion, he assumed the risk that on October 10, his luck would run out.

This case is distinguishable from Pioneer because encountering traffic in Orange County is in no way analogous to being misled by the "dramatic ambiguity" of a faulty notice of a bar date in a bankruptcy proceeding. When Mr. Moskus set out at 3:30 p.m. to travel to the Courthouse, it was entirely predictable that he might not arrive by 4:00 p.m. Even if Mr. Moskus assured Mr. Mersel that 45 minutes would be sufficient time to file the papers, Mr. Mersel was not the victim of any "dramatic ambiguity" in circumstances. Considering all of the circumstances and keeping in mind that the Pioneer test is an equitable one, the Court finds that TAIS' proffered reason for delay does not justify an enlargement of the time period for filing its motion.

Example Complaint and Answer

UNITED STATES DISTRICT COURT FOR THE
DISTRICT OF NEW MEXICO

TWO OLD HIPPIES, LLC,
Plaintiff,

     v.   No: _____

CATCH THE BUS, LLC,
GARY MACK And FALLON MACK,

Defendants.

COMPLAINT FOR BREACH OF CONTRACT, BREACH OF WARRANTY, VIOLATION OF THE NEW MEXICO DEALERS FRANCHISING ACT, VIOLATION OF THE NEW MEXICO UNFAIR PRACTICES ACT, VIOLATION OF THE COLORADO CONSUMER PROTECTION ACT, NEGLIGENT MISREPRESENTATION, AND RESCISSION

COMES NOW the Plaintiff, TWO OLD HIPPIES, LLC (hereinafter "TOH"), by and through its undersigned counsel, and for its Complaint against Defendants, CATCH THE BUS, LLC, ("CTB"), GARY MACK and FALLON MACK (hereinafter "CTB Defendants"), alleges as follows:

1. TOH is an Iowa limited liability company.

2. TOH does not transact business in New Mexico within the meaning of NMSA53-19-54.

3. TOH is wholly owned by the Thomas W. Bedell Revocable Trust ("Trust").

4. The trustee of the Trust is Thomas W. Bedell and the beneficiary of the trust is Thomas W. Bedell.

5. The Trust, trustee and beneficiary are citizens of Iowa.

6. CTB is a New Mexico limited liability company.

7. On information and belief, CTB is wholly owned by Gary Mack and Fallon Mack.

8. On information and belief, Gary Mack and Fallon Mack are citizens of New Mexico.

9. In July 2009, TOH contracted to purchase a restored VW bus from CTB for $41,424 ("Bus #1").

10. On Bus #1, TOH was overcharged $1,500 for air conditioning, and charged $1,000 for snow tires not provided.

11. In October 2009, TOH contracted to purchase a second restored VW bus from CTB for $33,624 ("Bus #2").

12. The purchase price of Bus #1 and Bus #2 together totals $75,048.

13. The CTB Defendants guaranteed TOH 100% satisfaction with the buses ("guarantee") which was a part of the contracts.

14. The CTB Defendants promised that the buses would be "ready to go" on delivery "whether for daily driver or for cross-country trips" ("promise") which was a part of the contracts.

15. The guarantee has been breached because TOH is not 100% satisfied with the buses and The CTB Defendants are unable or unwilling to provide 100% satisfaction to TOH.

16. The promise has been breached because buses were not "ready to go" on delivery "whether for daily driver or for cross-country trips".

17. TOH planned to use Bus #1 in its business and give away Bus #2 in a business promotion to an entrant who won Bus #2 in the promotion.

18. The CTB Defendants were informed of TOH's intended uses of the buses prior to the purchases of the buses.

19. After delivery of Bus #1 to TOH, Bus #1 was not safely operable and TOH determined that Bus #1 had many serious mechanical and physical defects.

20. After delivery of Bus #2, TOH conducted the business promotion and awarded the bus to its winning entrant.

21. After delivery of Bus #2 to TOH's winning entrant, the entrant, and subsequently TOH, determined that Bus #2 was not operable and had many serious mechanical and physical defects.

22. Because of the many serious mechanical and physical defects, TOH has never been able to use Bus #1.

23. Because of the many serious mechanical and physical defects, TOH reacquired Bus #2 from its winning entrant for $33,624 making the total amount paid for Bus#2 $67,248 and the total for both buses in the amount of $108,672.

24. The cost of transporting Bus #2 to the contest winner was $243.

25. The cost of transporting Bus #2 back to TOH is $1,384.

26. Because of the many serious mechanical and physical defects, TOH has spent $3,240.68 in repair costs on Bus #1 to attempt to make it safely operable, but despite the repairs, Bus #1 is not safely operable.

27. Because Bus #1 is not safely operable and Bus #2 is not operable and because of the many mechanical and physical defects, the buses have no value to TOH.

28. Because of the deplorable condition of the buses, TOH has lost reputation, lost use of Bus #1, and suffered distress.

29. TOH has demanded refund of the purchase price for the buses and other related compensation, and, upon payment, that the CTB Defendants retrieve the buses from their location.

30. Despite demand, the CTB Defendants have refused to refund the purchase price and compensate TOH for other related expenses.

31. Diversity of citizenship jurisdiction exists pursuant to 28 USC§1332(a) and venue is proper pursuant to 18 USC§ 1391(a)(2).

COUNT I–
BREACH OF CONTRACT

32. TOR incorporates the above allegations by reference.

33. CTB breached its contracts with TOH by failing to provide the buses to TOR's 100% satisfaction.

34. CTB breached its contracts with TOH by failing to deliver the buses "ready to go" "whether for daily driver or for cross-country trips".

35. CTB's breaches have damaged TOH.

COUNT II- BREACH OF WARRANTY

36. TOH incorporates the above allegations by reference.

37. The CTB Defendants gave express warranties under NMSA §57-2-313(1)(a) and (b) about the buses to TOH by its guarantee and promise.

38. The CTB Defendants breached their express warranties.

39. The CTB Defendants' breach of their express warranties have damaged TOH.

40. The CTB Defendants are a "merchant" under the New Mexico Uniform Commercial Code with respect to the sale of restored VW buses.

41. The CTB Defendants gave TOR implied warranties of merchantability pursuant to NMSA 55-2-314(2)(a) and (2)(c).

42. The CTB Defendants breached their implied warranties of merchantability.

43. TOH has been damaged by The CTB Defendants' breach of their implied warranties of merchantability.

COUNT III–
VIOLATION OF MOTOR DEALERS FRANCHISING ACT

44. The CTB Defendants are a "motor vehicle dealer" pursuant to NMSA 57-16-3 B.

45. The CTB Defendants committed fraud as defined by 57-16-3 I in connection with the sale of the buses to TOH in violation of NMSA 57-16-4 Band C.

46. TOH was damaged by the CTB Defendants' violations of NMSA 57-16-4.

COUNT IV–
VIOLATION OF THE NEW MEXICO UNFAIR PRACTICES ACT

47. TOH incorporates the above allegations by reference.

48. The CTB Defendants engaged in unfair or deceptive trade practices in violation of NMSA §57-12-2D by:

    a. representing the buses were of a particular standard, quality or grade subsection (subsection 7);

    b. using exaggeration, innuendo or ambiguity as to a material fact or failing to state a material fact which deceived or tended to deceive TOH (subsection 14);

    c. failing to deliver the quality of goods contracted for (subsection 17).

49. The CTB Defendants violated NMSA §57-12-6 by willfully misrepresenting the condition of buses.

50. The CTB Defendants' violations of NMSA §57-12-2D and §57-12-6 have damaged TOH.

COUNT V–
VIOLATION OF THE COLORADO CONSUMER PROTECTION ACT

51. TOH incorporates the above allegations by reference.

52. The CTB Defendants engaged in deceptive trade practices in bad faith in violation of Colorado's statute§ 61-105(1) by

    a) representing the buses were of a particular standard, quality or grade (subsection g;)

    b) representing the buses were guaranteed without clearly and conspicuously disclosing the nature and extent of the guarantee, any material conditions or limitations in the guarantee which are imposed by the guarantors, and the manner in which the guarantors will perform (subsection r).

53. CTB's violations of Colorado statute§ 61-105(1) have damaged TOH.

COUNT VI–
NEGLIGENT MISREPRESENTATION

54. TOH incorporates the above allegations by reference.

55. In the alternative, the CTB Defendants' guarantee and promise were material false misrepresentations of fact negligently made to TOH.

56. The CTB Defendants did not exercise ordinary care in making the material false misrepresentation of fact to TOH.

57. The CTB Defendants owed a duty to TOH not to make material false misrepresentations of fact to TOH.

58. TOH justifiably relied on the CTB Defendants' material false misrepresentations of fact.

59. TOH was damaged by the CTB Defendants to false misrepresentations of fact.

COUNT VII–RESCISSION

60. TOH incorporates the above allegations by reference.

61. The CTB Defendants misrepresent material facts to TOH.

62. The CTB Defendants intended TOH to rely on the misrepresentations.

63. TOH relied on the misrepresentations.

PRAYER FOR RELIEF

64. TOH prays for relief against the CTB Defendants as follows:

    a. Actual damages;

    b. Incidental and consequential damages;

    c. Punitive damages;

    d. In the alternative, treble damages for violation of NMSA §57-12-2D and §57-12-6 and Colorado statute§ 6-1-105(1);

    e. In the alternative, rescission plus refund of the purchase price plus damages;

    f. Reasonable attorneys' fees; and,

    g. Costs of suit.

Dated: May 7, 2010

> Respectfully submitted,
> BANNERMAN & JOHNSON, P.A.
> Thomas P. Gulley
> 2201 San Pedro, NE, Building 2, Suite 207
> Albuquerque, New Mexico 87110

**UNITED STATES DISTRICT COURT
FOR THE DISTRICT OF NEW MEXICO**

TWO OLD HIPPIES, LLC,
     Plaintiff,

         v.   Cause No. 10-CV-00459-WDS-RLP

CATCH THE BUS, LLC,
GARY MACK And FALLON MACK,
     Defendants.

DEFENDANTS' ANSWER TO COMPLAINT FOR BREACH OF CONTRACT, BREACH OF WARRANTY, VIOLATION OF THE NEW MEXICO DEALERS FRANCHISING ACT, VIOLATION OF THE NEW MEXICO UNFAIR PRACTICES ACT, VIOLATION OF THE COLORADO CONSUMER PROTECTION ACT, NEGLIGENT MISREPRESENTATION, AND RESCISSION

COMES NOW, Defendants, Catch the Bus, L.L.C., Gary Mack, and Fallon Mack, by and through their attorney, Roger E. Yarbro, of Yarbro & Associates, P.A., and submits their Answer to Complaint for Breach of Contract, Breach of Warranty, Violation of the New Mexico Dealers Franchising Act, Violation of the New Mexico Unfair Practices Act, Violation of the Colorado Consumer Protection Act, Negligent Misrepresentation, and Rescission and therefore STATES:

FIRST DEFENSE

Plaintiff has failed to plead sufficient facts in accordance with Fed. R. Civ. P. 8 (a) which, when taken as true, set forth plausible claims for relief under counts I – VII of the Complaint. The Complaint should, therefore, be dismissed pursuant to Fed. R. Civ. P. 12(b)(6).

SECOND DEFENSE

Plaintiff has failed to state with particularity the circumstances constituting fraud or mistake as is required by Fed. R. Civ. P.9(b) and has failed to set forth plausible claims for relief under Counts III, IV, V, and VII. Counts III, IV, V, and VII should, therefore be dismissed pursuant to Fed. R. Civ. P.12 (b)(6).

THIRD DEFENSE

Plaintiff has failed to plead sufficient facts and grounds for items of special damages as required by Fed. R. Civ. P. 12(b)(6) as Defendant has no notice of the grounds upon which such claims are based.

FOURTH DEFENSE

Plaintiff's Complaint fails to state a claim against Gary Mack and Fallon Mack individually.

FIFTH DEFENSE

Plaintiff's Complaint failed to state a claim for punitive damages.

ANSWER TO SPECIFIC ALLEGATIONS

1. Defendants admit the allegations contained in Paragraph 1 of Plaintiff's Complaint.

2. Defendants deny the allegations contained in Paragraph 2 of Plaintiff's Complaint.

3. Defendants are without knowledge sufficient to either admit or deny the allegations contained in Paragraph 3 of Plaintiff's Complaint, and therefore deny the same.

4. Defendants are without knowledge sufficient to either admit or deny the allegations contained in Paragraph 4 of Plaintiff's Complaint, and therefore deny the same.

5. Defendants are without knowledge sufficient to either admit or deny the allegations contained in Paragraph 5 of Plaintiff's Complaint, and therefore deny the same.

6. Defendants admit the allegations contained in Paragraph 6 of Plaintiff's Complaint.

7. Defendants admit the allegations contained in Paragraph 7 of Plaintiff's Complaint.

8. Defendants admit the allegations contained in Paragraph 8 of Plaintiff's Complaint.

9. Defendants admit the allegations contained in Paragraph 9 of Plaintiff's Complaint.

10. Defendants deny the allegations contained in Paragraph 10 of Plaintiff's Complaint.

11. Defendants admit the allegations contained in Paragraph 11 of Plaintiff's Complaint.

12. Defendants admit the allegations contained in Paragraph 12 of Plaintiff's Complaint.

13. Defendants deny the allegations contained in Paragraph 13 of Plaintiff's Complaint.

14. Defendants deny the allegations contained in Paragraph 14 of Plaintiff's Complaint.

15. Defendants deny the guarantee has been given and/or breached. Defendants are without knowledge regarding Plaintiff's satisfactions and therefore denies obligation to provide 100% satisfaction and states Plaintiff's alleged dissatisfaction is in bad faith.

16. Defendants deny the allegations contained in Paragraph 16 of Plaintiff's Complaint.

17. Defendants admit the allegations contained in Paragraph 17 of Plaintiff's Complaint.

18. Defendants admit the allegations contained in Paragraph 18 of Plaintiff's Complaint.

19. Defendants deny the allegations contained in Paragraph 19 of Plaintiff's Complaint.

20. Defendants are without knowledge sufficient to either admit or deny the allegations contained in Paragraph 20 of Plaintiff's Complaint, and therefore deny the same.

21. Defendants are without knowledge sufficient to either admit or deny the allegations contained in Paragraph 21 of Plaintiff's Complaint, and therefore deny the same.

22. Defendants deny the allegations contained in Paragraph 22 of Plaintiff's Complaint.

23. Defendants deny the allegations contained in Paragraph 23 of Plaintiff's Complaint.

24. Defendants are without knowledge sufficient to either admit or deny the allegations contained in Paragraph 24 of Plaintiff's Complaint, and therefore deny the same.

25. Defendants are without knowledge sufficient to either admit or deny the allegations contained in Paragraph 25 of Plaintiff's Complaint, and therefore deny the same.

26. Defendants deny the allegations contained in Paragraph 26 of Plaintiff's Complaint.

27. Defendants deny the allegations contained in Paragraph 27 of Plaintiff's Complaint.

28. Defendants deny the allegations contained in Paragraph 28 of Plaintiff's Complaint.

29. Defendants admit the allegations contained in Paragraph 29 of Plaintiff's Complaint.

30. Defendants admit they have refused to perform the unreasonable and unlawful demands of Plaintiff, but have offered to remedy any actual defects.

31. Defendants deny the allegations contained in Paragraph 31 of Plaintiff's Complaint.

COUNT I – BREACH OF CONTRACT

32. Defendants incorporate their response to Paragraphs 1-31 as though fully stated herein.

33. Defendants deny the allegations contained in Paragraph 33 of Plaintiff's Complaint.

34. Defendants deny the allegations contained in Paragraph 34 of Plaintiff's Complaint.

35. Defendants deny the allegations contained in Paragraph 35 of Plaintiff's Complaint.

COUNT II – BREACH OF WARRANTY

36. Defendants incorporate their response to Paragraphs 1-31 and Count I as though fully stated herein.

37. Defendants deny the allegations contained in Paragraph 37 of Plaintiff's Complaint.

38. Defendants deny the allegations contained in Paragraph 38 of Plaintiff's Complaint.

39. Defendants deny the allegations contained in Paragraph 39 of Plaintiff's Complaint.

40. Defendants admit the allegations contained in Paragraph 40 of Plaintiff's Complaint.

41. Defendants deny the allegations contained in Paragraph 41 of Plaintiff's Complaint.

42. Defendants deny the allegations contained in Paragraph 42 of Plaintiff's Complaint.

43. Defendants deny the allegations contained in Paragraph 43 of Plaintiff's Complaint.

COUNT III – VIOLATION OF MOTOR DEALERS FRANCHISING ACT

44. Defendants admit the allegations contained in Paragraph 44 of Plaintiff's Complaint.

45. Defendants deny the allegations contained in Paragraph 45 of Plaintiff's Complaint.

46. Defendants deny the allegations contained in Paragraph 46 of Plaintiff's Complaint.

COUNT IV –
VIOLATION OF THE NEW MEXICO UNFAIR PRACTICES ACT

47. Defendants incorporate their response to Paragraphs 1-31 and Counts I, II, and III as though fully stated herein.

48. Defendants deny the allegations contained in Paragraph 48 of Plaintiff's Complaint.

49. Defendants deny the allegations contained in Paragraph 49 of Plaintiff's Complaint.

50. Defendants deny the allegations contained in Paragraph 50 of Plaintiff's Complaint.

COUNT V – VIOLATION OF THE COLORADO PROTECTION ACT

51. Defendants incorporate their response to Paragraphs 1-31 and Counts I, II, III, and IV as though fully stated herein.

52. Defendants deny the allegations contained in Paragraph 52 of Plaintiff's Complaint.

53. Defendants deny the allegations contained in Paragraph 53 of Plaintiff's Complaint.

COUNT VI – NEGLIGENT MISREPRESENTATION

54. Defendants incorporate their response to Paragraphs 1-31 and Count I, II, III, IV, and V as though fully stated herein.

55. Defendants deny the allegations contained in Paragraph 55 of Plaintiff's Complaint.

56. Defendants deny the allegations contained in Paragraph 56 of Plaintiff's Complaint.

57. Defendants admit the allegations contained in Paragraph 57 of Plaintiff's Complaint.

58. Defendants deny the allegations contained in Paragraph 58 of Plaintiff's Complaint.

59. Defendants deny the allegations contained in Paragraph 59 of Plaintiff's Complaint.

COUNT VII – RESCISSION

60. Defendants incorporate their response to Paragraphs 1-31 and Counts I, II, II, IV, V, and VI as though fully stated herein.

61. Defendants deny the allegations contained in Paragraph 61 of Plaintiff's Complaint.

62. Defendants deny the allegations contained in Paragraph 62 of Plaintiff's Complaint.

63. Defendants deny the allegations contained in Paragraph 63 of Plaintiff's Complaint.

FIRST AFFIRMATIVE DEFENSE

Plaintiff failed to mitigate their damages.

SECOND AFFIRMATIVE DEFENSE

There exists failure of consideration with regard to Bus #2 repurchase.

THIRD AFFIRMATIVE DEFENSE

Defendants deny that Plaintiff had the right of 100% satisfaction. Defendants state the buses were ready to go, and Plaintiff's alleged dissatisfaction is in bad faith and unreasonable.

FOURTH AFFIRMATIVE DEFENSE

Defendants deny that the buses were defective but in the alternative, Plaintiff has refused to allow Defendants to fix any minor corrections.

SIXTH AFFIRMATIVE DEFENSE

Plaintiff has failed to plead consequential or special damages.

Respectfully Submitted,

/s/ Roger E. Yarbro   Roger E. Yarbro
Yarbro & Associates, P.A.,
Attorney for Defendants
109 James Canyon Hwy, Suite
A P.O. Box 480
Cloudcroft, NM 88317-0480
(575) 682-3614, (575) 682-3642 Facsimile
yarbrocc@tularosa.net

CERTIFICATE OF SERVICE

I HEREBY CERTIFY that on the 23rd day of June, 2010, I filed the foregoing electronically through the CM/ECF system, which caused the following parties or counsel to be served by electronic means, as more fully reflected on the Notice of Electronic Filing:

>Thomas P. Gulley
>Bannerman & Johnson, P.A.,
>Attorneys for Plaintiff
>*tpg@nmcounsel.com*

/s/ Roger E. Yarbro   Roger E. Yarbro
Yarbro & Associates, P.A.,
Attorney for Defendants
109 James Canyon Highway, Suite A P.O. Box 480
Cloudcroft, NM 88317
(575) 682-3614 | (575) 682-3642 Facsimile
yarbrocc@tularosa.net

EXPERIENTIAL ASSIGNMENTS

Draft a Complaint for the Frensch, Cash, or Williams case, as assigned by your professor. At your professor's discretion, some students in your class may draft Complaints and other students Answers that respond to one or more of them.

B. Joinder

There are two kinds of joinder, claim and party. For efficiency's and fairness' sake, it is sometimes possible and desirable to add claims or parties or both to a single civil action as it was originally brought by the plaintiff. Naturally, there must be some rules of the game defining which claims and which parties may be added. And there must also be rules for what happens when a party or parties that ought, in fairness, be joined, cannot be joined because, for example, the court cannot assert personal jurisdiction over them.

Rule Material

Rule 14 *Third Party Practice*

(a) When a Defending Party May Bring in a Third Party.

(1) *Timing of the Summons and Complaint.* A defending party may, as third-party plaintiff, serve a summons and complaint on a nonparty who is or may be liable to it for all or part of the claim against it. But the third-party plaintiff must, by motion, obtain the court's leave if it files the third-party complaint more than 14 days after serving its original answer.

(2) *Third-Party Defendant's Claims and Defenses.* The person served with the summons and third-party complaint—the "third-party defendant":

(A) must assert any defense against the third-party plaintiff's claim under Rule 12;

(B) must assert any counterclaim against the third-party plaintiff under Rule 13a, and may assert any counterclaim against the third-party plaintiff under Rule 13(b) or any cross-claim against another third-party defendant under Rule 13(g);

(C) may assert against the plaintiff any defense that the third-party plaintiff has to the plaintiff's claim; and

(D) may also assert against the plaintiff any claim arising out of the transaction or occurrence that is the subject matter of the plaintiff's claim against the third-party plaintiff.

(3) *Plaintiff's Claims Against a Third-Party Defendant.* The plaintiff may assert against the third-party defendant any claim arising out of the transaction or occurrence that is the subject matter of the plaintiff's claim against the third-party plaintiff. The third-party defendant must then assert any defense under Rule 12 and any counterclaim under Rule 13(a), and may assert any counterclaim under Rule 13(b) or any crossclaim under Rule 13(g).

(4) *Motion to Strike, Sever, or Try Separately.* Any party may move to strike the third-party claim, to sever it, or to try it separately.

(5) *Third-Party Defendant's Claim Against a Nonparty.* A third-party defendant may proceed under this rule against a nonparty who is or may be liable to the third-party defendant for all or part of any claim against it.

.   .   .

(b) When a Plaintiff May Bring in a Third Party. When a claim is asserted against a plaintiff, the plaintiff may bring in a third party if this rule would allow a defendant to do so.

. . .

Rule 18 Joinder of Claims

(a) In General. A party asserting a claim, counterclaim, cross-claim, or third-party claim may join, as independent or alternative claims, as many claims as it has against an opposing party.

(b) Joinder of Contingent Claims. A party may join two claims even though one of them is contingent on the disposition of the other; but the court may grant relief only in accordance with the parties' relative substantive rights. In particular, a plaintiff may state a claim for money and a claim to set aside a conveyance that is fraudulent as to that plaintiff, without first obtaining a judgment for the money.

Rule 19 Required Joinder of Parties

(a) Persons Required to Be Joined If Feasible.

(1) *Required Party.* A person who is subject to service of process and whose joinder will not deprive the court of subject-matter jurisdiction must be joined as a party if:

(A) in that person's absence, the court cannot accord complete relief among existing parties; or

(B) that person claims an interest relating to the subject of the action and is so situated that disposing of the action in the person's absence may:

(i) as a practical matter impair or impede the person's ability to protect the interest; or

(ii) leave an existing party subject to a substantial risk of incurring double, multiple, or otherwise inconsistent obligations because of the interest.

(2) *Joinder by Court Order.* If a person has not been joined as required, the court must order that the person be made a party. A person who refuses to join as a plaintiff may be made either a defendant or, in a proper case, an involuntary plaintiff.

(3) *Venue.* If a joined party objects to venue and the joinder would make venue improper, the court must dismiss that party.

(b) When Joinder Is Not Feasible. If a person who is required to be joined if feasible cannot be joined, the court must determine whether, in equity and good conscience, the action should proceed among the existing parties or should be dismissed. The factors for the court to consider include:

(1) the extent to which a judgment rendered in the person's absence might prejudice that person or the existing parties;

(2) the extent to which any prejudice could be lessened or avoided by:

(A) protective provisions in the judgment;

(B) shaping the relief; or

(C) other measures;

(3) whether a judgment rendered in the person's absence would be adequate; and

(4) whether the plaintiff would have an adequate remedy if the action were dismissed for nonjoinder.

(c) Pleading the Reasons for Nonjoinder. When asserting a claim for relief, a party must state:

(1) the name, if known, of any person who is required to be joined if feasible but is not joined; and

(2) the reasons for not joining that person.

(d) Exception for Class Actions. This rule is subject to Rule 23.

Rule 20 Permissive Joinder of Parties

(a) Persons Who May Join or Be Joined.

(1) *Plaintiffs.* Persons may join in one action as plaintiffs if:

(A) they assert any right to relief jointly, severally, or in the alternative with respect to or arising out of the same transaction, occurrence, or series of transactions or occurrences; and

(B) any question of law or fact common to all plaintiffs will arise in the action.

(2) *Defendants.* Persons—as well as a vessel, cargo, or other property subject to admiralty process *in rem*—may be joined in one action as defendants if:

> (A) any right to relief is asserted against them jointly, severally, or in the alternative with respect to or arising out of the same transaction, occurrence, or series of transactions or occurrences; and

> (B) any question of law or fact common to all defendants will arise in the action.

(3) *Extent of Relief.* Neither a plaintiff nor a defendant need be interested in obtaining or defending against all the relief demanded. The court may grant judgment to one or more plaintiffs according to their rights, and against one or more defendants according to their liabilities.

(b) Protective Measures. The court may issue orders—including an order for separate trials—to protect a party against embarrassment, delay, expense, or other prejudice that arises from including a person against whom the party asserts no claim and who asserts no claim against the party.

Rule 21 Misjoinder and Nonjoinder of Parties

Misjoinder of parties is not a ground for dismissing an action. On motion or on its own, the court may at any time, on just terms, add or drop a party. The court may also sever any claim against a party.

United Mine Workers Of America v. Gibbs

383 U.S. 715, 86 S.Ct. 1130 (1966)

Mr. Justice BRENNAN delivered the opinion of the Court.

Respondent Paul Gibbs was awarded compensatory and punitive damages in this action against petitioner United Mine Workers of America (UMW) for alleged violations of the Labor Management Relations Act, and of the common law of Tennessee. The case grew out of the rivalry between the United Mine Workers and the Southern Labor Union over representation of workers in the southern Appalachian coal fields. Tennessee Consolidated Coal Company, not a party here, laid off 100 miners of the UMW's Local 5881 when it closed one of its mines in southern Tennessee during the spring of 1960. Late that summer, Grundy Company, a wholly owned subsidiary of Consolidated, hired respondent as mine superintendent to attempt to open a new mine on Consolidated's property at nearby

Gray's Creek through use of members of the Southern Labor Union. As part of the arrangement, Grundy also gave respondent a contract to haul the mine's coal to the nearest railroad loading point.

On August 15 and 16, 1960, armed members of Local 5881 forcibly prevented the opening of the mine, threatening respondent and beating an organizer for the rival union. The members of the local believed Consolidated had promised them the jobs at the new mine; they insisted that if anyone would do the work, they would. At this time, no representative of the UMW, their international union, was present. There was no further violence at the mine site; a picket line was maintained there for nine months; and no further attempts were made to open the mine during that period.

Respondent lost his job as superintendent, and never entered into performance of his haulage contract. He testified that he soon began to lose other trucking contracts and mine leases he held in nearby areas. Claiming these effects to be the result of a concerted union plan against him, he sought recovery not against Local 5881 or its members, but only against petitioner, the international union. The suit was brought in the United States District Court for the Eastern District of Tennessee, and jurisdiction was premised on allegations of secondary boycotts under s 303. The state law claim, for which jurisdiction was based upon the doctrine of pendent jurisdiction, asserted 'an unlawful conspiracy and an unlawful boycott aimed at him and (Grundy) to maliciously, wantonly and willfully interfere with his contract of employment and with his contract of haulage.'

I.

A threshold question is whether the District Court properly entertained jurisdiction of the claim based on Tennessee law. [The Court explained that the state law claims were not pre-empted by the federal labor laws.]

The fact that state remedies were not entirely pre-empted does not, however, answer the question whether the state claim was properly adjudicated in the District Court absent diversity jurisdiction. The Court held in *Hurn v. Oursler*, 289 U.S. 238, 53 S.Ct. 586, that state law claims are appropriate for federal court determination if they form a separate but parallel ground for relief also sought in a substantial claim based on federal law. The Court distinguished permissible from non-permissible exercises of federal judicial power over state law claims by contrasting 'a case where two distinct grounds in support of a single cause of action are alleged, one only of which presents a federal question, and a case where two separate and distinct causes of action are alleged, one only of which is federal in character. In the former, where the federal question averred is not plainly wanting in substance, the federal court, even though the federal ground be not established, may nevertheless retain and dispose of the case upon the nonfederal ground; in the latter it may not do so upon the nonfederal cause of action.' 289 U.S., at 246, 53 S.Ct., at 589. The question is into which category the present action fell.

Hurn was decided in 1933, before the unification of law and equity by the Federal Rules of Civil Procedure. At the time, the meaning of 'cause of action' was a subject of serious dispute; the phrase might 'mean one thing for one purpose and something different for another.' *United States v. Memphis Cotton Oil Co.,* 288 U.S. 62, 67-68, 53 S.Ct. 278. The Court in Hurn identified what it meant by the term by citation of *Baltimore S.S. Co. v. Phillips,* 274 U.S. 316, 47 S.Ct. 600, a case in which 'cause of action' had been used to identify the operative scope of the doctrine of res judicata. In that case the Court had noted that "the whole tendency of our decisions is to require a plaintiff to try his whole cause of action and his whole case at one time," 274 U.S., at 320, 47 S.Ct., at 602.

With the adoption of the Federal Rules of Civil Procedure and the unified form of action, Fed.Rule Civ.Proc. 2, much of the controversy over 'cause of action' abated. The phrase remained as the keystone of the Hurn test, however, and, as commentators have noted, has been the source of considerable confusion. Under the Rules, the impulse is toward entertaining the broadest possible scope of action consistent with fairness to the parties; joinder of claims, parties and remedies is strongly encouraged.[5] Yet because the Hurn question involves issues of jurisdiction as well as convenience, there has been some tendency to limit its application to cases in which the state and federal claims are, as in Hurn, 'little more than the equivalent of different epithets to characterize the same group of circumstances.' 289 U.S., at 246, 53 S.Ct. at 590.

This limited approach is unnecessarily grudging. Pendent jurisdiction, in the sense of judicial power, exists whenever there is a claim 'arising under (the) Constitution, the Laws of the United States, and Treaties made, or which shall be made, under their Authority * * *,' U.S.Const., Art. III, s 2, and the relationship between that claim and the state claim permits the conclusion that the entire action before the court comprises but one constitutional 'case.' The federal claim must have substance sufficient to confer subject matter jurisdiction on the court. *Levering & Garrigues Co. v. Morrin,* 289 U.S. 103, 53 S.Ct. 549, 77 L.Ed. 1062. The state and federal claims must derive from a common nucleus of operative fact. But if, considered without regard to their federal or state character, a plaintiff's claims are such that he would ordinarily be expected to try them all in one judicial proceeding, then, assuming substantiality of the federal issues, there is power in federal courts to hear the whole.

---

5 *See,* e.g., Fed.Rules Civ.Proc. 2, 18-20, 42.

That power need not be exercised in every case in which it is found to exist. It has consistently been recognized that pendent jurisdiction [a name for one form of supplemental jurisdiction. Ed.] is a doctrine of discretion, not of plaintiff's right. Its justification lies in considerations of judicial economy, convenience and fairness to litigants; if these are not present a federal court should hesitate to exercise jurisdiction over state claims, even though bound to apply state law to them, *Erie R. Co. v. Tompkins*, 304 U.S. 64, 58 S.Ct. 817. Needless decisions of state law should be avoided both as a matter of comity and to promote justice between the parties, by procuring for them a surer-footed reading of applicable law. Certainly, if the federal claims are dismissed before trial, even though not insubstantial in a jurisdictional sense, the state claims should be dismissed as well. Similarly, if it appears that the state issues substantially predominate, whether in terms of proof, of the scope of the issues raised, or of the comprehensiveness of the remedy sought, the state claims may be dismissed without prejudice and left for resolution to state tribunals. There may, on the other hand, be situations in which the state claim is so closely tied to questions of federal policy that the argument for exercise of pendent jurisdiction is particularly strong. In the present case, for example, the allowable scope of the state claim implicates the federal doctrine of pre-emption; while this interrelationship does not create statutory federal question jurisdiction, *Louisville & N.R. Co. v. Mottley*, 211 U.S. 149, 29 S.Ct. 42, its existence is relevant to the exercise of discretion. Finally, there may be reasons independent of jurisdictional considerations, such as the likelihood of jury confusion in treating divergent legal theories of relief, that would justify separating state and federal claims for trial, Fed.Rule Civ.Proc. 42(b). If so, jurisdiction should ordinarily be refused.

The question of power will ordinarily be resolved on the pleadings. But the issue whether pendent jurisdiction has been properly assumed is one which remains open throughout the litigation. Pretrial procedures or even the trial itself may reveal a substantial hegemony of state law claims, or likelihood of jury confusion, which could not have been anticipated at the pleading stage. Although it will of course be appropriate to take account in this circumstance of the already completed course of the litigation, dismissal of the state claim might even then be merited. For example, it may appear that the plaintiff was well aware of the nature of his proofs and the relative importance of his claims; recognition of a federal court's wide latitude to decide ancillary questions of state law does not imply that it must tolerate a litigant's effort to impose upon it what is in effect only a state law case. Once it appears that a state claim constitutes the real body of a case, to which the federal claim is only an appendage, the state claim may fairly be dismissed.

We are not prepared to say that in the present case the District Court exceeded its discretion in proceeding to judgment on the state claim. Although s 303 limited recovery to compensatory damages based on secondary pressures, and state law allowed both compensatory and punitive damages, and allowed such damages as to both secondary and primary activity, the state and federal claims arose from the same nucleus of operative fact and reflected alternative remedies. Indeed, the verdict sheet sent in to the jury authorized only one award of damages, so that recovery could not be given separately on the federal and state claims.

It is true that the s 303 claims ultimately failed and that the only recovery allowed respondent was on the state claim. We cannot confidently say, however, that the federal issues were so remote or played such a minor role at the trial that in effect the state claim only was tried.

Painter, Plaintiff-Appellant, v. Harvey, Defendant-Appellee

863 F. 2d 329 (4th Cir. 1988)

WILKINSON, Circuit Judge:

In this case we must determine if the district court properly invoked its ancillary subject matter jurisdiction [the name previously used for one form of supplemental jurisdiction under 28 USC 1367. Ed.] to entertain a state libel counterclaim that arose in response to a federal action under 42 U.S.C. s 1983. Plaintiff Painter alleged that defendant Harvey violated her constitutional rights while arresting her for driving under the influence in November, 1984. Defendant counterclaimed, asserting that plaintiff slandered and libeled him by filing a fabricated complaint about the circumstances of her arrest with the Town Council of Luray, Virginia, and by distributing her complaint to the local news media. Following a jury verdict in defendant's favor, plaintiff moved to dismiss defendant's counterclaim for lack of subject matter jurisdiction. The district court held defendant's counterclaim compulsory because it involved substantially the same evidence as plaintiff's claim. It also denied defendant's motion for attorney's fees. We affirm both rulings.

I.

At 12:45 a.m. on the morning of November 9, 1984, police officer Larry Harvey stopped a vehicle driven erratically by plaintiff Florhline Painter in the Town of Luray, Virginia. Both plaintiff and a companion appeared intoxicated and Harvey called for additional assistance. After the assistance arrived, Harvey placed Painter under arrest for driving while intoxicated, handcuffed her, and, with the help of another officer, placed her in the back seat of his patrol car. A plastic shield separated the front and back seats.

Harvey transported Painter at once from the scene of the arrest to a local jail. Harvey's car was preceded and followed by two other police cars and was never out of their sight. When Painter arrived at the jail, her blouse was unbuttoned, one breast was exposed, and her shoes, panty hose, and underpants were removed. She claimed Officer Harvey had raped her and initially refused to cover herself when requested to do so.

On April 9, 1985, Painter appeared before the Luray Town Council to summarize her version of the events of her arrest and to file a formal complaint against Officer Harvey. She also issued a prepared written statement to a reporter from the local newspaper, the Page News and Courier. The statement contained the allegation that Harvey had "jerked me out of my car, tore my blouse, put marks on my breast, and I also sustained a head and neck injury from his excessive force he used...." Excerpts from the complaint were published in the Page News and Courier on April 12, 1985.

Painter filed suit in federal district court in February, 1985. She alleged that Harvey lacked probable cause to arrest her and had used excessive force during her arrest, all in violation of 42 U.S.C. s 1983.

Harvey counterclaimed against Painter for defamation. He alleged that Painter had falsely claimed that she was molested or raped during the November, 1984 arrest, and had submitted a false summary of the circumstances of her arrest to the Luray Town Council the following April. Harvey's version of events was starkly at variance with that of Painter. He testified that when he and Painter arrived at the jail, he noticed that Painter had opened her blouse, exposed one of her breasts, and had removed her shoes, panty hose, and underpants. Jerry Shiro, the former chief of police of the Luray Police Department, stated that the Page News and Courier article had created serious embarrassment for Harvey with the public, his fellow police officers, and members of the Town Council.

The case was tried before a jury. The jury found for Harvey on Painter's s 1983 claim. The jury also found in Harvey's favor on the defamation counterclaim, awarding compensatory damages of $5,000.00 and punitive damages of $15,000.00. Painter moved to set aside the verdict on the grounds that the court lacked subject matter jurisdiction over the counterclaim. Harvey moved for attorney's fees. The district court denied both motions. Painter appeals and Harvey cross-appeals.

II.

The sole question on Painter's appeal is the nature of Harvey's counterclaim.

If the counterclaim is compulsory, it is within the ancillary jurisdiction of the court to entertain and no independent basis of federal jurisdiction is required. If the counterclaim is permissive, however, it must have its own independent jurisdictional base. Since Painter and Harvey are both citizens of Virginia, and Harvey asserts no federal question, the designation of the counterclaim is critical.

In defining a compulsory counterclaim, Fed.R.Civ.P. 13(a) provides in pertinent part that:

> *A pleading shall state as a counterclaim any claim which at the time of serving the pleadings the pleader has against any opposing party, if it arises out of the transaction or occurrence that is the subject matter of the opposing party's claim.*

Fed.R.Civ.P. 13(b), in contrast, provides that:

> *A pleading may state as a counterclaim any claim against an opposing party not arising out of the transaction or occurrence that is the subject matter of the opposing party's claim.*

We hold that defendant's counterclaim is compulsory and that the district court properly exercised jurisdiction over it.

III.

In *Sue & Sam Mfg. Co. v. B-L-S Const. Co.*, 538 F.2d 1048 (4th Cir.1976), this circuit suggested four inquiries to determine if a counterclaim is compulsory:

(1) Are the issues of fact and law raised in the claim and counterclaim largely the same? (2) Would res judicata bar a subsequent suit on the party's counterclaim, absent the compulsory counterclaim rule? (3) Will substantially the same evidence support or refute the claim as well as the counterclaim? and (4) Is there any logical relationship between the claim and counterclaim? A court need not answer all these questions in the affirmative for the counterclaim to be compulsory. Rather, the tests are less a litmus, more a guideline.

Although the tests are four in number, there is an underlying thread to each of them in this case: evidentiary similarity. The claim and counterclaim both involved witness testimony directed toward the same critical event. Indeed, in applying the four Sue & Sam tests, the district court invariably returned to the same place. As to inquiry (1), the district court noted that: "The central issue in both the claim and counterclaim is identical: What transpired during Mrs. Painter's arrest on November 9, 1984? The jury, in essence, was faced with irreconcilably conflicting evidence and was required to choose which version to accept or reject."

As to inquiry (2), the district court stated: "Examining the facts here, one finds that the jury verdict against Mrs. Painter on her s 1983 claim necessarily determined the issue of what happened during her arrest. Thus, in subsequent state action she could well face an issue preclusion [Note the relationship between compulsoriness of counterclaims and issue preclusion, further explored in chapter 10. Ed.] bar as to relitigating those facts."

Inquiry (3) is explicitly evidentiary in nature. Not surprisingly, the district court concluded: "All of the witnesses, except the newspaper editor and witnesses testifying to damages, limited their testimony to a single factual issue—what transpired during Mrs. Painter's arrest on November 9, 1984? It is hard to imagine a case in which the evidence bearing on the two claims is so closely identical."

With regard to inquiry (4), the district court was once again led to the differing tales of the same evening underlying both claim and counterclaim. It concluded that: "In short, the truth of Officer Harvey's version of the events of November 9, 1984, is the central issue of fact in both the claim and counterclaim. They are inextricably and logically connected."

Where, as here, the same evidence will support or refute both the claim and counterclaim, the counterclaim will almost always be compulsory. The "same evidence" test thus accomplishes the purposes of Fed.R.Civ.P. 13(a), because the "very purpose of making certain types of counterclaims compulsory is to prevent the relitigation of the same set of facts. This rationale for ancillary jurisdiction over compulsory counterclaims, moreover, parallels the rationale for pendent jurisdiction—namely, that where different claims of law "derive from a common nucleus of operative fact," the justification for the exercise of federal jurisdiction "lies in considerations of judicial economy, convenience and fairness to litigants." *United Mine Workers of America v. Gibbs*, 383 U.S. 715, 725-26, 86 S.Ct. 1130, 1138-39, 16 L.Ed.2d 218 (1966). Holding counterclaims compulsory avoids the burden of multiple trials with their corresponding duplication of evidence and their drain on limited judicial resources. The "same evidence" test simply makes these concerns the focal point of its determination by requiring claims and counterclaims which involve the same evidence to be heard in a single proceeding.

Although the district court appeared to apply what in essence was the "same evidence test" in this case, courts have properly cautioned that this test should not be the exclusive determinant of compulsoriness under Fed.R.Civ.P. 13(a) because it is too narrow a definition of a single transaction or occurrence. Some counterclaims may thus be compulsory even though they do not involve a substantial identity of evidence with the claim. A counterclaim may still arise from the same "transaction or occurrence", as a logically related claim even though the evidence needed to prove the opposing claims may be quite different. Here, however, the claims both bear a logical relationship and an evidentiary similarity, and the problems of a divergence between the last two inquiries under Sue & Sam are not present.

IV.

The foregoing purposes of Fed.R.Civ.P. 13(a) lead us to reject Painter's assertion that Harvey's libel counterclaim was merely permissive. We address plaintiff's arguments in turn.

Plaintiff argues that defendant's counterclaim should be found permissive because plaintiff's claim involves federal law and defendant's counterclaim state libel law. The fact that the counterclaim may be one of state law, however, says nothing about its logical relationship to the federal claim or to the evidentiary overlap between them. Where a plaintiff asserts a claim based on federal law, a counterclaim based on state law may be adjudicated as a matter of ancillary jurisdiction so long as the counterclaim arises from the same transaction.

Similarly, we reject plaintiff's assertion that the counterclaim is permissive because the events of November 9, 1984 became relevant to the libel counterclaim only when plaintiff responded to that counterclaim with an affirmative defense of truth. The affirmative defense, however, followed the counterclaim much as night follows day, and indeed plaintiff could not have withheld the affirmative defense without repudiating the version of events as set forth in her original complaint. Since the counterclaim itself was not subject to the federal face of the complaint rule, the status of the counterclaim cannot be made to depend on the fact that issue is joined over the events of November 9, 1984 only by way of an affirmative defense to it. To decide otherwise would be to construct an artificial barrier to the comprehensive purposes of Rule 13(a).

We also cannot accept plaintiff's argument, based on the second inquiry under Sue & Sam, that defendant's counterclaim should be permissive because a withheld counterclaim would face no res judicata bar in a subsequent state proceeding. Assuming that Harvey's counterclaim might still be brought in state court, the res judicata test cannot be the controlling one. If the limits of the compulsory counterclaim are no broader than res judicata, then Fed.R.Civ.P. 13(a) would be superfluous. Commentators and courts have recognized the difficulty of using a res judicata test to distinguish between permissive and compulsory counterclaims and, in fact, the doctrines of preclusion have been adapted to the requirements of Fed.R.Civ.P. 13(a). That is to say, "absent a compulsory counterclaim rule, a pleader is never barred by res judicata from suing independently on a claim that he refrained from pleading as a counterclaim in a prior action."

For much the same reasons, we find unpersuasive plaintiff's assertion that the burden of multiple trials in federal and state courts is not implicated here. Plaintiff argues that an adverse verdict on her 1983 claim would collaterally stop her on the issue of liability in libel in state court and restrict any future state trial to the matter of damages. Although the danger of multiplicity of litigation may be lessened by issue preclusion, the use of issue preclusion is never analogous to having the same judge or jury try the entire cause. To require the defendant to pursue a state libel claim independently of this action, in which the only determination to be made would center on damages, is to ignore the value of having the same factfinder resolve all issues with an eye for consistency and an appreciation for the total context of the case.

Contrary to plaintiff's assertion, this case does not fall within the narrow line of exceptions to Fed.R.Civ.P. 13(a) holding that a counterclaim "which stems from the filing of the main action and subsequent alleged defamations is not a compulsory counterclaim...." We need not address whether Harris was properly decided because we believe it is distinguishable from the facts of this case. In Harris, the libel counterclaim related to publications which arguably were privileged as court filings. The Harris court thus regarded the libel counterclaim as little more than a claim of malicious prosecution which was "premature prior to the determination of the main action." Here, by contrast, the focus of the counterclaim was on Painter's activities before the Luray Town Council, which are distinct and apart from a filing of a lawsuit. To extend the Harris rule to this different set of facts would vitiate the general premise of Fed.R.Civ.P. 13(a)—that another logically related claim need only have accrued by the time a responsive pleading is filed in the first action, not by the time of the filing of the complaint. In addition, it would ignore the general purpose of Fed.R.Civ.P. 13(a)-to have all related actions heard at one time.

Plaintiff argues finally that holding this counterclaim to be compulsory will impermissibly chill the prosecution of actions under 42 U.S.C. s 1983. This argument is unpersuasive for several reasons. First, Fed.R.Civ.P. 13(a) is neutral in its terms and does not suggest that the characterization of counterclaims should be made to depend upon the type of cause of action alleged in the complaint. Second, the "substantial evidence" test employed to find this counterclaim compulsory is, if anything, underinclusive in its application. As we have noted, counterclaims that are logically related to the claim but require different evidence to prove, may also be compulsory where considerations of economy and fairness require, as they do here, that the controversy be settled in a single lawsuit.

. . .

The judgment of the district court is

AFFIRMED.

––––––––––––––

NOTES

1. May a plaintiff make multiple claims against a defendant in her Complaint? To be joined in one civil action, must the multiple claims be related to one another in some way? See FRCP 8(e)(2) and 18. If the plaintiff has multiple claims against the defendant and they are closely related, wouldn't it be terribly inefficient and perhaps unfair if they are not joined in one action? (More on this in chapter 10, where we will see that the preclusion doctrine may penalize a plaintiff who fails to join connected claims in one action.)

2. What if multiple plaintiffs want to sue the same defendant? Is the same efficiency rationale present as when a single plaintiff wants to state multiple claims against a defendant? If the multiple plaintiffs' claims are all related to the same events? If the multiple plaintiffs are combining their unrelated claims against a single defendant?

3. What about a defendant who has claims that could be brought against a plaintiff? Should he be permitted to bring them in the same action? Must he bring them in the same action? See FRCP 13.

4. Multiple defendants might have claims against one another. Note that allowing them to bring these claims does not require bringing anyone into the action who is not already in. Should these claims by one party against another party who is "on the same side of the v." have to be related to the main claim initially brought by the plaintiff? Why or why not?

5. Perhaps a defendant thinks that someone else is liable to the plaintiff instead of the defendant. Should the defendant be permitted to bring this new "third party" into the action? What if the "third party" would be liable to the defendant for damages the defendant is required to pay the plaintiff? Is this situation different? See FRCP 14.

6. Consider the various kinds of joined claims. Must the court find a new basis for personal and subject matter jurisdiction for them? Some but not all?

7. An especially complex situation is presented when a federal court sitting with diversity of citizenship subject matter jurisdiction for the main claim is asked to consider new claims brought by plaintiffs or defendants that would destroy the complete diversity required by Strawbridge or when the added plaintiffs failed to show a satisfactory amount in controversy. Should such a court be permitted to exercise Supplemental Jurisdiction over these joined claims? Review 28 USC 1367. The lower courts were split on how to interpret 1367 until the Supreme Court ruled in *Exxon Mobil v. Allapattah Services*, 125 S.Ct. 2611 (2005). In this 5-4 decision, the Court applied the somewhat odd language of 1367, saying that it had no idea why Congress chose to make the distinctions it made, but that those distinctions would be followed.

C

If possible under FRCP 14, draft allegations necessary for a Third-Party Complaint in either the Frensch or Cash case. Here are some additional facts.

Frensch Case: Nickel 'n Dime tells defense counsel that it has a contract with Acme maintenance and that the terms of the contract oblige Acme to keep the floors and aisles clean and clear of debris. The contract was executed one year prior to the Frensch incident, which is the first such slip and fall since the contract execution. Since contract execution, an Acme employee has come to the Nickel 'n Dime every day on which the store is open. The employee comes near the end of each store-day and cleans. The contract includes a clause that says:

> *Acme agrees that it will indemnify Nickel 'n Dime for any damages paid for claims that are the direct result of a failure of Acme to perform its duties under this contract.*

Cash Case: Cari Pearsall says that Wiscbeads agreed that she could return the beads if she could not use them for any or no reason. But after she became ill and Becky's order could not be filled, she asked and Wiscbeads refused to return her money. Does this help her frame a proper Third-Party Claim? If so, draft the allegations; if not, write a one-page explanation to your supervising lawyer explaining why it does not.

C. Affirmative Defenses

Review Rule 8. In many situations, a defendant will have a possible affirmative defense. The essence of an affirmative defense is that it stands on its own without regard to the truth of the plaintiff's claim. Classic affirmative defenses include the statute of limitations (even if the plaintiff's claim is true, it was filed too late), "accord and satisfaction" (defendant says she already reached an agreement about this claim and has paid it), and the classic tort defenses of contributory negligence (plaintiff contributed to his own harm and is barred from recovery) and assumption of risk (plaintiff knew of and accepted the risk of harm). Notice that none of them deny the truth of the plaintiff's allegations. As a result, a defendant must plead any affirmative defense he wishes to claim, or face the possibility of losing it. (Again, see Rule 8.)

Likewise, because the affirmative defense stands independently of the plaintiff's allegations, a defendant bears the burden of proof on an affirmative defense. (See chapter 8).

"Damage caps" is one example of a defense that may or may not be regarded as an affirmative defense. Many states have adopted damage caps on certain kinds of tort claims, limiting the recovery of the plaintiff. Should these be considered affirmative defenses and therefore waived if not asserted by the defendant? Some courts have treated them as affirmative defenses. Consistent with that view, federal courts in other contexts have refused to allow public entities to belatedly raise an affirmative defense to damages, notwithstanding the impact on innocent taxpayers. See, e.g., *Bentley v. Cleveland County Bd. of County Comm'rs.*, 41 F.3d 600, 604-05 (10th Cir. 1994) (concluding that county, having failed to raise affirmative defense of $ 100,000 statutory damages cap in discrimination suit until after $ 157,000 verdict was rendered, forfeited its right to that defense); *Ingraham v. United States*, 808 F.2d 1075, 1079 (5th Cir. 1987) (barring government from belatedly raising statutory cap on medical malpractice damages)

CHAPTER FIVE

Motions to Dismiss

THE MOTION TO DISMISS is the device for challenging the quality of a Complaint. Unlike an Answer, which responds to the Plaintiff's allegations of fact, a Motion to Dismiss asks the court to end the civil action in the defendant's favor because of some defect in the Complaint.

Not all Motions to Dismiss are created equal. Read the list of grounds for filing a Motion to Dismiss in FRCP 12(b). Then read the rest of the rule, carefully noting which grounds may be combined with an Answer, which grounds are waived if not raised before or in an Answer, and so on. Notice the connection in this regard to other topics already covered. Because a defect in the court's subject matter jurisdiction robs it of the basic power to resolve the dispute, a 12(b) objection to subject-matter jurisdiction can be raised at any time and cannot be waived.

Consider the other forms that FRCP 12 motions can take other than a Motion to Dismiss, such as the Motion for a More Definite Statement or the Motion for Judgment on the Pleadings.

Motions to Dismiss for Failure to State a Claim represent the first way in which an action can be terminated in favor of a defendant. It serves the same function as a "demur" or a "nonsuit" in older forms of pleading before the FRCPs. In any event, it is a sort of "legal so-what?" If, even assuming everything a plaintiff says is true and could be proven at trial, the law gives the plaintiff nothing, there is no point in going through the time and expense of discovery and trial. To be efficient, such a civil action should be ended at the first opportunity with a minimum of expense for the court or the parties. Let's say, for example, that your male professor comes to teach class dressed casually, without a jacket and tie. And let's further say that this offends your sensibilities in the extreme. Perhaps you would go to the dean's office to complain and get no satisfaction. Now that you know how to prepare a Complaint from chapter 4, you decide to start a civil action in the local court, claiming that the offense of your professor's casual dress should entitle you to damages of one million dollars. Your Complaint names both the professor and the law school as defendants (for failing to have a policy requiring more formal dress). Even if everything you have said in your Complaint is true, and even if you are truly distressed, the law provides no redress for your claim. Essentially, the law says to your allegations, "so what?" This is the classic situation for a Motion to Dismiss to succeed in ending a civil action.

Since the *Twombly* and *Iqbal* cases excerpted in this chapter, the likelihood for termination of actions by the Motion to Dismiss route has been increased.

Rule Material

Rule 12 Defenses and Objections: When and How Presented; Motion for Judgment on the Pleadings; Consolidating Motions; Waiving Defenses; Pretrial Hearing

(a) Time to Serve a Responsive Pleading.

(1) *In General.* Unless another time is specified by this rule or a federal statute, the time for serving a responsive pleading is as follows:

(A) A defendant must serve an answer:

(i) within 21 days after being served with the summons and complaint; or

(ii) if it has timely waived service under Rule 4(d), within 60 days after the request for a waiver was sent, or within 90 days after it was sent to the defendant outside any judicial district of the United States.

(B) A party must serve an answer to a counterclaim or cross-claim within 21 days after being served with the pleading that states the counterclaim or cross-claim.

(C) A party must serve a reply to an answer within 21 days after being served with an order to reply, unless the order specifies a different time.

. . .

(4) *Effect of a Motion.* Unless the court sets a different time, serving a motion under this rule alters these periods as follows:

(A) if the court denies the motion or postpones its disposition until trial, the responsive pleading must be served within 14 days after notice of the court's action; or

(B) if the court grants a motion for a more definite statement, the responsive pleading must be served within 14 days after the more definite statement is served.

(b) How to Present Defenses. Every defense to a claim for relief in any pleading must be asserted in the responsive pleading if one is required. But a party may assert the following defenses by motion:

(1) lack of subject-matter jurisdiction;

(2) lack of personal jurisdiction;

(3) improper venue;

(4) insufficient process;

(5) insufficient service of process;

(6) failure to state a claim upon which relief can be granted; and

(7) failure to join a party under Rule 19.

A motion asserting any of these defenses must be made before pleading if a responsive pleading is allowed. If a pleading sets out a claim for relief that does not require a responsive pleading, an opposing party may assert at trial any defense to that claim. No defense or objection is waived by joining it with one or more other defenses or objections in a responsive pleading or in a motion.

(c) Motion for Judgment on the Pleadings. After the pleadings are closed— but early enough not to delay trial—a party may move for judgment on the pleadings.

(d) Result of Presenting Matters Outside the Pleadings. If, on a motion under Rule 12(b)(6) or 12(c), matters outside the pleadings are presented to and not excluded by the court, the motion must be treated as one for summary judgment under Rule 56. All parties must be given a reasonable opportunity to present all the material that is pertinent to the motion.

(e) Motion for a More Definite Statement. A party may move for a more definite statement of a pleading to which a responsive pleading is allowed but which is so vague or ambiguous that the party cannot reasonably prepare a response. The motion must be made before filing a responsive pleading and must point out the defects complained of and the details desired. If the court orders a more definite statement and the order is not obeyed within 14 days after notice of the order or within the time the court sets, the court may strike the pleading or issue any other appropriate order.

(f) Motion to Strike. The court may strike from a pleading an insufficient defense or any redundant, immaterial, impertinent, or scandalous matter. The court may act:

(1) on its own; or

(2) on motion made by a party either before responding to the pleading or, if a response is not allowed, within 21 days after being served with the pleading.

(g) Joining Motions.

(1) *Right to Join.* A motion under this rule may be joined with any other motion allowed by this rule.

(2) *Limitation on Further Motions.* Except as provided in Rule 12 (h)(2) or (3), a party that makes a motion under this rule must not make another motion under this rule raising a defense or objection that was available to the party but omitted from its earlier motion.

(h) Waiving and Preserving Certain Defenses.

(1) *When Some Are Waived.* A party waives any defense listed in Rule 12(b)(2)–(5) by:

(A) omitting it from a motion in the circumstances described in Rule 12(g)(2); or

(B) failing to either:

(i) make it by motion under this rule; or

(ii) include it in a responsive pleading or in an amendment allowed by Rule 15(a)(1) as a matter of course.

(2) *When to Raise Others.* Failure to state a claim upon which relief can be granted, to join a person required by Rule 19(b), or to state a legal defense to a claim may be raised:

(A) in any pleading allowed or ordered under Rule 7(a);

(B) by a motion under Rule 12(c); or

(C) at trial.

(3) *Lack of Subject-Matter Jurisdiction.* If the court determines at any time that it lacks subject-matter jurisdiction, the court must dismiss the action.

(i) Hearing Before Trial. If a party so moves, any defense listed in Rule 12(b)(1)–(7)—whether made in a pleading or by motion—and a motion under Rule 12(c) must be heard and decided before trial unless the court orders a deferral until trial.

Bell Atlantic Corporation, et al. v. Twombly, et al.

550 U.S. 544, 127 S.Ct. 1955 (2007)

Justice SOUTER delivered the opinion of the Court.

Liability under § 1 of the Sherman Act, 15 U.S.C. § 1, requires a "contract, combination . . . , or conspiracy, in restraint of trade or commerce." The question in this putative class action is whether a § 1 complaint can survive a motion to dismiss when it alleges that major telecommunications providers engaged in certain parallel conduct unfavorable to competition, absent some factual context suggesting agreement, as distinct from identical, independent action. We hold that such a complaint should be dismissed.

I

Respondents William Twombly and Lawrence Marcus (hereinafter plaintiffs) represent a putative class consisting of all "subscribers of local telephone and/or high speed internet services . . . from February 8, 1996 to present." Complaint. In this action against petitioners, a group of ILECs[1] plaintiffs seek treble damages and declaratory and injunctive relief for claimed violations of § 1 of the Sherman Act which prohibits "[e]very contract, combination in the form of trust or otherwise, or conspiracy, in restraint of trade or commerce among the several States, or with foreign nations."

---

1 The 1984 divestiture of AT & T's local telephone service created seven Regional Bell Operating Companies. Through a series of mergers and acquisitions, those seven companies were consolidated into the four ILECs named in this suit: BellSouth Corporation, Qwest Communications International, Inc., SBC Communications, Inc., and Verizon Communications, Inc. (successor-in-interest to Bell Atlantic Corporation). Complaint ¶ 21, App. 16. Together, these ILECs allegedly control 90 percent or more of the market for local telephone service in the 48 contiguous States. *Id.*, ¶ 48, App. 26.

The complaint alleges that the ILECs conspired to restrain trade in two ways, each supposedly inflating charges for local telephone and high-speed Internet services. Plaintiffs say, first, that the ILECs "engaged in parallel conduct" in their respective service areas to inhibit the growth of upstart CLECs. Their actions allegedly included making unfair agreements with the CLECs for access to ILEC networks, providing inferior connections to the networks, overcharging, and billing in ways designed to sabotage the CLECs' relations with their own customers. According to the complaint, the ILECs' "compelling common motivatio[n]" to thwart the CLECs' competitive efforts naturally led them to form a conspiracy; "[h]ad any one [ILEC] not sought to prevent CLECs . . . from competing effectively . . ., the resulting greater competitive inroads into that [ILEC's] territory would have revealed the degree to which competitive entry by CLECs would have been successful in the other territories in the absence of such conduct."

Second, the complaint charges agreements by the ILECs to refrain from competing against one another. These are to be inferred from the ILECs' common failure "meaningfully [to] pursu[e]" "attractive business opportunit[ies]" in contiguous markets where they possessed "substantial competitive advantages," and from a statement of Richard Notebaert, chief executive officer (CEO) of the ILEC Qwest, that competing in the territory of another ILEC " 'might be a good way to turn a quick dollar but that doesn't make it right,' "

The complaint couches its ultimate allegations this way:

> "In the absence of any meaningful competition between the [ILECs] in one another's markets, and in light of the parallel course of conduct that each engaged in to prevent competition from CLECs within their respective local telephone and/or high speed internet services markets and the other facts and market circumstances alleged above, Plaintiffs allege upon information and belief that [the ILECs] have entered into a contract, combination or conspiracy to prevent competitive entry in their respective local telephone and/or high speed internet services markets and have agreed not to compete with one another and otherwise allocated customers and markets to one another." *Id.*, ¶ 51, App. 27.

The United States District Court for the Southern District of New York dismissed the complaint for failure to state a claim upon which relief can be granted.

The Court of Appeals for the Second Circuit reversed, holding that the District Court tested the complaint by the wrong standard.

We granted certiorari to address the proper standard for pleading an antitrust conspiracy through allegations of parallel conduct, and now reverse.

II

A

Because § 1 of the Sherman Act "does not prohibit [all] unreasonable restraints of trade . . . but only restraints effected by a contract, combination, or conspiracy," *Copperweld Corp. v. Independence Tube Corp.*, 467 U.S. 752, 775, 104 S.Ct. 2731, 81 L.Ed.2d 628 (1984), "[t]he crucial question" is whether the challenged anticompetitive conduct "stem[s] from independent decision or from an agreement, tacit or express," Theatre Enterprises, 346 U.S., at 540, 74 S.Ct. 257. While a showing of parallel "business behavior is admissible circumstantial evidence from which the fact finder may infer agreement," it falls short of "conclusively establish[ing] agreement or . . . itself constitut[ing] a Sherman Act offense." *Id.*, at 540–541, 74 S.Ct. 257.

B

This case presents the antecedent question of what a plaintiff must plead in order to state a claim under § 1 of the Sherman Act. Federal Rule of Civil Procedure 8(a)(2) requires only "a short and plain statement of the claim showing that the pleader is entitled to relief," in order to "give the defendant fair notice of what the . . . claim is and the grounds upon which it rests," *Conley v. Gibson*, 355 U.S. 41, 47, 78 S.Ct. 99 (1957). While a complaint attacked by a Rule 12(b)(6) motion to dismiss does not need detailed factual allegations, a plaintiff's obligation to provide the "grounds" of his "entitle[ment] to relief" requires more than labels and conclusions, and a formulaic recitation of the elements of a cause of action will not do. Factual allegations must be enough to raise a right to relief above the speculative level, on the assumption that all the allegations in the complaint are true (even if doubtful in fact). ("Rule 12(b)(6) does not countenance . . . dismissals based on a judge's disbelief of a complaint's factual allegations"); *Scheuer v. Rhodes*, 416 U.S. 232, 236, 94 S.Ct. 1683 (1974) (a well-pleaded complaint may proceed even if it appears "that a recovery is very remote and unlikely").

In applying these general standards to a § 1 claim, we hold that stating such a claim requires a complaint with enough factual matter (taken as true) to suggest that an agreement was made. Asking for plausible grounds to infer an agreement does not impose a probability requirement at the pleading stage; it simply calls for enough fact to raise a reasonable expectation that discovery will reveal evidence of illegal agreement. And, of course, a well-pleaded complaint may proceed even if it strikes a savvy judge that actual proof of those facts is improbable, and "that a recovery is very remote and unlikely." Ibid. In identifying facts that are suggestive enough to render a § 1 conspiracy plausible, we have the benefit of the prior rulings and considered views of leading commentators, already quoted, that lawful parallel conduct fails to bespeak unlawful agreement. It makes sense to say, therefore, that an allegation of parallel conduct and a bare assertion of conspiracy will not suffice. Without more, parallel conduct does not suggest conspiracy, and a conclusory allegation of agreement at some unidentified point does not supply facts adequate to show illegality. Hence, when allegations of parallel conduct are set out in order to make a § 1 claim, they must be placed in a context that raises a suggestion of a preceding agreement, not merely parallel conduct that could just as well be independent action.

The need at the pleading stage for allegations plausibly suggesting (not merely consistent with) agreement reflects the threshold requirement of Rule 8(a)(2) that the "plain statement" possess enough heft to "sho[w] that the pleader is entitled to relief." A statement of parallel conduct, even conduct consciously undertaken, needs some setting suggesting the agreement necessary to make out a § 1 claim; without that further circumstance pointing toward a meeting of the minds, an account of a defendant's commercial efforts stays in neutral territory. An allegation of parallel conduct is thus much like a naked assertion of conspiracy in a § 1 complaint: it gets the complaint close to stating a claim, but without some further factual enhancement it stops short of the line between possibility and plausibility of "entitle[ment] to relief."

We alluded to the practical significance of the Rule 8 entitlement requirement in *Dura Pharmaceuticals, Inc. v. Broudo,* 544 U.S. 336, 125 S.Ct. 1627 (2005), when we explained that something beyond the mere possibility of loss causation must be alleged, lest a plaintiff with " 'a largely groundless claim' " be allowed to " 'take up the time of a number of other people, with the right to do so representing an in terrorem increment of the settlement value.' " *Id.,* at 347, 125 S.Ct. 1627 (quoting *Blue Chip Stamps v. Manor Drug Stores,* 421 U.S. 723, 741, 95 S.Ct. 1917 (1975)). So, when the allegations in a complaint, however true, could not raise a claim of entitlement to relief, "this basic deficiency should . . . be exposed at the point of minimum expenditure of time and money by the parties and the court." *Daves v. Hawaiian Dredging Co.,* 114 F.Supp. 643, 645 (D.Hawai 1953)); see also *Dura,* supra, at 346, 125 S.Ct. 1627; *Asahi Glass Co. v. Pentech Pharmaceuticals, Inc.,* 289 F.Supp.2d 986, 995 (N.D.Ill.2003) (Posner, J., sitting by designation) ("[S]ome threshold of plausibility must be crossed at the outset before a patent antitrust case should be permitted to go into its inevitably costly and protracted discovery phase").

It is no answer to say that a claim just shy of a plausible entitlement to relief can, if groundless, be weeded out early in the discovery process through "careful case management," post, at 1975, given the common lament that the success of judicial supervision in checking discovery abuse has been on the modest side. And it is self-evident that the problem of discovery abuse cannot be solved by "careful scrutiny of evidence at the summary judgment stage," much less "lucid instructions to juries," post, at 1975; the threat of discovery expense will push cost-conscious defendants to settle even anemic cases before reaching those proceedings. Probably, then, it is only by taking care to require allegations that reach the level suggesting conspiracy that we can hope to avoid the potentially enormous expense of discovery in cases with no " 'reasonably founded hope that the [discovery] process will reveal relevant evidence' " to support a § 1 claim. *Dura*, 544 U.S., at 347, 125 S.Ct. 1627, 161 L.Ed.2d 577, (quoting *Blue Chip Stamps, supra*, at 741, 95 S.Ct. 1917; alteration in *Dura*).

Plaintiffs main argument against the plausibility standard at the pleading stage is its ostensible conflict with an early statement of ours construing Rule 8. Justice Black's opinion for the Court in *Conley v. Gibson* spoke not only of the need for fair notice of the grounds for entitlement to relief but of "the accepted rule that a complaint should not be dismissed for failure to state a claim unless it appears beyond doubt that the plaintiff can prove no set of facts in support of his claim which would entitle him to relief." 355 U.S., at 45–46, 78 S.Ct. 99. This "no set of facts" language can be read in isolation as saying that any statement revealing the theory of the claim will suffice unless its factual impossibility may be shown from the face of the pleadings; and the Court of Appeals appears to have read *Conley* in some such way when formulating its understanding of the proper pleading standard, see 425 F.3d, at 106, 114 (invoking *Conley*'s "no set of facts" language in describing the standard for dismissal).

On such a focused and literal reading of *Conley*'s "no set of facts," a wholly conclusory statement of claim would survive a motion to dismiss whenever the pleadings left open the possibility that a plaintiff might later establish some "set of [undisclosed] facts" to support recovery. So here, the Court of Appeals specifically found the prospect of unearthing direct evidence of conspiracy sufficient to preclude dismissal, even though the complaint does not set forth a single fact in a context that suggests an agreement. It seems fair to say that this approach to pleading would dispense with any showing of a " 'reasonably founded hope' " that a plaintiff would be able to make a case, see *Dura*, 544 U.S., at 347, 125 S.Ct. 1627 (quoting *Blue Chip Stamps*, 421 U.S., at 741, 95 S.Ct. 1917); Mr. Micawber's optimism would be enough.

Seeing this, a good many judges and commentators have balked at taking the literal terms of the *Conley* passage as a pleading standard.

We could go on, but there is no need to pile up further citations to show that *Conley*'s "no set of facts" language has been questioned, criticized, and explained away long enough. To be fair to the *Conley* Court, the passage should be understood in light of the opinion's preceding summary of the complaint's concrete allegations, which the Court quite reasonably understood as amply stating a claim for relief. But the passage so often quoted fails to mention this understanding on the part of the Court, and after puzzling the profession for 50 years, this famous observation has earned its retirement. The phrase is best forgotten as an incomplete, negative gloss on an accepted pleading standard: once a claim has been stated adequately, it may be supported by showing any set of facts consistent with the allegations in the complaint.

III

When we look for plausibility in this complaint, we agree with the District Court that plaintiffs' claim of conspiracy in restraint of trade comes up short. To begin with, the complaint leaves no doubt that plaintiffs rest their § 1 claim on descriptions of parallel conduct and not on any independent allegation of actual agreement among the ILECs. Although in form a few stray statements speak directly of agreement on fair reading these are merely legal conclusions resting on the prior allegations. Thus, the complaint first takes account of the alleged "absence of any meaningful competition between [the ILECs] in one another's markets," "the parallel course of conduct that each [ILEC] engaged in to prevent competition from CLECs," "and the other facts and market circumstances alleged [earlier]"; "in light of" these, the complaint concludes "that [the ILECs] have entered into a contract, combination or conspiracy to prevent competitive entry into their . . . markets and have agreed not to compete with one another." The nub of the complaint, then, is the ILECs' parallel behavior, consisting of steps to keep the CLECs out and manifest disinterest in becoming CLECs themselves, and its sufficiency turns on the suggestions raised by this conduct when viewed in light of common economic experience.

We think that nothing contained in the complaint invests either the action or inaction alleged with a plausible suggestion of conspiracy. As to the ILECs' supposed agreement to disobey the 1996 Act and thwart the CLECs' attempts to compete, we agree with the District Court that nothing in the complaint intimates that the resistance to the upstarts was anything more than the natural, unilateral reaction of each ILEC intent on keeping its regional dominance. The 1996 Act did more than just subject the ILECs to competition; it obliged them to subsidize their competitors with their own equipment at wholesale rates. The economic incentive to resist was powerful, but resisting competition is routine market conduct, and even if the ILECs flouted the 1996 Act in all the ways the plaintiffs allege, there is no reason to infer that the companies had agreed among themselves to do what was only natural anyway; so natural, in fact, that if alleging parallel decisions to resist competition were enough to imply an antitrust conspiracy, pleading a § 1 violation against almost any group of competing businesses would be a sure thing.

We agree with the District Court's assessment that antitrust conspiracy was not suggested by the facts adduced under either theory of the complaint, which thus fails to state a valid § 1 claim.[2]

Here, we do not require heightened fact pleading of specifics, but only enough facts to state a claim to relief that is plausible on its face. Because the plaintiffs here have not nudged their claims across the line from conceivable to plausible, their complaint must be dismissed.

*   *   *

The judgment of the Court of Appeals for the Second Circuit is reversed, and the case is remanded for further proceedings consistent with this opinion.

It is so ordered.

Justice STEVENS, with whom Justice GINSBURG joins except as to Part IV, dissenting.

In the first paragraph of its 23–page opinion the Court states that the question to be decided is whether allegations that "major telecommunications providers engaged in certain parallel conduct unfavorable to competition" suffice to state a violation of § 1 of the Sherman Act. The answer to that question has been settled for more than 50 years. If that were indeed the issue, a summary reversal would adequately resolve this case. [P]arallel conduct is circumstantial evidence admissible on the issue of conspiracy, but it is not itself illegal.

Thus, this is a case in which there is no dispute about the substantive law. If the defendants acted independently, their conduct was perfectly lawful. If, however, that conduct is the product of a horizontal agreement among potential competitors, it was unlawful. The plaintiffs have alleged such an agreement and, because the complaint was dismissed in advance of answer, the allegation has not even been denied. Why, then, does the case not proceed? Does a judicial

---

2 In reaching this conclusion, we do not apply any "heightened" pleading standard, nor do we seek to broaden the scope of Federal Rule of Civil Procedure 9, which can only be accomplished " 'by the process of amending the Federal Rules, and not by judicial interpretation.' " *Swierkiewicz v. Sorema N. A.*, 534 U.S. 506, 515, 122 S.Ct. 992, 152 L.Ed.2d 1 (2002) (quoting *Leatherman v. Tarrant County Narcotics Intelligence and Coordination Unit*, 507 U.S. 163, 168, 113 S.Ct. 1160, 122 L.Ed.2d 517 (1993)). On certain subjects understood to raise a high risk of abusive litigation, a plaintiff must state factual allegations with greater particularity than Rule 8 requires. Fed. Rules Civ. Proc. 9(b)-(c). Here, our concern is not that the allegations in the complaint were insufficiently "particular[ized]," ibid.; rather, the complaint warranted dismissal because it failed in toto to render plaintiffs' entitlement to relief plausible.

opinion that the charge is not "plausible" provide a legally acceptable reason for dismissing the complaint? I think not.

Two practical concerns presumably explain the Court's dramatic departure from settled procedural law. Private antitrust litigation can be enormously expensive, and there is a risk that jurors may mistakenly conclude that evidence of parallel conduct has proved that the parties acted pursuant to an agreement when they in fact merely made similar independent decisions. Those concerns merit careful case management, including strict control of discovery, careful scrutiny of evidence at the summary judgment stage, and lucid instructions to juries; they do not, however, justify the dismissal of an adequately pleaded complaint without even requiring the defendants to file answers denying a charge that they in fact engaged in collective decisionmaking. More importantly, they do not justify an interpretation of Federal Rule of Civil Procedure 12(b)(6) that seems to be driven by the majority's appraisal of the plausibility of the ultimate factual allegation rather than its legal sufficiency.

I

Rule 8(a)(2) of the Federal Rules requires that a complaint contain "a short and plain statement of the claim showing that the pleader is entitled to relief." The Rule did not come about by happenstance, and its language is not inadvertent.

Under the relaxed pleading standards of the Federal Rules, the idea was not to keep litigants out of court but rather to keep them in. The merits of a claim would be sorted out during a flexible pretrial process and, as appropriate, through the crucible of trial. See Swierkiewicz, 534 U.S., at 514, 122 S.Ct. 992 ("The liberal notice pleading of Rule 8(a) is the starting point of a simplified pleading system, which was adopted to focus litigation on the merits of a claim"). Charles E. Clark, the "principal draftsman" of the Federal Rules, put it thus:

"Experience has shown . . . that we cannot expect the proof of the case to be made through the pleadings, and that such proof is really not their function. We can expect a general statement distinguishing the case from all others, so that the manner and form of trial and remedy expected are clear, and so that a permanent judgment will result."

The pleading paradigm under the new Federal Rules was well illustrated by the inclusion in the appendix of Form 9, a complaint for negligence. As relevant, the Form 9 complaint states only: "On June 1, 1936, in a public highway called Boylston Street in Boston, Massachusetts, defendant negligently drove a motor vehicle against plaintiff who was then crossing said highway." Form 9, Complaint for Negligence, Forms App.,

Fed. Rules Civ. Proc., 28 U.S.C.App., p. 829 (hereinafter Form 9). The complaint then describes the plaintiff's injuries and demands judgment. The asserted ground for relief [is] the defendant's negligent driving. But that bare allegation suffices under a system that "restrict[s] the pleadings to the task of general notice-giving and invest[s] the deposition-discovery process with a vital role in the preparation for trial." [3]

We have consistently reaffirmed that basic understanding of the Federal Rules in the half century since *Conley*. For example, in *Scheuer v. Rhodes,* 416 U.S. 232, 94 S.Ct. 1683, 40 L.Ed.2d 90 (1974), we reversed the Court of Appeals' dismissal on the pleadings when the respondents, the Governor and other officials of the State of Ohio, argued that the petitioners' claims were barred by sovereign immunity. In a unanimous opinion by then-Justice Rehnquist, we emphasized:

> "When a federal court reviews the sufficiency of a complaint, before the reception of any evidence either by affidavit or admissions, its task is necessarily a limited one. The issue is not whether a plaintiff will ultimately prevail but whether the claimant is entitled to offer evidence to support the claims. *Indeed it may appear on the face of the pleadings that a recovery is very remote and unlikely but that is not the test." Id.,* at 236, 94 S.Ct. 1683 (emphasis added).

The Rhodes plaintiffs had "alleged generally and in conclusory terms" that the defendants, by calling out the National Guard to suppress the Kent State University student protests, "were guilty of wanton, wilful and negligent conduct." *Krause v. Rhodes,* 471 F.2d 430, 433 (C.A.6 1972). We reversed the Court of Appeals on the ground that "[w]hatever the plaintiffs may or may not be able to establish as to the merits of their allegations, their claims, as stated in the complaints, given the favorable reading required by the Federal Rules of Civil Procedure," were not barred by the Eleventh Amendment because they were styled as suits against the defendants in their individual capacities.

Accordingly, I respectfully dissent.

---

3   The Federal Rules do impose a "particularity" requirement on "all averments of fraud or mistake," Fed. Rule Civ. Proc. 9(b), neither of which has been alleged in this case. We have recognized that the canon of *expresio unius est exclusio alterius* applies to Rule 9(b).

Ashcroft et al. v. Iqbal et al.

556 U.S. 662, 129 S.Ct. 1937 (2009)

KENNEDY, J., delivered the opinion of the Court, in which ROBERTS, C.J., and SCALIA, THOMAS, and ALITO, JJ., joined. SOUTER, J., filed a dissenting opinion, in which STEVENS, GINSBURG, and BREYER, JJ., joined. BREYER, J., filed a dissenting opinion.

Justice KENNEDY delivered the opinion of the Court.

Respondent Javaid Iqbal is a citizen of Pakistan and a Muslim. In the wake of the September 11, 2001, terrorist attacks he was arrested in the United States on criminal charges and detained by federal officials. Respondent claims he was deprived of various constitutional protections while in federal custody. To redress the alleged deprivations, respondent filed a complaint against numerous federal officials, including John Ashcroft, the former Attorney General of the United States, and Robert Mueller, the Director of the Federal Bureau of Investigation (FBI). Ashcroft and Mueller are the petitioners in the case now before us. As to these two petitioners, the complaint alleges that they adopted an unconstitutional policy that subjected respondent to harsh conditions of confinement on account of his race, religion, or national origin.

In the District Court petitioners raised the defense of qualified immunity and moved to dismiss the suit, contending the complaint was not sufficient to state a claim against them. The District Court denied the motion to dismiss, concluding the complaint was sufficient to state a claim despite petitioners' official status at the times in question. Petitioners brought an interlocutory appeal in the Court of Appeals for the Second Circuit. The court, without discussion, assumed it had jurisdiction over the order denying the motion to dismiss; and it affirmed the District Court's decision.

Respondent's account of his prison ordeal could, if proved, demonstrate unconstitutional misconduct by some governmental actors. But the allegations and pleadings with respect to these actors are not before us here. This case instead turns on a narrower question: Did respondent, as the plaintiff in the District Court, plead factual matter that, if taken as true, states a claim that petitioners deprived him of his clearly established constitutional rights. We hold respondent's pleadings are insufficient.

I

Following the 2001 attacks, the FBI and other entities within the Department of Justice began an investigation of vast reach to identify the assailants and prevent them from attacking anew. The FBI dedicated more than 4,000 special agents and 3,000 support personnel to the endeavor. By September 18 "the FBI had received more than 96,000 tips or potential leads from the public."

In the ensuing months the FBI questioned more than 1,000 people with suspected links to the attacks in particular or to terrorism in general. Of those individuals, some 762 were held on immigration charges; and a 184–member subset of that group was deemed to be "of 'high interest' " to the investigation. The high-interest detainees were held under restrictive conditions designed to prevent them from communicating with the general prison population or the outside world.

Respondent was one of the detainees. According to his complaint, in November 2001 agents of the FBI and Immigration and Naturalization Service arrested him on charges of fraud in relation to identification documents and conspiracy to defraud the United States. Pending trial for those crimes, respondent was housed at the Metropolitan Detention Center (MDC) in Brooklyn, New York. Respondent was designated a person "of high interest" to the September 11 investigation and in January 2002 was placed in a section of the MDC known as the Administrative Maximum Special Housing Unit (ADMAX SHU). As the facility's name indicates, the ADMAX SHU incorporates the maximum security conditions allowable under Federal Bureau of Prison regulations. ADMAX SHU detainees were kept in lockdown 23 hours a day, spending the remaining hour outside their cells in handcuffs and leg irons accompanied by a four-officer escort.

Respondent pleaded guilty to the criminal charges, served a term of imprisonment, and was removed to his native Pakistan. He then filed a *Bivens* action in the United States District Court for the Eastern District of New York.

The 21-cause-of-action complaint does not challenge respondent's arrest or his confinement in the MDC's general prison population. Rather, it concentrates on his treatment while confined to the ADMAX SHU. The complaint sets forth various claims against defendants who are not before us. For instance, the complaint alleges that respondent's jailors "kicked him in the stomach, punched him in the face, and dragged him across" his cell without justification, subjected him to serial strip and body-cavity searches when he posed no safety risk to himself or others, and refused to let him and other Muslims pray because there would be "[n]o prayers for terrorists."

The allegations against petitioners are the only ones relevant here. The complaint contends that petitioners designated respondent a person of high interest on account of his race, religion, or national origin, in contravention of the First and Fifth Amendments to the Constitution. The complaint alleges that "the [FBI], under the direction of Defendant MUELLER, arrested and detained thousands of Arab Muslim men . . . as part of its investigation of the events of September 11." It further alleges that "[t]he policy of holding post–September–11th detainees in highly restrictive conditions of confinement until they were 'cleared' by the FBI was approved by Defendants ASHCROFT and MUELLER in discussions in the weeks after September 11, 2001." Lastly, the complaint posits that petitioners "each knew of, condoned, and willfully and maliciously agreed to subject" respondent to harsh conditions of confinement "as a matter of policy, solely on account of [his] religion, race, and/or national origin and for no legitimate penological interest." The pleading names Ashcroft as the "principal architect" of the policy, and identifies Mueller as "instrumental in [its] adoption, promulgation, and implementation."

Petitioners moved to dismiss the complaint for failure to state sufficient allegations to show their own involvement in clearly established unconstitutional conduct. The District Court denied their motion. Accepting all of the allegations in respondent's complaint as true, the court held that "it cannot be said that there [is] no set of facts on which [respondent] would be entitled to relief as against" petitioners. (relying on *Conley v. Gibson,* 355 U.S. 41, 78 S.Ct. 99, 2 L.Ed.2d 80 (1957)). Invoking the collateral-order doctrine petitioners filed an interlocutory appeal in the United States Court of Appeals for the Second Circuit. While that appeal was pending, this Court decided *Bell Atlantic Corp. v. Twombly,* 550 U.S. 544, 127 S.Ct. 1955, 167 L.Ed.2d 929 (2007), which discussed the standard for evaluating whether a complaint is sufficient to survive a motion to dismiss.

The Court of Appeals considered *Twombly*'s applicability to this case. Acknowledging that *Twombly* retired the Conley no-set-of-facts test relied upon by the District Court, the Court of Appeals' opinion discussed at length how to apply this Court's "standard for assessing the adequacy of pleadings." It concluded that *Twombly* called for a "flexible 'plausibility standard,' which obliges a pleader to amplify a claim with some factual allegations in those contexts where such amplification is needed to render the claim plausible." The court found that petitioners' appeal did not present one of "those contexts" requiring amplification. As a consequence, it held respondent's pleading adequate to allege petitioners' personal involvement in discriminatory decisions which, if true, violated clearly established constitutional law.

We granted certiorari and now reverse.

II

We first address whether the Court of Appeals had subject-matter jurisdiction to affirm the District Court's order denying petitioners' motion to dismiss. Respondent disputed subject-matter jurisdiction in the Court of Appeals, but the court hardly discussed the issue. We are not free to pretermit the question. Subject-matter jurisdiction cannot be forfeited or waived and should be considered when fairly in doubt. *Arbaugh v. Y & H Corp.*, 546 U.S. 500, 514, 126 S.Ct. 1235, 163 L.Ed.2d 1097 (2006) (citing *United States v. Cotton,* 535 U.S. 625, 630, 122 S.Ct. 1781, 152 L.Ed.2d 860 (2002)). According to respondent, the District Court's order denying petitioners' motion to dismiss is not appealable under the collateral-order doctrine. We disagree.

III

In *Twombly*, the Court found it necessary first to discuss the antitrust principles implicated by the complaint. Here too we begin by taking note of the elements a plaintiff must plead to state a claim of unconstitutional discrimination against officials entitled to assert the defense of qualified immunity.

In *Bivens*—proceeding on the theory that a right suggests a remedy—this Court "recognized for the first time an implied private action for damages against federal officers alleged to have violated a citizen's constitutional rights."

In the limited settings where *Bivens* does apply, the implied cause of action is the "federal analog to suits brought against state officials under 42 U.S.C. § 1983."

The factors necessary to establish a *Bivens* violation will vary with the constitutional provision at issue. Where the claim is invidious discrimination in contravention of the First and Fifth Amendments, our decisions make clear that the plaintiff must plead and prove that the defendant acted with discriminatory purpose. Under extant precedent purposeful discrimination requires more than "intent as volition or intent as awareness of consequences." It instead involves a decision-maker's undertaking a course of action " 'because of,' not merely 'in spite of,' [the action's] adverse effects upon an identifiable group." It follows that, to state a claim based on a violation of a clearly established right, respondent must plead sufficient factual matter to show that petitioners adopted and implemented the detention policies at issue not for a neutral, investigative reason but for the purpose of discriminating on account of race, religion, or national origin.

IV

A

We turn to respondent's complaint. Under Federal Rule of Civil Procedure 8(a)(2), a pleading must contain a "short and plain statement of the claim showing that the pleader is entitled to relief." As the Court held in *Twombly*, 550 U.S. 544, 127 S.Ct. 1955, the pleading standard Rule 8 announces does not require "detailed factual allegations," but it demands more than an unadorned, the-defendant-unlawfully-harmed-me accusation. *Id.*, at 555, 127 S.Ct. 1955 (citing *Papasan v. Allain*, 478 U.S. 265, 286, 106 S.Ct. 2932 (1986)). A pleading that offers "labels and conclusions" or "a formulaic recitation of the elements of a cause of action will not do." 550 U.S., at 555, 127 S.Ct. 1955. Nor does a complaint suffice if it tenders "naked assertion[s]" devoid of "further factual enhancement." *Id.*, at 557, 127 S.Ct. 1955.

To survive a motion to dismiss, a complaint must contain sufficient factual matter, accepted as true, to "state a claim to relief that is plausible on its face." *Id.*, at 570, 127 S.Ct. 1955. A claim has facial plausibility when the plaintiff pleads factual content that allows the court to draw the reasonable inference that the defendant is liable for the misconduct alleged. *Id.*, at 556, 127 S.Ct. 1955. The plausibility standard is not akin to a "probability requirement," but it asks for more than a sheer possibility that a defendant has acted unlawfully. Where a complaint pleads facts that are "merely consistent with" a defendant's liability, it "stops short of the line between possibility and plausibility of 'entitlement to relief.' " *Id.*, at 557, 127 S.Ct. 1955 (brackets omitted).

Two working principles underlie our decision in *Twombly*. First, the tenet that a court must accept as true all of the allegations contained in a complaint is inapplicable to legal conclusions. Threadbare recitals of the elements of a cause of action, supported by mere conclusory statements, do not suffice. (Although for the purposes of a motion to dismiss we must take all of the factual allegations in the complaint as true, we "are not bound to accept as true a legal conclusion couched as a factual allegation." Rule 8 marks a notable and generous departure from the hyper-technical, code-pleading regime of a prior era, but it does not unlock the doors of discovery for a plaintiff armed with nothing more than conclusions. Second, only a complaint that states a plausible claim for relief survives a motion to dismiss. Determining whether a complaint states a plausible claim for relief will, as the Court of Appeals observed, be a context-specific task that requires the reviewing court to draw on its judicial experience and common sense. But where the well-pleaded facts do not permit the court to infer more than the mere possibility of misconduct, the complaint has alleged—but it has not "show[n]"—"that the pleader is entitled to relief." Fed. Rule Civ. Proc. 8(a)(2).

In keeping with these principles a court considering a motion to dismiss can choose to begin by identifying pleadings that, because they are no more than conclusions, are not entitled to the assumption of truth. While legal conclusions can provide the framework of a complaint, they must be supported by factual allegations. When there are well-pleaded factual allegations, a court should assume their veracity and then determine whether they plausibly give rise to an entitlement to relief.

B

Under *Twombly*'s construction of Rule 8, we conclude that respondent's complaint has not "nudged [his] claims" of invidious discrimination "across the line from conceivable to plausible."

We begin our analysis by identifying the allegations in the complaint that are not entitled to the assumption of truth. Respondent pleads that petitioners "knew of, condoned, and willfully and maliciously agreed to subject [him]" to harsh conditions of confinement "as a matter of policy, solely on account of [his] religion, race, and/or national origin and for no legitimate penological interest." The complaint alleges that Ashcroft was the "principal architect" of this invidious policy, and that Mueller was "instrumental" in adopting and executing it. These bare assertions, much like the pleading of conspiracy in *Twombly*, amount to nothing more than a "formulaic recitation of the elements" of a constitutional discrimination claim, 550 U.S., at 555, 127 S.Ct. 1955, namely, that petitioners adopted a policy " 'because of,' not merely 'in spite of,' its adverse effects upon an identifiable group." *Feeney*, 442 U.S., at 279, 99 S.Ct. 2282. As such, the allegations are conclusory and not entitled to be assumed true. *Twombly*, supra, 550 U.S., at 554–555, 127 S.Ct. 1955. To be clear, we do not reject these bald allegations on the ground that they are unrealistic or nonsensical. We do not so characterize them any more than the Court in *Twombly* rejected the plaintiffs' express allegation of a " 'contract, combination or conspiracy to prevent competitive entry,' " *id.*, at 551, 127 S.Ct. 1955, because it thought that claim too chimerical to be maintained. It is the conclusory nature of respondent's allegations, rather than their extravagantly fanciful nature, that disentitles them to the presumption of truth.

We next consider the factual allegations in respondent's complaint to determine if they plausibly suggest an entitlement to relief. The complaint alleges that "the [FBI], under the direction of Defendant MUELLER, arrested and detained thousands of Arab Muslim men . . . as part of its investigation of the events of September 11. It further claims that "[t]he policy of holding post–September–11th detainees in highly restrictive conditions of confinement until they were 'cleared' by the FBI was approved by Defendants ASHCROFT and MUELLER in discussions in the weeks after September 11, 2001." Taken as true, these allegations are consistent with petitioners' purposefully designating detainees "of high interest" because of their race, religion, or national origin. But given more likely explanations, they do not plausibly establish this purpose.

The September 11 attacks were perpetrated by 19 Arab Muslim hijackers who counted themselves members in good standing of al Qaeda, an Islamic fundamentalist group. Al Qaeda was headed by another Arab Muslim—Osama bin Laden—and composed in large part of his Arab Muslim disciples. It should come as no surprise that a legitimate policy directing law enforcement to arrest and detain individuals because of their suspected link to the attacks would produce a disparate, incidental impact on Arab Muslims, even though the purpose of the policy was to target neither Arabs nor Muslims. On the facts respondent alleges the arrests Mueller oversaw were likely lawful and justified by his nondiscriminatory intent to detain aliens who were illegally present in the United States and who had potential connections to those who committed terrorist acts. As between that "obvious alternative explanation" for the arrests, *Twombly*, supra, at 567, 127 S.Ct. 1955, and the purposeful, invidious discrimination respondent asks us to infer, discrimination is not a plausible conclusion.

But even if the complaint's well-pleaded facts give rise to a plausible inference that respondent's arrest was the result of unconstitutional discrimination, that inference alone would not entitle respondent to relief. It is important to recall that respondent's complaint challenges neither the constitutionality of his arrest nor his initial detention in the MDC. Respondent's constitutional claims against petitioners rest solely on their ostensible "policy of holding post–September–11th detainees" in the ADMAX SHU once they were categorized as "of high interest." To prevail on that theory, the complaint must contain facts plausibly showing that petitioners purposefully adopted a policy of classifying post–September–11 detainees as "of high interest" because of their race, religion, or national origin.

This the complaint fails to do. Though respondent alleges that various other defendants, who are not before us, may have labeled him a person "of high interest" for impermissible reasons, his only factual allegation against petitioners accuses them of adopting a policy approving "restrictive conditions of confinement" for post–September–11 detainees until they were " 'cleared' by the FBI." Accepting the truth of that allegation, the complaint does not show, or even intimate, that petitioners purposefully housed detainees in the ADMAX SHU due to their race, religion, or national origin. All it plausibly suggests is that the Nation's top law enforcement officers, in the aftermath of a devastating terrorist attack, sought to keep suspected terrorists in the most secure conditions available until the suspects could be cleared of terrorist activity. Respondent does not argue, nor can he, that such a motive would violate petitioners' constitutional obligations. He would need to allege more by way of factual content to "nudg[e]" his claim of purposeful discrimination "across the line from conceivable to plausible." *Twombly*, 550 U.S., at 570, 127 S.Ct. 1955.

To be sure, respondent can attempt to draw certain contrasts between the pleadings the Court considered in *Twombly* and the pleadings at issue here. In *Twombly*, the complaint alleged general wrongdoing that extended over a period of years, whereas here the complaint alleges discrete wrongs—for instance, beatings—by lower level Government actors. The allegations here, if true, and if condoned by petitioners, could be the basis for some inference of wrongful intent on petitioners' part. Despite these distinctions, respondent's pleadings do not suffice to state a claim. Unlike in *Twombly*, where the doctrine of *respondeat superior* could bind the corporate defendant, here, as we have noted, petitioners cannot be held liable unless they themselves acted on account of a constitutionally protected characteristic. Yet respondent's complaint does not contain any factual allegation sufficient to plausibly suggest petitioners' discriminatory state of mind. His pleadings thus do not meet the standard necessary to comply with Rule 8.

It is important to note, however, that we express no opinion concerning the sufficiency of respondent's complaint against the defendants who are not before us. Respondent's account of his prison ordeal alleges serious official misconduct that we need not address here. Our decision is limited to the determination that respondent's complaint does not entitle him to relief from petitioners.

C

Respondent offers three arguments that bear on our disposition of his case, but none is persuasive.

1

Respondent first says that our decision in *Twombly* should be limited to pleadings made in the context of an antitrust dispute. This argument is not supported by *Twombly* and is incompatible with the Federal Rules of Civil Procedure. Though *Twombly* determined the sufficiency of a complaint sounding in antitrust, the decision was based on our interpretation and application of Rule 8. 550 U.S., at 554, 127 S.Ct. 1955. That Rule in turn governs the pleading standard "in all civil actions and proceedings in the United States district courts." Fed. Rule Civ. Proc. 1. Our decision in *Twombly* expounded the pleading standard for "all civil actions," ibid., and it applies to antitrust and discrimination suits alike.

2

Respondent next implies that our construction of Rule 8 should be tempered where, as here, the Court of Appeals has "instructed the district court to cabin discovery in such a way as to preserve" petitioners' defense of qualified immunity "as much as possible in anticipation of a summary judgment motion." We have held, however, that the question presented by a motion to dismiss a complaint for insufficient pleadings does not turn on the controls placed upon the discovery process. *Twombly*, supra, at 559, 127 S.Ct. 1955 ("It is no answer to say that a claim just shy of a plausible entitlement to relief can, if groundless, be weeded out early in the discovery process through careful case management given the common lament that the success of judicial supervision in checking discovery abuse has been on the modest side" (internal quotation marks and citation omitted)).

Our rejection of the careful-case-management approach is especially important in suits where Government-official defendants are entitled to assert the defense of qualified immunity. The basic thrust of the qualified-immunity doctrine is to free officials from the concerns of litigation, including "avoidance of disruptive discovery." *Siegert v. Gilley*, 500 U.S. 226, 236, 111 S.Ct. 1789, 114 L.Ed.2d 277 (1991) (KENNEDY, J., concurring in judgment).

We decline respondent's invitation to relax the pleading requirements on the ground that the Court of Appeals promises petitioners minimally intrusive discovery. That promise provides especially cold comfort in this pleading context, where we are impelled to give real content to the concept of qualified immunity for high-level officials who must be neither deterred nor detracted from the vigorous performance of their duties. Because respondent's complaint is deficient under Rule 8, he is not entitled to discovery, cabined or otherwise.

3

Respondent finally maintains that the Federal Rules expressly allow him to allege petitioners' discriminatory intent "generally," which he equates with a conclusory allegation. (citing Fed. Rule Civ. Proc. 9). It follows, respondent says, that his complaint is sufficiently well pleaded because it claims that petitioners discriminated against him "on account of [his] religion, race, and/or national origin and for no legitimate penological interest." Were we required to accept this allegation as true, respondent's complaint would survive petitioners' motion to dismiss. But the Federal Rules do not require courts to credit a complaint's conclusory statements without reference to its factual context.

It is true that Rule 9(b) requires particularity when pleading "fraud or mistake," while allowing "[m]alice, intent, knowledge, and other conditions of a person's mind [to] be alleged generally." But "generally" is a relative term. In the context of Rule 9, it is to be compared to the particularity requirement applicable to fraud or mistake. Rule 9 merely excuses a party from pleading discriminatory intent under an elevated pleading standard. It does not give him license to evade the less rigid—though still operative—strictures of Rule 8. And Rule 8 does not empower respondent to plead the bare elements of his cause of action, affix the label " general allegation," and expect his complaint to survive a motion to dismiss.

V

We hold that respondent's complaint fails to plead sufficient facts to state a claim for purposeful and unlawful discrimination against petitioners. The Court of Appeals should decide in the first instance whether to remand to the District Court so that respondent can seek leave to amend his deficient complaint.

The judgment of the Court of Appeals is reversed, and the case is remanded for further proceedings consistent with this opinion.

It is so ordered.

Justice SOUTER, with whom Justice STEVENS, Justice GINSBURG, and Justice BREYER join, dissenting.

The majority misapplies the pleading standard under *Bell Atlantic Corp. v. Twombly*, to conclude that the complaint fails to state a claim. I respectfully dissent.

I

A

Respondent Iqbal was arrested in November 2001 on charges of conspiracy to defraud the United States and fraud in relation to identification documents, and was placed in pretrial detention at the Metropolitan Detention Center in Brooklyn, New York. He alleges that FBI officials carried out a discriminatory policy by designating him as a person "'of high interest'" in the investigation of the September 11 attacks solely because of his race, religion, or national origin. Owing to this designation he was placed in the detention center's Administrative Maximum Special Housing Unit for over six months while awaiting the fraud trial. As I will mention more fully below, Iqbal contends that Ashcroft and Mueller were at the very least aware of the discriminatory detention policy and condoned it (and perhaps even took part in devising it), thereby violating his First and Fifth Amendment rights.

Iqbal claims that on the day he was transferred to the special unit, prison guards, without provocation, "picked him up and threw him against the wall, kicked him in the stomach, punched him in the face, and dragged him across the room." First Amended Complaint. He says that after being attacked a second time he sought medical attention but was denied care for two weeks. According to Iqbal's complaint, prison staff in the special unit subjected him to unjustified strip and body cavity searches, verbally berated him as a " 'terrorist' " and " 'Muslim killer,' " refused to give him adequate food, and intentionally turned on air conditioning during the winter and heating during the summer. He claims that prison staff interfered with his attempts to pray and engage in religious study.

The District Court denied Ashcroft and Mueller's motion to dismiss Iqbal's discrimination claim, and the Court of Appeals affirmed. Ashcroft and Mueller then asked this Court to grant certiorari on two questions:

> "1. Whether a conclusory allegation that a cabinet-level officer or other high-ranking official knew of, condoned, or agreed to subject a plaintiff to allegedly unconstitutional acts purportedly committed by subordinate officials is sufficient to state individual-capacity claims against those officials under *Bivens*.

> "2. Whether a cabinet-level officer or other high-ranking official may be held personally liable for the allegedly unconstitutional acts of subordinate officials on the ground that, as high-level supervisors, they had constructive notice of the discrimination allegedly carried out by such subordinate officials."

The Court granted certiorari on both questions. The first is about pleading; the second goes to the liability standard.

In the first question, Ashcroft and Mueller did not ask whether "a cabinet-level officer or other high-ranking official" who "knew of, condoned, or agreed to subject a plaintiff to allegedly unconstitutional acts committed by subordinate officials" was subject to liability under *Bivens*. In fact, they conceded in their petition for certiorari that they would be liable if they had "actual knowledge" of discrimination by their subordinates and exhibited " 'deliberate indifference' " to that discrimination. Instead, they asked the Court to address whether Iqbal's allegations against them (which they call conclusory) were sufficient to satisfy Rule 8(a)(2), and in particular whether the Court of Appeals misapplied our decision in *Twombly* construing that rule.

The briefing at the merits stage was no different. Iqbal argued that the allegations in his complaint were sufficient under Rule 8(a)(2) and *Twombly*, and conceded that as a matter of law he could not recover under a theory of respondeat superior. Thus, the parties agreed as to a proper standard of supervisory liability, and the disputed question was whether Iqbal's complaint satisfied Rule 8(a)(2).

II

Given petitioners' concession, the complaint satisfies Rule 8(a)(2). Ashcroft and Mueller admit they are liable for their subordinates' conduct if they "had actual knowledge of the assertedly discriminatory nature of the classification of suspects as being 'of high interest' and they were deliberately indifferent to that discrimination." Brief for Petitioners 50. Iqbal alleges that after the September 11 attacks the Federal Bureau of Investigation (FBI) "arrested and detained thousands of Arab Muslim men," that many of these men were designated by high-ranking FBI officials as being " 'of high interest,' " and that in many cases, including Iqbal's, this designation was made "because of the race, religion, and national origin of the detainees, and not because of any evidence of the detainees' involvement in supporting terrorist activity." The complaint further alleges that Ashcroft was the "principal architect of the policies and practices challenged," and that Mueller "was instrumental in the adoption, promulgation, and implementation of the policies and practices challenged." According to the complaint, Ashcroft and Mueller "knew of, condoned, and willfully and maliciously agreed to subject [Iqbal] to these conditions of confinement as a matter of policy, solely on account of [his] religion, race, and/or national origin and for no legitimate penological interest." The complaint thus alleges, at a bare minimum, that Ashcroft and Mueller knew of and condoned the discriminatory policy their subordinates carried out. Actually, the complaint goes further in alleging that Ashcroft and Muller affirmatively acted to create the discriminatory detention policy. If these factual allegations are true, Ashcroft and Mueller were, at the very least, aware of the discriminatory policy being implemented and deliberately indifferent to it.

Ashcroft and Mueller argue that these allegations fail to satisfy the "plausibility standard" of *Twombly*. They contend that Iqbal's claims are implausible because such high-ranking officials "tend not to be personally involved in the specific actions of lower-level officers down the bureaucratic chain of command." Brief for Petitioners 28. But this response bespeaks a fundamental misunderstanding of the enquiry that *Twombly* demands. *Twombly* does not require a court at the motion-to-dismiss stage to consider whether the factual allegations are probably true. We made it clear, on the contrary, that a court must take the allegations as true, no matter how skeptical the court may be. See *Twombly*, 550 U.S., at 555, 127 S.Ct. 1955 (a court must proceed "on the assumption that all the allegations in the complaint are true (even if doubtful in fact)"); *id.,* at 556, 127 S.Ct. 1955 ("[A] well-pleaded complaint may proceed even if it strikes a savvy judge that actual proof of the facts alleged is improbable"); see also *Neitzke v. Williams,* 490 U.S. 319, 327, 109 S.Ct. 1827, 104 L.Ed.2d 338 (1989) ("Rule 12(b)(6) does not countenance . . . dismissals based on a judge's disbelief of a complaint's factual allegations"). The sole exception to this rule lies with allegations that are sufficiently fantastic to defy reality as we know it: claims about little green men, or the plaintiff's recent trip to Pluto, or experiences in time travel. That is not what we have here.

Under *Twombly,* the relevant question is whether, assuming the factual allegations are true, the plaintiff has stated a ground for relief that is plausible. That is, in *Twombly* 's words, a plaintiff must "allege facts" that, taken as true, are "suggestive of illegal conduct." 550 U.S., at 564, n. 8, 127 S.Ct. 1955. In *Twombly,* we were faced with allegations of a conspiracy to violate § 1 of the Sherman Act through parallel conduct. The difficulty was that the conduct alleged was "consistent with conspiracy, but just as much in line with a wide swath of rational and competitive business strategy unilaterally prompted by common perceptions of the market." *Id.,* at 554, 127 S.Ct. 1955. We held that in that sort of circumstance, "[a]n allegation of parallel conduct is . . . much like a naked assertion of conspiracy in a § 1 complaint: it gets the complaint close to stating a claim, but without some further factual enhancement it stops short of the line between possibility and plausibility of 'entitlement to relief.' " *Id.,* at 557, 127 S.Ct. 1955 (brackets omitted). Here, by contrast, the allegations in the complaint are neither confined to naked legal conclusions nor consistent with legal conduct. The complaint alleges that FBI officials discriminated against Iqbal solely on account of his race, religion, and national origin, and it alleges the knowledge and deliberate indifference that, by Ashcroft and Mueller's own admission, are sufficient to make them liable for the illegal action. Iqbal's complaint therefore contains "enough facts to state a claim to relief that is plausible on its face." *Id.,* at 570, 127 S.Ct. 1955.

I do not understand the majority to disagree with this understanding of "plausibility" under *Twombly.* Rather, the majority discards the allegations discussed above with regard to Ashcroft and Mueller as conclusory, and is left considering only two statements in the complaint: that "the [FBI], under the direction of Defendant MUELLER, arrested and detained thousands of Arab Muslim men . . . as part of its investigation of the events of September 11," and that "[t]he policy of holding post–September–11th detainees in highly restrictive conditions of confinement until they were 'cleared' by the FBI was approved by Defendants ASHCROFT and MUELLER in discussions in the weeks after

September 11, 2001." See ante, at 1951. I think the majority is right in saying that these allegations suggest only that Ashcroft and Mueller "sought to keep suspected terrorists in the most secure conditions available until the suspects could be cleared of terrorist activity," and that this produced "a disparate, incidental impact on Arab Muslims." And I agree that the two allegations selected by the majority, standing alone, do not state a plausible entitlement to relief for unconstitutional discrimination.

But these allegations do not stand alone as the only significant, nonconclusory statements in the complaint, for the complaint contains many allegations linking Ashcroft and Mueller to the discriminatory practices of their subordinates.

The majority says that these are "bare assertions" that, "much like the pleading of conspiracy in *Twombly,* amount to nothing more than a 'formulaic recitation of the elements' of a constitutional discrimination claim" and therefore are "not entitled to be assumed true." The fallacy of the majority's position, however, lies in looking at the relevant assertions in isolation. The complaint contains specific allegations that, in the aftermath of the September 11 attacks, the Chief of the FBI's International Terrorism Operations Section and the Assistant Special Agent in Charge for the FBI's New York Field Office implemented a policy that discriminated against Arab Muslim men, including Iqbal, solely on account of their race, religion, or national origin. Viewed in light of these subsidiary allegations, the allegations singled out by the majority as "conclusory" are no such thing. Iqbal's claim is not that Ashcroft and Mueller "knew of, condoned, and willfully and maliciously agreed to subject" him to a discriminatory practice that is left undefined; his allegation is that "they knew of, condoned, and willfully and maliciously agreed to subject" him to a particular, discrete, discriminatory policy detailed in the complaint. Iqbal does not say merely that Ashcroft was the architect of some amorphous discrimination, or that Mueller was instrumental in an ill-defined constitutional violation; he alleges that they helped to create the discriminatory policy he has described. Taking the complaint as a whole, it gives Ashcroft and Mueller " 'fair notice of what the . . . claim is and the grounds upon which it rests.' "

That aside, the majority's holding that the statements it selects are conclusory cannot be squared with its treatment of certain other allegations in the complaint as nonconclusory. For example, the majority takes as true the statement that "[t]he policy of holding post–September–11th detainees in highly restrictive conditions of confinement until they were 'cleared' by the FBI was approved by Defendants ASHCROFT and MUELLER in discussions in the weeks after September 11, 2001." This statement makes two points: (1) after September 11, the FBI held certain detainees in highly restrictive conditions, and (2) Ashcroft and Mueller discussed and approved these conditions. If, as the majority says, these allegations are not conclusory, then I cannot see why the majority deems it merely conclusory when Iqbal alleges that (1) after September 11, the FBI designated Arab Muslim detainees as being of " 'high interest' " "because of the race, religion, and national origin of the detainees, and not because of any evidence of the detainees' involvement in supporting terrorist activity," and (2) Ashcroft and Mueller "knew of, condoned, and willfully and maliciously agreed" to that discrimination. By my lights, there is no principled basis for the majority's disregard of the allegations linking Ashcroft and Mueller to their subordinates' discrimination.

I respectfully dissent.

[A dissenting opinion of Justice BREYER is omitted.]

Iqbal and *Twombly* Transform Federal Litigation: Courts Are Unevenly Applying Two Infamous Supreme Court Decisions

By Adele Nicholas
April 30, 2012; *InsideCounsel* Magazine [reprinted with permission]

In a now infamous pair of decisions, *Bell Atlantic v. Twombly* in 2007 and *Ashcroft v. Iqbal* in 2009, the Supreme Court announced a new pleading standard that shook the foundations of federal litigation. The decisions allow district court judges to dismiss a complaint if it does not set out a "plausible" claim—a departure from the rule established in the 1957 case *Conley v. Gibson* that a court cannot dismiss a complaint unless it is apparent that the plaintiff could prove "no set of facts" that would entitle him to relief.

The defense bar heralded the decisions as a path to early dismissal of frivolous cases. Meanwhile, plaintiffs decried *Iqbal* as a barrier to legitimate claims. But according to a recent study by the Federal Judicial Center (FJC), neither prediction has come true.

The FJC studied data from 23 federal district courts and found that although defendants are filing more motions to dismiss—a 2.2 percent increase over pre-*Twombly* levels—those motions aren't resulting in more cases being dismissed with prejudice. Rather, courts are giving plaintiffs a chance to replead. A study published by the Washington College of Law at American University showed that the percentage of motions to dismiss that were granted with leave to amend "increased from 6 percent under Conley to 9 percent under *Twombly* to 19 percent under *Iqbal*."

In practice, the data doesn't tell the whole story. Although most cases aren't summarily dismissed, defendants are successfully invoking *Iqbal* to whittle down claims and ultimately to get courts to throw out amended complaints. But litigants also are discovering that not every jurisdiction gives *Iqbal* equal force.

"It depends what part of the country you're in whether you can get through the courthouse door with the same complaint," says University of Pennsylvania law professor Stephen Burbank.

Chipping Away

Even when motions citing *Iqbal* do not result in dismissal, there are several ways in which the decision helps defendants. The first is narrowing the theories asserted.

"The plaintiff might file a complaint with seven counts, and some will get chopped off," says Max Kennerly, an attorney with the Beasley Firm. "For instance, in a recent breach of fiduciary duty case, the court cut off the plaintiff's claim for consequential damages, ruling that it wasn't pleaded with enough specificity."

Likewise, courts may dismiss certain defendants without throwing out the whole case. In the 2011 breach of contract case *Two Old Hippies v. Catch the Bus*, for example, the District of New Mexico dismissed claims against the individual defendants, ruling that under Conley, it was acceptable to attribute allegations to all of the defendants, but that collective pleading did not satisfy *Iqbal*.

Iqbal also made it harder for plaintiffs to piggyback class actions on government antitrust investigations.

"It used to be that plaintiffs would see a government investigation and rush to file a bare-bones complaint regurgitating the language of the federal statute and hope to learn more in discovery," says Caroline Mitchell, a partner at Jones Day. "Now, you can't force a company to come to court and spend millions on its defense without first having facts."

Mitchell also points out that although most dismissals under *Iqbal* are without prejudice, they often result in outright dismissal if the plaintiff can't discover additional facts. This is particularly true in employment cases, in which plaintiffs rely on employers' records to prove their claims. For instance, in the Southern District of Florida case *Desrouleaux v. Quest Diagnostics,* the court dismissed the initial complaint and allowed the plaintiff to replead. Although she added more specifics, the court ultimately wasn't satisfied.

"Often, the plaintiff cannot get enough information without discovery into the employer's personnel records," Kennerly points out.

Uneven Application

Burbank is critical of how district courts are applying *Iqbal* and *Twombly*. He calls the situation "lawlessness cubed."

"First, the Supreme Court amended the federal rules without going through the legal process for doing so," he says. "Second, you have a number of federal courts continuing to apply a heightened pleading standard where they're not supposed to; and third, you have some federal courts ignoring the clear implications of *Iqbal* and *Twombly*."

The 7th Circuit, for example, has pushed back against the idea that *Iqbal* raised pleading standards. In *Swanson v. Citibank,* the court reversed the district court's dismissal and wrote, "It is not necessary to stack up inferences side by side and allow the case to go forward only if the plaintiff's inferences seem more compelling than the opposing inferences."

Some state courts have declined to follow *Iqbal*. Delaware announced in the January case *Cambium v. Trilantic Capital Partners III* that it would continue to follow its "reasonable conceivability" standard.

Meanwhile, certain district courts apply *Iqbal* stringently. The American University study showed that district judges in the 2nd Circuit granted 60 percent of motions to dismiss, whereas courts in the 7th Circuit granted only 33 percent.

District courts exercise significant discretion in applying the "plausibility" standard. If a court denies a motion to dismiss, the defendant doesn't have an immediate appeal, so there's no choice but to litigate the case.

"There's not a good mechanism for enforcing it," Mitchell says.

In a strange twist, the Federal Circuit rejected the applicability of *Iqbal* to patent cases, where so-called "trolls" famously drag defendants to court with little factual support. Patent plaintiffs may still initiate a case by filling out a form identifying the patent and stating that the defendant is infringing on it without additional details.

"The disparity is shocking and grossly unfair," Kennerly says.

Affirmative Defenses

Defendants need to be aware that *Iqbal* can be a sword as well as a shield. District courts remain divided on whether *Iqbal* also applies to affirmative defenses. Of the approximately 30 courts that have weighed in on the issue, about half apply *Iqbal* to affirmative defenses. No appellate courts have ruled on the issue.

"In their wake, *Twombly* and *Iqbal* have provoked a frenzy of district court opinions reexamining . . . the pleading standard by which a court should judge a defendant's affirmative defenses," wrote Western District of Kentucky Chief District Judge Thomas Russell.

Example Documents

UNITED STATES DISTRICT COURT
FOR THE DISTRICT OF NEW MEXICO

TWO OLD HIPPIES, LLC,
      Plaintiff,

          v.   No.   CIV-10-00459 WDS/RLP

CATCH THE BUS, LLC,
GARY MACK
and FALLON MACK,
      Defendants.

MOTION TO DISMISS

COME NOW Defendants, Catch The Bus, LLC, Gary Mack, and Fallon Mack, by and through their attorney, Roger E. Yarbro, Yarbro & Associates, P.A., and pursuant to F.R.C.P.12(b)(6) respectfully move the Court to dismiss Counts II through VII of Plaintiff's Complaint and as grounds therefore STATE:

1.   Defendants, Gary Mack and Fallon Mack move to dismiss with prejudice all counts of the Complaint made against them individually pursuant to F.R.C.P. 12(b)(6). Plaintiff has failed to aver specific facts to establish a plausible claim against the individual Defendants, Gary Mack and Fallon Mack, and all claims and counts against them individually should be dismissed.

2.   Defendants, Catch the Bus LLC, Gary Mack, and Fallon Mack, move to dismiss Counts II through VII of Plaintiff's Complaint pursuant to F.R.C.P. 12(b)(6) for failure to state a claim upon which relief can be granted. Plaintiff has failed to state with particularity specific factual allegations establishing plausible claims under Counts II through VII and the claims should be dismissed.

3.   Plaintiffs have failed to comply with the mandate of Fed. R. Civ. P. 9(b) requiring that when a Complaint alleges fraud or mistake, a party must state with particularity the circumstances constituting fraud or mistake. Counts III, IV, V, and VII of Plaintiff's Complaint should be dismissed for failure to meet the pleading requirements of Fed. R. Civ. P. 9(b) and Fed. R. Civ. P. 8.

4.   Plaintiffs have failed to specifically state items of special damages and the grounds for the assessment of special damages in accordance with Fed. R. Civ. P. 9(g). Plaintiff's prayer for items of special damages should be dismissed.

WHEREFORE, Defendants, Catch the Bus, LLC, Gary Mack and Fallon Mack, respectfully move the Court to dismiss Counts II through VII of Plaintiff's Complaint for the foregoing reasons as more specifically set out in Defendants' Memorandum Brief in Support of Defendants' Motion to Dismiss which is being filed simultaneously herewith.

Respectfully submitted,

/s/ Roger E. Yarbro   Roger E. Yarbro
Yarbro & Associates, P.A.,
Attorney for Defendants
109 James Canyon Hwy. Suite A.
Post Office Box 480
Cloudcroft, New Mexico 88317-0480
(575) 682-3614 | (575) 682-3642 Facsimile

**UNITED STATES DISTRICT COURT
FOR THE DISTRICT OF NEW MEXICO**

TWO OLD HIPPIES, LLC,
      Plaintiff,

        v.   No.   CIV-10-00459 WDS/RLP

CATCH THE BUS, LLC,
GARY MACK
and FALLON MACK,
      Defendants.

**DEFENDANTS' MEMORANDUM BRIEF IN SUPPORT OF
DEFENDANTS' MOTION TO DISMISS**

TABLE OF CONTENTS

TABLE OF AUTHORITIES

Cases Cited:

Federal Rules of Civil Procedure:

Statutes:

COME NOW Defendants Catch the Bus, LLC., Gary Mack, and Fallon Mack, by and through their attorney, Roger E. Yarbro of Yarbro & Associates, P.A., and pursuant to Fed. R. Civ. P. 12(b)(6) respectfully submit the following memorandum of law in support of Defendants' Motion to Dismiss.

I. Introduction

In July of 2009, Two Old Hippies, LLC ordered a customized 1965 Volkswagen Bus from Catch the Bus, LLC. In October of 2009, Two Old Hippies ordered an additional customized Volkswagen Bus from Catch the Bus, LLC.

II. Failure to State a Claim
On Counts II – VII of Complaint

Plaintiff has brought this diversity action alleging claims under New Mexico state law for breach of contract, breach of warranty, violation of the New Mexico Motor Dealers Franchising Act, N.M.S.A. 1978, §57-16-1 et seq., violation of the New Mexico Unfair Trade Practices Act, N.M.S.A. 1978, §57-12-1, negligent misrepresentation, and for rescission. Plaintiff includes in its complaint a claim under Colorado state law for alleged violations of the Colorado Consumer Protection Act, C.R.S. §6-1-101 et seq. The generalized and conclusory statements of facts contained within the Complaint coupled with incomplete recitations of the elements of the claims fail to meet the pleading requirements of Fed. R. Civ. P. 8(b). Counts II through VII of the Complaint should be dismissed pursuant to Fed. R. Civ. P. 12(b)(6) as Plaintiff has failed to state specific facts, when taken as true, to establish plausible claims for relief.

A. Plaintiff Has Failed to Meet the Pleading Standard
of Rule 8(a)(2) : *Iqbal* and *Twombly*

Under Fed. R. Civ. P. 8(a)(2) in order to state a claim for relief a pleading must contain a short and plain statement of the claim showing that the pleader is entitled to relief.

To meet the requirements of Rule 8 and to survive a motion to dismiss, a complaint must contain sufficient factual matter, accepted as true, to "state a claim for relief that is plausible on its face." *Ashcroft v. Iqbal*, U.S. , 129 S.Ct. 1937, 1949, 173 L. Ed. 2d 868 (2009) (quoting *Bell Atlantic Corp. v. Twombly*, 550 U.S. 544, 570, 127 S.Ct. 1955, 167 L. Ed. 2d 929 (2007)). When addressing a Rule 12(b)(6) motion, a court must accept as true all well-pleaded factual allegations in the complaint, view those allegations in the light most favorable to the non-moving party, and draw all reasonable inferences in the plaintiff's favor. *Moore v. Guthrie*, 438 F. 3d 1036, 1039 (10th Cir. 2006). However, "[t]he tenet that a court must accept as true all of the allegations contained in a complaint is inapplicable to legal conclusions. Threadbare recitals of the elements of a cause of action, supported by mere conclusory statements, do not suffice." *Bixler v. Foster*, 596 F. 3d 751, 756 (10th Cir. 2010) (quoting *Iqbal*, 129 S.Ct. at 1949).

As was set forth by the Supreme Court in *Iqbal*, the sufficiency of a complaint is analyzed using a two part process which may begin with the identification of claims which are no more than conclusions and are, therefore, not entitled to the assumption of truth. *Iqbal*, 129 S.Ct. at 1950. "While legal conclusions can provide the framework of a complaint, they must be supported by factual allegations". *Id.* When there are well-pleaded factual allegations, a court should assume their veracity and then determine whether they plausible give rise to an entitlement to relief. *Id.*

When Plaintiff's Complaint and Counts II – VII are examined according to the standards set forth in *Iqbal* and *Twombly*, Plaintiff fails to state plausible claims for relief.

B. Plaintiff Fails to State a Claim on Count II – Breach of Warranty

Plaintiff in its Complaint, Count II, alleges that Defendants breached express and implied warranties for two Volkswagen Buses which Plaintiff ordered from Defendant, Catch the Bus, LLC. Although Plaintiff did not include with its Complaint copies of the order documentation related to the transactions, Defendant has attached them hereto as Exhibits A and B. Defendant asks that the Court take judicial notice of the order forms. [4]

1. Plaintiff Fails to Plead Sufficient Facts to Show Express Warranty and Breach

Plaintiff's Complaint (Complaint, Doc. 1) sets forth only the following conclusory factual statements relevant to its claims of Defendants breach of an express warranty: in July and October of 2009, Plaintiff contracted to purchase two restored Volkswagen buses from Catch the Bus, LLC (Complaint at 2, ¶¶ 9, 11); "[t]he CTB Defendants guaranteed TOH 100% satisfaction with the buses ("guarantee") which was a part of the contracts" (Complaint at 2, ¶ 13); "[t]he CTB Defendants promised that the buses would be ready to go on delivery whether for daily driver or for cross-country trips (promise) which was a part of the contracts" (Complaint at 2, ¶14); the guarantee has been breached because TOH is not 100% satisfied with the buses (Complaint at 2, ¶ 15); the promise has been breached (because) "buses were not ready to go on delivery whether for daily driver or for cross-country trips" (Complaint at 2, ¶ 16).

The plain language of the order forms, (Ex. A, Ex. B., attached), coupled with Plaintiff's assertion that "the Defendants promised that the buses would be ready to go on delivery whether for daily driver or for cross-country trips (promise) which was a part of the contracts" (Complaint at 2, ¶ 14) provide insufficient

---

1 "It is accepted practice that, if a plaintiff does not incorporate by reference or attach a document to its complaint, but the document is referred to in the complaint and is central to the plaintiff's claim, a defendant may submit an indisputably authentic copy to the court to be considered on a motion to dismiss." *Pace v. Swerdlow,* 519 F. 3d 1067, 1072 (10th Cir. 2008) (quoting *Dean Witter Reynolds, Inc. v. Howsam,* 261 F. 3d 956, 961 (10th Cir. 2001) (internal quotation omitted).

notice to Defendants of the circumstances alleged by Plaintiff to have created an express warranty. N.M.S.A. 1978, § 55-2-313(1)(a)(b) provides that express warranties by the seller are created by affirmations of fact or promise made by the seller to the buyer which relate to the goods and become part of the basis of the bargain and also by description of the goods which is made part of the basis of the bargain. N.M.S.A. 1978, §55-2-313(c)(2) expressly provides that an affirmation of the value of the goods or a statement purporting to be merely the seller's opinion or commendation of the goods does not create a warranty.

Plaintiff has averred no specific facts identifying the time, place, manner, or person making any representation to Plaintiff. Further, Plaintiff has averred no specific facts from which it can be shown that any such statements made were part of the basis of the bargain, thus creating an express warranty under N.M.S.A. 1978, §55-2-213. Plaintiff's bare assertion that a promise that the buses were ready to go became part of the contract, (Complaint at 2, ¶ 14) is the type of "'naked assertion' devoid of 'further factual enhancement'" which is insufficient to meet the pleading requirements of Rule 8. *Iqbal*, 129 S.Ct. at 1949 (quoting *Twombly*, 550 U.S. 544, 557, 127 S.Ct. 1955).

In addition to having failed to provide specific factual content to identify the circumstances under which an express warranty was allegedly made, Plaintiff has not presented factual information from which a breach can be inferred. While Plaintiff has asserted that the buses were not "ready to go" upon delivery and that Plaintiffs were not 100% satisfied with the buses, (Complaint at 2, ¶¶ 15, 16), Plaintiff has not provided any specific facts regarding alleged defects or deficiencies which would provide notice to Defendants of the basis of the claim.

Plaintiff has not stated a plausible claim for relief under Count II of its Complaint. "A claim has facial plausibility when the plaintiff pleads factual content that allows the court to draw the reasonable inference that the defendant is liable for the misconduct alleged." *Iqbal*, 129 S.Ct. at 1949 (quoting *Twombly*, 550 U.S. at 556). Because the threadbare recitals of Count II are supported by mere conclusory statements not entitled to an assumption of truth, the facts as pleaded do not "permit the court to infer more than the mere possibility of misconduct" and Plaintiff has not shown that it is entitled to relief for purposes of Fed. R. Civ. P. 8(a)(2). Count II of the Complaint should be dismissed.

2. Plaintiff Fails to Plead Sufficient Facts to Show Implied Warranties and Breach

Plaintiff's Complaint (Complaint, Doc. 1) sets forth only the following conclusory factual statements relevant to its claims of Defendants' breach of implied warranties of merchantability and fitness: in July and October of 2009, Plaintiff contracted to purchase two restored Volkswagen buses from Catch the Bus, LLC (Complaint at 2, ¶¶ 9, 11); TOH planned to use Bus #1 in its business and give away bus #2 in a business promotion (Complaint at 2, ¶ 17); the CTB Defendants were informed of TOH's intended uses of the buses prior to the purchase of the buses (Complaint at 3, ¶ 18); after delivery of bus #1 to TOH Bus #1 was not "safely operable and TOH determined that Bus # 1 had many serious mechanical and physical defects" (Complaint at 3, ¶ 19); after delivery of Bus #2 to TOH's winning entrant, the entrant and subsequently TOH, "determined that Bus #2 was not operable and had many serious mechanical and physical defects" (Complaint at 3, ¶ 21).

a. Plaintiff Fails to Plead Facts to Show Existence of Implied Warranty of Fitness

N.M.S.A. 1978, §55-2-315 states that "[w]here the seller at the time of contracting has reason to know any particular purpose for which the goods are required and that the buyer is relying on the seller's skill or judgment to select or furnish suitable goods, there is unless excluded or modified...an implied warranty that the goods shall be fit for such purpose". While Plaintiff has alleged that they ordered bus #2 for the purpose of giving it away in a business promotion, Plaintiff has failed to set forth specific fact showing that such a purpose created requirements beyond those normally associated with the sale of an automobile and incorporated into an implied warranty of merchantability.

b. Plaintiff Fails to Plead Facts to Show Alleged Breach of Implied Warranties

Plaintiff's bare assertions that the buses had "serious mechanical and physical defects" provide insufficient notice to Defendants of the circumstances alleged by Plaintiff to have constituted a breach of either an implied warranty of merchantability or fitness for a particular purpose. Plaintiff has not set forth specific factual content indicating alleged deficiencies which would establish a breach of the implied warranty of merchantability under N.M.S.A. 1978, §55-2-314(a)(c): that the goods would not pass without objection in the trade under the contract description or fit for the ordinary purposes for which such goods are used. Plaintiff has not set forth specific factual content indicating alleged deficiencies which would establish a breach of an implied warranty of fitness for a particular purpose under N.M.S.A. 1978, §55-2-315: that the goods were not fit for a particular purpose.

Plaintiff has not stated a plausible claim for relief under Count II of its Complaint for breach of implied warranties of merchantability and fitness. Because the threadbare recitals of Count II are supported by mere conclusory statements not entitled to an assumption of truth, the facts as pleaded do not "permit the court to infer more than the mere possibility of misconduct" and Plaintiff has not shown that it is entitled to relief for purposes of Fed. R. Civ. P. 8(a)(2). Count II of the Complaint should be dismissed.

C. Plaintiff Fails to State a Claim on Count III – Violation of the New Mexico Motor Dealers Franchising Act

Plaintiff has failed to state with particularity specific factual allegations establishing the elements of a plausible claim under N.M.S.A. 1978, §57-16-4(B) and (C). The provisions of N.M.S.A. 1978, §57-16-4(B) and (C) address unlawful acts by a "dealer" as that term is defined by N.M.S.A. 1978, §57-16-3(B) Under that provision, a dealer is defined as being any person who sells or solicits or advertises the sale of new or used motor vehicles. "Persons making casual sales of their own vehicles duly registered and licensed to them by the state" are not dealers for purposes of the Motor Vehicle Dealers Franchising Act. N.M.S.A. 1978, §57-16-3(B)(3). Plaintiff has failed to set forth specific factual allegations related to the nature of Defendant, Catch the Bus LLC's business from which the Court can infer that Defendant is a "dealer" within the meaning of the applicable statute.

Plaintiff has failed to set forth specific allegations of fact to state a plausible claim for relief under N.M.S.A. 1978, §57-16-4 (B) which makes it unlawful for any dealer to use false, deceptive, or misleading advertising in connection with his business. Plaintiff has made no specific allegations of fact to show that Defendant, Catch the Bus LLC engaged in any advertising activity in relation to the transactions in question.

As is discussed further in Section III of this Memorandum Brief, Plaintiff has failed to set forth specific allegations of fact to state a plausible claim for relief under N.M.S.A. 1978, §57-16-4 (C) which makes it unlawful for a dealer to willfully defraud any retail buyer to the buyer's damage. For purposes of the Motor Vehicle Dealers Franchising Act, fraud is defined under N.M.S.A. 1978, §57-16-3 (I) as "(1) a misrepresentation in any manner, whether intentionally false or due to gross negligence, of a material fact; (2) a promise or representation not made honestly and in good faith; and (3) an intentional failure to disclose a material fact". Plaintiff has not set forth specific factual averments alleging a specific misrepresentation allegedly made by Defendant, Catch the Bus, LLC, which it knew to be false. Plaintiff has not set forth specific factual averments alleging a specific misrepresentation negligently made by Defendant, Catch the Bus. Plaintiff has not set forth specific factual allegations which tend to show that Defendant, Catch the Bus, made a promise or representation that was not honest and made in good faith. Plaintiff has failed to specifically allege through factual averments that Defendant, Catch the Bus, intentionally failed to disclose any material fact.

Because the threadbare recitals of Count III are not supported by factual allegations, the claim as pleaded does not "permit the court to infer more than the mere possibility of misconduct". Plaintiff has not shown that it is entitled to relief for purposes of Fed. R. Civ. P. 8(a)(2) and Count III of the Complaint should be dismissed.

D. Plaintiff Fails to State a Claim on Count IV – Violation of the New Mexico Trade Practices Act

Count IV of the Complaint alleges that Defendants violated the New Mexico Unfair Trade Practices Act, N.M.S.A. 1978, §§57-12-2, 57-12-6 by representing that the buses were of a particular standard, quality or grade and willfully misrepresenting the condition of the buses. (Complaint, Doc. 1 at 5, ¶ 49). In addition to having failed to meet the pleading requirements of Fed. R. Civ. P. 9(b), as is discussed in Section III of this Memorandum Brief, Plaintiff has failed to aver sufficient factual detail to sustain a claim under Rule 8(a)(2).

As was discussed in Section II (B) of this Memorandum Brief in relation to Plaintiff's claims of breach of warranty, Plaintiff has failed to set forth specific facts to establish any deficiencies in the condition of the buses. The Complaint fails to provide notice to Defendants of the nature of the deficiencies alleged by Plaintiff and fails to present a plausible claim for relief. Count IV of Plaintiff's Complaint should be dismissed for failure to state a claim under Fed. R. Civ. P. 12(b)(6).

E. Plaintiff Fails to State a Claim on Count V – Colorado Consumer Protection Act

Defendants move the dismissal of Count V with prejudice pursuant to F.R.C.P. 12(b)(6) for failure to state a claim upon which relief can be granted as Plaintiff has failed to set forth specific factual allegations establishing the elements and a plausible claim of recovery under C.R.S. §6-1-101 et seq.

Plaintiff has failed to set forth any factual allegations or legal references providing Defendants notice of the grounds upon which Defendant asserts that the Colorado Consumer Protection Act is applicable to their claims. To the contrary, Plaintiff has asserted that venue is proper in this Court pursuant to 28 U.S.C. §1391 (a)(2) alleging that a substantial part of the events or omissions giving rise to the claim occurred within this judicial District. (Complaint, Doc. 1, ¶ 31). Plaintiff has averred that Defendant, Catch the Bus, LLC is a New Mexico limited liability company. (Complaint, Doc. 1, ¶ 6). Plaintiff has averred that Plaintiff is an Iowa limited liability company, is wholly owned by the Thomas W. Bedell Revocable Trust, and that the Trust, trustee and beneficiary are citizens of Iowa. (Complaint, Doc. 1, ¶¶ 1,3-5).

Plaintiff has not stated any facts from which the Court can infer that Catch the Bus, LLC conducts business within Colorado as set forth in C.R.S. §70-90-801 such as to make the Colorado Consumer Protection Act applicable. Plaintiff has failed to plead a necessary element of a claim under Count V of the Complaint and said Count should be dismissed.

Count V of Plaintiff's Complaint should be dismissed with prejudice as even had Plaintiff set forth facts sufficient to show that the Colorado Consumer Protection Act might apply to the transactions at issue, under no interpretation of the facts could Plaintiff establish liability on such a claim. To sustain a claim under the Colorado Consumer Protection Act, a plaintiff must show: (1) that defendants engaged in an unfair or deceptive trade practice; (2) that the challenged practice occurred in the course of defendants' business; (3) that it significantly impacts the public as actual or potential consumers of defendant's goods, services, or property; (4) that plaintiff suffered injury in fact to a legally protected interests; and (5) that the challenged practice caused Plaintiff's injury. *Cache la Poudre Feeds, LLC v. Land O'Lakes, In c* ., 438 F.Supp.2d 1288 (D. Colo., 2006).

If a wrong is private in nature and does not affect the public, the claim is not actionable under the act. *Dean Witter Reynolds, Inc. v. Variable Annuity Life Ins. Co.*, 373 F. 3d 1100 (D. Colo., 2004). To determine whether a practice challenged under the Colorado Act significantly impacts the public, courts should consider "(1) the number of consumers directly affected by the challenged practice, (2) the relative sophistication and bargaining power of the consumer affected by the challenged practice, and (3) evidence that the challenged practice has previously impacted other consumers or has the significant potential to do so in the future". *Alpine Bank v. Hubbell*, 555 F. 3d 1097 (10th Cir. 2009). Plaintiff has averred no facts in its complaint from which such a showing of public impact can be made.

Because the facts as pleaded do not permit the court to infer even a possibility of misconduct, Plaintiff has not shown that it is entitled to relief for purposes of Fed. R. Civ. P. 8(a)(2) and Count V of the Complaint should be dismissed with prejudice.

III. Failure to Plead as Required Under Fed. R. Civ. P. 9(b)

Fed. R. Civ. P. 9(b) states that "[i]n alleging fraud or mistake, a party must state with particularity the circumstances constituting fraud or mistake . . .". More specifically, a complaint alleging fraud must "'set forth the time, place and contents of the false representation, the identity of the party making the false statements and the consequences thereof.'" *Koch v. Koch Industries Inc.*, 203 F. 3d 1202, 1236 (10th Cir. 2000) (quoting *Lawrence Nat'l. Bank v. Edmonds* (In re Edmonds), 924 F.2d 176, 180 10th Cir. 1991)), accord United States ex rel. *Lacy v. New Horizons, Inc.*, 2009 WL 324129, 2 (10th Cir. 2009) (unpublished opinion) (plaintiff must set forth the who, what, when, where and how of the alleged fraud). Counts III, IV, V, and VII of the Complaint which are predicated upon allegations that Defendants willfully and intentionally made false representations of fact to Defendants should be dismissed pursuant to Rules 12(b)(6) and 9(b) as Plaintiffs have failed to meet the specific pleading requirements of Fed. R. Civ. P. 9(b).

Count III of Plaintiff's Complaint (Complaint, Doc. 1 at 5, ¶ 45) alleges a violation by Defendants of the New Mexico Motor Dealers Franchising Act, N.M.S.A. 1978, §57-16-4 (C). N.M.S.A. 1978, §57-16-4 (C) makes it unlawful for a dealer to willfully defraud any retail buyer to the buyer's damage. For purposes of the Motor Vehicle Dealers Franchising Act, fraud is defined under N.M.S.A. 1978, §57-16-3 (I) as "(1) a misrepresentation in any manner, whether intentionally false or due to gross negligence, of a material fact; (2) a promise or representation not made honestly and in good faith; and (3) an intentional failure to disclose a material fact".

Count IV of the Complaint alleges that Defendants violated the New Mexico Unfair Trade Practices Act, N.M.S.A. 1978, §§57-12-2, 57-12-6 by representing that the buses were of a particular standard, quality or grade and willfully misrepresenting the condition of the buses. (Complaint, Doc. 1 at 5, ¶ 49). Count V of the Complaint alleges a violation of the Colorado Consumer Protection Act, C.R.S. §6-1-105(g) which includes as a deceptive trade practice the representation that goods are of a particular standard, quality, or grade, or that the goods are of a particular style or model, if one "knows that they are of another". In Count VII of the Complaint, Plaintiff alleges that Defendant misrepresented material facts warranting the rescission of the purchase contracts.

While Plaintiff has alleged that "Defendants promised that the buses would be ready to go "on delivery" (Complaint, Doc. 1 at 2, ¶ 14), Plaintiff has not set forth the time at which the alleged representation was made to Plaintiff, where and in what context the representation was made, in what manner the representation was false, the identity of the party alleged to have made the representation, or the consequences of the alleged false representation.

As was discussed in Section II of this Memorandum Brief, the statements that Plaintiff was not satisfied with the buses and that the buses were not safely operable or had serious mechanical and physical defects (Complaint, Doc. 1 at 2-3, ¶¶ 15, 19, 21), are conclusory and are not entitled to the assumption of truth for purposes of this Motion to Dismiss under Fed. R. Civ. P. 12(b)(6).

In *Koch v. Koch Industries Inc.*, 203 F. 3d 1202 (10th Cir. 2000) a case involving allegations of fraud in the sale of securities, the Tenth Circuit affirmed the dismissal of the Plaintiff's fraud claims. The Court held that broad allegations which did not identify a precise time frame, place at which misrepresentations were made, and the content of the alleged misrepresentations failed to meet the pleading requirements of Fed. R. Civ. P. 9(b). Id. at 1237. The purpose of Rule 9(b) is "to afford defendant fair notice of plaintiff's claims and the factual ground upon which they are based". Id. at 1237 (quoting *Farlow v. Peat, Marwick, Mitchell & Co.*, 956 F.2d 982, 987 (10th Cir. 1992). Similarly, the general statements made by Plaintiff are insufficient to provide Defendants notice of the factual grounds upon which its claim is based and should, therefore, be dismissed pursuant to Fed. R. Civ. P. 9(b).

IV. Plaintiff Fails to State Claims Against Individual Defendants, Gary Mack and Fallon Mack

Pursuant to N.M.S.A. 1978, §53-19-14, a member of a limited liability company is not a proper party to a proceeding by or against the limited liability company solely by reason of being a member of the limited liability company. N.M.S.A. 1978, §53-19-13 provides that "the debts, obligations and liabilities of a limited liability company, whether arising in contract, tort or otherwise, shall be solely the debts, obligations and liabilities of the limited liability company".

No member or manager of a limited liability company shall be obligated personally for any debt, obligation or liability of a limited liability company solely by reason of being a member or manager of the limited liability company. *Id.*

Plaintiff in its Complaint (Complaint, Doc. 1) sets forth no facts upon which the individual liability of Gary Mack or Fallon Mack might be premised. While Plaintiff asserts that Gary Mack and Fallon Mack are "owners" of Catch the Bus, LLC (Complaint, Doc. 1 at 2, ¶ 7), N.M.S.A. 1978, §53-19-14 establishes that they are not proper parties to this suit on the basis that they are members of Catch the Bus, LLC. Plaintiff's claims against Gary Mack and Fallon Mack should be dismissed with prejudice as they are not a proper party to suits brought against Catch the Bus, LLC.

WHEREFORE, Defendants, Catch the Bus, LLC, Gary Mack and Fallon Mack, respectfully move the Court to dismiss Counts II through IV of Plaintiff's Complaint pursuant to Fed. R. Civ. P. 12(b)(6).

Respectfully submitted,

/s/ Roger E. Yarbro   Roger E. Yarbro
Yarbro & Associates, P.A.,
Attorney for Defendants
109 James Canyon Hwy. Suite A.
Post Office Box 480
Cloudcroft, New Mexico 88317
(575) 682-3614 | (575) 682-3642 Facsimile

EXPERIENTIAL ASSIGNMENTS

Here is the official form for a Motion to Dismiss provided by the FRCP. Such a Motion will ordinarily be accompanied by a Memorandum of Law in Support of Defendant's Motion to Dismiss. The memorandum will have a caption and document title. It will then briefly focus the judge's attention on the issue with an Introductory Statement or a Question Presented, or both. It will briefly summarize the facts in a Statement of Facts. Then the meat of the document will be an Argument section, in which the writer persuasively conveys the legal argument that supports the Motion. The opposing party will file a Memorandum in Opposition to the Defendant's Motion to Dismiss. It will include all the same elements as the Memorandum in Support.

UNITED STATES DISTRICT COURT
FOR THE
<_____> DISTRICT OF <_____>

<Name(s) of plaintiff(s)>,
    Plaintiff(s)
  v.
<Name(s) of defendant(s)>,
    Defendant(s)
	)
	)
	)
	)
	)
	)

Civil Action No. <Number>

MOTION TO DISMISS UNDER RULE 12(b) FOR LACK OF JURISDICTION, IMPROPER VENUE, INSUFFICIENT SERVICE OF PROCESS, OR FAILURE TO STATE A CLAIM

The defendant moves to dismiss the action because:

1. the amount in controversy is less than the sum or value specified by 28 U.S.C. § 1332;

2. the defendant is not subject to the personal jurisdiction of this court;

3. venue is improper (this defendant does not reside in this district and no part of the events or omissions giving rise to the claim occurred in the district);

4. the defendant has not been properly served, as shown by the attached affidavits of <_____>; or

5. the complaint fails to state a claim upon which relief can be granted.

Date: <Date>

<Signature of the attorney or unrepresented party>

_____

<Printed name>
<Address>
<E-mail address>
<Telephone number>

Here are Complaints that might have been filed in the Frensch, Cash, and Williams cases.

UNITED STATES DISTRICT COURT
FOR THE NORTHERN DISTRICT OF OHIO

Carlene Frensch,	)
Plaintiff	)
v.	)
Nickel 'n Dime Inc.,	)
Defendant	)

Civil Action No. <Number>

COMPLAINT

1. Plaintiff is a citizen of Ohio.

2. Defendant is a citizen of Pennsylvania and Delaware.

3. On July 29, (year 0), the Plaintiff, was severely and permanently injured when she fell at Nickel 'n Dime in Cary, Ohio. The store was owned and operated by the Defendant and employees and agents of the Defendant.

4. The Plaintiff fell due to the negligence of the Defendants' agents and employees who negligently failed to remove the liquid from the floor and had negligently failed to place warning signs to alert and warn the Plaintiff of the wet floor. The Defendants through its employees breached their duty to warn the Plaintiff of the dangerous wet floor.

5. As a direct result of the negligence of the Defendants' agents and employees, acting in the scope of their employment, the Plaintiff was severely and permanently injured. She lost many of the pleasures of life. She suffered pain. She has incurred medical and hospital bills of $139,476. Her ability to earn an income was dissipated.

6. The Plaintiff seeks a judgment in the amount of Three Hundred Thousand Dollars ($300,000.00) against the Defendant.

> Date: <Date>

> <Signature of the attorney or unrepresented party>

<Printed name>
<Address>
<E-mail address>
<Telephone number>

UNITED STATES DISTRICT COURT
FOR THE EASTERN DISTRICT OF NORTH CAROLINA

Becky Cash,	)
Plaintiff	)
v.	)
Cari Pearsall,	)
Defendant	)

Civil Action No. <Number>

COMPLAINT TO RECOVER ON A CONTRACT

1. The plaintiff is a citizen of North Carolina. The defendant is a citizen of Wisconsin.

2. The amount in controversy, without interest and costs, exceeds the sum or value specified by 28 U.S.C. § 1332.

3. Plaintiff and Defendant entered a contract for the sale of jewelry to be made by Defendant.

4. The Plaintiff paid the Defendant $ 82,000 for jewelry that Defendant promised to deliver to Plaintiff.

5. Defendant has not delivered the contracted-for jewelry to Plaintiff.

6. In reliance on Defendant's promise to deliver the contracted-for jewelry, Plaintiff entered into a one-year lease for retail space at $700/month.

7. The retail space referred to in paragraph 6 has no value to Plaintiff absent the jewelry promised and not delivered by Defendant.

DEMAND FOR JUDGMENT

Therefore, the plaintiff demands judgment against the defendant for $90,400, plus interest and costs.

Date: <Date>

<Signature of the attorney or unrepresented party>

_____

<Printed name>
<Address>
<E-mail address>
<Telephone number>

UNITED STATES DISTRICT COURT
FOR THE EASTERN DISTRICT OF NORTH CAROLINA

Terry Williams, Plaintiff	))))	No. _____
v.	)	Civil Action
Gerry Mancini, Defendant	))))	JURY TRIAL DEMANDED

COMPLAINT

Plaintiff Terry Williams complains of Defendant Gerry Mancini and Defendant FastGas Station (collectively, as "Defendants") as follows:

STATEMENT OF FACTS

1. Jurisdiction in this case is based on diversity of citizenship. Plaintiff is a

citizen of North Carolina. Defendant is a citizen of the Commonwealth of Virginia. Venue is proper pursuant to the local rules of this Court.

2. Plaintiff Terry Williams ("Williams") was employed by Defendant Gerry Mancini ("Mancini") as a gas station attendant for FastGas Station ("FastGas"). FastGas was located in Emporia, Virginia, and was owned by Mancini. Williams was hired in May of 2011 as an at-will employee, but then fired in May of 2012.

3. While Williams worked at FastGas, it was his duty to turn the wooden hand-crank in order to pump gas from the storage facility located in the rear of FastGas to the reserve tank, and ultimately to the pumps used by customers.

4. Williams notified Mancini on more than one occasion to address safety concerns Williams had regarding the wooden hand-crank leaking gas and regarding the proximity of individuals smoking on the premises to the leaking gas.

5. Mancini took no remedial action, which prompted Williams to bring these safety violations to the attention of the State Regulatory Agency ("Agency") on May 18, 2011.

6. The Agency conducted an inspection of FastGas's premises, but on May 20, 2012, only two days after Williams initially contacted the Agency, Williams was fired by Mancini.

7. No safety or health violations were found in the affidavit submitted by the Agency upon the completion of the inspection.

8. On multiple occasions, Mancini has been seen in the company of the Mayor and several of these Agency officials.

9. Many gas stations in Emporia, Virginia, use a more modernized electric pump that is safer but less cost effective compared to Mancini's older wooden hand-crank.

CAUSES OF ACTION

10. Although the Commonwealth of Virginia follows the common-law doctrine of employment-at-will, the rule is not absolute and has exceptions. Virginia courts recognize an exception to the employment-at-will doctrine when the discharge violates public policy.

11. Pursuant to Va. Code Ann. § 40.1-51.2 (d), no person shall be discharged by his or her employer on the basis of participating in any safety and health inspection.

DAMAGES

12. As a result of Williams' retaliatory discharge, Williams has suffered loss of wages.

RELIEF

13. WHEREFORE, Plaintiff Terry Williams demands judgment against Defendant Gerry Mancini for the sum of $80,000 and granting any and all other relief as this Court deems proper or just.

Dated: August 28, 2012
/s/ Audrey Karman

Audrey Karman, Esquire
Sydney Lewis Hall, CJC
Lexington, VA 24450
(202) 213-3551
Attorney for Plaintiff

PLAINTIFF DEMANDS TRIAL BY JURY

Having read *Twombly, Iqbal* and FRCP 12(b)(6), draft a Motion to Dismiss in one or more of the cases, as assigned by your professor. Now write a two-page argument for and a two-page argument against the Motion.

CHAPTER 6

Case Management, ADR

DURING THE LATTER HALF of the 1970s and continuing through the 1980s, a wide range of phenomena were swept under the rubric of the "litigation boom," or, sometimes, "litigation explosion." Either term implied dramatic, powerful forces that were changing the American litigation landscape. Increased court filings (especially in federal court), astronomical jury verdicts, and excessive pretrial, discovery and trial maneuvering were all decried as symptomatic of America's litigation crisis. The air was full of talk about justice system and lawyer failures. Some of it was about so-called preposterous claims against fast food giants for spilled coffee and obesity. Some of it was about two-year-long trials.

The wide range of phenomena gathered under the litigation boom umbrella was matched by the range of causes to blame for it. Too many lawyers, too many greedy lawyers, too many new "rights-laws," judges who failed to use their powers of remitittur, an American culture of blame and expectation of a legal remedy for every wrong, lawyer advertising, an uptick of frivolous claims, and civil discovery abuses, all were said to be to blame for the destructive forces of excessive litigation.

The negative results attributed to this boom were also quite diverse: a breakdown in social responsibility, escalating malpractice and products liability insurance premiums, increases in court costs and lessening of court efficiency, advantage-taking by contingent fee lawyers, and professional embarrassment in the public eye. Doctors were being driven from their practices by the cost of insurance and the misery of defending malpractice claims. Drug companies said they would stop making critical vaccination drugs because of lawsuits over side effects. The economy was being dampened by the cost of law.

The official data from a given year, 1979, show a dramatic increase in federal court filings, but not of the type to cause alarm:

> The 162,469 civil cases filed in the district courts during the twelve month period ended December 31, 1979, represents the largest influx of cases during any comparable twelve month period. A number of districts showed tremendous increases in civil filings over the same period a year ago. . . . The most substantial increase in filings in the district courts was in U.S. plaintiff cases, which increased 46.7 percent over 1978. This is directly related to the increased activity on the part of the federal government in filing cases for recovery of overpayments and enforcement of judgments. This increased activity, related mostly to delinquent or defaulted student loans, caused the number of such cases to jump from 4,666 in 1978 to 13,223 in 1979, a rise of 183.4 percent.[1]

The huge increase in filings was substantially attributable to filings by the United States to recover debts and overpayments. There were also less significant increases in some other types of filings, giving something for each side of the debate to highlight.

> Other case types with significant increases over 1978 were cases related to medical malpractice (up 60.0 percent), negotiable instruments (up 30.8 percent), banks and banking (up 25.7 percent) and the Freedom of Information Act of 1974 (up 24.5 percent).[2]

Statistics on the number of court filings can mislead, but they mislead in both directions. First, a massive increase in low-engagement civil actions occurred, driving the number of filings up, but without a commensurate workload consequence. Prisoner petitions in federal court increased rapidly, but they require far less judicial time than ordinary civil actions. Most are dismissed early, involve little or no discovery and proceed to trial at a miniscule rate.[3] It is also

---

1 Admin. Office of the U.S. Courts, Statistics Division 5-9 (1979).

2 *Id.*

3 See Lewis F. Powell, Jr., Are the Federal Courts Becoming Bureaucracies?, 68 A.B.A. J. 1370, 1372 (1982) ("To be sure, as is true of Section 1983 suits, most of the Section 2254 cases are not burdensome and can be disposed of on order.").

true, however, that there was an increase in complex cases. Rights cases and class actions increased significantly, and require significant measures of discovery and judicial resources. These are not simply contract disputes or basic tort cases.

Individual courts and federal judges took matters into their own hands and succeeded at reforms within their particular fiefdoms. In Cleveland, Federal District Judge Thomas Lambros brought techniques to resolve disputes without significant litigation from his state court judge experience. In state court, his claim to fame was a domestic relations reconciliation program that produced fewer final orders of divorce and reduced the measure of litigation in those that proceeded to final judgment. In federal court, it was a wide range of innovative ADR techniques, including use of mock juries to inform parties and hasten their willingness to settle.[4] In the mid-1960s in the Eastern District of Virginia, Judge Alvin Bryan created the now-famed "rocket docket." The court has consistently been the fastest to judgment in civil matters of all federal district courts and high in the criminal pace rankings. The solution in the EDVA is simple: the schedule for the case's development is managed by a judge from the outset; no continuance is a good continuance. The joke among lawyers practicing in the court is that the only successful excuse for gaining a continuance is a death in the family. But it has to be the lawyer's death.[5]

Change took the form of civil procedure reforms of essentially two types: toughened sanctions devices and increased court management of litigation.

In 1983, to combat the perception that more frivolous claims were being filed, Congress amended Federal Rule of Civil Procedure 11 to make judges more likely to impose sanctions on lawyers who file frivolous claims or motions. The goal was to "discourage dilatory or abusive tactics and to streamline the litigation process by lessening the amount of frivolous matters brought before the federal courts."[6] Most states followed with their own versions of the same. The trouble with the new Rule 11 was that it was used. Now, with its encouragement for judges to impose sanctions, more and more lawyers filed motions under the newly amended rule asking judges to sanction opposing counsel.

---

4 See Carl E. Feather, Bar Association Honors Retired Judge Tom Lambros, Star Beacon (Oct. 10, 2010), http://starbeacon.com/local/x921681626/Bar-Association-honors-retired-Judge-Tom-Lambros.

5Jerry Markon, Docket, Wash. Post, Oct. 3, 2004 at C04, available at http://www.washingtonpost.com/wp-dyn/articles/A3007-2004Oct2.html (recounting two celebrated criminal matters that have slowed even the rocket docket).

6 Fed. R. Civ. P. 11 advisory committee's note (1983).

Pursuing the themes of the litigation boom worriers, Congress adopted the Judicial Improvements and Access to Justice Act of 1988[7] and the Civil Justice Reform Act of 1990 (CJRA).[8] The former raised the diversity of citizenship amount in controversy requirement from 10 to 50 thousand dollars. The latter introduced greater judicial control over pretrial procedures including discovery and tracking into ADR and the latter.

The CJRA ushered in a new era of court efficiency efforts. As a result of the CJRA, federal district judges are monitored for their efficiency, with regular reports being published of the length of time it takes for each individual district judge to resolve motions, and close cases. New measures of efficiency have been devised and judges compete with one another to push civil actions through their courts. The pressure transferred from judges to lawyers, as judges pushed lawyers to complete discovery on time and settle matters.

Use of mediation and other ADR techniques increased sharply, with judges now having the power to order parties to engage in good faith mediation and settlement efforts.

The CJRA requires judges to set up schedules for discovery and motion practice, and to hold initial and pretrial conferences with the parties for the purpose of streamlining the schedule and process for resolving the action. The judges' efforts to set up schedules devolve largely to the parties and their lawyers. Judges ask the parties to agree on various aspects of discovery and schedules and resolve on their own as many disputes as possible, leaving the judge to resolve only the thorniest issues on which the parties cannot seem to agree. Judges are displeased when it appears that the parties and their lawyers have not made serious efforts to resolve matters on their own.

Rule Material

Rule 16 Pretrial Conferences; Scheduling; Management

(a) Purposes of a Pretrial Conference. In any action, the court may order the attorneys and any unrepresented parties to appear for one or more pretrial conferences for such purposes as:

(1) expediting disposition of the action;

---

7 See Judicial Improvements and Access to Justice Act of 1988, Pub. L. No. 100-702, 102 Stat. 4642 (codified as amended in scattered sections of 28 U.S.C.).

8 Civil Justice Reform Act of 1990.

(2) establishing early and continuing control so that the case will not be protracted because of lack of management;

(3) discouraging wasteful pretrial activities;

(4) improving the quality of the trial through more thorough preparation; and

(5) facilitating settlement.

(b) Scheduling.

(1) *Scheduling Order.* Except in categories of actions exempted by local rule, the district judge—or a magistrate judge when authorized by local rule—must issue a scheduling order:

(A) after receiving the parties' report under Rule 26(f); or

(B) after consulting with the parties' attorneys and any unrepresented parties at a scheduling conference or by telephone, mail, or other means.

(2) *Time to Issue.* The judge must issue the scheduling order as soon as practicable, but in any event within the earlier of 120 days after any defendant has been served with the complaint or 90 days after any defendant has appeared.

(3) *Contents of the Order.*

(A) Required Contents. The scheduling order must limit the time to join other parties, amend the pleadings, complete discovery, and file motions.

(B) Permitted Contents. The scheduling order may:

(i) modify the timing of disclosures under Rules 26(a) and 26(e)(1);

(ii) modify the extent of discovery;

(iii) provide for disclosure or discovery of electronically stored information;

(iv) include any agreements the parties reach for asserting claims of privilege or of protection as trial-preparation material after information is produced;

(v) set dates for pretrial conferences and for trial; and

(vi) include other appropriate matters.

(4) *Modifying a Schedule.* A schedule may be modified only for good cause and with the judge's consent.

(c) Attendance and Matters for Consideration at a Pretrial Conference.

(1) *Attendance.* A represented party must authorize at least one of its attorneys to make stipulations and admissions about all matters that can reasonably be anticipated for discussion at a pretrial conference. If appropriate, the court may require that a party or its representative be present or reasonably available by other means to consider possible settlement.

(2) *Matters for Consideration.* At any pretrial conference, the court may consider and take appropriate action on the following matters:

(A) formulating and simplifying the issues, and eliminating frivolous claims or defenses;

(B) amending the pleadings if necessary or desirable;

(C) obtaining admissions and stipulations about facts and documents to avoid unnecessary proof, and ruling in advance on the admissibility of evidence;

(D) avoiding unnecessary proof and cumulative evidence, and limiting the use of testimony under Federal Rule of Evidence 702;

(E) determining the appropriateness and timing of summary adjudication under Rule 56;

(F) controlling and scheduling discovery, including orders affecting disclosures and discovery under Rule 26 and Rules 29 through 37;

(G) identifying witnesses and documents, scheduling the filing and exchange of any pretrial briefs, and setting dates for further conferences and for trial;

(H) referring matters to a magistrate judge or a master;

(I) settling the case and using special procedures to assist in resolving the dispute when authorized by statute or local rule;

(J) determining the form and content of the pretrial order;

(K) disposing of pending motions;

(L) adopting special procedures for managing potentially difficult or protracted actions that may involve complex issues, multiple parties, difficult legal questions, or unusual proof problems;

(M) ordering a separate trial under Rule 42(b) of a claim, counter-claim, cross-claim, third-party claim, or particular issue;

(N) ordering the presentation of evidence early in the trial on a manageable issue that might, on the evidence, be the basis for a judgment as a matter of law under Rule 50(a) or a judgment on partial findings under Rule 52(c);

(O) establishing a reasonable limit on the time allowed to present evidence; and

(P) facilitating in other ways the just, speedy, and inexpensive dis-position of the action.

(d) Pretrial Orders. After any conference under this rule, the court should issue an order reciting the action taken. This order controls the course of the action unless the court modifies it.

(e) Final Pretrial Conference and Orders. The court may hold a final pre-trial conference to formulate a trial plan, including a plan to facilitate the admission of evidence. The conference must be held as close to the start of trial as is reasonable, and must be attended by at least one attorney who will conduct the trial for each party and by any unrepresented party. The court may modify the order issued after a final pretrial conference only to prevent manifest injustice.

(f) Sanctions.

(1) *In General.* On motion or on its own, the court may issue any just orders, including those authorized by Rule 37(b)(2)(A)(ii)–(vii), if a party or its attorney:

(A) fails to appear at a scheduling or other pretrial conference;

(B) is substantially unprepared to participate—or does not par-ticipate in good faith—in the conference; or

(C) fails to obey a scheduling or other pretrial order.

(2) *Imposing Fees and Costs.* Instead of or in addition to any other sanction, the court must order the party, its attorney, or both to pay the reasonable expenses—including attorney's fees—incurred because of any noncompliance with this rule, unless the noncom-pliance was substantially justified or other circumstances make an award of expenses unjust.

Rule 41 Dismissal of Actions

(a) Voluntary Dismissal.

(1) *By the Plaintiff.*

(A) Without a Court Order. Subject to Rules 23(e), 23.1(c), 23.2, and 66 and any applicable federal statute, the plaintiff may dismiss an action without a court order by filing:

(i) a notice of dismissal before the opposing party serves either an answer or a motion for summary judgment; or

(ii) a stipulation of dismissal signed by all parties who have appeared.

(B) Effect. Unless the notice or stipulation states otherwise, the dismissal is without prejudice. But if the plaintiff previously dismissed any federal- or state-court action based on or including the same claim, a notice of dismissal operates as an adjudication on the merits.

(2) *By Court Order; Effect.* Except as provided in Rule 41(a)(1), an action may be dismissed at the plaintiff's request only by court order, on terms that the court considers proper. If a defendant has pleaded a counterclaim before being served with the plaintiff's motion to dismiss, the action may be dismissed over the defendant's objection only if the counterclaim can remain pending for independent adjudication. Unless the order states otherwise, a dismissal under this paragraph (2) is without prejudice.

(b) Involuntary Dismissal; Effect. If the plaintiff fails to prosecute or to comply with these rules or a court order, a defendant may move to dismiss the action or any claim against it. Unless the dismissal order states otherwise, a dismissal under this subdivision (b) and any dismissal not under this rule—except one for lack of jurisdiction, improper venue, or failure to join a party under Rule 19—operates as an adjudication on the merits.

(c) Dismissing a Counterclaim, Crossclaim, or Third-Party Claim. This rule applies to a dismissal of any counterclaim, cross-claim, or third-party claim. A claimant's voluntary dismissal under Rule 41(a)(1)(A)(i) must be made:

(1) before a responsive pleading is served; or

(2) if there is no responsive pleading, before evidence is introduced at a hearing or trial.

(d) Costs of a Previously Dismissed Action. If a plaintiff who previously dismissed an action in any court files an action based on or including the same claim against the same defendant, the court:

> (1) may order the plaintiff to pay all or part of the costs of that previous action; and

> (2) may stay the proceedings until the plaintiff has complied.

Rule 68 Offer of Judgment

(a) Making an Offer; Judgment on an Accepted Offer. At least 14 days before the date set for trial, a party defending against a claim may serve on an opposing party an offer to allow judgment on specified terms, with the costs then accrued. If, within 14 days after being served, the opposing party serves written notice accepting the offer, either party may then file the offer and notice of acceptance, plus proof of service. The clerk must then enter judgment.

(b) Unaccepted Offer. An unaccepted offer is considered withdrawn, but it does not preclude a later offer. Evidence of an unaccepted offer is not admissible except in a proceeding to determine costs.

(c) Offer After Liability Is Determined. When one party's liability to another has been determined but the extent of liability remains to be determined by further proceedings, the party held liable may make an offer of judgment. It must be served within a reasonable time—but at least 14 days—before the date set for a hearing to determine the extent of liability.

(d) Paying Costs After an Unaccepted Offer. If the judgment that the offeree finally obtains is not more favorable than the unaccepted offer, the offeree must pay the costs incurred after the offer was made.

Marek v. Chesny

473 U.S. 1, 105 S.Ct. 3012 (1985)

Syllabus[9]*

Petitioner police officers, in answering a call on a domestic disturbance, shot and killed respondent's adult son. Respondent, in his own behalf and as administrator of his son's estate, filed suit against petitioners in Federal District Court under 42 U.S.C. § 1983 and state tort law. Prior to trial, petitioners made a timely offer of settlement of $100,000, expressly including accrued costs and attorney's fees, but respondent did not accept the offer. The case went to trial and respondent was awarded $5,000 on the state-law claim, $52,000 for the § 1983 violation, and $3,000 in punitive damages. Respondent then filed a request for attorney's fees under 42 U.S.C. § 1988, which provides that a prevailing party in a § 1983 action may be awarded attorney's fees "as part of the costs." The claimed attorney's fees included fees for work performed subsequent to the settlement offer. The District Court declined to award these latter fees pursuant to Federal Rule of Civil Procedure 68, which provides that if a timely pretrial offer of settlement is not accepted and "the judgment finally obtained by the offeree is not more favorable than the offer, the offeree must pay the costs incurred after the making of the offer." The Court of Appeals reversed.

Donald G. Peterson argued the cause for petitioners. With him on the brief was *Elizabeth Hubbard.*

Jerrold J. Ganzfried argued the cause for the United States as amicus curiae urging reversal. On the brief were *Solicitor General Lee, Acting Assistant Attorney General Willard, Deputy Solicitor General Geller, Deputy Assistant Attorney General Kuhl, Katheryn A. Oberly, Robert S. Greenspan,* and *Barbara S. Woodall.*

Victor J. Stone argued the cause for respondent. On the brief was *James D. Montgomery.*

Briefs of *amici curiae* urging reversal were filed for the State of Florida by *Jim Smith,* Attorney General, *Mitchell D. Franks,* and *Linda K. Huber* and *Bruce A. Minnick,* Assistant Attorneys General; for the City of New York by *Frederick A.O. Schwarz, Jr., Leonard Koerner, Ronald E. Sternberg, Evelyn Jonas,* and *John P.*

---

9 The syllabus constitutes no part of the opinion of the Court but has been prepared by the Reporter of Decisions for the convenience of the reader.

Woods; and for the Equal Employment Advisory Council by *Robert E. Williams, Douglas S. McDowell,* and *Thomas R. Bagby.*

Briefs of *amici curiae* urging affirmance were filed for the Alliance for Justice by *Laura Macklin;* for the American Civil Liberties Union et al. by *Roger Pascal, Burt Neuborne, E. Richard Larson,* and *Harvey Grossman;* for the Lawyers' Committee for Civil Rights Under Law by *Fred N. Fishman, Robert H. Kapp, Norman Redlich, William L. Robinson, Norman J. Chachkin, Harold R. Tyler, Jr.,* and *Sara E. Lister;* for the Committee on the Federal Courts of the Association of the Bar of the City of New York by *Sheldon H. Elsen, Michael W. Schwartz, Sidney S. Rosdeitcher, Edmund H. Kerr,* and *John G. Koeltl;* and for the NAACP Legal Defense and Educational Fund, Inc., by *Barry L. Goldstein, Julius LeVonne Chambers,* and *Charles Stephen Ralston.*[10]

Chief Justice BURGER delivered the opinion of the Court.

We granted certiorari to decide whether attorney's fees incurred by a plaintiff subsequent to an offer of settlement under Federal Rule of Civil Procedure 68 must be paid by the defendant under 42 U.S.C. § 1988, when the plaintiff recovers a judgment less than the offer.

II

Rule 68 provides that if a timely pretrial offer of settlement is not accepted and "the judgment finally obtained by the offeree is not more favorable than the offer, the offeree must pay the costs incurred after the making of the offer." (Emphasis added.) The plain purpose of Rule 68 is to encourage settlement and avoid litigation. The Rule prompts both parties to a suit to evaluate the risks and costs of litigation, and to balance them against the likelihood of success upon trial on the merits. This case requires us to decide whether the offer in this case was a proper one under Rule 68, and whether the term "costs" as used in Rule 68 includes attorney's fees awardable under 42 U.S.C. § 1988.

A

The first question we address is whether petitioners' offer was valid under Rule 68. Respondent contends that the offer was invalid because it lumped petitioners' proposal for damages with their proposal for costs. Respondent argues that Rule 68 requires that an offer must separately recite the amount that the defendant is offering in settlement of the substantive claim and the amount he is offering to cover accrued costs.

---

10 The affiliations of those filing amici curiae briefs on both sides of important litigation can be revealing about the interests at play in a case. Ed.

We do not read Rule 68 to require that a defendant's offer itemize the respective amounts being tendered for settlement of the underlying substantive claim and for costs.

B

The second question we address is whether the term "costs" in Rule 68 includes attorney's fees awardable under 42 U.S.C. § 1988. By the time the Federal Rules of Civil Procedure were adopted in 1938, federal statutes had authorized and defined awards of costs to prevailing parties for more than 85 years. Unlike in England, such "costs" generally had not included attorney's fees; under the "American Rule," each party had been required to bear its own attorney's fees. The "American Rule" as applied in federal courts, however, had become subject to certain exceptions by the late 1930's. Some of these exceptions had evolved as a product of the "inherent power in the courts to allow attorney's fees in particular situations." But most of the exceptions were found in federal statutes that directed courts to award attorney's fees as part of costs in particular cases.

The authors of Federal Rule of Civil Procedure 68 were fully aware of these exceptions to the American Rule. The Advisory Committee's Note to Rule 54(d) contains an extensive list of the federal statutes which allowed for costs in particular cases; of the 35 "statutes as to costs" set forth in the final paragraph of the Note, no fewer than 11 allowed for attorney's fees as part of costs. Against this background of varying definitions of "costs," the drafters of Rule 68 did not define the term; nor is there any explanation whatever as to its intended meaning in the history of the Rule.

In this setting, given the importance of "costs" to the Rule, it is very unlikely that this omission was mere oversight; on the contrary, the most reasonable inference is that the term "costs" in Rule 68 was intended to refer to all costs properly awardable under the relevant substantive statute or other authority. In other words, all costs properly awardable in an action are to be considered within the scope of Rule 68 "costs." Thus, absent congressional expressions to the contrary, where the underlying statute defines "costs" to include attorney's fees, we are satisfied such fees are to be included as costs for purposes of Rule 68.

Here, respondent sued under 42 U.S.C. § 1983. Pursuant to the Civil Rights Attorney's Fees Awards Act of 1976, 90 Stat. 2641, as amended, 42 U.S.C. § 1988, a prevailing party in a § 1983 action may be awarded attorney's fees "as part of the costs." Since Congress expressly included attorney's fees as "costs" available to a plaintiff in a § 1983 suit, such fees are subject to the cost-shifting provision of Rule 68. This "plain meaning" interpretation of the interplay between Rule

68 and § 1988 is the only construction that gives meaning to each word in both Rule 68 and § 1988.

Unlike the Court of Appeals, we do not believe that this "plain meaning" construction of the statute and the Rule will frustrate Congress' objective in § 1988 of ensuring that civil rights plaintiffs obtain " 'effective access to the judicial process.' " Merely subjecting civil rights plaintiffs to the settlement provision of Rule 68 does not curtail their access to the courts, or significantly deter them from bringing suit. Application of Rule 68 will serve as a disincentive for the plaintiff's attorney to continue litigation after the defendant makes a settlement offer. There is no evidence, however, that Congress, in considering § 1988, had any thought that civil rights claims were to be on any different footing from other civil claims insofar as settlement is concerned. Indeed, Congress made clear its concern that civil rights plaintiffs not be penalized for "helping to lessen docket congestion" by settling their cases out of court.

Moreover, Rule 68's policy of encouraging settlements is neutral, favoring neither plaintiffs nor defendants; it expresses a clear policy of favoring settlement of all lawsuits. Civil rights plaintiffs—along with other plaintiffs—who reject an offer more favorable than what is thereafter recovered at trial will not recover attorney's fees for services performed after the offer is rejected. But, since the Rule is neutral, many civil rights plaintiffs will benefit from the offers of settlement encouraged by Rule 68. Some plaintiffs will receive compensation in settlement where, on trial, they might not have recovered, or would have recovered less than what was offered. And, even for those who would prevail at trial, settlement will provide them with compensation at an earlier date without the burdens, stress, and time of litigation. In short, settlements rather than litigation will serve the interests of plaintiffs as well as defendants.

To be sure, application of Rule 68 will require plaintiffs to "think very hard" about whether continued litigation is worthwhile; that is precisely what Rule 68 contemplates. This effect of Rule 68, however, is in no sense inconsistent with the congressional policies underlying § 1983 and § 1988. Section 1988 authorizes courts to award only "reasonable" attorney's fees to prevailing parties. In a case where a rejected settlement offer exceeds the ultimate recovery, the plaintiff—although technically the prevailing party—has not received any monetary benefits from the postoffer services of his attorney. This case presents a good example: the $139,692 in postoffer legal services resulted in a recovery $8,000 less than petitioners' settlement offer. Given Congress' focus on the success achieved, we are not persuaded that shifting the postoffer costs to respondent in these circumstances would in any sense thwart its intent under § 1988.

Rather than "cutting against the grain" of § 1988, as the Court of Appeals held, we are convinced that applying Rule 68 in the context of a § 1983 action is consistent with the policies and objectives of § 1988. Section 1988 encourages plaintiffs to bring meritorious civil rights suits; Rule 68 simply encourages settlements. There is nothing incompatible in these two objectives.

III

Congress, of course, was well aware of Rule 68 when it enacted § 1988, and included attorney's fees as part of recoverable costs. The plain language of Rule 68 and § 1988 subjects such fees to the cost-shifting provision of Rule 68. Nothing revealed in our review of the policies underlying § 1988 constitutes "the necessary clear expression of congressional intent" required "to exempt . . . [the] statute from the operation of" Rule 68. We hold that petitioners are not liable for costs of $139,692 incurred by respondent after petitioners' offer of settlement.

The judgment of the Court of Appeals is

Reversed.

[Concurring opinions of Justices POWELL and REHNQUIST are omitted.]

Justice BRENNAN, with whom Justice MARSHALL and Justice BLACKMUN join, dissenting.

The question presented by this case is whether the term "costs" as it is used in Rule 68 of the Federal Rules of Civil Procedure and elsewhere throughout the Rules refers simply to those taxable costs defined in 28 U.S.C. § 1920 and traditionally understood as "costs"—court fees, printing expenses, and the like —or instead includes attorney's fees when an underlying fees-award statute happens to refer to fees "as part of" the awardable costs. Relying on what it recurrently emphasizes is the "plain language" of one such statute, 42 U.S.C. § 1988,[11] the Court today holds that a prevailing civil rights litigant entitled to fees under that statute is *per se* barred by Rule 68 from recovering any fees for work performed after rejecting a settlement offer where he ultimately recovers less than the proffered amount in settlement.

I dissent. The Court's reasoning is wholly inconsistent with the history and structure of the Federal Rules, and its application to the over 100 attorney's fees

---

11 Civil Rights Attorney's Fees Awards Act of 1976, 90 Stat. 2641, as amended, 42 U.S.C. § 1988. That section provides in relevant part that "[i]n any action or proceeding to enforce a provision of sections 1981, 1982, 1983, 1985, and 1986 of this title, title IX of Public Law 92–318, or title VI of the Civil Rights Act of 1964, the court, in its discretion, may allow the prevailing party, other than the United States, a reasonable attorney's fee as part of the costs."

statutes enacted by Congress will produce absurd variations in Rule 68's operation based on nothing more than picayune differences in statutory phraseology. Neither Congress nor the drafters of the Rules could possibly have intended such inexplicable variations in settlement incentives. Moreover, the Court's interpretation will "seriously undermine the purposes behind the attorney's fees provisions" of the civil rights laws. . . .

I

The Court's "plain language" analysis goes as follows: Section 1988 provides that a "prevailing party" may recover "a reasonable attorney's fee as part of the costs." Rule 68 in turn provides that, where an offeree obtains a judgment for less than the amount of a previous settlement offer, "the offeree must pay the costs incurred after the making of the offer." Because "attorney's fees" are "costs," the Court concludes, the "plain meaning" of Rule 68 *per se* prohibits a prevailing civil rights plaintiff from recovering fees incurred after he rejected the proposed out-of-court settlement.

The Court's "plain language" approach is, as Judge Posner's opinion for the court below noted, "in a sense logical." However, while the starting point in interpreting statutes and rules is always the plain words themselves, "[t]he particular inquiry is not what is the abstract force of the words or what they may comprehend, but in what sense were they intended to be understood or what understanding they convey when used in the particular act."

For a number of reasons, "costs" as that term is used in the Federal Rules should be interpreted uniformly in accordance with the definition of costs set forth in § 1920:

First. The limited history of the costs provisions in the Federal Rules suggests that the drafters intended "costs" to mean only taxable costs traditionally allowed under the common law or pursuant to the statutory predecessor of § 1920.

Second. The Rules provide that "costs" may automatically be taxed by the clerk of the court on one day's notice, Fed.Rule Civ.Proc. 54(d)—strongly suggesting that "costs" were intended to refer only to those routine, readily determinable charges that could appropriately be left to a clerk, and as to which a single day's notice of settlement would be appropriate. Attorney's fees, which are awardable only by the court and which frequently entail lengthy disputes and hearings, obviously do not fall within that category.

Third. When particular provisions of the Federal Rules are intended to encompass attorney's fees, they do so explicitly. Eleven different provisions of the Rules authorize a court to award attorney's fees as "expenses" in particular circumstances, demonstrating that the drafters knew the difference, and intended a difference, between "costs," "expenses," and "attorney's fees."

Fourth. With the exception of one recent Court of Appeals opinion and two recent District Court opinions, the Court can point to no authority suggesting that courts or attorneys have ever viewed the cost-shifting provisions of Rule 68 as including attorney's fees. Yet Rule 68 has been in effect for 47 years.

Fifth. We previously have held that words and phrases in the Federal Rules must be given a consistent usage and be read *in pari materia*, reasoning that to do otherwise would "attribute a schizophrenic intent to the drafters." Applying the Court's "plain language" approach consistently throughout the Rules, however, would produce absurd results that would turn statutes like § 1988 on their heads and plainly violate the restraints imposed on judicial rulemaking by the Rules Enabling Act.

Sixth. As with all of the Federal Rules, the drafters intended Rule 68 to have a uniform, consistent application in *all* proceedings in federal court. Yet today's decision will lead to dramatically different settlement incentives depending on minor variations in the phraseology of the underlying fees-award statutes—distinctions that would appear to be nothing short of irrational and for which the Court has no plausible explanation.

Congress has enacted well over 100 attorney's fees statutes, many of which would appear to be affected by today's decision. As the Appendix to this dissent illustrates, Congress has employed a variety of slightly different wordings in these statutes.

The result is to sanction a senseless patchwork of fee shifting that flies in the face of the fundamental purpose of the Federal Rules—the provision of uniform and consistent procedure in federal courts. Such a construction will "introduce into [Rule 68] distinctions unrelated to its goal . . . and [will] result in virtually random application of the Rule."

In sum, there is nothing in the history and structure of the Rules or in the history of any of the underlying attorney's fee statutes to justify such incomprehensible distinctions based simply on fine linguistic variations among the underlying fees-award statutes.

II

A

Although the Court's opinion fails to discuss any of the problems reviewed above, it does devote some space to arguing that its interpretation of Rule 68 "is in no sense inconsistent with the congressional policies underlying § 1983 and § 1988."

The Court is wrong. Congress has instructed that attorney's fee entitlement under § 1988 be governed by a *reasonableness* standard. Until today the Court always has recognized that this standard precludes reliance on any mechanical "bright-line" rules automatically denying a portion of fees, acknowledging that such "mathematical approach[es]" provide "little aid in determining what is a reasonable fee in light of all the relevant factors." Although the starting point is always "the number of hours *reasonably* expended on the litigation," this "does not end the inquiry": a number of considerations set forth in the legislative history of § 1988 "may lead the district court to adjust the fee upward or downward." We also have emphasized that district court "necessarily has discretion in making this equitable judgment" because of its "superior understanding of the litigation." Section 1988's reasonableness standard is, in sum, "acutely sensitive to the merits of an action and to antidiscrimination policy."

Rule 68, on the other hand, is not "sensitive" at all to the merits of an action and to antidiscrimination policy. It is a mechanical *per se* provision automatically shifting "costs" incurred after an offer is rejected, and it deprives a district court of all discretion with respect to the matter by using "the strongest verb of its type known to the English language—'must.' "

Of course, a civil rights plaintiff who *unreasonably* fails to accept a settlement offer, and who thereafter recovers less than the proffered amount in settlement, is barred under § 1988 itself from recovering fees for unproductive work performed in the wake of the rejection. This is because "the extent of a plaintiff's success is a crucial factor in determining the proper amount of an award of attorney's fees," hours that are "excessive, redundant, or otherwise unnecessary" must be excluded from that calculus. To this extent, the results might sometimes be the same under either § 1988's reasonableness inquiry or the Court's wooden application of Rule 68.

But the results under § 1988 and Rule 68 will *not* always be congruent, because § 1988 mandates the careful consideration of a broad range of other factors and accords appropriate leeway to the district court's informed discretion. Contrary to the Court's protestations, it is not at all clear that "[t]his case presents a good example" of the smooth interplay of § 1988 and Rule 68, ante, at 9, because there has never been an evidentiary consideration of the reasonableness or unreasonableness of the respondent's fee request. It *is* clear, however, that under the Court's interpretation of Rule 68 a plaintiff who ultimately recovers only slightly less than the proffered amount in settlement will *per se* be barred from recovering trial fees even if he otherwise "has obtained excellent results" in litigation that will have far-reaching benefit to the public interest. Today's decision necessarily will require the disallowance of some fees that otherwise would have passed muster under § 1988's reasonableness standard, and there is *nothing* in § 1988's legislative history even vaguely suggesting that Congress intended such a result.

The Court argues, however, that its interpretation of Rule 68 "is neutral, favoring neither plaintiffs nor defendants." This contention is also plainly wrong. As the Judicial Conference Advisory Committee on the Federal Rules of Civil Procedure has noted twice in recent years, Rule 68 "is a 'one-way street,' available only to those defending against claims and not to claimants." Interpreting Rule 68 in its current version to include attorney's fees will lead to a number of skewed settlement incentives that squarely conflict with Congress' intent. To discuss but one example, Rule 68 allows an offer to be made any time after the complaint is filed and gives the plaintiff only 10 days to accept or reject. The Court's decision inevitably will encourage defendants who know they have violated the law to make "low-ball" offers immediately after suit is filed and before plaintiffs have been able to obtain the information they are entitled to by way of discovery to assess the strength of their claims and the reasonableness of the offers. The result will put severe pressure on plaintiffs to settle on the basis of inadequate information in order to avoid the risk of bearing all of their fees even if reasonable discovery might reveal that the defendants were subject to far greater liability. Indeed, because Rule 68 offers may be made recurrently without limitation, defendants will be well advised to make ever-slightly larger offers throughout the discovery process and before plaintiffs have conducted all reasonably necessary discovery.

This sort of so-called "incentive" is fundamentally incompatible with Congress' goals. Congress intended for "private citizens . . . to be able to assert their civil rights" and for "those who violate the Nation's fundamental laws" not to be able "to proceed with impunity." Accordingly, civil rights plaintiffs "'appear before the court cloaked in a mantle of public interest'"; to promote the "*vigorous* enforcement of modern civil rights legislation," Congress has directed that such "private attorneys general" shall not "be deterred from bringing good faith actions to vindicate the fundamental rights here involved." Yet requiring plaintiffs to make wholly uninformed decisions on settlement offers, at the risk of *automatically* losing all of their postoffer fees no matter what the circumstances and notwithstanding the "excellent" results they might achieve after the full picture emerges, will work just such a deterrent effect.

Example Documents

Here is the Scheduling Order for the Two Old Hippies case.

IN THE UNITED STATES DISTRICT COURT
FOR THE DISTRICT OF NEW MEXICO

TWO OLD HIPPIES, LLC,
      Plaintiff,

       v.   No. CIV 10-459 JB/RLP

CATCH THE BUS, LLC, et al.,
      Defendants.

SCHEDULING ORDER

In accordance with the Civil Justice Expense and Delay Reduction Plan adopted in compliance with the Civil Justice Reform Act, and pursuant to Title 28 U.S.C. § 473(a)(1), this case is assigned to a **"standard"** track classification. Accordingly, the termination date for discovery is **May 31, 2011**, and discovery shall not be reopened, nor shall case management deadlines be modified, except by an order of the Court upon a showing of good cause. This deadline shall be construed to require that discovery be <u>completed</u> on or before the above date. Service of interrogatories or requests for production shall be considered timely only if the responses are due prior to the deadline. A notice to take deposition shall be considered timely only if the deposition takes place prior to the deadline. The pendency of dispositive motions shall not stay discovery.

Plaintiff shall be allowed until March 2, 2011 to amend the pleadings and to join additional parties. Defendants shall be allowed until April 4, 2011 to amend the pleadings and to join additional parties.

Motions relating to discovery (including, but not limited to, motions to compel and motions for protective order) shall be filed with the Court and served on opposing parties by **June 20, 2011**. See D.N.M.LR-Civ. 7 for motion practice requirements and timing of responses and replies. This deadline shall not be construed to extend the twenty-day time limit in D.N.M.LR-Civ. 26.6.

Plaintiff shall identify to all parties in writing any expert witness to be used by Plaintiff at trial and to provide expert reports pursuant to Fed. R. Civ. P. 26(a)(2)(B) no later than **April 30, 2011**. All other parties shall identify in writing any expert witness to be used by such parties at trial and to provide expert reports pursuant to Fed. R. Civ. P. 26(a)(2)(B) no later than **May 15, 2011**.

The parties shall have their experts ready to be deposed at the time they identify them and produce their reports.

Pretrial motions, other than discovery motions, shall be filed with the Court and served on opposing party by **June 30, 2011**. See D.N.M.LR-Civ. 7 for motion practice requirements and timing of responses and replies. Any pretrial motions, other than discovery motions, filed after the above dates shall, in the discretion of the Court, be considered untimely.

If documents are attached as exhibits to motions, affidavits or briefs, those parts of the exhibits that counsel want to bring to the attention of the Court must be highlighted in accordance with D.N.M.LR-Civ. 10.6.

Counsel are directed to file a consolidated final Pretrial Order as follows: Plaintiff to Defendants on or before **August 11, 2011;** Defendants to Court on or before **August 18, 2011**. Counsel are directed that the Pretrial Order will provide that no witnesses except rebuttal witnesses whose testimony cannot be anticipated, will be permitted to testify unless the name of the witness is furnished to the Court and opposing counsel no later than thirty (30) days prior to the time set for trial. Any exceptions thereto must be upon order of the Court for cause shown.

A motion hearing is scheduled in this matter on **August 2, 2011 at 1:30 p.m.**

This matter is set for a Pretrial Conference on **August 19, 2011 at 1:30 p.m.**

This matter is set for a **Jury Selection/Trial** on a trailing calendar beginning on **August 29, 2011 at 9:00 a.m. (Albuquerque/Vermejo Courtroom).**

IT IS SO ORDERED this 23rd day of February, 2011.

_____
UNITED STATES DISTRICT JUDGE

Courts require the parties to prepare and file reports on the status of the action and discovery plans. Here is an example of such a report and plan in a somewhat complex matter. Notice that at the end of the parties plan submission, the district judge turns the parties' submission into a Scheduling Order by adding the judge's signature. Once the document has become an Order, the parties are bound to follow it upon pain of contempt of court or sanctions. Consider when reading the RMR case to follow, how closely courts should adhere to a Final Pretrial Order.

UNITED STATES DISTRICT COURT
NORTHERN DISTRICT OF GEORGIA

ADVENTURE OUTDOORS, INC.; JAY
WALLACE, a Georgia Resident; and CECILIA
WALLACE, a Georgia Resident;

Plaintiffs,

– against –

MICHAEL BLOOMBERG, a New York Resident
and Mayor of New York City; TANYA MARIE
NOONER, a Georgia Resident; MELISA
MERCED, a Georgia Resident, of the Nooner
Investigative Group, a/k/a Nooner Initiatives
Inc.; JOSEPH TOUNSEL, a Georgia Resident, of
the Nooner Investigative Group, a/k/a Nooner
Initiatives Inc.; THE NOONER INVESTI-
GATIVE GROUP, a/k/a Nooner Initiative
Inc. a Georgia Corporation, and; THE JAMES
MINTZ GROUP, and JAMES MINTZ individu-
ally, Certain of Its other Principals & Agents,
As Yet Unidentified; MICHAEL CARDOZO,
Corporation Counsel of the City of New York;
and JOHN FEINBLATT, Criminal Justice
Coordinator of the of the City of New York; and
RAYMOND KELLY, a New York Resident and
Chief of the New York City Police Department,

Defendants.

Civil Action File No.
1 06 CV 2897-JOF

JOINT PRELIMINARY REPORT AND DISCOVERY PLAN

1. Description of Case:

(a) Describe briefly the nature of this action.

Plaintiff:

Pursuant to this Court's Order of September 20, 2007 (as amended
September 21, 2007), the remaining Plaintiff Adventure Outdoors, Inc. has
asserted a claim for Libel and Slander against Michael Bloomberg, Michael

Cardozo, John Feinblatt and Raymond Kelly, individually and as conspirators, all residents of the State of New York, each of which made public and published statements alleging criminal behavior on the part of the Plaintiff. The same statements, and the underlying and concomitant conduct of the named Defendants form the basis of the allegation of tortious interference with business relations, which also includes the other Defendants, including also the corporate Defendants.

Defendants:

In this suit, as refined by the Court's order of September 20, 2007, granting, in part, Defendants' Motion to Dismiss, Plaintiff Adventure Outdoors Inc. asserts claims for libel and slander and tortious interference with business relations based on public statements made by the Defendant New York public officials in which they described litigation brought against Plaintiff by the City of New York, aimed at curbing the flow of illegal guns into the City.

(b) Summarize, in the space provided below, the facts of this case. The summary should not be argumentative nor recite evidence.

Plaintiff:

Plaintiff Adventure Outdoors, Inc., alleges that, at a press conference and by other means of information distribution, including the internet, Michael Bloomberg, Michael Cardozo, John Feinblatt, and Raymond Kelly made and caused to be published statements that were libelous and slanderous as toward the Plaintiff.

The said statements were made at press conference on May 15, 2006 and were disseminated immediately and thereafter and were published in Atlanta and Georgia generally. The Plaintiff alleges that the statements made accuse it of violations of the criminal laws of the United State, and of disreputable and illicit behavior. The Plaintiff alleges that these statements were ultra vires and their underlying behavior, as it relates to any of the official duties of the individuals named above and were not fair comment on the lawsuit filed in the Eastern District of New York (06 CV 2233 (JBW) (CLP)) and that no privilege protects these statements.

The Plaintiff also alleges that all of the individual Defendants and the corporate Defendants, including the Georgia citizens, conspired together and acted to tortiously interfere with its business relations by the course of conduct of entering the Plaintiff's place of business and by lying on federal BATF Form

4473 on or about April 8, 2006, in order to justify the lawsuit in the Eastern District of New York (06 CV 2233 (JBW) (CLP)), and then by publication cast the Plaintiff's business and its business practices in a disparaging light and, in fact, did so. This conduct tortiously interfered with the Plaintiff's business, the Plaintiff alleges.

Defendants:

Plaintiff Adventure Outdoors, Inc. alleges that, at a press conference called to describe the filing of a lawsuit by the City of New York, and in subsequent press releases issued for the same reason, the Defendant New York public officials made certain statements that defamed it and tortiously interfered with its business relations.

The lawsuit being discussed at the press conference and in the press releases giving rise to Plaintiff's claims was part of the City of NewYork's efforts to curb the flow of illegal guns into the City. Information made available to the City showed that firearms sold by Plaintiff wound up being used in New York crimes in disproportionately high numbers. Through the use of integrity testing, the City uncovered further information regarding gun-sale practices at Plaintiff's business. Specifically, investigators entered Plaintiff's gun store and engaged in, and videotaped, a simulated "straw purchase" of a gun from Plaintiff. This simulated straw purchase had the appearance of an actual straw purchase, but differed from an actual straw purchase because the individual posing as the straw purchaser did not intend to transfer the gun immediately to another person and in fact retained possession of the firearm.

On May 15, 2006, the City of New York filed suit for negligence and public nuisance against Plaintiff and fourteen other gun dealers who contributed to the flow of illegal guns into the City at disproportionately high rates. A press conference was held that same day to announce the filing of the lawsuit and to describe the lawsuit's role in stemming the flow of illegal guns into the City. On May 15 and May 21, 2006, press releases further announcing and describing the lawsuit were issued. Plaintiff Adventure Outdoors, Inc. claims that statements made in the press conference and press releases defamed it and tortiously interfered with its business relations.

(c) The legal issues to be tried are as follows:

Plaintiff:

1.   Whether the statements made by the Defendants are Libelous and Slanderous.

2. Whether the statements made by the Defendants were Libel and Slander *per se*.

3. Whether the statement (and conduct) of the individual New York Defendants was ultra vires.

4. Whether any privilege exists and if so whether the individual Defendants or any of them, are protected by such a privilege.

5. Whether the May 15, 2006 statements of the Defendants was "fair" comment on the lawsuit filed in the Eastern District of New York (06 CV 2233 (JBW) (CLP)).

6. Whether the conduct of all Defendants, individually, and/or collectively in a conspiracy, tortiously interfered with the Plaintiff business.

Defendants:

1) Whether the statements giving rise to Plaintiff's claims are privileged.

2) Whether Plaintiff's claims are barred by the doctrine of official immunity.

3) Whether Plaintiff can establish the elements of their libel and slander claim, including but not limited to publication, whether the statements giving rise to that claim are "of and concerning" Plaintiff, whether the statements are false, whether Defendants made the statements with the requisite degree of fault depending on its status as a public or private figure, and whether the statements were the proximate cause of any compensable harm to Plaintiff.

4) Whether Plaintiff can establish the elements of their tortious interference claim, including but not limited to whether the statements giving rise to that claim were privileged, whether Defendants acted with malice and an intent to injure, whether any third parties have been induced to not enter or to discontinue a business relationship with Plaintiff, and whether Defendants' statements were the proximate cause of any compensable harm to Plaintiff.

(d) The cases listed below (include both style and action number)are:

(1) Pending Related Cases:

City of New York v. A-1 Jewelry & Pawn, Inc., et al, No. 1:06-cv-02233 (E.D.N.Y., filed May 15, 2006).

(2) Previously Adjudicated Related Cases:

Adventure Outdoors, et al. v. Michael Bloomberg, et al., No 1:06-cv-1931-JOF (N.D. Ga., filed in Cobb County Superior Court on July 20, 2006, removed to this Court on August 18, 2006) (voluntarily dismissed by plaintiffs therein on October 13, 2006).

2.   This case is complex because it possesses one (1) or more of the features listed below (please check)

_____ (1) Unusually large number of parties

_____ (2) Unusually large number of claims or defenses

_____ (3) Factual issues are exceptionally complex

_____ (4) Greater than normal volume of evidence

_____ (5) Extended discovery period is needed

_____ (6) Problems locating or preserving evidence

_____ (7) Pending parallel investigations or action by government

___X___ (8) Multiple use of experts

_____ (9) Need for discovery outside United States boundaries

___X___ (10) Existence of highly technical issues and proof

3.   Counsel:

The following individually-named attorneys are hereby designated as lead counsel for the parties:

Plaintiff:

Edwin Marger
Law Offices of Edwin Marger
44 North Main Street
Jasper, Georgia 30143

Defendants:

Peter Canfield
Dow Lohnes PLLC
Six Concourse Parkway, Suite 1800
Atlanta, Georgia 30328

4.   Jurisdiction:

Is there any question regarding this court's jurisdiction?

____ Yes   _____ No

Plaintiff:

No; however, there is an Appeal in the 11th Circuit 07-14966-HH, which asserts that this Court has lost jurisdiction by issuing a "final" order.

Defendants:

Yes. As previously asserted in Defendants' January 5, 2007 motion to dismiss, Defendants maintain that this Court lacks personal jurisdiction over Defendants. Moreover, as indicated in Defendants' response to 10 below and in their pending motion for stay of discovery pending appeal, the Court's jurisdiction is limited by virtue of Defendants' Eleventh Circuit appeals. See, e.g., *Griggs v. Provident Consumer Discount Co.*, 459 U.S. 56 (1982).

If "yes," please attach a statement, not to exceed one (1) page, explaining the jurisdictional objection. When there are multiple claims, identify and discuss separately the claim(s) on which the objection is based. Each objection should be supported by authority.

Please see Defendants' January 5, 2007, Motion to Dismiss and February 25, 2008 Motion for Stay of Discovery.

5.   Parties to This Action:

(a)   The following persons are necessary parties who have not been joined:
None.

(b)   The following persons are improperly joined as parties:
None.

(c) The names of the following parties are either inaccurately stated or necessary portions of their names are omitted:
None.

(d) The parties shall have a continuing duty to inform the court of any contentions regarding unnamed parties necessary to this action or any contentions regarding misjoinder of parties or errors in the statement of a party's name.

6. Amendments to the Pleadings: Amended and supplemental pleadings must be filed in accordance with the time limitations and other provisions of Fed.R.Civ.P. 15. Further instructions regarding amendments are contained in LR 15.

(a) List separately any amendments to the pleadings which the parties anticipate will be necessary:

At this time, the parties do not anticipate that any amendments to the pleadings will be necessary.

(b) Amendments to the pleading submitted LATER THAN THIRTY (30) DAYS after the Joint Preliminary Report and Discovery Plan is filed, or should have been filed, will not be accepted for filing, unless otherwise permitted by law.

7. Filing Times for Motions:

All motions should be filed as soon as possible. The local rules set specific filing limits for some motions. These times are restated below.

All other motions must be filed WITHIN THIRTY (30) DAYS after the beginning of discovery, unless the filing party has obtained prior permission of the court to file later. Local Rule 7.1A(2).

(a) *Motions to Compel:* before the close discovery or within the extension period allowed in some instances. Local Rule 37.1.

(b) *Summary Judgment Motions:* within twenty (20) days after the close of discovery, unless otherwise permitted by court order. Local Rule 56.1.

(c) *Other Limited Motions:* Refer to Local Rules 7.2A; 7.2B, and 7.2E, respectively, regarding filing limitations for motions pending on removal, emergency motions, and motions for reconsideration.

(d) *Motions Objecting to Expert Testimony:* Daubert motions with regard to expert testimony no later than the date that the proposed pretrial order is submitted. Refer to Local Rule 7.2F.

8. Initial Disclosures:

The parties are required to serve initial disclosures in accordance with Fed.R.Civ.P. 26. If any party objects that initial disclosures are not appropriate, state the party and basis for the party's objection.

See response to 10 below.

9. Request for Scheduling Conference:

Does any party request a scheduling conference with the Court? If so, please state the issues which could be addressed and the position of each party.

No scheduling conference is requested at this time.

10. Discovery Period:

The discovery period commences thirty (30) days after the appearance of the first defendant by answer to the complaint. As stated in LR 26.2A, responses to initiated discovery must be completed before expiration of the assigned discovery period.

Cases in this court are assigned to one of the following three (3) discovery tracks: (a) zero (0)-months discovery period, (b) four (4)- months discovery period, and (c) eight (8)-months discovery period. A chart showing the assignment of cases to a discovery track by filing category is contained in Appendix F. The track to which a particular case is assigned is also stamped on the complaint and service copies of the complaint at the time of filing.

Please state below the subjects on which discovery may be needed:

Plaintiff:

1. The identity of the people who conceived of the plan partially executed on April 8, 2006, and the parameters of the said plan.

2. The identity of the persons who attended meetings in preparation of the plan partially executed on April 8, 2006.

3. The names, if any, of the attorneys from whom advice was sought concerning the plan partially executed on April 8, 2006.

4. Any investigation that the Defendants utilized to determine if their statements of May 15, 2006 were true.

5. The existence or non-existence of any evidence that would support or refute the statements of May 15, 2006 concerning the Plaintiff.

6. The existence or non-existence of the personal economic contributions by Michael Bloomberg to a separate non- governmental entity that purports to limit the distribution of firearms.

7. The extent to which employees of New York City engaged in non- governmental efforts in support of the said non-governmental entity that purports to limit the distribution of firearms.

8. The state of the knowledge of each of the speakers on May 15, 2006 concerning the Plaintiff, Adventure Outdoors Inc.

9. Any and all meetings that took place prior to April 8, 2006 by any purported agent of New York City and the persons who entered the place of business of the Plaintiff on April 8, 2006.

10. The training, if any, and the identities of the trainers, of those persons who entered the place of business of the Plaintiff on April 8, 2006.

11. Any experience or involvement with law enforcement of those people who trained the persons who entered the place of business of the Plaintiff on April 8, 2006.

12. The payment, if any, that was made, and by whom, to those persons who entered the Plaintiff's place of business on April 8, 2006.

13. Disclosure of the unedited version of any tape and/or video recordings made within the context of the plan, partially executed on April 8, 2006, and if edited, the identity and procedures of those persons editing.

Defendants:

Should the Eleventh Circuit resolve Defendants' appeals in Plaintiff's favor, discovery will be necessary with regard to the issues listed in Section 1(c), above.

If the parties anticipate that additional time beyond that allowed by the assigned discovery will be needed to complete discovery or that discovery should be conducted in phases or be limited to or focused upon particular issues, please state those reasons in detail below:

Plaintiff:

Plaintiff has directed Counsel to proceed as expeditiously as the court will allow in light of the almost 18 month delay prior to the commencement of discovery in this matter. Therefore, plaintiff does not agree to hold discovery pending the outcome in the 11th circuit. Defendants note that all of the matters listed by Plaintiffs as subjects of discovery have already been the subject of extensive discovery in the related action pending in the Eastern District of New York.

Defendants:

In light of the Eleventh Circuit's January 31, 2008 decision to proceed with Defendants' potentially dispositive appeals, and Plaintiff's refusal to agree to defer the commencement of the discovery period until their resolution, Defendants have moved the Court for a stay of discovery. See, e.g., *Blinco v. Green Tree Servicing, LLC*, 366 F.3d 1249, 1251 (11th Cir. 2004) (recognizing that "[a] district court properly stays discovery pending appeal of a denial of immunity").

11. Discovery Limitation:

What changes should be made in the limitations on discovery imposed under the Federal Rules of Civil Procedure or Local Rules of this Court, and what other limitations should be imposed?

See response to 10 above.

12. Other Orders:

What other orders do the parties think that the Court should enter under Rule 26(c) or under Rule 16(b) and (c)?

None at this time.

13. Settlement Potential:

(a) Lead counsel for the parties certify by their signatures below that they conducted a Rule 26(f) conference that was held on February 11, 2008, and that they participated in settlement discussions. Other persons who participated in the settlement discussions are listed according to party.

For Plaintiff:

Lead counsel:	*Edwin Marger (signature below)*
Other participants:	*Bob Barr*

For Defendant:

Lead counsel:	*Peter Canfield (signature below)*
Other participants:	*Eric Proshansky, Kenneth Taber and Dayna Harmelin*

(b) All parties were promptly informed of all offers of settlement and **following discussion by all counsel, it appears that there is now:**

See response to 13(c) below.

(___) **A possibility of settlement before discovery.**

(___) **A possibility of settlement after discovery.**

(___) **A possibility of settlement, but a conference with the judge is needed.**

(___) **No possibility of settlement.**

(c) Counsel (X) do or (__) do not intend to hold additional settlement conference among themselves prior to the close of discovery.

The parties intend to make use of the Eleventh Circuit's mediation process.

(d)   The following specific problems have created a hindrance to settlement of this case.

14.   **Trial by Magistrate Judge:**

Note: Trial before a Magistrate Judge will be by jury trial if a party is otherwise entitled to a jury trial.

(a)   The parties (   ) do consent to having this case tried before a magistrate judge of this court.

(b)   The parties (X) do not consent to having this case tried before a magistrate judge of this court.

/s/ Edwin Marger	/s/ Peter C. Canfield
Edwin Marger	Peter C. Canfield
Georgia Bar No. 470400	Georgia Bar No. 107748
Bob Barr	Michael Kovaka
Georgia Bar No. 039475	Georgia Bar No. 300197
	Matthew D. Crawford
	Georgia Bar No. 190109
Law Offices of Edwin Marger, LLC	
44 North Main Street	
Jasper, Georgia 30143	Dow Lohnes, PLLC
	Six Concourse Parkway
Attorneys for Plaintiff	Suite 1800
	Atlanta, Georgia 30328-6117
	(770) 901-8800
	Attorneys for Defendants

Of Counsel:

Michael A. Cardozo
Eric Proshansky
Corporation Counsel
of the City of New York
New York City Law Department
100 Church Street
New York, New York 10007
(212) 788-1324

Kenneth Taber
Pillsbury Winthrop Shaw Pittman,
LLP
1540 Broadway
New York, NY 10036 (212) 858-1000

Attorneys for Defendants Michael
Bloomberg, Michael Cardozo,
John Feinblatt and Raymond Kelly

Steven F. Reich
(Admitted Pro Hac Vice)
Kimo S. Peluso
(Admitted Pro Hac Vice)

Manatt, Phelps & Phillips, LLP
7 Times Square
New York, NY 10036
(212) 790-4500

Attorneys for Defendants James
Mintz and the James Mintz Group

* * * * *

SCHEDULING ORDER

Upon review of the information contained in the Joint Preliminary Report and Discovery Plan form completed and filed by the parties, the court orders that the time limits for adding parties, amending the pleadings, filing motions, completing discovery, and discussing settlement are as set out in the Federal Rules of Civil Procedure and the Local Rules of this Court, except as herein modified:

See response to 10 above.

IT IS ORDERED, this _____ day of _____, 2008

_____

UNITED STATES DISTRICT JUDGE

How Strictly Should Pretrial Orders Be Adhered to?

R.M.R., *Plaintiff-Appellant v.*
Muscogee County School District, Defendants-Appellees

165 F.3d 812 (1999)

Before TJOFLAT, BIRCH and MARCUS, Circuit Judges.

TJOFLAT, Circuit Judge:

Thirteen-year-old R.M.R. was sexually molested at school by his music teacher. R.M.R. then brought this suit against the Muscogee County School District ("Muscogee"), alleging that Muscogee was vicariously liable for this abuse under Title IX of the Education Amendments and under 42 U.S.C. s 1983. The jury returned a verdict in favor of Muscogee. Robbie and his mother appeal, claiming that the district court erred by: (1) denying their motion to compel discovery of certain student records before trial, (2) barring certain testimony of other witnesses at trial, and (3) improperly excluding a last-minute witness who was not listed in the pretrial order. We affirm the district court's judgment for the reasons set forth below.

I.

A.

In 1993, R.M.R. was a student at Richards Middle School, where he attended a boys' chorus class taught by Herman Larry Carr. Carr had been teaching at the school since 1982, and he was both well-respected by other teachers and well-liked by the students. Carr and R.M.R. shared a particularly strong rapport; Carr had shown special interest in R.M.R.'s music instruction, and R.M.R.

thought of Carr as his "idol." Consequently, when Carr asked R.M.R. to come to school on a student vacation day, March 12, 1993, to assist with some work, R.M.R. readily agreed.

While the two were alone in Carr's office on March 12, Carr molested R.M.R.; he pulled R.M.R. down onto his knee and held R.M.R. against his chest. Carr then touched R.M.R.'s groin with his hand, and moved R.M.R.'s hand onto Carr's own groin. Moments later there was a noise in the adjoining room, and Carr threw R.M.R. off his lap.

R.M.R. did not immediately tell anyone about the incident. Around Friday, April 23, however, he told both his girlfriend and Mrs. Becker, the mother of another friend, about the attack. Then on Monday, April 26, accompanied by his girlfriend, R.M.R. explained to the school counselor what Carr had done. The school counselor immediately reported the incident to the principal, William Arrington. The next morning, Arrington confronted Carr with R.M.R.'s claim and when Carr did not deny the charges, Arrington suspended him from teaching classes. Later that same day, Carr directly admitted to the Muscogee superintendent that he had molested R.M.R. The superintendent gave Carr the option of resigning or facing termination, and on May 4 Carr tendered his resignation.

Meanwhile, the word had spread around the school that R.M.R. was responsible for Carr's suspension. Some students speculated about what had happened, and frequently told R.M.R. that they believed he was lying. Arrington did not inform the students or their parents that Carr had confessed to the attack.

Carr was arrested for child molestation on May 19. The arrest, including the fact that R.M.R. was Carr's accuser, received considerable media attention. On May 20, R.M.R. left the school, and on May 29, he and his mother moved from Georgia to Alabama.

B.

Appellants filed this suit on July 17, 1994. The complaint alleged that Carr's sexual harassment interfered with R.M.R.'s school activities and was sufficiently severe and pervasive to constitute a hostile school environment in violation of Title IX. The complaint asserted that Muscogee was liable under Title IX because it knew or should have known that Carr had molested boys in the past, and therefore constituted a danger to the children entrusted to his care. (Although Carr was originally named as a defendant along with Muscogee, appellants settled their claim against Carr after the first day of trial.) Despite knowledge of Carr's proclivity to molest boys, the complaint asserted, Muscogee failed to take action to protect R.M.R.

The complaint also alleged that Carr's sexual contact violated R.M.R.'s "constitutional right to be free from intrusion into his body and the right to be free from the infliction of unnecessary pain." Because Carr engaged in this sexual contact while acting under color of state law, Muscogee was liable under 42 U.S.C. s 1983.

In defense to appellants' claims, Muscogee responded that it did not know, and could not reasonably have known, that Carr posed a danger to children. Consequently, it was not liable for Carr's misconduct.

In order to prove that Muscogee had prior knowledge of Carr's propensity to molest children, appellants decided to contact each of Carr's former students and ask whether Carr had molested them. To accomplish this goal, appellants served on Muscogee a set of discovery requests, including the following interrogatories:

2. Identify by title each document, including, but not limited to, class rolls, which lists the names of students who were enrolled in each class [taught by Carr]. State the location of each such document, each form in which it exists (i.e., paper record, computer file, etc.), and the name of its custodian.

3. Identify by title each document, including, but not limited to, student directories, containing "directory information" such as name, address, and/or phone number, which lists the names of students who were enrolled in each class [taught by Carr]. State the location of each such document, each form in which it exists (i.e., paper record, computer file, etc.), and the name of its custodian.

Appellants also served on Muscogee a request to produce all documents identified in response to these two interrogatories.

Muscogee responded to Interrogatory 2 and the corresponding request for document production by identifying and producing grade books that listed the name of each student taught by Carr. In response to Interrogatory 3 and its corresponding document request, however, Muscogee objected that the discovery request was "overly broad, burdensome, and is not reasonably calculated to lead to the discovery of admissible evidence." Subject to that objection, Muscogee identified Rolodex cards for each student taught by Carr between 1988 and 1993. Muscogee refused, however, to produce the Rolodex cards.[12] Appellants moved the district court to compel production of the cards but the court denied the motion, concluding that the discovery request was "overly broad."

---

12 Muscogee refused to produce the Rolodex cards even after R.M.R.'s counsel offered to hire a copy service to photocopy the cards, or alternatively, to pay Muscogee to make the photocopies.

The case went to trial before a jury on September 23, 1996.

On the third day of trial, after appellants had rested their case and Muscogee had presented most of its defense—four of its six witnesses (including Arrington)—appellants moved the court for leave to reopen their case in order to call a witness whom they had not listed in the pretrial order. This witness, D.L.J., had appeared at the courthouse that morning, after hearing about the case in the media. D.L.J. had been a student in Carr's class in 1984, and, according to D.L.J., had been molested by Carr approximately 50 times. D.L.J. claimed that he repeatedly told Arrington about this sexual abuse.

Muscogee opposed appellants' motion, arguing that allowing D.L.J. to testify without first giving it an opportunity to depose him and conduct whatever investigation might be required to rebut his testimony would be highly prejudicial. The district court agreed, and therefore denied appellants' motion.

After Muscogee rested its case, appellants attempted to call D.L.J. to the tand to rebut Arrington's testimony. Arrington had testified (during Muscogee's case) that he "[a]bsolutely [did] not" have prior notice that "Carr had previously engaged in any behavior similar to what R.M.R. was saying was done. ..." Muscogee objected, reiterating the argument it made in opposition to appellants' motion for leave to reopen their case. The court sustained their objection.

Appellants presented no rebuttal, and the evidence was closed. Following counsels' summations and the court's instructions, the jury returned a verdict for Muscogee.

II.

Appellants first challenge the court's denial of their motion to compel production of the student Rolodex cards. Appellants had requested that Muscogee produce student directories and other documents containing the addresses and phone numbers of Carr's former students. Although Muscogee had identified student Rolodex cards in response to this document request, the court upheld Muscogee's objection to this request as being overly broad. We review a court's refusal to compel discovery under an abuse of discretion standard. We find no such abuse here.

Appellants argue that they were required to prove that Muscogee knew or should have known that Carr posed a danger to his students in order for their claim against Muscogee to succeed. Consequently, it was vital for appellants to find other students who were molested by Carr and ask whether they had reported Carr's sexual abuse to Muscogee officials. Because student directories that listed the address and phone number of former students would have helped appellants find these potential witnesses, appellants contend that the document request for student directories was reasonably calculated to lead to admissible evidence.

Furthermore, appellants assert that they needed student directories (such as the Rolodex cards) to find Carr's former students. Although Muscogee produced grade books that included the names of Carr's students, appellants argue that they could not locate most of Carr's former students using these grade books alone. The grade books listed students by the names that they used when they attended Richards Middle School. Many of those students, however, used different names by the time the case went to trial.[13] Consequently, appellants argue, they successfully contacted only ten percent of Carr's former students based on the names listed in the grade books.

We conclude, however, that the district court did not abuse its discretion by refusing to compel production of the student Rolodex cards, because the requested discovery was overly broad. Appellants' purpose in requesting this discovery was to learn the identity of students who had complained to Muscogee that Carr sexually abused them. Although appellants requested the addresses and phone numbers of hundreds of students in order to gain this information, there was a much narrower and less burdensome manner of discovery available: appellants could have asked, by interrogatory, for the names (as well as the addresses and phone numbers) of all students who complained that Carr sexually abused them. Only if Muscogee balked at this request would appellants have been justified in requesting student directory information for all of Carr's former students.

Furthermore, we note that appellants never informed the district court that they were able to locate only ten percent of Carr's former students using the grade books. In their motion to compel discovery of the Rolodex cards, appellants argued that the Rolodex cards were discoverable because they would lead to admissible evidence, but they did not argue that the cards were necessary to find that evidence. We cannot assume that the district court would have turned a deaf ear to that argument, had appellants presented it to the court. Consequently, we affirm the district court's denial of appellants' motion to compel discovery of the student Rolodex cards.

.   .   .

---

13 For example, D.L.J. was listed by his middle name rather than his first name in the grade books.

IV.

Third, appellants claim that the district court improperly barred D.L.J. from testifying. A district court's decision to exclude a witness not listed on the pretrial order is reviewable only for abuse of discretion We have previously stated that an appellate court that is reviewing the decision to exclude a witness should consider: (1) the importance of the testimony, (2) the reason for the failure to disclose the witness earlier, and (3) the prejudice to the opposing party if the witness had been allowed to testify.

Appellants assert that the court should have allowed D.L.J. to testify because his testimony was of crucial importance. If D.L.J. was allowed to testify, he would have stated that Carr molested him approximately 50 times, and that he repeatedly told Arrington about the abuse. Consequently, D.L.J.'s testimony would have refuted Muscogee's assertion that its officials did not have prior notice of Carr's propensity to molest children. Appellants argue that the importance of D.L.J.'s testimony outweighed any prejudice that would have resulted to Muscogee because D.L.J. was not listed on the pretrial order.

Furthermore, appellants contend that D.L.J. should not have been excluded because appellants had a good excuse for failing to discover his identity before he appeared on the third day of trial: at the time of trial, D.L.J. went by a different name from that which he used as a student at Richards Middle School. Although D.L.J. used his middle name while attending Richards, at the time of the trial he instead was using his first name. Consequently, appellants failed to locate D.L.J. from the grade books produced by Muscogee.

We conclude, however, that the court did not abuse its discretion in excluding D.L.J.'s testimony. It would have been extremely prejudicial to Muscogee to allow D.L.J. to testify. If Muscogee had received notice before the trial that Jordan would testify, Muscogee could have structured its defense to counter what D.L.J. had to say. By the time D.L.J. was discovered, however, Muscogee had already presented most of its defense to the jury. Had D.L.J. been allowed to testify in the middle of Muscogee's presentation of its case, it would have disrupted the flow of Muscogee's defense, and forced Muscogee to scramble at the last minute to counter his testimony.

Appellants had several options available that would have minimized the prejudice to Muscogee. First, after appellants discovered D.L.J. they could have requested that the court grant a continuance. This option would have allowed Muscogee the opportunity to depose D.L.J., investigate D.L.J.'s story, prepare cross-examination, and find witnesses to rebut his testimony. A continuance, in short, would have provided Muscogee the opportunity to counter D.L.J.'s testimony in some meaningful way. Second, appellants could have requested a mistrial.

This option would have allowed both parties to investigate D.L.J.'s claims and reargue their case from the beginning, taking D.L.J.'s testimony into account.

Appellants, however, eschewed both of these less prejudicial alternatives. Instead, they presented the judge with a narrow choice: allow D.L.J. to testify immediately—and thus deny Muscogee the opportunity to depose him and prepare cross-examination—or exclude his testimony entirely.[14] In light of the extreme prejudice to Muscogee if D.L.J. were allowed to testify, as well as appellants' failure to move for a continuance or request a mistrial in an effort to ameliorate the prejudice to Muscogee, we conclude that the district court did not abuse its discretion in barring D.L.J.'s testimony.

V.

For the forgoing reasons, the district court's judgment is AFFIRMED.

EXPERIENTIAL ASSIGNMENTS

1. Draft a proposed Scheduling Order for the Cash, Frensch or Williams case as assigned, accounting for the major items included in Rule 16 and in the sample documents provided.

2. E-mail from your Partner:

"I need to dismiss one of the three claims stated in a Complaint I filed six weeks ago. Explain in plain English under what circumstances I may do so and how I should best go about dismissing the claim. I need to know by 5 pm tomorrow."

---

14 Because it was appellants who sought D.L.J.'s testimony, the obligation to request a continuance or a mistrial fell on appellants, not Muscogee.

CHAPTER SEVEN

Discovery Practice

THIS CHAPTER WILL COVER the mechanics, scope and compulsion of discovery. Discovery can be an expensive aspect of litigation and it produces some of the most virulent conflict and disagreement between parties and their lawyers. It was once thought that a litigator was a trial lawyer. But with the reduction in the percentage of civil actions that proceed all the way to trial, litigators are now thought of more as discovery managers and motion practice lawyers.

The major devices for formal discovery are well known: depositions, written and oral; interrogatories; requests for admission; and inspection and production of documents. There are others for specialized circumstances. Informal forms of discovery should never be ignored. Informal witness interviews, public records searches, Internet searches, visual inspections of places and things, social network information-mining, and more, all provide invaluable information to the litigator.

The threshold standard for the scope of discovery is "any nonprivileged matter that is relevant to any party's claim or defense." FRCP 26(b). The court may expand the scope to include any matter relevant to the subject matter of the action. To be discoverable, material need not be admissible as evidence as long as it is reasonably calculated to lead to admissible evidence. The scope of discovery is thus very broad.

Many pieces of information are subject to mandatory, automatic disclosure, very early in the litigation. FRCP 26(a). These mandatory disclosures are meant to streamline the discovery process by relieving parties of using other discovery devices to obtain very basic information. The disclosures come in two main phases, initial disclosures and pretrial disclosures. They include contact information on people who are likely to have relevant information about the action, calculations of plaintiff's damages, copies of documents that the disclosing party is likely to use to support her claims or defenses, and more. Much of this material would be discovered by use of interrogatories and requests for production of documents if it was not subject to the relatively new mandatory disclosure requirements.

Parties must disclose the name of experts they expect to call as a witness at trial, and those persons must produce a written report summarizing their findings. FRCP 26(a)(2).

Beyond the various mandatory disclosures, an initial conference will be held at which the court will order volume and time limits for discovery. An end date for all discovery, and limits on the number of interrogatories, depositions and requests for admission and production of documents will typically be ordered at this conference.

From here, the parties will proceed mostly without court supervision to pose interrogatories, requests for admission and production of documents, and take depositions within the terms of the court's order. The terms on which each device may be used can be found by reading the appropriate specific discovery rule. FRCP 27-36. Local court rules will also include such limitations. They may be found on court websites. No good litigator fails to search the local court rules. When disputes occur, parties may file motions for a protective order or motions to compel discovery. FRCP 26(c), FRCP 37. Sanctions may be imposed by the court against particularly belligerent or recalcitrant parties for their abuses of the discovery process. FRCP 37. The sanctions can range from repeated orders to cooperate to money sanctions to dismissal of claims or defenses.

Rule Material

Rule 26 Duty to Disclose; General Provisions Governing Discovery

(a) Required Disclosures.

(1) *Initial Disclosure.*

(A) *In General.* Except as exempted by Rule 26(a)(1)(B) or as otherwise stipulated or ordered by the court, a party must, without awaiting a discovery request, provide to the other parties:

(i) the name and, if known, the address and telephone number of each individual likely to have discoverable information—along with the subjects of that information—that the disclosing party may use to support its claims or defenses, unless the use would be solely for impeachment;

(ii) a copy—or a description by category and location—of all documents, electronically stored information, and tangible things that the disclosing party has in its possession, custody, or control and may use to support its claims or defenses, unless the use would be solely for impeachment;

(iii) a computation of each category of damages claimed by the disclosing party—who must also make available for inspection and copying as under Rule 34 the documents or other evidentiary material, unless privileged or protected from disclosure, on which each computation is based, including materials bearing on the nature and extent of injuries suffered; and

(iv) for inspection and copying as under Rule 34, any insurance agreement under which an insurance business may be liable to satisfy all or part of a possible judgment in the action or to indemnify or reimburse for payments made to satisfy the judgment.

. . .

(C) *Time for Initial Disclosures—In General.* A party must make the initial disclosures at or within 14 days after the parties' Rule 26(f) conference unless a different time is set by stipulation or court order, or unless a party objects during the conference that initial disclosures are not appropriate in this action and states the objection in the proposed discovery plan. In ruling on the objection, the court must determine what disclosures, if any, are to be made and must set the time for disclosure.

. . .

(E) *Basis for Initial Disclosure; Unacceptable Excuses.* A party must make its initial disclosures based on the information then reasonably available to it. A party is not excused from making its disclosures because it has not fully investigated the case or because it challenges the sufficiency of another party's disclosures or because another party has not made its disclosures.

(2) *Disclosure of Expert Testimony.*

(A) *In General.* In addition to the disclosures required by Rule

26(a)(1), a party must disclose to the other parties the identity of any witness it may use at trial to present evidence under Federal Rule of Evidence 702, 703, or 705.

(B) *Witnesses Who Must Provide a Written Report.* Unless otherwise stipulated or ordered by the court, this disclosure must be accompanied by a written report—prepared and signed by the witness—if the witness is one retained or specially employed to provide expert testimony in the case or one whose duties as the party's employee regularly involve giving expert testimony. The report must contain:

(i) a complete statement of all opinions the witness will express and the basis and reasons for them;

(ii) the facts or data considered by the witness in forming them;

(iii) any exhibits that will be used to summarize or support them;

(iv) the witness's qualifications, including a list of all publications authored in the previous 10 years;

(v) a list of all other cases in which, during the previous 4 years, the witness testified as an expert at trial or by deposition; and

(vi) a statement of the compensation to be paid for the study and testimony in the case.

(C) *Witnesses Who Do Not Provide a Written Report.* Unless otherwise stipulated or ordered by the court, if the witness is not required to provide a written report, this disclosure must state:

(i) the subject matter on which the witness is expected to present evidence under Federal Rule of Evidence 702, 703, or 705; and

(ii) a summary of the facts and opinions to which the witness is expected to testify.

(D) *Time to Disclose Expert Testimony.* A party must make these disclosures at the times and in the sequence that the court orders. Absent a stipulation or a court order, the disclosures must be made:

(i) at least 90 days before the date set for trial or for the case to be ready for trial; or

(ii) if the evidence is intended solely to contradict or rebut evidence on the same subject matter identified by another party under Rule 26(a)(2)(B) or (C), within 30 days after the other party's disclosure.

(E) *Supplementing the Disclosure.* The parties must supplement these disclosures when required under Rule 26(e).

(3) *Pretrial Disclosures.*

(A) *In General.* In addition to the disclosures required by Rule 26(a)(1) and (2), a party must provide to the other parties and promptly file the following information about the evidence that it may present at trial other than solely for impeachment:

(i) the name and, if not previously provided, the address and telephone number of each witness—separately identifying those the party expects to present and those it may call if the need arises;

(ii) the designation of those witnesses whose testimony the party expects to present by deposition and, if not taken stenographically, a transcript of the pertinent parts of the deposition; and

(iii) an identification of each document or other exhibit, including summaries of other evidence—separately identifying those items the party expects to offer and those it may offer if the need arises.

(B) *Time for Pretrial Disclosures; Objections.* Unless the court orders otherwise, these disclosures must be made at least 30 days before trial. Within 14 days after they are made, unless the court sets a different time, a party may serve and promptly file a list of the following objections: any objections to the use under Rule 32(a) of a deposition designated by another party under Rule 26(a)(3)(A)(ii); and any objection, together with the grounds for it, that may be made to the admissibility of materials identified under Rule 26(a)(3)(A)(iii). An objection not so made—except for one under Federal Rule of Evidence 402 or 403—is waived unless excused by the court for good cause.

(4) *Form of Disclosures.* Unless the court orders otherwise, all disclosures under Rule 26(a) must be in writing, signed, and served.

(b) Discovery Scope and Limits.

(1) *Scope in General.* Unless otherwise limited by court order, the scope of discovery is as follows: Parties may obtain discovery regarding any nonprivileged matter that is relevant to any party's claim or defense—including the existence, description, nature, custody, condition, and location of any documents or other tangible things and the identity and location of persons who know of any discoverable matter. For good cause, the court may order discovery of any matter relevant to the subject matter involved in the action. Relevant information need not be admissible at the trial if the discovery appears reasonably calculated to lead to the discovery of admissible evidence. All discovery is subject to the limitations imposed by Rule 26(b)(2)(C).

(2) *Limitations on Frequency and Extent.*

(A) *When Permitted.* By order, the court may alter the limits in these rules on the number of depositions and interrogatories or on the length of depositions under Rule 30. By order or local rule, the court may also limit the number of requests under Rule 36.

(B) *Specific Limitations on Electronically Stored Information.* A party need not provide discovery of electronically stored information from sources that the party identifies as not reasonably accessible because of undue burden or cost. On motion to compel discovery or for a protective order, the party from whom discovery is sought must show that the information is not reasonably accessible because of undue burden or cost. If that showing is made, the court may nonetheless order discovery from such sources if the requesting party shows good cause, considering the limitations of Rule 26(b)(2)(C). The court may specify conditions for the discovery.

(C) *When Required.* On motion or on its own, the court must limit the frequency or extent of discovery otherwise allowed by these rules or by local rule if it determines that:

(i) the discovery sought is unreasonably cumulative or duplicative, or can be obtained from some other source that is more convenient, less burdensome, or less expensive;

(ii) the party seeking discovery has had ample opportunity to obtain the information by discovery in the action; or

(iii) the burden or expense of the proposed discovery outweighs its likely benefit, considering the needs of the case, the amount in controversy, the parties' resources, the importance of the issues at stake in the action, and the importance of the discovery in resolving the issues.

(3) *Trial Preparation: Materials.*

(A) *Documents and Tangible Things.* Ordinarily, a party may not discover documents and tangible things that are prepared in anticipation of litigation or for trial by or for another party or its representative (including the other party's attorney, consultant, surety, indemnitor, insurer, or agent). But, subject to Rule 26(b)(4), those materials may be discovered if:

(i) they are otherwise discoverable under Rule 26(b)(1); and

(ii) the party shows that it has substantial need for the materials to prepare its case and cannot, without undue hardship, obtain their substantial equivalent by other means.

(B) *Protection Against Disclosure.* If the court orders discovery of those materials, it must protect against disclosure of the mental impressions, conclusions, opinions, or legal theories of a party's attorney or other representative concerning the litigation.

(C) *Previous Statement.* Any party or other person may, on request and without the required showing, obtain the person's own previous statement about the action or its subject matter. If the request is refused, the person may move for a court order, and Rule 37(a)(5) applies to the award of expenses. A previous statement is either:

(i) a written statement that the person has signed or otherwise adopted or approved; or

(ii) a contemporaneous stenographic, mechanical, electrical, or other recording—or a transcription of it—that recites substantially verbatim the person's oral statement.

(4) Trial Preparation: Experts.

(A) *Deposition of an Expert Who May Testify.* A party may depose any person who has been identified as an expert whose opinions may be presented at trial. If Rule 26(a)(2)(B) requires a report from the expert, the deposition may be conducted only after the report is provided.

(B) *Trial-Preparation Protection for Draft Reports or Disclosures.* Rules 26(b)(3)(A) and (B) protect drafts of any report or disclosure required under Rule 26(a)(2), regardless of the form in which the draft is recorded.

(C) *Trial-Preparation Protection for Communications Between a Party's Attorney and Expert Witnesses.* Rules 26(b)(3)(A) and (B) protect communications between the party's attorney and any witness required to provide a report under Rule 26(a)(2)(B), regardless of the form of the communications, except to the extent that the communications:

(i) relate to compensation for the expert's study or testimony;

(ii) identify facts or data that the party's attorney provided and that the expert considered in forming the opinions to be expressed; or

(iii) identify assumptions that the party's attorney provided and that the expert relied on in forming the opinions to be expressed.

(D) *Expert Employed Only for Trial Preparation.* Ordinarily, a party may not, by interrogatories or deposition, discover facts known or opinions held by an expert who has been retained or specially employed by another party in anticipation of litigation or to prepare for trial and who is not expected to be called as a witness at trial. But a party may do so only:

(i) as provided in Rule 35(b); or

(ii) on showing exceptional circumstances under which it is impracticable for the party to obtain facts or opinions on the same subject by other means.

(E) *Payment.* Unless manifest injustice would result, the court must require that the party seeking discovery:

(i) pay the expert a reasonable fee for time spent in responding to discovery under Rule 26(b)(4)(A) or (D); and

(ii) for discovery under (D), also pay the other party a fair portion of the fees and expenses it reasonably incurred in obtaining the expert's facts and opinions.

(5) *Claiming Privilege or Protecting Trial-Preparation Materials.*

(A) *Information Withheld.* When a party withholds information otherwise discoverable by claiming that the information is privileged or subject to protection as trial-preparation material, the party must:

(i) expressly make the claim; and

(ii) describe the nature of the documents, communications, or tangible things not produced or disclosed—and do so in a manner that, without revealing information itself privileged or protected, will enable other parties to assess the claim.

(B) *Information Produced.* If information produced in discovery is subject to a claim of privilege or of protection as trial-preparation material, the party making the claim may notify any party that received the information of the claim and the basis for it. After being notified, a party must promptly return, sequester, or destroy the specified information and any copies it has; must not use or disclose the information until the claim is resolved; must take reasonable steps to retrieve the information if the party disclosed it before being notified; and may promptly present the information to the court under seal for a determination of the claim. The producing party must preserve the information until the claim is resolved.

(c) Protective Orders.

(1) *In General.* A party or any person from whom discovery is sought may move for a protective order in the court where the action is pending—or as an alternative on matters relating to a deposition, in the court for the district where the deposition will be taken. The motion must include a certification that the movant has in good faith conferred or attempted to confer with other affected parties in an effort to resolve the dispute without court action. The court may, for good cause, issue an order to protect a party or person from annoyance, embarrassment, oppression, or undue burden or expense, including one or more of the following:

(A) forbidding the disclosure or discovery;

(B) specifying terms, including time and place, for the disclosure or discovery;

(C) prescribing a discovery method other than the one selected by the party seeking discovery;

(D) forbidding inquiry into certain matters, or limiting the scope of disclosure or discovery to certain matters;

(E) designating the persons who may be present while the discovery is conducted;

(F) requiring that a deposition be sealed and opened only on court order;

(G) requiring that a trade secret or other confidential research, development, or commercial information not be revealed or be revealed only in a specified way; and

(H) requiring that the parties simultaneously file specified documents or information in sealed envelopes, to be opened as the court directs.

(2) *Ordering Discovery.* If a motion for a protective order is wholly or partly denied, the court may, on just terms, order that any party or person provide or permit discovery.

(3) *Awarding Expenses.* Rule 37(a)(5) applies to the award of expenses.

(d) Timing and Sequence of Discovery.

(1) *Timing.* A party may not seek discovery from any source before the parties have conferred as required by Rule 26(f), except in a proceeding exempted from initial disclosure under Rule 26(a)(1)(B), or when authorized by these rules, by stipulation, or by court order.

(2) *Sequence.* Unless, on motion, the court orders otherwise for the parties' and witnesses' convenience and in the interests of justice:

(A) methods of discovery may be used in any sequence; and

(B) discovery by one party does not require any other party to delay its discovery.

(e) Supplementing Disclosures and Responses.

(1) *In General.* A party who has made a disclosure under Rule 26(a)— or who has responded to an interrogatory, request for production, or request for admission—must supplement or correct its disclosure or response:

(A) in a timely manner if the party learns that in some material respect the disclosure or response is incomplete or incorrect, and if the additional or corrective information has not otherwise been made known to the other parties during the discovery process or in writing; or

(B) as ordered by the court.

(2) Expert Witness. For an expert whose report must be disclosed under Rule 26(a)(2)(B), the party's duty to supplement extends both to information included in the report and to information given during the expert's deposition. Any additions or changes to this information must be disclosed by the time the party's pretrial disclosures under Rule 26(a)(3) are due.

(f) Conference of the Parties; Planning for Discovery.

(1) *Conference Timing.* Except in a proceeding exempted from initial disclosure under Rule 26(a)(1)(B) or when the court orders otherwise, the parties must confer as soon as practicable—and in any event at least 21 days before a scheduling conference is to be held or a scheduling order is due under Rule 16(b).

(2) *Conference Content; Parties' Responsibilities.* In conferring, the parties must consider the nature and basis of their claims and defenses and the possibilities for promptly settling or resolving the case; make or arrange for the disclosures required by Rule 26(a)(1); discuss any issues about preserving discoverable information; and develop a proposed discovery plan. The attorneys of record and all unrepresented parties that have appeared in the case are jointly responsible for arranging the conference, for attempting in good faith to agree on the proposed discovery plan, and for submitting to the court within 14 days after the conference a written report outlining the plan. The court may order the parties or attorneys to attend the conference in person.

(3) *Discovery Plan.* A discovery plan must state the parties' views and proposals on:

(A) what changes should be made in the timing, form, or requirement for disclosures under Rule 26(a), including a statement of when initial disclosures were made or will be made;

(B) the subjects on which discovery may be needed, when discovery should be completed, and whether discovery should be conducted in phases or be limited to or focused on particular issues;

(C) any issues about disclosure or discovery of electronically stored information, including the form or forms in which it should be produced;

(D) any issues about claims of privilege or of protection as trial-preparation materials, including—if the parties agree on a procedure to assert these claims after production—whether to ask the court to include their agreement in an order;

(E) what changes should be made in the limitations on discovery imposed under these rules or by local rule, and what other limitations should be imposed; and

(F) any other orders that the court should issue under Rule 26(c) or under Rule 16(b) and (c).

(4) *Expedited Schedule.* If necessary to comply with its expedited schedule for Rule 16(b) conferences, a court may by local rule:

(A) require the parties' conference to occur less than 21 days before the scheduling conference is held or a scheduling order is due under Rule 16(b); and

(B) require the written report outlining the discovery plan to be filed less than 14 days after the parties' conference, or excuse the parties from submitting a written report and permit them to report orally on their discovery plan at the Rule 16(b) conference.

(g) Signing Disclosures and Discovery Requests, Responses, and Objections.

(1) *Signature Required; Effect of Signature.* Every disclosure under Rule 26(a)(1) or (a)(3) and every discovery request, response, or objection must be signed by at least one attorney of record in the attorney's own name—or by the party personally, if unrepresented—and must state the signer's address, e-mail address, and telephone number. By signing, an attorney or party certifies that to the best of the person's knowledge, information, and belief formed after a reasonable inquiry:

(A) with respect to a disclosure, it is complete and correct as of the time it is made; and

(B) with respect to a discovery request, response, or objection, it is:

(i) consistent with these rules and warranted by existing law or by a nonfrivolous argument for extending, modifying, or reversing existing law, or for establishing new law;

(ii) not interposed for any improper purpose, such as to harass, cause unnecessary delay, or needlessly increase the cost of litigation; and

(iii) neither unreasonable nor unduly burdensome or expensive, considering the needs of the case, prior discovery in the case, the amount in controversy, and the importance of the issues at stake in the action.

(2) *Failure to Sign.* Other parties have no duty to act on an unsigned disclosure, request, response, or objection until it is signed, and the court must strike it unless a signature is promptly supplied after the omission is called to the attorney's or party's attention.

(3) *Sanction for Improper Certification.* If a certification violates this rule without substantial justification, the court, on motion or on its own, must impose an appropriate sanction on the signer, the party on whose behalf the signer was acting, or both. The sanction may include an order to pay the reasonable expenses, including attorney's fees, caused by the violation.

Rule 27 Depositions to Perpetuate Testimony

(a) Before an Action Is Filed.

(1) *Petition.* A person who wants to perpetuate testimony about any matter cognizable in a United States court may file a verified petition in the district court for the district where any expected adverse party resides. The petition must ask for an order authorizing the petitioner to depose the named persons in order to perpetuate their testimony. The petition must be titled in the petitioner's name and must show:

(A) that the petitioner expects to be a party to an action cognizable in a United States court but cannot presently bring it or cause it to be brought;

(B) the subject matter of the expected action and the petitioner's interest;

(C) the facts that the petitioner wants to establish by the proposed testimony and the reasons to perpetuate it;

(D) the names or a description of the persons whom the petitioner expects to be adverse parties and their addresses, so far as known; and

(E) the name, address, and expected substance of the testimony of each deponent.

. . .

Rule 28 Persons Before Whom Depositions May Be Taken

(a) Within the United States.

(1) *In General.* Within the United States or a territory or insular possession subject to United States jurisdiction, a deposition must be taken before:

(A) an officer authorized to administer oaths either by federal law or by the law in the place of examination; or

(B) a person appointed by the court where the action is pending to administer oaths and take testimony.

. . .

Rule 29 Stipulations About Discovery Procedures

Unless the court orders otherwise, the parties may stipulate that:

(a) a deposition may be taken before any person, at any time or place, on any notice, and in the manner specified—in which event it may be used in the same way as any other deposition; and

(b) other procedures governing or limiting discovery be modified—but a stipulation extending the time for any form of discovery must have court approval if it would interfere with the time set for completing discovery, for hearing a motion, or for trial.

Rule 30 Depositions by Oral Examination

(a) When a Deposition May Be Taken.

(1) *Without Leave.* A party may, by oral questions, depose any person, including a party, without leave of court except as provided in Rule 30(a)(2). The deponent's attendance may be compelled by subpoena under Rule 45.

(2) *With Leave.* A party must obtain leave of court, and the court must grant leave to the extent consistent with Rule 26(b)(2):

(A) if the parties have not stipulated to the deposition and:

(i) the deposition would result in more than 10 depositions being taken under this rule or Rule 31 by the plaintiffs, or by the defendants, or by the third-party defendants;

(ii) the deponent has already been deposed in the case; or

(iii) the party seeks to take the deposition before the time specified in Rule 26(d), unless the party certifies in the notice, with supporting facts, that the deponent is expected to leave the United States and be unavailable for examination in this country after that time; or

(B) if the deponent is confined in prison.

(b) Notice of the Deposition; Other Formal Requirements.

(1) *Notice in General.* A party who wants to depose a person by oral questions must give reasonable written notice to every other party. The notice must state the time and place of the deposition and, if known, the deponent's name and address. If the name is unknown, the notice must provide a general description sufficient to identify the person or the particular class or group to which the person belongs.

(2) *Producing Documents.* If a subpoena duces tecum is to be served on the deponent, the materials designated for production, as set out in the subpoena, must be listed in the notice or in an attachment. The notice to a party deponent may be accompanied by a request under Rule 34 to produce documents and tangible things at the deposition.

. . .

(6) *Notice or Subpoena Directed to an Organization.* In its notice or subpoena, a party may name as the deponent a public or private corporation, a partnership, an association, a governmental agency, or other entity and must describe with reasonable particularity the matters for examination. The named organization must then designate one or more officers, directors, or managing agents, or designate other persons who consent to testify on its behalf; and it may set out the matters on which each person designated will testify. A subpoena must advise a nonparty organization of its duty to make this designation. The persons designated must testify about information known or

reasonably available to the organization. This paragraph (6) does not preclude a deposition by any other procedure allowed by these rules.

(c) Examination and Cross-Examination; Record of the Examination; Objections; Written Questions.

(1) *Examination and Cross-Examination.* The examination and cross-examination of a deponent proceed as they would at trial under the Federal Rules of Evidence, except Rules 103 and 615. After putting the deponent under oath or affirmation, the officer must record the testimony by the method designated under Rule 30(b)(3)(A). The testimony must be recorded by the officer personally or by a person acting in the presence and under the direction of the officer.

(2) *Objections.* An objection at the time of the examination—whether to evidence, to a party's conduct, to the officer's qualifications, to the manner of taking the deposition, or to any other aspect of the deposition—must be noted on the record, but the examination still proceeds; the testimony is taken subject to any objection. An objection must be stated concisely in a nonargumentative and nonsuggestive manner. A person may instruct a deponent not to answer only when necessary to preserve a privilege, to enforce a limitation ordered by the court, or to present a motion under Rule 30(d)(3).

(3) *Participating Through Written Questions.* Instead of participating in the oral examination, a party may serve written questions in a sealed envelope on the party noticing the deposition, who must deliver them to the officer. The officer must ask the deponent those questions and record the answers verbatim.

(d) Duration; Sanction; Motion to Terminate or Limit.

(1) *Duration.* Unless otherwise stipulated or ordered by the court, a deposition is limited to 1 day of 7 hours. The court must allow additional time consistent with Rule 26(b)(2) if needed to fairly examine the deponent or if the deponent, another person, or any other circumstance impedes or delays the examination.

(2) *Sanction.* The court may impose an appropriate sanction—including the reasonable expenses and attorney's fees incurred by any party—on a person who impedes, delays, or frustrates the fair examination of the deponent.

(3) *Motion to Terminate or Limit.*

(A) *Grounds.* At any time during a deposition, the deponent or a party may move to terminate or limit it on the ground that it is being conducted in bad faith or in a manner that unreasonably annoys, embarrasses, or oppresses the deponent or party. The motion may be filed in the court where the action is pending or the deposition is being taken. If the objecting deponent or party so demands, the deposition must be suspended for the time necessary to obtain an order.

(B) *Order.* The court may order that the deposition be terminated or may limit its scope and manner as provided in Rule 26(c). If terminated, the deposition may be resumed only by order of the court where the action is pending.

(C) *Award of Expenses.* Rule 37(a)(5) applies to the award of expenses.

(e) Review by the Witness; Changes.

(1) *Review; Statement of Changes.* On request by the deponent or a party before the deposition is completed, the deponent must be allowed 30 days after being notified by the officer that the transcript or recording is available in which:

(A) to review the transcript or recording; and

(B) if there are changes in form or substance, to sign a statement listing the changes and the reasons for making them.

. . .

(g) Failure to Attend a Deposition or Serve a Subpoena; Expenses. A party who, expecting a deposition to be taken, attends in person or by an attorney may recover reasonable expenses for attending, including attorney's fees, if the noticing party failed to:

(1) attend and proceed with the deposition; or

(2) serve a subpoena on a nonparty deponent, who consequently did not attend.

Rule 31 Depositions by Written Questions

(a) When a Deposition May Be Taken.

(1) *Without Leave.* A party may, by written questions, depose any person, including a party, without leave of court except as provided in Rule 31(a)(2). The deponent's attendance may be compelled by subpoena under Rule 45.

(2) *With Leave.* A party must obtain leave of court, and the court must grant leave to the extent consistent with Rule 26(b)(2):

(A) if the parties have not stipulated to the deposition and:

(i) the deposition would result in more than 10 depositions being taken under this rule or Rule 30 by the plaintiffs, or by the defendants, or by the third-party defendants;

(ii) the deponent has already been deposed in the case; or

(iii) the party seeks to take a deposition before the time specified in Rule 26(d); or

(B) if the deponent is confined in prison.

(3) *Service; Required Notice.* A party who wants to depose a person by written questions must serve them on every other party, with a notice stating, if known, the deponent's name and address. If the name is unknown, the notice must provide a general description sufficient to identify the person or the particular class or group to which the person belongs. The notice must also state the name or descriptive title and the address of the officer before whom the deposition will be taken.

(4) *Questions Directed to an Organization.* A public or private corporation, a partnership, an association, or a governmental agency may be deposed by written questions in accordance with Rule 30(b)(6).

(5) *Questions from Other Parties.* Any questions to the deponent from other parties must be served on all parties as follows: cross-questions, within 14 days after being served with the notice and direct questions; redirect questions, within 7 days after being served with cross-questions; and recross-questions, within 7 days after being served with redirect questions. The court may, for good cause, extend or shorten these times.

. . .

Rule 33 Interrogatories to Parties

(a) In General.

(1) *Number.* Unless otherwise stipulated or ordered by the court, a party may serve on any other party no more than 25 written interrogatories, including all discrete subparts. Leave to serve additional interrogatories may be granted to the extent consistent with Rule 26(b)(2).

(2) *Scope.* An interrogatory may relate to any matter that may be inquired into under Rule 26(b). An interrogatory is not objectionable merely because it asks for an opinion or contention that relates to fact or the application of law to fact, but the court may order that the interrogatory need not be answered until designated discovery is complete, or until a pretrial conference or some other time.

(b) Answers and Objections.

(1) *Responding Party.* The interrogatories must be answered:

(A) by the party to whom they are directed; or

(B) if that party is a public or private corporation, a partnership, an association, or a governmental agency, by any officer or agent, who must furnish the information available to the party.

(2) *Time to Respond.* The responding party must serve its answers and any objections within 30 days after being served with the interrogatories. A shorter or longer time may be stipulated to under Rule 29 or be ordered by the court.

(3) *Answering Each Interrogatory.* Each interrogatory must, to the extent it is not objected to, be answered separately and fully in writing under oath.

(4) *Objections.* The grounds for objecting to an interrogatory must be stated with specificity. Any ground not stated in a timely objection is waived unless the court, for good cause, excuses the failure.

(5) *Signature.* The person who makes the answers must sign them, and the attorney who objects must sign any objections.

(c) Use. An answer to an interrogatory may be used to the extent allowed by the Federal Rules of Evidence.

(d) Option to Produce Business Records. If the answer to an interrogatory may be determined by examining, auditing, compiling, abstracting, or summarizing a party's business records (including electronically stored information), and if the burden of deriving or ascertaining the answer will be substantially the same for either party, the responding party may answer by:

(1) specifying the records that must be reviewed, in sufficient detail to enable the interrogating party to locate and identify them as readily as the responding party could; and

(2) giving the interrogating party a reasonable opportunity to examine and audit the records and to make copies, compilations, abstracts, or summaries.

Rule 34 Producing Documents, Electronically Stored Information, and Tangible Things, or Entering onto Land, for Inspection and Other Purposes

(a) In General. A party may serve on any other party a request within the scope of Rule 26(b):

(1) to produce and permit the requesting party or its representative to inspect, copy, test, or sample the following items in the responding party's possession, custody, or control:

(A) any designated documents or electronically stored information—including writings, drawings, graphs, charts, photographs, sound recordings, images, and other data or data compilations—stored in any medium from which information can be obtained either directly or, if necessary, after translation by the responding party into a reasonably usable form; or

(B) any designated tangible things; or

(2) to permit entry onto designated land or other property possessed or controlled by the responding party, so that the requesting party may inspect, measure, survey, photograph, test, or sample the property or any designated object or operation on it.

(b) Procedure.

(1) *Contents of the Request.* The request:

(A) must describe with reasonable particularity each item or category of items to be inspected;

(B) must specify a reasonable time, place, and manner for the inspection and for performing the related acts; and

(C) may specify the form or forms in which electronically stored information is to be produced.

(2) Responses and Objections.

(A) *Time to Respond.* The party to whom the request is directed must respond in writing within 30 days after being served. A shorter or longer time may be stipulated to under Rule 29 or be ordered by the court.

(B) *Responding to Each Item.* For each item or category, the response must either state that inspection and related activities will be permitted as requested or state an objection to the request, including the reasons.

(C) *Objections.* An objection to part of a request must specify the part and permit inspection of the rest.

(D) *Responding to a Request for Production of Electronically Stored Information.* The response may state an objection to a requested form for producing electronically stored information. If the responding party objects to a requested form—or if no form was specified in the request—the party must state the form or forms it intends to use.

(E) *Producing the Documents or Electronically Stored Information.* Unless otherwise stipulated or ordered by the court, these procedures apply to producing documents or electronically stored information:

(i) A party must produce documents as they are kept in the usual course of business or must organize and label them to correspond to the categories in the request;

(ii) If a request does not specify a form for producing electronically stored information, a party must produce it in a form or forms in which it is ordinarily maintained or in a reasonably usable form or forms; and

(iii) A party need not produce the same electronically stored information in more than one form.

(c) Nonparties. As provided in Rule 45, a nonparty may be compelled to produce documents and tangible things or to permit an inspection.

Rule 35 Physical and Mental Examinations

(a) Order for an Examination.

(1) *In General.* The court where the action is pending may order a party whose mental or physical condition—including blood group—is in controversy to submit to a physical or mental examination by a suitably licensed or certified examiner. The court has the same authority to order a party to produce for examination a person who is in its custody or under its legal control.

(2) Motion and Notice; Contents of the Order. The order:

(A) may be made only on motion for good cause and on notice to all parties and the person to be examined; and

(B) must specify the time, place, manner, conditions, and scope of the examination, as well as the person or persons who will perform it.

(b) Examiner's Report.

(1) *Request by the Party or Person Examined.* The party who moved for the examination must, on request, deliver to the requester a copy of the examiner's report, together with like reports of all earlier examinations of the same condition. The request may be made by the party against whom the examination order was issued or by the person examined.

(2) *Contents.* The examiner's report must be in writing and must set out in detail the examiner's findings, including diagnoses, conclusions, and the results of any tests.

(3) *Request by the Moving Party.* After delivering the reports, the party who moved for the examination may request—and is entitled to receive—from the party against whom the examination order was issued like reports of all earlier or later examinations of the same condition. But those reports need not be delivered by the party with custody or control of the person examined if the party shows that it could not obtain them.

(4) *Waiver of Privilege.* By requesting and obtaining the examiner's report, or by deposing the examiner, the party examined waives any privilege it may have—in that action or any other action involving the same controversy—concerning testimony about all examinations of the same condition.

(5) *Failure to Deliver a Report.* The court on motion may order—on just terms—that a party deliver the report of an examination. If the report is not provided, the court may exclude the examiner's testimony at trial.

(6) *Scope.* This subdivision (b) applies also to an examination made by the parties' agreement, unless the agreement states otherwise. This subdivision does not preclude obtaining an examiner's report or deposing an examiner under other rules.

Rule 36 Requests for Admission

(a) Scope and Procedure.

(1) *Scope.* A party may serve on any other party a written request to admit, for purposes of the pending action only, the truth of any matters within the scope of Rule 26(b)(1) relating to:

(A) facts, the application of law to fact, or opinions about either; and

(B) the genuineness of any described documents.

(2) *Form; Copy of a Document.* Each matter must be separately stated. A request to admit the genuineness of a document must be accompanied by a copy of the document unless it is, or has been, otherwise furnished or made available for inspection and copying.

(3) *Time to Respond; Effect of Not Responding.* A matter is admitted unless, within 30 days after being served, the party to whom the request is directed serves on the requesting party a written answer or objection addressed to the matter and signed by the party or its attorney. A shorter or longer time for responding may be stipulated to under Rule 29 or be ordered by the court.

(4) *Answer.* If a matter is not admitted, the answer must specifically deny it or state in detail why the answering party cannot truthfully admit or deny it. A denial must fairly respond to the substance of the matter; and when good faith requires that a party qualify an answer or deny only a part of a matter, the answer must specify the part admitted and qualify or deny the rest. The answering party may assert lack of knowledge or information as a reason for failing to admit or deny only if the party states that it has made reasonable inquiry and that the information it knows or can readily obtain is insufficient to enable it to admit or deny.

(5) *Objections.* The grounds for objecting to a request must be stated. A party must not object solely on the ground that the request presents a genuine issue for trial.

(6) *Motion Regarding the Sufficiency of an Answer or Objection.* The requesting party may move to determine the sufficiency of an answer or objection. Unless the court finds an objection justified, it must order that an answer be served. On finding that an answer does not comply with this rule, the court may order either that the matter is admitted or that an amended answer be served. The court may defer its final decision until a pretrial conference or a specified time before trial. Rule 37(a)(5) applies to an award of expenses.

(b) Effect of an Admission; Withdrawing or Amending It. A matter admitted under this rule is conclusively established unless the court, on motion, permits the admission to be withdrawn or amended. Subject to Rule 16(e), the court may permit withdrawal or amendment if it would promote the presentation of the merits of the action and if the court is not persuaded that it would prejudice the requesting party in maintaining or defending the action on the merits. An admission under this rule is not an admission for any other purpose and cannot be used against the party in any other proceeding.

A. Mechanics

Analyze the mechanics of the discovery rules by completing this chart. Every discovery device has its place. Each one is more useful than the others for some particular purpose. Completion of this chart will help you understand the advantages and disadvantages of each device.

Figure 7-1 Discovery Rules Organization Chart

	Oral Deposition	Written Deposition	Interrogatories	Request for Production	Physical/ Mental Exam	Request for Admission
Which Federal Rule(s) create this device?						
From whom may information be sought when using this device?						
In what form is the information obtained?						
Are there limits on number or frequency of requests?						
Is prior court approval required?						
What strategic advantages or weaknesses for this device?						
Who pays the cost of providing information?						

B. Scope of Discovery

Take a close look at FRCP 26(b)(1) and (5), as well as 26(c).

The basic limitation on the subject matter scope of discovery is "relevance." Notice that relevance is not the same as admissibility at trial under the evidence rules. What is the difference between information that is relevant to claims or defenses and information that is relevant to the subject matter of the action?

Beyond the basic limitation on subject matter scope, 26(b)(1) exempts privileged material from disclosure and (b)(3) and (b)(5) explain the protection for attorney work product. The Upjohn case explains the privilege and work product doctrine generally and applies those concepts in the corporate setting.

Even discovery of nonprivileged material that is within the subject matter scope of discovery may sometimes be prohibited if the discovery amounts to "annoyance, embarrassment, oppression, or undue burden or expense. . . ." FRCP 26(c). Do not take too much from this limitation. Much of discovery annoys, embarrasses and burdens the party whose information is sought. Only extreme forms of these attributes will produce the protective order under 26(c).

Upjohn Company et al. v. United States et al.

449 U.S. 383, 101 S.Ct. 677 (1981)

Justice REHNQUIST delivered the opinion of the Court.

We granted certiorari in this case to address important questions concerning the scope of the attorney-client privilege in the corporate context and the applicability of the work-product doctrine in proceedings to enforce tax summonses. With respect to the privilege question the parties and various amici have described our task as one of choosing between two "tests" which have gained adherents in the courts of appeals. We are acutely aware, however, that we sit to decide concrete cases and not abstract propositions of law. We decline to lay down a broad rule or series of rules to govern all conceivable future questions in this area, even were we able to do so. We can and do, however, conclude that the attorney-client privilege protects the communications involved in this case from compelled disclosure and that the work-product doctrine does apply in tax summons enforcement proceedings.

I

Petitioner Upjohn Co. manufactures and sells pharmaceuticals here and abroad. In January 1976 independent accountants conducting an audit of one of Upjohn's foreign subsidiaries discovered that the subsidiary made payments to or for the benefit of foreign government officials in order to secure government business. The accountants, so informed petitioner, Mr. Gerard Thomas, Upjohn's Vice President, Secretary, and General Counsel. Thomas is a member of the Michigan and New York Bars, and has been Upjohn's General Counsel for 20 years. He consulted with outside counsel and R. T. Parfet, Jr., Upjohn's Chairman of the Board. It was decided that the company would conduct an internal investigation of what were termed "questionable payments." As part of this investigation the attorneys prepared a letter containing a questionnaire which was sent to "All Foreign General and Area Managers" over the Chairman's signature. The letter began by noting recent disclosures that several American companies made "possibly illegal" payments to foreign government officials and emphasized that the management needed full information concerning any such payments made by Upjohn. The letter indicated that the Chairman had asked Thomas, identified as "the company's General Counsel," "to conduct an investigation." The questionnaire sought detailed information concerning such payments. Managers were instructed to treat the investigation as "highly confidential" and not to discuss it with anyone other than Upjohn employees who might be helpful in providing the requested information. Responses were to be sent directly to Thomas. Thomas and outside counsel also interviewed the recipients of the questionnaire and some 33 other Upjohn officers or employees as part of the investigation.

On March 26, 1976, the company voluntarily submitted a preliminary report to the Securities and Exchange Commission on Form 8-K disclosing certain questionable payments. A copy of the report was simultaneously submitted to the Internal Revenue Service, which immediately began an investigation to determine the tax consequences of the payments. Special agents conducting the investigation were given lists by Upjohn of all those interviewed and all who had responded to the questionnaire. On November 23, 1976, the Service issued a summons pursuant to 26 U.S.C. § 7602 demanding production of:

"All files relative to the investigation conducted under the supervision of Gerard Thomas to identify payments to employees of foreign governments and any political contributions made by the Upjohn Company or any of its affiliates since January 1, 1971 and to determine whether any funds of the Upjohn Company had been improperly accounted for on the corporate books during the same period.

"The records should include but not be limited to written questionnaires sent to managers of the Upjohn Company's foreign affiliates, and memorandums or notes of the interviews conducted in the United States and abroad with officers and employees of the Upjohn Company and its subsidiaries."

The company declined to produce the documents specified in the second paragraph on the grounds that they were protected from disclosure by the attorney-client privilege and constituted the work product of attorneys prepared in anticipation of litigation. On August 31, 1977, the United States filed a petition seeking enforcement of the summons in the United States District Court for the Western District of Michigan. That court adopted the recommendation of a Magistrate who concluded that the summons should be enforced. Petitioners appealed to the Court of Appeals for the Sixth Circuit which rejected the Magistrate's finding of a waiver of the attorney-client privilege, but agreed that the privilege did not apply "[t]o the extent that the communications were made by officers and agents not responsible for directing Upjohn's actions in response to legal advice . . . for the simple reason that the communications were not the 'client's.' " The court reasoned that accepting petitioners' claim for a broader application of the privilege would encourage upper-echelon management to ignore unpleasant facts and create too broad a "zone of silence." Noting that Upjohn's counsel had interviewed officials such as the Chairman and President, the Court of Appeals remanded to the District Court so that a determination of who was within the "control group" could be made.

II

Federal Rule of Evidence 501 provides that "the privilege of a witness . . . shall be governed by the principles of the common law as they may be interpreted by the courts of the United States in light of reason and experience." The attorney-client privilege is the oldest of the privileges for confidential communications known to the common law. 8 J. Wigmore, Evidence § 2290 (McNaughton rev. 1961). Its purpose is to encourage full and frank communication between attorneys and their clients and thereby promote broader public interests in the observance of law and administration of justice. The privilege recognizes that sound legal advice or advocacy serves public ends and that such advice or advocacy depends upon the lawyer's being fully informed by the client. As we stated last Term in *Trammel v. United States*, 445 U.S. 40, 51, 100 S.Ct. 906, 913 (1980): "The lawyer-client privilege rests on the need for the advocate and counselor to know all that relates to the client's reasons for seeking representation if the professional mission is to be carried out." And in *Fisher v. United States*, 425 U.S. 391, 403, 96 S.Ct. 1569, 1577 (1976), we recognized the purpose of the privilege to be "to encourage clients to make full disclosure to their attorneys."

The Court of Appeals, however, considered the application of the privilege in the corporate context to present a "different problem," since the client was an inanimate entity and "only the senior management, guiding and integrating the several operations, ... can be said to possess an identity analogous to the corporation as a whole."

Such a view, we think, overlooks the fact that the privilege exists to protect not only the giving of professional advice to those who can act on it but also the giving of information to the lawyer to enable him to give sound and informed advice. The first step in the resolution of any legal problem is ascertaining the factual background and sifting through the facts with an eye to the legally relevant. See ABA Code of Professional Responsibility, Ethical Consideration 4-1:

"A lawyer should be fully informed of all the facts of the matter he is handling in order for his client to obtain the full advantage of our legal system. It is for the lawyer in the exercise of his independent professional judgment to separate the relevant and important from the irrelevant and unimportant. The observance of the ethical obligation of a lawyer to hold inviolate the confidences and secrets of his client not only facilitates the full development of facts essential to proper representation of the client but also encourages laymen to seek early legal assistance." See also *Hickman v. Taylor,* 329 U.S. 495, 511, 67 S.Ct. 385, 393-394 (1947).

In the case of the individual client the provider of information and the person who acts on the lawyer's advice are one and the same. In the corporate context, however, it will frequently be employees beyond the control group as defined by the court below—"officers and agents ... responsible for directing [the company's] actions in response to legal advice"—who will possess the information needed by the corporation's lawyers. Middle-level—and indeed lower-level—employees can, by actions within the scope of their employment, embroil the corporation in serious legal difficulties, and it is only natural that these employees would have the relevant information needed by corporate counsel if he is adequately to advise the client with respect to such actual or potential difficulties.

The control group test adopted by the court below thus frustrates the very purpose of the privilege by discouraging the communication of relevant information by employees of the client to attorneys seeking to render legal advice to the client corporation. The attorney's advice will also frequently be more significant to noncontrol group members than to those who officially sanction the advice, and the control group test makes it more difficult to convey full and frank legal advice to the employees who will put into effect the client corporation's policy.

The narrow scope given the attorney-client privilege by the court below not only makes it difficult for corporate attorneys to formulate sound advice when their client is faced with a specific legal problem but also threatens to limit the valuable efforts of corporate counsel to ensure their client's compliance with the law. In light of the vast and complicated array of regulatory legislation confronting the modern corporation, corporations, unlike most individuals, "constantly go to lawyers to find out how to obey the law," Burnham, The Attorney-Client Privilege in the Corporate Arena, 24 Bus.Law. 901, 913 (1969), particularly since compliance with the law in this area is hardly an instinctive matter, see, e. g., *United States v. United States Gypsum Co.,* 438 U.S. 422, 440-441, 98 S.Ct. 2864, 2875-2876 (1978) ("the behavior proscribed by the [Sherman] Act is often difficult to distinguish from the gray zone of socially acceptable and economically justifiable business conduct").[1] The test adopted by the court below is difficult to apply in practice, though no abstractly formulated and unvarying "test" will necessarily enable courts to decide questions such as this with mathematical precision. But if the purpose of the attorney-client privilege is to be served, the attorney and client must be able to predict with some degree of certainty whether particular discussions will be protected. An uncertain privilege, or one which purports to be certain but results in widely varying applications by the courts, is little better than no privilege at all. The very terms of the test adopted by the court below suggest the unpredictability of its application. The test restricts the availability of the privilege to those officers who play a "substantial role" in deciding and directing a corporation's legal response.

The communications at issue were made by Upjohn employees[2] to counsel for Upjohn acting as such, at the direction of corporate superiors in order to secure legal advice from counsel. As the Magistrate found, "Mr. Thomas consulted with the Chairman of the Board and outside counsel and thereafter conducted a factual investigation to determine the nature and extent of the questionable payments and to be in a position to give legal advice to the company with respect to the payments." (Emphasis supplied.). Information, not available

---

1 The Government argues that the risk of civil or criminal liability suffices to ensure that corporations will seek legal advice in the absence of the protection of the privilege. This response ignores the fact that the depth and quality of any investigations, to ensure compliance with the law would suffer, even were they undertaken. The response also proves too much, since it applies to all communications covered by the privilege: an individual trying to comply with the law or faced with a legal problem also has strong incentive to disclose information to his lawyer, yet the common law has recognized the value of the privilege in further facilitating communications.

2 Seven of the eighty-six employees interviewed by counsel had terminated their employment with Upjohn at the time of the interview. App. 33a-38a. Petitioners argue that the privilege should nonetheless apply to communications by these former employees concerning activities during their period of employment. Neither the District Court nor the Court of Appeals had occasion to address this issue, and we decline to decide it without the benefit of treatment below.

from upper-echelon management, was needed to supply a basis for legal advice concerning compliance with securities and tax laws, foreign laws, currency regulations, duties to shareholders, and potential litigation in each of these areas. The communications concerned matters within the scope of the employees' corporate duties, and the employees themselves were sufficiently aware that they were being questioned in order that the corporation could obtain legal advice. The questionnaire identified Thomas as "the company's General Counsel" and referred in its opening sentence to the possible illegality of payments such as the ones on which information was sought. A statement of policy accompanying the questionnaire clearly indicated the legal implications of the investigation. The policy statement was issued "in order that there be no uncertainty in the future as to the policy with respect to the practices which are the subject of this investigation." It began "Upjohn will comply with all laws and regulations," and stated that commissions or payments "will not be used as a subterfuge for bribes or illegal payments" and that all payments must be "proper and legal." Any future agreements with foreign distributors or agents were to be approved "by a company attorney" and any questions concerning the policy were to be referred "to the company's General Counsel." This statement was issued to Upjohn employees worldwide, so that even those interviewees not receiving a questionnaire were aware of the legal implications of the interviews. Pursuant to explicit instructions from the Chairman of the Board, the communications were considered "highly confidential" when made, and have been kept confidential by the company.[3] Consistent with the underlying purposes of the attorney-client privilege, these communications must be protected against compelled disclosure.

The Court of Appeals declined to extend the attorney-client privilege beyond the limits of the control group test for fear that doing so would entail severe burdens on discovery and create a broad "zone of silence" over corporate affairs. Application of the attorney-client privilege to communications such as those involved here, however, puts the adversary in no worse position than if the communications had never taken place. The privilege only protects disclosure of communications; it does not protect disclosure of the underlying facts by those who communicated with the attorney:

"[T]he protection of the privilege extends only to communications and not to facts. A fact is one thing and a communication concerning that fact is an entirely different thing. The client cannot be compelled to answer the question, 'What did you say or write to the attorney?' but may not refuse to disclose any rel-

---

3 See Magistrate's opinion: "The responses to the questionnaires and the notes of the interviews have been treated as confidential material and have not been disclosed to anyone except Mr. Thomas and outside counsel."

evant fact within his knowledge merely because he incorporated a statement of such fact into his communication to his attorney." *Philadelphia v. Westinghouse Electric Corp.*, 205 F.Supp. 830, 831.

Here the Government was free to question the employees who communicated with Thomas and outside counsel. Upjohn has provided the IRS with a list of such employees, and the IRS has already interviewed some 25 of them. While it would probably be more convenient for the Government to secure the results of petitioner's internal investigation by simply subpoenaing the questionnaires and notes taken by petitioner's attorneys, such considerations of convenience do not overcome the policies served by the attorney-client privilege.

Needless to say, we decide only the case before us, and do not undertake to draft a set of rules which should govern challenges to investigatory subpoenas. Any such approach would violate the spirit of Federal Rule of Evidence 501. While such a "case-by-case" basis may to some slight extent undermine desirable certainty in the boundaries of the attorney-client privilege, it obeys the spirit of the Rules. At the same time we conclude that the narrow "control group test" sanctioned by the Court of Appeals, in this case cannot, consistent with "the principles of the common law as ... interpreted ... in the light of reason and experience," Fed. Rule Evid. 501, govern the development of the law in this area.

III

Our decision that the communications by Upjohn employees to counsel are covered by the attorney-client privilege disposes of the case so far as the responses to the questionnaires and any notes reflecting responses to interview questions are concerned. The summons reaches further, however, and Thomas has testified that his notes and memoranda of interviews go beyond recording responses to his questions. To the extent that the material subject to the summons is not protected by the attorney-client privilege as disclosing communications between an employee and counsel, we must reach the ruling by the Court of Appeals [regarding] the work-product doctrine.

The "strong public policy" underlying the work-product doctrine was reaffirmed recently in *United States v. Nobles*, 422 U.S. 225, 236-240, 95 S.Ct. 2160, 2169-2171 (1975), and has been substantially incorporated in Federal Rule of Civil Procedure 26(b)(3).

The Government stresses that interviewees are scattered across the globe and that Upjohn has forbidden its employees to answer questions it considers irrelevant. Forcing an attorney to disclose notes and memoranda of witnesses' oral statements is particularly disfavored because it tends to reveal the attorney's mental processes, 329 U. S., at 513, 67 S.Ct., at 394-395 ("what he saw fit to write down regarding witnesses' remarks"); id, at 516-517, 67 S.Ct., at 396 ("the statement would be his [the attorney's] language, permeated with his inferences") (Jackson, J., concurring).[4]

Rule 26 accords special protection to work product revealing the attorney's mental processes. The Rule permits disclosure of documents and tangible things constituting attorney work product upon a showing of substantial need and inability to obtain the equivalent without undue hardship. Rule 26 goes on, however, to state that "[i]n ordering discovery of such materials when the required showing has been made, the court shall protect against disclosure of the mental impressions, conclusions, opinions or legal theories of an attorney or other representative of a party concerning the litigation." Although this language does not specifically refer to memoranda based on oral statements of witnesses, the Hickman court stressed the danger that compelled disclosure of such memoranda would reveal the attorney's mental processes. It is clear that this is the sort of material the draftsmen of the Rule had in mind as deserving special protection.

Based on the foregoing, some courts have concluded that no showing of necessity can overcome protection of work product which is based on oral statements from witnesses. Those courts declining to adopt an absolute rule have nonetheless recognized that such material is entitled to special protection.

We do not decide the issue at this time. It is clear that the Magistrate applied the wrong standard when he concluded that the Government had made a sufficient showing of necessity to overcome the protections of the work-product doctrine. The Magistrate applied the "substantial need" and "without undue hardship" standard articulated in the first part of Rule 26(b)(3). The notes and memoranda sought by the Government here, however, are work product based on oral statements. If they reveal communications, they are, in this case, protected by the attorney-client privilege. To the extent they do not reveal communications, they reveal the attorneys' mental processes in evaluating the communications. As Rule 26 and Hickman make clear, such work product cannot be disclosed simply on a showing of substantial need and inability to obtain the equivalent without undue hardship.

While we are not prepared at this juncture to say that such material is always protected by the work-product rule, we think a far stronger showing of necessity

---

4 Thomas described his notes of the interviews as containing "what I considered to be the important questions, the substance of the responses to them, my beliefs as to the importance of these, my beliefs as to how they related to the inquiry, my thoughts as to how they related to other questions. In some instances they might even suggest other questions that I would have to ask or things that I needed to find elsewhere."

and unavailability by other means than was made by the Government or applied by the Magistrate in this case would be necessary to compel disclosure.

Accordingly, the judgment of the Court of Appeals is reversed, and the case remanded for further proceedings.

It is so ordered.

[The opinion of Chief Justice BURGER, concurring in part and concurring in the judgment is omitted.]

Preparing a deposition index

A very common assignment for a beginning lawyer is preparation of a deposition index, an absolute necessity for use in trial or complex negotiations. Depositions in even a moderately complex matter can consume a thousand pages, and none of the information in them is valuable unless a lawyer can quickly and easily access the information.

In general, an index begins with a three column description of the content of the deposition, something like this:

Deposition of Mary Bernard

pp.	Topic	Summary
3-4	Initial meetings with Nick P.	M.B. first met N.P. at a diner in Girard OH. N.P. was a truck driver and M.B. a waitress. First topic of conversation: weather.
6	Suggestion of collaboration	N.P. suggests that when he leaves town, he needs help with his number-running racket. M.B. agrees to assist.
9	M.B. background	M.B. born in Western PA; moved to OH as a young girl to care for her brother and sister-in-law when sister-in-law broke her hip
Etc.	Etc.	Etc.

To prepare an intelligible index, the beginning lawyer needs to study the pleadings and any motions that have been filed to understand what the fact and legal issues are in the matter. Once the entire deposition or set of depositions has been indexed as indicated in the three-column format, the next step is to create an alphabetical index cross-referencing the important topics and specific facts and witnesses' names. This alphabetical index allows any lawyer who uses the index to quickly access information.

Typically, a lawyer making a deposition index will include a list of questions that the witness refused or otherwise never answered. This alerts the lawyer to the need to follow up with other sources of information and also serves as a useful list of possibly impeaching references if the witness does speak to those topics at trial.

Lawyers also include in an index a list of any claims of privilege, again for the purpose of following up and possibly contesting the privilege claims.

EXPERIENTIAL ASSIGNMENTS

1. As plaintiff or defendant, create a discovery plan for the Frensch or Cash case as assigned.

- What information would you want to learn?
- What parts of this information could you learn by informal (that is, "cheaper,") means?
- What among this information is already covered by the required disclosures?
- What formal discovery device would best enable you to learn the other information? (Consider the chart you produced earlier.)

Write one page to explain your plan to a supervising lawyer.

2. Draft Interrogatories

Consider what information you would like to learn in the Frensch, Cash or Williams cases. What pieces of information could you learn from the opposing party? Draft 3 interrogatories for one or more of the cases, as assigned by your professor. Now consider how the opposing parties might view your questions. Would your questions be easy to evade or to answer so vaguely that the answers would be meaningless? How might you make your questions more precise?

3. View video of a deposition or consider the following deposition and other discovery excerpts from the Cash, Frensch and Williams cases and create an index that would allow you to quickly and accurately access the deposition information during a hearing or trial.

If assigned to view a video of a deposition, consider the difficulties posed in trying to craft a deposition index of some of Lil Wayne's depositions in his lawsuit against Quincy Jones III. If these links do not work, there are plenty of other sites available upon searching.

- http://www.complex.com/music/2012/09/video-lil-wayne-deposition-footage-from-quincy-jones-iii-lawsuit

- http://www.complex.com/music/2012/09/lil-wayne-suing-quincy-jones-iii-over-copyright-infringement

- http://www.huffingtonpost.com/2012/09/26/lil-wayne-deposition-attorney-pete-ross_n_1916596.html

- http://blogs.miaminewtimes.com/crossfade/2012/09/lil_wayne_deposition_quincy_jones_iii_lawsuit.php

Frensch v. Nickel 'n Dime Discovery

Deposition of Fresch
■ *Examination by Counsel for Defendant Nickel 'n Dime.*

Q: What is your name, please?
A: Carlene Frensch.

Q: Where do you live?
A: Cary, Ohio.

Q: What do you do for employment?
A: I own a small business.

Q: What is the nature of that business?
A: Farming.

Q: Do you own a farm?
A: Yes.

Q: What do you produce on the farm?
A: Corn. I sell it for feed, for human consumption and for ethanol production.

Q: Do you have employees?
A: No. I work the farm myself along with family members.

Q: Where were you on July 16, (year 0)?
A: I guess you mean the Nickel 'n Dime store in Cary.

Q: Why were you there?
A: To shop for household items.

Q: You were distracted then, as you looked for items?
A: No more than usual.

Q: Were you alone?
A: Yes.

Q: What had you done the evening before?
A: I don't remember.

Q: You had been drinking, correct?
A: I suppose.

Q: With your friends at Joe s All-Star Café, correct?
A: Uh-huh.

Q: And you didn't get home until after 2 am, right?
A: That's about right.

Q: And you arrived at Nickel 'n Dime at about 9:20 am, right?
A: That sounds right.

Q: After a long night of drinking and a short night of sleep?
A: I got enough sleep.

Q: At the Nickel 'n Dime, what were you shopping for?
A: Just household things. Detergent, tissues, things like that.

Q: You are just guessing, though, aren't you?
A: Well, I don't remember everything I was shopping for, so I am just saying things that I might have been shopping for because I always seem to be out of detergent and tissues and that's what I usually get at Nickel 'n Dime.

Q: In your Complaint, you claim that you fell at Nickel 'n Dime. Where do you claim this happened?
A: In the outdoor/picnic aisle.

Q: It was raining outside that morning, wasn't it?
A: I don't recall.

Q: What kind of shoes were you wearing that morning?
A: I don't recall.

Q: Same ones you wore out drinking the night before?
A: I don't remember.

Q: Just to be clear, then, you may have been wearing shoes that were wet from outside or may have been wet from drinking at a bar the night before?
A: I don't think so.

Q: But you don't know for sure?
A: That's right.

Q: Now you say you were hospitalized later that day.
A: I was taken from Nickel 'n Dime in an ambulance.

Q: And you say you were treated for back pain.
A: I was.

Q: You had some back problems before this incident, didn't you?
A: Minor pain and stiffness sometimes, yes.

Q: Enough that you had visited a doctor about the pain?
A: Once, yes. Just as a precaution.

Q: And you once fell at a Pizza Dream restaurant, didn't you?

A: Several years ago, yes.

Q: And you had back pain then?

A: Very much so.

Q: And you filed a claim against Pizza Dream for negligence, didn't you?

A: Yes. Their insurance company paid my medical bills, unlike yours.

That's all I have.

■ *Examination by counsel for Carlene Frensch.*

Q: Good morning, Ms. Frensch. How are you feeling?

A: I've been better.

Q: On July 16, year-0, you went to Nickel 'n Dime.

A: Yes, that's right.

Q: What happened at Nickel 'n Dime that morning?

A: I was walking down the outdoor/picnic aisle. I noticed a can on the floor at one end of the aisle. I carefully walked past it. Near the other end of the same aisle, I slipped. My shoes were wet from whatever was spilled on the floor. I fell flat on my back, landing hard. I heard someone working at the store say, "damn it, that should have been cleaned up!" Very excitedly like.

Q: What happened next?

A: There was some customer standing over me and he said, "Just stay still. I called 911."

Q: After that?

A: Some time passed. The ambulance came and they loaded me up and took me to the hospital emergency room.

Q: And then?

A: I was in the hospital about two weeks, then physical therapy, a back brace, lots of pain. And no corn. I wound up way behind on getting my corn crop in. I lost money.

Q: What did you slip on at the Nickel 'n Dime?

A: Some liquid that came from the spilled container in the aisle where I slipped. I think it was lighter fluid.

Thank you.

Deposition of Customer

■ *Examination by counsel for Carlene Frensch.*

Q: What is your name, please?
A: Chris Patterson.

Q: Where were you on the morning of July 16, year-0?
A: In the Nickel 'n Dime store in Cary.

Q: Did anything unusual happen?
A: I saw a woman fall.

Q: Could you explain?
A: Sure. I was near the front of the store, and out of the corner of my eye I saw this woman, another customer like me, have her feet go flying out from under her. She fell flat on her back and screamed, and then moaned in pain.

Q: Did you hear anything else?
A: I heard an employee say, "I told Joey to clean that up!" She was mad.

Q: How do you know she was an employee?
A: She had a name tag and uniform.

Q: What happened next?
A: I could see she was in pain, so I called 911 and told them to send an ambulance. I then told the woman who fell to relax that help was coming. The last I saw, she was being taken away on a stretcher to the ambulance.

Thanks.

■ *Examination by counsel for Nickel 'n Dime*

Q: You don't know why the woman fell, do you?
A: I saw her feet slip.

Q: But you don't know if her shoes were wet from being outdoors, do you?
A: No.

Q: And you don't know where her shoes might have gotten slippery, do you?
A: No, I guess not.

Q: You don't know what kind of shoes she was wearing, do you?
A: No, I didn't notice that.

Q: Do you know that she claimed back injuries from a fall at a restaurant?

A: How would I know that?

Q: So you don't know.

A: That's right.

Q: You know nothing about what happened before you saw her, do you?

A: No. You mean nothing about her and her fall? I mean, I know a lot of things about what happened before I saw her.

Q: Right. About her.

A: Correct. I know nothing about her before she fell.

Q: And you don't know anything about what happened when she left the store, do you?

A: No.

Q: And you don't know anything about whose job it was to maintain the store, do you?

A: No, of course not.

Thank you, that's all.

Deposition of Employee

■ *Examination by counsel for Carlene Frensch.*

Q: Tell us your name, please.

A: Melissa Progresso.

Q: Where do you work?

A: At the Nickel 'n Dime store in Cary, Ohio.

Q: Were you on duty there on July 16, year-0?

A: Yes.

Q: Were there other employees on duty that morning?

A: Not employees, but someone was there from Acme earlier that morning.

Q: Who was that?

A: Joey Amletto.

Q: Anyone else?

A: No.

Q: Did you see Ms. Frensch in the store that morning?

A: Yes.

Q: Did you see her fall?
A: No.

Q: Did you see her on the floor?
A: Yes.

Q: Did you hear her fall?
A: I heard a thud, and then some moaning.

Q: Did you say anything at that time?
A: Yes, I said that I had told Joey to clean up the spill on that aisle.

Q: What had spilled?
A: I'm not sure. It was some clear liquid and I mentioned it to Joey earlier that morning.

Q: What was Joey doing at the store?
A: He worked for Acme Maintenance, and his job was to clean the store.

Q: Did he clean the store that morning?
A: I guess not all of it.

Q: But he was there for the purpose of cleaning the store that morning?
A: Yes.

Q: You work for Nickel 'n Dime, correct?
A: Yes.

Q: And you were on duty that morning, correct?
A: Yes.

Q: And you were aware of the spill, weren't you?
A: Yes. I told Joey to clean it up.

Q: Was Joey still at the store when the Plaintiff fell?
A: No.

Q: And you knew of the spill?
A: Yeah. But I thought maybe Joey had cleaned it up until I heard the thud.

Q: At the time you heard the thud, you assumed the person had slipped on that same spill, didn't you?
A: Yes. I remember being mad that Joey had missed it.

Q: And you said something to that effect, didn't you?
A: I think I did. Yes.

Q: Did Ms. Frensch appear to be in pain?
A: Yes.

Q: Enough that a customer called an ambulance, right?
A: Yes.

Q: You didn't call an ambulance, did you?
A: No, but I knew one had been called, so why call another?

Q: Others have slipped and fallen at the store, haven't they?
A: I know of a couple other incidents, yes.

Q: How long had you worked there at the time of this incident?
A: About six months.

Q: And you knew of a couple other falls?
A: That's right.

Q: Did you fill out any report about the fall?
A: No, I just told my boss about it later that day.

Q: And your boss' name is?
A: Andrea MacShay.

Q: Do you know what she did as a result?
A: I have no idea.

Q: Does she still work at Nickel 'n Dime?
A: No, she moved to Tanzania to do some kind of public service thing—
    kind of like Peace Corps or something.

Q: Did you as an employee ever receive any notices or instructions as a result
    of prior falls at the store?
A: No. They hired Acme to clean. I think that's what they did.

Thank you. Nothing further.

Counsel for Nickel 'n Dime had no questions.

Deposition of Acme employee
■ *Questioning by counsel for Carlene Frensch.*

Q: What is your name, please?
A: Joey Amletto.

Q: What was your employment on July 16, year-0?
A: I worked for Acme, cleaning stores and offices.

Q: Was one of your jobs to clean the Nickel 'n Dime store in Cary, Ohio?
A: Yes, it was.

Q: At what time of day would you normally clean the store?
A: Various times, but most often I cleaned in the morning before the store opened for the day.

Q: Did you clean that store on July 16?
A: Yes.

Q: In the morning?
A: Yes.

Q: Do you recall seeing a spill on the outdoor/picnic aisle?
A: Yes, I do. I cleaned it up. Dried the wet spot. Made sure it was perfectly safe.

Q: Do you recall what had produced the spill?
A: There was a can of lighter fluid on the floor, laying on its side. I guess that's where the liquid came from.

Q: Did you pick that can up?
A: Of course. I wouldn't just leave it there like that.

Q: Did you dispose of the can or put it back on the shelf for sale?
A: That I don't recall.

Q: You finished your duties and left before the store opened, correct?
A: That's right.

Q: You would have no idea what happened after you left?
A: I heard later that someone slipped and fell, but I wasn't there when it happened.

Thank you. That's all.

Counsel for Nickel 'n Dime had no questions.

Figure 7-2 Depostion Hospital Bill

Consolidated Hospital Bill   August 16, year 0

Patient: Carlene Frensch

Date Admitted: July 16, year 0

Date Discharged: August 1, year 0

Services rendered by: emergency room staff;
ortho staff; ward staff

Products/devices: back brace; cane; pharma; misc.

Costs by provider:

E-Room	$ 37,692
Ortho staff	$ 69,475
Ward staff (daily stay rate)	19,660
Med devices	$ 2,987
Pharma	$ 9,672
Outpatient care to date	$ 3,000
Total	**$ 139,476**

Figure 7-3 Defenadant's Response to Plaintiff's Interrogatories

UNITED STATES DISTRICT COURT
NORTHERN DISTRICT OF OHIO

CARLENE FRENSCH,	)	
Plaintiff,	)	
	)	
--against--	)	Civil Case No.
	)	
Nickel 'n Dime, Inc.	)	
Defendant.	)	

DEFENDANT'S RESPONSES TO PLAINTIFF'S INTERROGATORIES

INSTRUCTIONS

(a) These Interrogatories and Request for Productions of Documents are continuing in character and require you to supplement answers materials if you obtain further or different information before trial, pursuant to the Federal Rules of the Civil Procedure.

(b) Unless otherwise stated, these Interrogatories and Request for Production of Documents refer to the time, place, and circumstances of the occurrence mentioned or complained of in the Plaintiff's Complaint and the Defendant's Counterclaim.

(c) Where name and identity of a person is required, please state full name, home address and also business address, if known.

(d) Where knowledge or information in possession of a party is requested, such request includes knowledge of the party's agents, representatives, and unless privileged, the Defendant's attorney.

(e) The pronouns "you" and/or "your" refer to the party to whom the Interrogatories and Request for Production of Documents are addressed and the parties mentioned in clause (d).

INTERROGATORIES

1. Does Nickel 'n Dime operate stores in Ohio? Is so, how many?
A: Yes, Nickel 'n Dime operates 12 stores in Ohio.

2. Does Nickel 'n Dime have a maintenance contract with Acme regarding the Cary, Ohio store?
A: Yes.

3. Have there been reports of falls by customers at the Cary, Ohio store in addition to the report of Plaintiff's fall?
A: Yes.

. . .

Cash v. Pearsall Discovery

Deposition of Cari Pearsall
Questioning by counsel for Becky Cash

Q: What is your name, please?
A: Cari Pearsall.

Q: Where do you live?
A: Wisconsin.

Q: Be a little more specific, please?
A: Eau Claire, Wisconsin. 635 Wausau Street.

Q: Did you start a business called Carisbeads?
A: Yes.

Q: Advertised on the Internet?
A: Yes.

Q: Everywhere the Internet reaches?
A: I guess.

Q: What do you sell on this website?
A: Jewelry made from beads and strings.

Q: Who makes the jewelry?
A: I did until I got sick.

Q: Did anyone else make the jewelry?

A: In the summer of year 0, I hired four employees and trained them. But they can't do the work without my close supervision.

Q: How old are you, Cari?

A: Eighteen.

Q: When you hired these employees, were you seventeen?

A: That's right. My birthday is August 8, year -18.

Q: Did you fulfill your contract with these employees?

A: What?

Q: Did you pay them what you agreed to pay them for their work?

A: Of course I did. Do you think I cheated them?

Q: Did you also enter a contract with Wiscbeads to obtain materials for the jewelry-making?

A: Yes.

Q: When did you enter that contract?

A: Summer of year 0.

Q: When you were seventeen?

A: Yes. I was still seventeen then.

Q: Did you pay Wiscbeads what you owed them for the beads?

A: Yes.

Q: Do you have a credit card?

A: Yes.

Q: How did you get a credit card before you were eighteen?

A: I don't know. I applied for it.

Q: And you lied about your age, didn't you?

A: I don't remember.

Q: If I show you your credit card application would that refresh your memory?

A: OK, so I lied about my age a little.

Q: Did you pay what you owe on the credit card?

A: Always.

Q: Before you were eighteen?

A: Yes.

Q: And after you turned eighteen?

A: Yes.

Q: Now, you were pleased when you received Becky Cash's initial order in May of year 0, weren't you?

A: Yes.

Q: And you fulfilled that order, didn't you?

A: Yes.

Q: And she paid you?

A: Yes.

Q: All this happened before your eighteenth birthday?

A: Yes.

Q: And you were further thrilled when her second order came in, weren't you?

A: And scared, too. I wasn't sure I could do it.

Q: You didn't tell Becky that you were scared, did you?

A: No.

Q: You didn't tell her you were seventeen, did you?

A: No.

Q: Had you ever met Becky Cash in person?

A: No.

Q: You accepted her money for the second order, didn't you?

A: Yes.

Q: And you started to fulfill the order, didn't you?

A: Yes, but I got sick.

Q: And you contacted Becky Cash to tell her you would neither fulfill the order nor return her money?

A: Right. I didn't see any choice at that time.

Q: You didn't have your employees complete the order, did you?

A: No, I was sick and couldn't supervise them.

Q: You didn't ask Becky Cash if she could wait until you were out of the hospital, did you?

A: No, I was feeling overwhelmed.

Q: You were feeling overwhelmed and just decided to keep the money and quit your business, right?

A: I didn't know what else to do.

Thank you, that's all for now.

■ Deposition of Becky Cash

Questioning by counsel for Cari Pearsall.

Q: Your name please?
A: Becky Cash.

Q: Your business please?
A: I have retail space where I sell jewelry in Duck, North Carolina.

Q: Did you have any interactions with Cari Pearsall's website while in North Carolina?
A: No. Just by coincidence, both times I ordered from her, I was visiting my daughter in Virginia.

Q: Your first order of jewelry from Carisbeads went well?
A: Exceedingly so. I sold the entire product group very quickly. People loved the products.

Q: Then you made the second order, right?
A: Well, first, I rented additional space.

Q: Before you made the second order?
A: Yes, I wanted to get ready for expansion.

Q: Cari didn't do anything to encourage you to expand your business, did she?
A: She made great jewelry that sold fast.

Q: But she didn't say anything to you to encourage you to expand?
A: No, I guess not. I did expand in substantial and reasonable reliance on her promise to fill the second order, though.

Q: Your lawyer gave you that phrase?
A: I talked with her about it, yes.

Q: Thank you for your honesty. Better if you say your own words rather than repeat your lawyer's.

Objection. I will give my client advice and she doesn't need any from Defendant's counsel.

Q: I'm sorry. Let's move on. Cari didn't demand the payment up front did she?
A: No. I wanted to show my good faith and make substantial performance.

Q: Right. That's how you would have said it at the time?
A: I don't know.

Q: But back to my question. Cari did not demand payment up front did she?
A: No.

Q: You knew Cari was a young person, didn't you?
A: Oh yes. I could tell by the youthful flair in the design that she was young and spirited.

Thank you that's all I have.

■ Examination by counsel for Becky Cash

Q: Just a few questions. When you say you knew Cari Pearsall was young, you mean youthful, is that correct?
A: Yes.

Q: Did you know her actual age?
A: Oh no. I didn't.

Q: Were all your answers today your own answers?
A: Yes. I mean, we chatted and I learned a lot from you. But the answers are mine alone.

Thank you.

■ Deposition of Melinda Cash

Questioning by counsel for Cari Pearsall.

Q: Your name, please?
A: Melinda Cash.

Q: Do you know the Plaintiff in this matter?
A: She's my mother.

Q: Does she visit you often?
A: Yes.

Q: And where do you live?
A: Lynchburg, Virginia.

Q: It's pretty there in the mountains.
A: Yes, it is.

Q: Where does your mother live?
A: In Duck, North Carolina.

Q: Was she visiting you on May 8, year 0?
A: Yes.

Q: And was she visiting you on July 15, year 0?
A: Yes.

Q: Do you recall her talking about buying beaded jewelry from Carisbeads?
A: Yes, both times. She was very excited, even more so the second visit. She used my computer to order the jewelry.

Q: As far as you know, did she have any other interaction with the website?
A: I have no idea.

Thank you, that's all.

Williams v. Mancini Discovery

Excerpt from the deposition of Martin Fletcher.

Q: What is your name?
A: Martin Fletcher.

Q: Do you know Gerry Mancini?
A: Yes, I do. I used to run Mancini's gasoline station with him/her.

Q: When and where was that?
A: This was in the late 90's or so in Norman, Oklahoma.

Q: By the way, do you still run a gasoline station now?
A: No, I drive a flower truck.

Q: How did you work with Mancini?
A: Well, he worked the books, and I set work schedules and manned the cash register a lot.

Q: Had you worked in other stations before this?
A: Yes, two or three others, first as a pump person and then at the register.

Q: Did you notice anything different about Mancini's station from the others you worked for?
A: Yes, Mancini used all old equipment even after new stuff was mandated by the state laws.

Q: Did anything ever come of these actions?
A: Sure, at one point there was a fire, and one of the employees was burned.

Q: Do you know how this happened.

A: Yea, we used some old jugs to store used oil and it leaked and caught fire from a welding torch in the shop. Mancini would never pay to get new stuff until something happened to prove to him/her that the old stuff didn't work.

Q: What happened then?

A: He wouldn't say, but I heard he paid the employee a lot to settle out of court.

Q. Did anyone ever speak to you regarding the situation?

A: The prosecutor. Somehow, the prosecutor got wind of what kind of shape the place was in and I was questioned. I thought they were going to bring charges against Mancini, but they never did. I honestly don't know why.

Q: Did Mancini ever clean up the station?

A: Not that I know of, but I left town a month or two after that and moved to Miami.

Q: How long after the prosecutor talked to you did you remain in Norman?

A: Only a month or two. Then I moved.

Q: Do you know what happened to Mancini?

A: No, the next time I heard the name was when you guys called me.

You may inquire.

■ Cross examination by Mancini counsel:

Q: Do you know Terry Williams?

A: No.

Q: Did you have anything to do with running the Oklahoma station?

A: Yes.

Q: And you made money doing this?

A: Yes.

Q: Did you say anything to Mancini about the jugs before the fire?

A: No, he never wanted to hear about anything that would mean spending money, so I didn't waste my breath.

Q: When did you last see Mancini?

A: I guess it would have been year -8. When Mancini left Norman.

Q: Have you had any contact with Mancini in the last 8 years?

A: None.

Q: You know nothing about Mancini's practices as an employer, do you?

A: No.

Q: You never threatened to tell or actually told the authorities about any dangerous conditions back in year -8, did you?

A: Nope.

Q: You have no idea how Mancini is running his current shop, do you?

A: No.

Q: And you have no idea what Mancini would do about an employee who would report, rightly or wrongly, that Mancini was running a dangerous store?

A: Well, he wouldn't be too happy about it, at least when I knew him.

I have nothing further.

■ Deposition of Billy Rossland

Questioning by counsel for Mancini

Q: What is your name and occupation?

A: My name is Billy Rossland and I am the Mayor of Emporia, Virginia.

Q: Do you know Gerry Mancini?

A: I have known Gerry Mancini for 8 years, since s/he moved to Emporia and opened FastGas.

Q: Can you please describe your sense of Mancini's character?

A: Mancini is a first-rate person in every way. Honest, considerate of others, smart. One of the characteristics I like most about Gerry is that he is always willing to give anybody a chance. One example of this is the way he gave Terry Williams a job as soon as he met him, even though Terry looked like some gypsy-vagrant when he arrived.

Q: Thank you. Did you have any discussions with Mancini regarding Mancini's employment relation with Terry Williams?

A: I did. Gerry made one thing clear when he hired Terry: he said Terry was only extra help around the station who would have to be let go if the downward trend in Mancini's profits continued. Gerry fired Terry recently because profits are down, and he had to cut costs wherever he could. Terry shouldn't be causing such a fuss; he told Gerry he didn't want a formal employment contract so that he could move on at any time.

That's all.

■ Questioning by counsel for Williams

Q: Were you present when Mancini hired Williams?
A: No.

Q: So whatever you claim to know about their employment relationship, you have heard from Mancini.
A: That's true, but as I said, Mancini is honest as the day is long. And I did see Williams that same day he was hired—he looked like a bum.

Q: Mayor Rossland, you are good friends with Mancini, correct?
A: Yes.

Q: And you are also friends with officials at the state regulatory commission?
A: I have lots of friends.

Q: Yes, but these in particular. You are friends with officials at the state regulatory commission?
A: I am.

Q: And Mancini knows these officials as well, yes?
A: Yes.

Q: Do you, Mancini and these officials share drinks together at times?
A: Fridays at 5.

Q: And you play golf together, correct?
A: Sunday mornings.

Q: Wouldn't want to see your foursome broken up, would you, Mayor?
A: We have been together for six years.

Q: On the golf course, and at the bar, there was discussion of Williams' complaint about the old pump leaking fuel, wasn't there?
A: Maybe. We talk about a lot of things. I don't recall.

Q: Neither you nor the regulatory officials would like to see Mancini in any trouble, would you?
A: He doesn't deserve this trouble.

Q: To your knowledge, has Mancini ever been found in violation of any safety, health, consumer or administrative violation of codes here in Emporia?
A: Never.

Q: Does Mancini donate to your election campaigns?
A: Yes.

Nothing further.

■ Further questioning by counsel for Mancini

Q: Did you encourage the regulatory officials to find a lack of safety violations at FastGas?

A: No.

Q: Did the officials ever say to you that there would be no adverse findings at FastGas?

A: No.

Q: Did you in any way influence the investigation of Williams' complaint?

A: Absolutely not.

■ Deposition of Stacy Duvall

Questioning by counsel for Mancini

Q: What is your name and occupation?

A: My name is Stacy Duvall, and I have run Emporia Gas for the last ten years. The station has been in my family for forty years.

Q: Do you know Terry Williams or Gerry Mancini?

A: When Terry Williams moved into town last year, I wanted to help him since he seemed like a nice kid, but I explained that my profit margin was too low to expand my staff. Terry and I became friends, though, and we have lunch together once or twice a week. Gerry is a business competitor, but we get along fine.

Q: As between you and Gerry, who has been the more successful financially?

A: Gerry.

Q: You have some envy of Gerry?

A: Like I said, we get along fine.

Q: You said you and Terry have become friends. But you were not present when Terry was hired by Gerry were you?

A: No.

Q: So whatever you think you know about their employment relationship, you know from Terry, right?

A: True.

Nothing further.

■ Questioning by counsel for Williams

Q: You said that Gerry has been more successful financially.
   Do you know why?

A: It has puzzled me for a long time how Gerry Mancini has continued to make profits with FastGas, particularly with the ups and downs of the oil market and all the free benefits Mancini continuously offers to his customers. Now I understand, though: it's easy to make a profit when you don't worry about the safety of your employees. Terry made this discovery and because he disclosed Mancini's neglect, Mancini fired Terry. That has to be the reason for Terry's termination because Terry is a conscientious, honest person who follows all rules and is a dependable, hard worker. If I could have afforded it, I would have hired Terry.

That's all.

Further by counsel for Mancini

Q: When Terry stopped working at FastGas, did you hire him?
A: No.

Q: Because despite all the profits for the oil companies, profits for local gas stations are tight right now, aren't they?
A: At least mine are. I wouldn't know about Mancini's profits. I just know Mancini has a better house and car than I do. Property in the mountains. A boat. I have none of that.

Thank you, nothing further.

■ Deposition of Frankie Fortunato
Questioning by counsel for Williams

Q: Please tell us your name and occupation.
A: My name is Frankie Fortunato. I own Frankie's, a local watering hole in Emporia. My place is very popular. I pour a lot of beer and hear a lot of talk. That's my occupation: listen, talk, pour.

Q: Do you know either Gerry Mancini or Terry Williams?
A: Terry Williams I only know from what people have said in my saloon, and they said alot. Mancini is one of my regulars. Mancini is in my place a couple times a week, minimum. On Fridays, he is in with the Mayor, and usually with some of the officials at the state regulatory commission.

Q: You say that customers said a lot about Terry. What did Mancini say,
    if anything?

A: From shortly after Terry Williams started at FastGas, Mancini started com-
    plaining about this new employee who was pestering customers with whin-
    ing about environmental stuff. Williams was driving Mancini nuts. I got sick
    of hearing about it from Mancini and told him to pipe down or do something
    about Williams. I hate it when people complain about something and do
    nothing to fix the situation.

Q: Did Mancini say any of this on the Fridays when the mayor and the
    officials were drinking with him?

A: I am open seven days a week, so the days run together for me. No concept
    of weekends. So I just don't remember exactly what day it was. I do
    remember Mancini saying that Williams was costing him money. And I
    know he talked
    a lot about Williams. So I would guess he said something on Fridays here
    and there. Sure.

Q: Are you aware of Mancini firing Williams?

A: Eventually, Mancini did say he was going to fire Williams. I said, "It's about
    time." The day Mancini said he was going to fire Williams was early to mid-
    May.

Q: Did Mancini mention any complaint filed by Williams?

A: It did come up. But honestly I can't remember if it was before or after
    Williams got the boot.

Thank you.

■ Questioning by counsel for Mancini

Q: You said that you heard a lot about Williams. That wasn't all from
    Mancini, was it?

A: Mancini wasn't the only one who ever came into my place talking about
    Williams. That's for sure. Once when Mancini was in my place a local guy
    named Taylor started a rant about Williams. Taylor said he was sick and
    tired of having Williams hack on him at the station about safety and envi-
    ronmental things. Taylor told Mancini that he would take his gas purchas-
    ing and small car repairs elsewhere to get away from having to listen to
    Williams. I remember a few others muttering about Williams and his envi-
    ronmental causes.

Q: You said you don't recall with certainty hearing Mancini talk about
    Williams with his Friday night group, correct?

A: With "certainty"? No. But Williams was such a regular part of Mancini's subject matter, I would say there had to have been some talk of Williams on Fridays.

Q: Ever heard anything from a customer about Mancini's station being unsafe?
A: No.

Q: But you have heard plenty about Williams being overbearing with Mancini's customers about environmental and safety issues. Correct?
A: That's true.

Nothing further.

■ Deposition of Louise Cos
Questioning by counsel for Mancini

Q: Your name and occupation, please?
A: My name is Louise Cos. I am a massage therapist in Emporia.

Q: Do you know Terry Williams or Gerry Mancini?
A: Not directly.

Q: Are you familiar with Peter Bargman?
A: I used to date a guy named Peter Bargman. He works for the State Regulatory Commission. They investigate safety issues at various businesses.

Q: And to your knowledge, did Peter investigate a safety complain at FastGas?
A: Yes, Peter was assigned to check out a complaint filed against FastGas about some gas pump issue.

Q: Do you know if Peter was friends with Mayor Rossland?
A: I don't believe so.

Q: Was Peter friends with Mancini?
A: I don't believe so.

Q: How long did you date Peter?
A: About six months.

Q: Did Peter go drinking with friends on Friday evenings?
A: No. We spent most evenings together.

Q: Does Peter play golf?
A: Hah! Sorry. I didn't mean to laugh. Peter is very uncoordinated. The thought of him swinging a golf club made me laugh. No, Peter was not a golfer.

Q: I gather you and Peter are not together now?
A: That's correct.

Q: Do you know the outcome of the investigation at FastGas?
A: No, I'm sorry. I don't.

Q: Did you come to any opinion regarding Peter's character for honesty?
A: I know Peter is an honest guy and very respectable and would never be unduly influenced.

Nothing further.

■ Questioning by counsel for Williams

Q: Don't feel badly about laughing at Peter golfing. I am a terrible golfer myself.
A: I'm sorry if I hurt your feelings.

Q: Not at all. I am terrible but I love to play. So maybe Peter played on Sunday mornings before you met him?
A: I guess that's possible.

Q: And after you broke up, . . . when was that?
A: Late April or early May.

Q: Maybe he played golf after that?
A: He never talked about golf.

Q: Did you spend every evening together?
A: No. But most every evening.

Q: Isn't it possible that there were some Friday evenings you didn't spend together?

A: I don't know. I guess so.

Q: So you don't really know what Peter did on every Friday evening during your six months together?
A: I guess that's right.

Q: And you have no idea what he did on Friday nights before you met him and after you broke up.
A: That would be true.

Q: Regarding the investigation of FastGas, didn't Peter confess some worry about that to you?
A: He did. Peter told me that it could be a problem because Gerry Mancini, the owner of FastGas, is well-connected. The mayor is some good friend

of Mancini and through the mayor, Mancini knows some state officials in Peter's office. Peter said to me that he was worried about the results if he found Mancini in violation of the state safety code. But as I said, Peter is very honest and he would not be unduly influenced by all that.

Thank you, nothing further.

Figure 7-4 Regualtory Report

REPORT OF STATE REGULATORY AGENCY

In today's investigation of FastGas in Emporia, no safety or health violations were discovered and it was determined that neither employees nor customers had been placed in danger.

This agency has closed its investigation of FastGas. At this time, no further action is planned.

Peter Bargman
Peter Bargman
May 23, Year 0
State Regulatory Agency

■ Excerpt from the deposition of Terry Williams

Q: What is your name?
A: Terry Williams.

Q: Do you know Gerry Mancini?
A: Yes. He was my boss when I worked at FastGas.

Q: Where is FastGas located?
A: Emporia, Virginia.

Q: When did you work for FastGas?
A: I started working for him in May year -1 and continued working for him until May year 0.

Q: Did you live in Emporia, Virginia before you began working for Mr. Mancini?
A: No.

Q: Where did you live before then?
A: I moved all over the country.

Q: In the past six years, have you lived in any one place for more than a year?
A: No. I did live in Emporia, VA for a year though.

Q: Do you still live in Emporia?
A: No. After Mr. Mancini fired me I moved to Raleigh, North Carolina.

Q: At the time that Mr. Mancini hired you, did he know that you moved a lot?
A: I don't recall talking too much about it, but I guess he might have surmised that since I never unpacked my suitcase.

Q: When you started working for Mr. Mancini, did you sign a written contract?
A: No.

Q: What did Mr. Mancini tell you were the terms of employment?
A: Well, he hired me with a handshake and told me that I could work for him as long as I was doing my job.

Q: But you did not have any form of written agreement stating how long you would work for him?
A: No.

Q: So you could have left your position at anytime with no consequences?
A: Yeah I guess so.

Q: Did you talk to any of the customers while you were pumping gas?
A: Yes. I would often talk to them about my thoughts on politics and the environment.

Q: What kinds of things would you talk about?
A: I would talk to them about how driving gas-guzzling cars was destroying the environment by causing oil spills and pollution. And I told them that Mancini runs a dangerous operation. I told them he is putting the employees and the public in danger of being burned or blown up.

Q: Did Mr. Mancini know that you talked to customers about this?
A: Yes.

Q: How did Mr. Mancini react?
A: He got mad at me and told me that I was turning away some customers, but I told Mr. Mancini that I have a right to freedom of speech. He was still angry with me and told me not to talk to customers about my radical views, which of course are not "radical" at all.

Q: Did you ever talk with Mr. Mancini about the storage tank pump?
A: Yes, I told him it was dangerous.

Q: Did you conclude on your own that it was dangerous?
A: Yes.

Q: Are you an expert about fuel pump safety?
A: No, but it leaked when it was used. I would be standing in a little puddle of gas when I used the pump, so I don't think it takes an expert to know it's dangerous. On top of that, people were allowed to smoke near it.

Q: When you concluded on your own that the gas pump might be dangerous what did you do?
A: I had a conversation with Mr. Mancini about it and told him that I would not work for him if he did not get a newer pump.

Q: On how many occasions did you discuss this with Mr. Mancini?
A: Just once, but I also left him a note.

Q: How long was your conversation with Mr. Mancini?
A: Probably not more than a couple of minutes.

Q: What did the note that you left him say?
A: It basically just reiterated our conversation that I thought the pump was dangerous and should be replaced.

Q: Why did you leave him a note if it said no more than you had already told him in person?
A: I don't know. I guess I didn't need to leave a note.

Q: Did Mr. Mancini ever mention receiving the note?
A: No.

Q: So is it possible that Mr. Mancini never received the note?
A: Well, I suppose so.

Q: What did you do next?
A: I called the state inspection agency and told them about the pump. I was fired by Mr. Mancini two days after the state sent a representative to investigate.

Q: Did Mr. Mancini give you a reason when he fired you.
A: Yeah he told me it was due to sinking profits. I don't buy it though. I think he fired me because I reported him.

Thank you. That's all I have.

■ Deposition of Gerry Mancini

Q: What is your name?

A: Gerry Mancini.

Q: Do you know Terry Williams?

A: Yes. He worked for me at FastGas.

Q: Where is FastGas located?

A: Emporia, Virginia.

Q: Do you own FastGas?

A: Yes, I opened the station about 8 years ago.

Q: When did Williams work for you?

A: I would say from about May year -1 until May year 0.

Q: So he worked for you for about a year?

A: Right, and he did a good enough job as far as his duties would go.

Q: I see. So he was a good employee?

A: Not exactly. I didn't say that. I said he was good at doing his duties. In other ways he was a pain.

Q: Tell me all the ways in which he was what you would call, "a pain."

A: He would bother customers, talking to them about how driving gas-guzzling cars was destroying the environment by causing oil spills and pollution. He criticized the oil industry and told people that I was careless in the way I ran the station.

Q: How did you react to that?

A: I got mad and told him to stop it.

Q: Did he stop?

A: No. Instead he gave me some line about freedom of speech. Hell, even I know that doesn't apply unless the government is trying to shut you up. I remember that from The Big Lebowski. .

Q: Well, thank you for the legal analysis, Mr. Mancini, but we'll just move on from there. Did you fire Mr. Williams when he failed to stop as you told him to do?

A: Well, not right then, no.

Q: Did Mr. Williams ever talk with you about the storage tank pump?

A: I don't recall. Maybe once.

Q: When did you buy the storage pump?

A: When I opened the station.

Q: Was the pump new at that time?
A: No, I bought it at an equipment auction.

Q: Do you know how old it was when you bought it eight years ago?
A: I don't know.

Q: Did you have the pump safety inspected when you installed
   it at the station?
A: No.

Q: Where is the pump located at the station?
A: In the pump house behind the station..

Q: Do you ever operate that pump?
A: No.

Q: Who does operate that pump?
A: Employees.

Q: Including Mr. Williams when he worked for you?
A: Yes.

Q: So would Mr. Williams have more experience operating the pump
   than you do?
A: Well, I suppose so.

Q: Did Mr. Williams give you a note regarding the pump?
A: No.

Q: To your knowledge, did Williams tell anyone else about the pump and
   his safety concerns?
A: I believe he called the state inspection agency and told them about the
   pump.

Q: Why do you think that?
A: They came to inspect the pump, and they found it is ok. They said Williams
   had contacted them to report it.

Q: Did you actually meet with the state inspector?
A: No.

Q: Did you see what they did during their inspection?
A: No. I did not participate in the inspection.

Q: When did you fire Mr. Williams?
A: I'm not exactly sure. Around that time.

Q: After the inspection?
A: I think so.

Q: And not long after the inspection?
A: Yeah.

Q: What reason did you give Williams for the firing?
A: I told him it was due to sinking profits. I was also fed up with him telling customers his crazy, radical nonsense.

Q: Do you know Stacy Duvall?
A: Stacy Duvall is a whiny loser. Always complaining that I am doing better
with the business than she does.

Q: Do you know Martin Fletcher?
A: No. Wait, I'm not sure. Is that the guy who worked for me in Oklahoma?

Q: As an employee of yours in Oklahoma, what do you remember
about Fletcher?
A: Just that he complained all the time.

Q: As you say Williams did?
A: Well, yes, sort of the same.

Q: Did you have a fire at the Oklahoma station you owned?
A: Yes.

Q: Did someone get hurt?

A: Yes, a worker was burned. Gas stations have oil and gas. They burn easily.
Gas stations have auto repair equipment, like torches. A torch set off some
oil, and we had a fire. Simple as that.

Q: Were you then contacted by any state authorities?
A: The prosecutor in town asked me some questions, but nothing came of it.

Q: Did that cause you to become more aware of safety issues?
A: I suppose so.

Thank you. That's all I have.

C. Compulsion

Most of the discovery process takes place between the lawyers and parties and outside the view of the judge. But as in all matters, sometimes the parties and their lawyers disagree about the obligation of a party to produce some discovery. When that happens, the rules allow the aggrieved party to ask the judge to order the recalcitrant party to produce the discovery. Notice the preference of the rules for having the parties solve their own problems before asking the judge. Notice also, that there are sanctions available for the judge to impose on a party who is frustrating the goals of the discovery process. Notice, too, that once the judge has issued an Order to produce some discovery, the sanctions for failing to comply increase.

Rule Material

Rule 37 *Failure to Make Disclosures or to Cooperate in Discovery; Sanctions*

(a) Motion for an Order Compelling Disclosure or Discovery.

(1) *In General.* On notice to other parties and all affected persons, a party may move for an order compelling disclosure or discovery. The motion must include a certification that the movant has in good faith conferred or attempted to confer with the person or party failing to make disclosure or discovery in an effort to obtain it without court action.

(2) *Appropriate Court.* A motion for an order to a party must be made in the court where the action is pending. A motion for an order to a nonparty must be made in the court where the discovery is or will be taken.

(3) *Specific Motions.*

(A) *To Compel Disclosure.* If a party fails to make a disclosure required by Rule 26(a), any other party may move to compel disclosure and for appropriate sanctions.

(B) *To Compel a Discovery Response.* A party seeking discovery may move for an order compelling an answer, designation, production, or inspection. This motion may be made if:

(i) a deponent fails to answer a question asked under Rule 30 or 31;

(ii) a corporation or other entity fails to make a designation under Rule 30(b)(6) or 31(a)(4);

(iii) a party fails to answer an interrogatory submitted under Rule 33; or

(iv) a party fails to respond that inspection will be permitted—or fails to permit inspection—as requested under Rule 34.

(C) *Related to a Deposition.* When taking an oral deposition, the party asking a question may complete or adjourn the examination before moving for an order.

(4) *Evasive or Incomplete Disclosure, Answer, or Response.* For purposes of this subdivision (a), an evasive or incomplete disclosure, answer, or response must be treated as a failure to disclose, answer, or respond.

(5) *Payment of Expenses; Protective Orders.*

(A) *If the Motion Is Granted (or Disclosure or Discovery Is Provided After Filing).* If the motion is granted—or if the disclosure or requested discovery is provided after the motion was filed—the court must, after giving an opportunity to be heard, require the party or deponent whose conduct necessitated the motion, the party or attorney advising that conduct, or both to pay the movant's reasonable expenses incurred in making the motion, including attorney's fees. But the court must not order this payment if:

(i) the movant filed the motion before attempting in good faith to obtain the disclosure or discovery without court action;

(ii) the opposing party's nondisclosure, response, or objection was substantially justified; or

(iii) other circumstances make an award of expenses unjust.

(B) *If the Motion Is Denied.* If the motion is denied, the court may issue any protective order authorized under Rule 26(c) and must, after giving an opportunity to be heard, require the movant, the attorney filing the motion, or both to pay the party or deponent who opposed the motion its reasonable expenses incurred in opposing the motion, including attorney's fees. But the court must not order this payment if the motion was substantially justified or other circumstances make an award of expenses unjust.

(C) *If the Motion Is Granted in Part and Denied in Part.* If the motion is granted in part and denied in part, the court may issue any protective order authorized under Rule 26(c) and may, after giving an opportunity to be heard, apportion the reasonable expenses for the motion.

(b) Failure to Comply with a Court Order.

(1) *Sanctions in the District Where the Deposition Is Taken.* If the court where the discovery is taken orders a deponent to be sworn or to answer a question and the deponent fails to obey, the failure may be treated as contempt of court.

(2) *Sanctions in the District Where the Action Is Pending.*

(A) *For Not Obeying a Discovery Order.* If a party or a party's officer, director, or managing agent—or a witness designated under Rule 30(b)(6) or 31(a)(4)—fails to obey an order to provide or permit discovery, including an order under Rule 26(f), 35, or 37(a), the court where the action is pending may issue further just orders. They may include the following:

(i) directing that the matters embraced in the order or other designated facts be taken as established for purposes of the action, as the prevailing party claims;

(ii) prohibiting the disobedient party from supporting or opposing designated claims or defenses, or from introducing designated matters in evidence;

(iii) striking pleadings in whole or in part;

(iv) staying further proceedings until the order is obeyed;

(v) dismissing the action or proceeding in whole or in part;

(vi) rendering a default judgment against the disobedient party; or

(vii) treating as contempt of court the failure to obey any order except an order to submit to a physical or mental examination.

(B) *For Not Producing a Person for Examination.* If a party fails to comply with an order under Rule 35(a) requiring it to produce another person for examination, the court may issue any of the orders listed in Rule 37(b)(2)(A)(i)–(vi), unless the disobedient party shows that it cannot produce the other person.

(C) *Payment of Expenses.* Instead of or in addition to the orders above, the court must order the disobedient party, the attorney advising that party, or both to pay the reasonable expenses, including attorney's fees, caused by the failure, unless the failure was substantially justified or other circumstances make an award of expenses unjust.

(c) Failure to Disclose, to Supplement an Earlier Response, or to Admit.

(1) *Failure to Disclose or Supplement.* If a party fails to provide informa-

tion or identify a witness as required by Rule 26(a) or (e), the party is not allowed to use that information or witness to supply evidence on a motion, at a hearing, or at a trial, unless the failure was substantially justified or is harmless. In addition to or instead of this sanction, the court, on motion and after giving an opportunity to be heard:

(A) may order payment of the reasonable expenses, including attorney's fees, caused by the failure;

(B) may inform the jury of the party's failure; and

(C) may impose other appropriate sanctions, including any of the orders listed in Rule 37(b)(2)(A)(i)–(vi).

(2) *Failure to Admit.* If a party fails to admit what is requested under Rule 36 and if the requesting party later proves a document to be genuine or the matter true, the requesting party may move that the party who failed to admit pay the reasonable expenses, including attorney's fees, incurred in making that proof. The court must so order unless:

(A) the request was held objectionable under Rule 36(a);

(B) the admission sought was of no substantial importance;

(C) the party failing to admit had a reasonable ground to believe that it might prevail on the matter; or

(D) there was other good reason for the failure to admit.

(d) Party's Failure to Attend Its Own Deposition, Serve Answers to Interrogatories, or Respond to a Request for Inspection.

(1) *In General.*

(A) *Motion; Grounds for Sanctions.* The court where the action is pending may, on motion, order sanctions if:

(i) a party or a party's officer, director, or managing agent—or a person designated under Rule 30(b)(6) or 31(a)(4)—fails, after being served with proper notice, to appear for that person's deposition; or

(ii) a party, after being properly served with interrogatories under Rule 33 or a request for inspection under Rule 34, fails to serve its answers, objections, or written response.

(B) *Certification.* A motion for sanctions for failing to answer or respond must include a certification that the movant has in good faith conferred or attempted to confer with the party failing to act in an effort to obtain the answer or response without court action.

> (2) *Unacceptable Excuse for Failing to Act.* A failure described in Rule 37(d)(1)(A) is not excused on the ground that the discovery sought was objectionable, unless the party failing to act has a pending motion for a protective order under Rule 26(c).

> (3) *Types of Sanctions.* Sanctions may include any of the orders listed in Rule 37(b)(2)(A)(i)–(vi). Instead of or in addition to these sanctions, the court must require the party failing to act, the attorney advising that party, or both to pay the reasonable expenses, including attorney's fees, caused by the failure, unless the failure was substantially justified or other circumstances make an award of expenses unjust.

(e) Failure to Provide Electronically Stored Information. Absent exceptional circumstances, a court may not impose sanctions under these rules on a party for failing to provide electronically stored information lost as a result of the routine, good-faith operation of an electronic information system.

(f) Failure to Participate in Framing a Discovery Plan. If a party or its attorney fails to participate in good faith in developing and submitting a proposed discovery plan as required by Rule 26(f), the court may, after giving an opportunity to be heard, require that party or attorney to pay to any other party the reasonable expenses, including attorney's fees, caused by the failure.

Zubulake v. UBS Warburg LLC

217 F.R.D. 309 (S.D.N.Y. 2003)

OPINION AND ORDER

SCHEINDLIN, District Judge.

The world was a far different place in 1849, when Henry David Thoreau opined (in an admittedly broader context) that "[t]he process of discovery is very simple." That hopeful maxim has given way to rapid technological advances, requiring new solutions to old problems. The issue presented here is one such problem, recast in light of current technology: To what extent is inaccessible electronic data discoverable, and who should pay for its production?

I. INTRODUCTION

The Supreme Court recently reiterated that our "simplified notice pleading standard relies on liberal discovery rules and summary judgment motions to define disputed facts and issues and to dispose of unmeritorious claims." Thus, it is now beyond dispute that "[b]road discovery is a cornerstone of the litigation process contemplated by the Federal Rules of Civil Procedure." The Rules contemplate a minimal burden to bringing a claim; that claim is then fleshed out through vigorous and expansive discovery.

In one context, however, the reliance on broad discovery has hit a road-block. As individuals and corporations increasingly do business electronically using computers to create and store documents, make deals, and exchange e-mails—the universe of discoverable material has expanded exponentially. The more information there is to discover, the more expensive it is to discover all the relevant information until, in the end, "discovery is not just about uncovering the truth, but also about how much of the truth the parties can afford to disinter."

This case provides a textbook example of the difficulty of balancing the competing needs of broad discovery and manageable costs. Laura Zubulake is suing UBS Warburg LLC, UBS Warburg, and UBS AG (collectively, "UBS" or the "Firm") under Federal, State and City law for gender discrimination and illegal retaliation. Zubulake's case is certainly not frivolous[5] and if she prevails, her damages may be substantial. She contends that key evidence is located in various e-mails exchanged among UBS employees that now exist only on backup tapes and perhaps other archived media. According to UBS, restoring those e-mails would cost approximately $175,000.00, exclusive of attorney time in reviewing the e-mails. Zubulake now moves for an order compelling UBS to produce those e-mails at its expense.

II. BACKGROUND

A. Zubulake's Lawsuit

UBS hired Zubulake on August 23, 1999, as a director and senior salesperson on its U.S. Asian Equities Sales Desk (the "Desk"), where she reported to Dominic Vail, the Desk's manager. At the time she was hired, Zubulake was told that she would be considered for Vail's position if and when it became vacant.

---

5 Indeed, Zubulake has already produced a sort of "smoking gun": an e-mail suggesting that she be fired "ASAP" after her EEOC charge was filed, in part so that she would not be eligible for year-end bonuses. See 8/21/01 e-mail from Mike Davies to Rose Tong ("8/21/01 e-Mail"), Ex. G to the 3/17/03 Affirmation of James A. Batson, counsel for Zubulake ("Batson Aff.").

In December 2000, Vail indeed left his position to move to the Firm's London office. But Zubulake was not considered for his position, and the Firm instead hired Matthew Chapin as director of the Desk. Zubulake alleges that from the outset Chapin treated her differently than the other members of the Desk, all of whom were male. In particular, Chapin "undermined Ms. Zubulake's ability to perform her job by, inter alia: (a) ridiculing and belittling her in front of co-workers; (b) excluding her from work-related outings with male co-workers and clients; (c) making sexist remarks in her presence; and (d) isolating her from the other senior salespersons on the Desk by seating her apart from them." No such actions were taken against any of Zubulake's male co-workers.

Zubulake ultimately responded by filing a Charge of (gender) Discrimination with the EEOC on August 16, 2001. On October 9, 2001, Zubulake was fired with two weeks' notice.

B. The Discovery Dispute

Discovery in this action commenced on or about June 3, 2002, when Zubulake served UBS with her first document request. At issue here is request number twenty-eight, for "[a]ll documents concerning any communication by or between UBS employees concerning Plaintiff." The term *document* in Zubulake's request "includ[es], without limitation, electronic or computerized data compilations." On July 8, 2002, UBS responded by producing approximately 350 pages of documents, including approximately 100 pages of e-mails. UBS also objected to a substantial portion of Zubulake's requests.

On September 12, 2002—after an exchange of angry letters and a conference before United States Magistrate Judge Gabriel W. Gorenstein—the parties reached an agreement (the "9/12/02 Agreement"). With respect to document request twenty-eight, the parties reached the following agreement, in relevant part:

Defendants will [ ] ask UBS about how to retrieve e-mails that are saved in the firm's computer system and will produce responsive e-mails if retrieval is possible and Plaintiff names a few individuals.

Pursuant to the 9/12/02 Agreement, UBS agreed unconditionally to produce responsive e-mails from the accounts of five individuals named by Zubulake: Matthew Chapin, Rose Tong (a human relations representation who was assigned to handle issues concerning Zubulake), Vinay Datta (a co-worker on the Desk), Andrew Clarke (another co-worker on the Desk), and Jeremy Hardisty (Chapin's supervisor and the individual to whom Zubulake originally complained about Chapin). UBS was to produce such e-mails sent between August 1999 (when Zubulake was hired) and December 2001 (one month after her termination), to the extent possible.

338 EXPERIENCING CIVIL PROCEDURE

UBS, however, produced no additional e-mails and insisted that its initial production (the 100 pages of e-mails) was complete. As UBS's opposition to the instant motion makes clear—although it remains unsaid—UBS never searched for responsive e-mails on any of its backup tapes. To the contrary, UBS informed Zubulake that the cost of producing e-mails on backup tapes would be prohibitive (estimated at the time at approximately $300,000.00).

Zubulake, believing that the 9/12/02 Agreement included production of e-mails from backup tapes, objected to UBS's nonproduction. In fact, Zubulake knew that there were additional responsive e-mails that UBS had failed to produce because she herself had produced approximately 450 pages of e-mail correspondence. Clearly, numerous responsive e-mails had been created and deleted[6] at UBS, and Zubulake wanted them.

.   .   .

C. UBS's E-Mail Backup System

In the first instance, the parties agree that e-mail was an important means of communication at UBS during the relevant time period. Each salesperson, including the salespeople on the Desk, received approximately 200 e-mails each day. Given this volume, and because Securities and Exchange Commission regulations require it,[7] UBS implemented extensive e-mail backup and preservation protocols. In particular, e-mails were backed up in two distinct ways: on backup tapes and on optical disks.

---

6 The term "deleted" is sticky in the context of electronic data. " 'Deleting' a file does not actually erase that data from the computer's storage devices. Rather, it simply finds the data's entry in the disk directory and changes it to a 'not used' status—thus permitting the computer to write over the 'deleted' data. Until the computer writes over the 'deleted' data, however, it may be recovered by searching the disk itself rather than the disk's directory. Accordingly, many files are recoverable long after they have been deleted—even if neither the computer user nor the computer itself is aware of their existence. Such data is referred to as 'residual data.' " Shira A. Scheindlin & Jeffrey Rabkin, Electronic Discovery in Federal Civil Litigation: Is Rule 34 Up to the Task?, 41 B.C. L.Rev. 327, 337 (2000) (footnotes omitted). Deleted data may also exist because it was backed up before it was deleted. Thus, it may reside on backup tapes or similar media. Unless otherwise noted, I will use the term "deleted" data to mean residual data, and will refer to backed-up data as "backup tapes."

7 SEC Rule 17a-4, promulgated pursuant to Section 17(a) of the Securities Exchange Act of 1934, provides in pertinent part: Every [ ] broker and dealer shall preserve for a period of not less than 3 years, the first two years in an accessible place ... [o]riginals of all communications received and copies of all communications sent by such member, broker or dealer (including inter-office memoranda and communications) relating to his business as such. 17 C.F.R. s 240.17a-4(b) and (4).

1. Backup Tape Storage

UBS employees used a program called HP OpenMail, manufactured by Hewlett-Packard, for all work-related e-mail communications. With limited exceptions, all e-mails sent or received by any UBS employee are stored onto backup tapes. To do so, UBS employs a program called Veritas NetBackup, which creates a "snapshot" of all e-mails that exist on a given server at the time the backup is taken. Except for scheduling the backups and physically inserting the tapes into the machines, the backup process is entirely automated.

UBS used the same backup protocol during the entire relevant time period, from 1999 through 2001. Using NetBackup, UBS backed up its e-mails at three intervals: (1) daily, at the end of each day, (2) weekly, on Friday nights, and (3) monthly, on the last business day of the month. Nightly backup tapes were kept for twenty working days, weekly tapes for one year, and monthly tapes for three years. After the relevant time period elapsed, the tapes were recycled.

Once e-mails have been stored onto backup tapes, the restoration process is lengthy. Each backup tape routinely takes approximately five days to restore, although resort to an outside vendor would speed up the process (at greatly enhanced costs, of course). Because each tape represents a snapshot of one server's hard drive in a given month, each server/month must be restored separately onto a hard drive. Then, a program called Double Mail is used to extract a particular individual's e-mail file. That mail file is then exported into a Microsoft Outlook data file, which in turn can be opened in Microsoft Outlook, a common e-mail application. A user could then browse through the mail file and sort the mail by recipient, date or subject, or search for key words in the body of the e-mail.

Fortunately, NetBackup also created indexes of each backup tape. Thus, Behny was able to search through the tapes from the relevant time period and determine that the e-mail files responsive to Zubulake's requests are contained on a total of ninety-four backup tapes.

2. Optical Disk Storage

In addition to the e-mail backup tapes, UBS also stored certain e-mails on optical disks. For certain "registered traders," probably including the members of the Desk, a copy of all e-mails sent to or received from outside sources (i.e., e-mails from a "registered trader" at UBS to someone at another entity, or vice versa) was simultaneously written onto a series of optical disks. Internal e-mails, however, were not stored on this system.

UBS has retained each optical disk used since the system was put into place in mid-1998. Moreover, the optical disks are neither erasable nor rewritable.

Thus, UBS has every e-mail sent or received by registered traders (except internal e-mails) during the period of Zubulake's employment, even if the e-mail was deleted instantaneously on that trader's system.

The optical disks are easily searchable using a program called Tumbleweed. Using Tumbleweed, a user can simply log into the system with the proper credentials and create a plain language search. Search criteria can include not just "header" information, such as the date or the name of the sender or recipient, but can also include terms within the text of the e-mail itself. For example, UBS personnel could easily run a search for e-mails containing the words "Laura" or "Zubulake" that were sent or received by Chapin, Datta, Clarke, or Hardisty.

. . .

IV. DISCUSSION

A. Should Discovery of UBS's Electronic Data Be Permitted?

Under Rule 34, a party may request discovery of any document, "including writings, drawings, graphs, charts, photographs, phonorecords, and other data compilations...." The "inclusive description" of the term *document* "accord[s] with changing technology." "It makes clear that Rule 34 applies to electronics [sic] data compilations." Thus, "[e]lectronic documents are no less subject to disclosure than paper records." This is true not only of electronic documents that are currently in use, but also of documents that may have been deleted and now reside only on backup disks.

That being so, Zubulake is entitled to discovery of the requested e-mails so long as they are relevant to her claims, which they clearly are. As noted, e-mail constituted a substantial means of communication among UBS employees. To that end, UBS has already produced approximately 100 pages of e-mails, the contents of which are unquestionably relevant.

Nonetheless, UBS argues that Zubulake is not entitled to any further discovery because it already produced all responsive documents, to wit, the 100 pages of e-mails. This argument is unpersuasive for two reasons. First, because of the way that UBS backs up its e-mail files, it clearly could not have searched all of its e-mails without restoring the ninety-four backup tapes (which UBS admits that it has not done). UBS therefore cannot represent that it has produced all responsive e-mails. Second, Zubulake herself has produced over 450 pages of relevant e-mails, including e-mails that would have been responsive to her discovery requests but were never produced by UBS. These two facts strongly suggest that there are e-mails that Zubulake has not received that reside on UBS's backup media.

B. Should Cost-Shifting Be Considered?

Because it apparently recognizes that Zubulake is entitled to the requested discovery, UBS expends most of its efforts urging the court to shift the cost of production to "protect [it] ... from undue burden or expense." Faced with similar applications, courts generally engage in some sort of cost-shifting analysis, whether the refined eight-factor Rowe test or a cruder application of Rule 34's proportionality test, or something in between.

The first question, however, is whether cost-shifting must be considered in every case involving the discovery of electronic data, which—in today's world—includes virtually all cases. In light of the accepted principle, stated above, that electronic evidence is no less discoverable than paper evidence, the answer is, "No." The Supreme Court has instructed that "the presumption is that the responding party must bear the expense of complying with discovery requests...." Any principled approach to electronic evidence must respect this presumption. Courts must remember that cost-shifting may effectively end discovery, especially when private parties are engaged in litigation with large corporations. As large companies increasingly move to entirely paper-free environments, the frequent use of cost-shifting will have the effect of crippling discovery in discrimination and retaliation cases. This will both undermine the "strong public policy favor[ing] resolving disputes on their merits," and may ultimately deter the filing of potentially meritorious claims.

Thus, cost-shifting should be considered only when electronic discovery imposes an "undue burden or expense" on the responding party.FN46 The burden or expense of discovery is, in turn, "undue" when it "outweighs its likely benefit, taking into account the needs of the case, the amount in controversy, the parties' resources, the importance of the issues at stake in the litigation, and the importance of the proposed discovery in resolving the issues."

Many courts have automatically assumed that an undue burden or expense may arise simply because electronic evidence is involved. This makes no sense. Electronic evidence is frequently cheaper and easier to produce than paper evidence because it can be searched automatically, key words can be run for privilege checks, and the production can be made in electronic form obviating the need for mass photocopying.

In fact, whether production of documents is unduly burdensome or expensive turns primarily on whether it is kept in an accessible or inaccessible format (a distinction that corresponds closely to the expense of production). In the world of paper documents, for example, a document is accessible if it is readily available in a usable format and reasonably indexed. Examples of inaccessible paper documents could include (a) documents in storage in a difficult to reach place; (b) documents converted to microfiche and not easily readable; or (c) documents kept haphazardly, with no indexing system, in quantities that make page-by-page searches impracticable. But in the world of electronic data, thanks to search engines, any data that is retained in a machine readable format is typically accessible.

Whether electronic data is accessible or inaccessible turns largely on the media on which it is stored. Five categories of data, listed in order from most accessible to least accessible, are described in the literature on electronic data storage: [*lengthy descriptions of each omitted. Ed.*]

1. Active, online data;

2. Near-line data;

3. Offline storage/archives;

4. Backup tapes;

5. Erased, fragmented or damaged data.

Of these, the first three categories are typically identified as accessible, and the latter two as inaccessible. The difference between the two classes is easy to appreciate. Information deemed "accessible" is stored in a readily usable format. Although the time it takes to actually access the data ranges from milliseconds to days, the data does not need to be restored or otherwise manipulated to be usable. "Inaccessible" data, on the other hand, is not readily usable. Backup tapes must be restored using a process similar to that previously described, fragmented data must be de-fragmented, and erased data must be reconstructed, all before the data is usable. That makes such data inaccessible.[8]

The case at bar is a perfect illustration of the range of accessibility of electronic data. As explained above, UBS maintains e-mail files in three forms: (1) active user e-mail files; (2) archived e-mails on optical disks; and (3) backup data stored on tapes. The active (HP OpenMail) data is obviously the most accessible: it is online data that resides on an active server, and can be accessed immediately. The optical disk (Tumbleweed) data is only slightly less accessible, and falls into either the second or third category. The e-mails are on optical disks that need to be located and read with the correct hardware, but the system is

---

8 A report prepared by the Sedona Conference recently propounded "Best Practices" for electronic discovery. See The Sedona Conference, The Sedona Principles: Best Practices Recommendations & Principles for Addressing Electronic Document Production (March 2003), ("Sedona Principles"), available at *http://www.thesedonaconference.org/publications.html* .

configured to make searching the optical disks simple and automated once they are located. For these sources of e-mails—active mail files and e-mails stored on optical disks—it would be wholly inappropriate to even consider cost-shifting. UBS maintains the data in an accessible and usable format, and can respond to Zubulake's request cheaply and quickly. Like most typical discovery requests, therefore, the producing party should bear the cost of production.

E-mails stored on backup tapes (via NetBackup), however, are an entirely different matter. Although UBS has already identified the ninety-four potentially responsive backup tapes, those tapes are not currently accessible. In order to search the tapes for responsive e-mails, UBS would have to engage in the costly and time-consuming process detailed above. It is therefore appropriate to consider cost-shifting.

C. What Is the Proper Cost-Shifting Analysis?

In the year since Rowe was decided, its eight factor test has unquestionably become the gold standard for courts resolving electronic discovery disputes. But there is little doubt that the Rowe factors will generally favor cost-shifting. Indeed, of the handful of reported opinions that apply Rowe or some modification thereof, all of them have ordered the cost of discovery to be shifted to the requesting party.

In order to maintain the presumption that the responding party pays, the cost-shifting analysis must be neutral; close calls should be resolved in favor of the presumption. The Rowe factors, as applied, undercut that presumption for three reasons. First, the Rowe test is incomplete. Second, courts have given equal weight to all of the factors, when certain factors should predominate. Third, courts applying the Rowe test have not always developed a full factual record.

1. The Rowe Test Is Incomplete

a. A Modification of Rowe: Additional Factors

[The court discusses the Rowe test and announces the following new test that it will employ.]

c. A New Seven-Factor Test

Set forth below is a new seven-factor test based on the modifications to Rowe discussed in the preceding sections.

1. The extent to which the request is specifically tailored to discover relevant information;

2. The availability of such information from other sources;

3. The total cost of production, compared to the amount in controversy;

4. The total cost of production, compared to the resources available to each party;

5. The relative ability of each party to control costs and its incentive to do so;

6. The importance of the issues at stake in the litigation; and

7. The relative benefits to the parties of obtaining the information.

2. The Seven Factors Should Not Be Weighted Equally

Whenever a court applies a multi-factor test, there is a temptation to treat the factors as a check-list, resolving the issue in favor of whichever column has the most checks. But "we do not just add up the factors." When evaluating cost-shifting, the central question must be, does the request impose an "undue burden or expense" on the responding party? Put another way, "how important is the sought-after evidence in comparison to the cost of production?" The seven-factor test articulated above provide some guidance in answering this question, but the test cannot be mechanically applied at the risk of losing sight of its purpose.

Weighting the factors in descending order of importance may solve the problem and avoid a mechanistic application of the test. The first two factors—comprising the marginal utility test—are the most important. These factors include: (1) The extent to which the request is specifically tailored to discover relevant information and (2) the availability of such information from other sources.

The second group of factors addresses cost issues: "How expensive will this production be?" and, "Who can handle that expense?" These factors include: (3) the total cost of production compared to the amount in controversy, (4) the total cost of production compared to the resources available to each party and (5) the relative ability of each party to control costs and its incentive to do so. The third "group"—(6) the importance of the litigation itself—stands alone, and as noted earlier will only rarely come into play. But where it does, this factor has the potential to predominate over the others. Collectively, the first three groups correspond to the three explicit considerations of Rule 26(b)(2)(iii). Finally, the last factor—(7) the relative benefits of production as between the requesting and producing parties—is the least important because it is fair to presume that the response to a discovery request generally benefits the requesting party. But in the unusual case where production will also provide a tangible or strategic benefit to the responding party, that fact may weigh against shifting costs.

D. A Factual Basis Is Required to Support the Analysis

Courts applying Rowe have uniformly favored cost-shifting largely because of assumptions made concerning the likelihood that relevant information will be found. . . .

But such proof will rarely exist in advance of obtaining the requested discovery. The suggestion that a plaintiff must not only demonstrate that probative evidence exists, but also prove that electronic discovery will yield a "gold mine," is contrary to the plain language of Rule 26(b)(1), which permits discovery of "any matter" that is "relevant to [a] claim or defense."

Requiring the responding party to restore and produce responsive documents from a small sample of backup tapes will inform the cost-shifting analysis laid out above. When based on an actual sample, the marginal utility test will not be an exercise in speculation—there will be tangible evidence of what the backup tapes may have to offer. There will also be tangible evidence of the time and cost required to restore the backup tapes, which in turn will inform the second group of cost-shifting factors. Thus, by requiring a sample restoration of backup tapes, the entire cost-shifting analysis can be grounded in fact rather than guesswork.

IV. CONCLUSION AND ORDER

. . . Accordingly, UBS is ordered to produce all responsive e-mails that exist on its optical disks or on its active servers (i.e., in HP OpenMail files) at its own expense. UBS is also ordered to produce, at its expense, responsive e-mails from any five backups tapes selected by Zubulake. UBS should then prepare an affidavit detailing the results of its search, as well as the time and money spent. After reviewing the contents of the backup tapes and UBS's certification, the Court will conduct the appropriate cost-shifting analysis.

A conference is scheduled in Courtroom 12C at 4:30 p.m. on June 17, 2003.

Example Documents

UNITED STATES DISTRICT COURT
FOR THE DISTRICT OF NEW MEXICO

TWO OLD HIPPIES, LLC,
        Plaintiff,

        v.   No: 10-CV-459 JB/RLP

CATCH THE BUS, LLC,
GARY MACK And FALLON MACK,
        Defendants.

PLAINTIFF'S MOTION TO COMPEL DISCOVERY RESPONSES

Plaintiff served interrogatories and requests for production on all Defendants on July 21, 2010. Defendants have not answered or responded. Plaintiff moves to compel answers and responses.

1.   Plaintiff's discovery was served by mail July 21, 2010.

2.   Settlement discussions began and Plaintiff suspended the due date of Defendants' answers and responses while settlement discussions were pending.

3.   Settlement discussions resulted in a settlement agreement, but Defendants did not meet the requirements of the agreement so the settlement collapsed.

4.   After the collapse, Plaintiff notified Defendants on 11/4/10 that their answers and responses would be due 11/19/10.

5.   Defendants have still not answered or responded.

6.   Plaintiff has no working phone numbers for Defendants. Plaintiff notified Defendants about this motion by e-mail and regular mail on 1/19/11 to attempt to confer but Defendants have not responded.

Wherefore, Plaintiff moves to compel Defendants to answer and respond to Plaintiff's discovery and for its attorneys' fees and costs related to this motion and for such other and further relief as proper.

Respectfully submitted,
BANNERMAN & JOHNSON, P.A.

By: /s/ Thomas P. Gulley
Thomas P. Gulley
Rebecca L. Avitia
2201 San Pedro, NE,
Building 2, Suite 207
Albuquerque, New Mexico 87110
(505) 837-1900

Attorneys for Plaintiff

**IN THE UNITED STATES DISTRICT COURT
FOR THE DISTRICT OF NEW MEXICO**

TWO OLD HIPPIES, LLC,
      Plaintiff,
        vs.   No. CIV 10-0459 JB/RLP
CATCH THE BUS, LLC,
GARY MACK
and FALLON MACK,
      Defendants.

MEMORANDUM OPINION AND ORDER

THIS MATTER comes before the Court on the Plaintiff's Motion to Compel Discovery Responses, filed January 25, 2011 (Doc. 33)("Motion"). The Court held a hearing on March 11, 2011. The primary issue is whether the Court should compel Defendant Catch the Bus, LLC, to answer and respond to Plaintiff Two Old Hippies, LLC's discovery, and award Two Old Hippies' attorneys' fees and costs related to this Motion. Because Catch the Bus has not responded to Two Old Hippies' Motion and thereby consented to the Motion, and because the Court concludes that Two Old Hippies' discovery is reasonably calculated to lead to relevant evidence, the Court grants the Motion.

PROCEDURAL HISTORY

On July 21, 2010, Two Old Hippies served the Defendants with discovery via the United States Postal Service. The parties began settlement discussions, and Two Old Hippies suspended the due date of Defendants' answers and responses while settlement discussions were pending. The parties reached a settlement agreement, but the Defendants did not meet the requirements of the agreement, so the settlement collapsed. After the collapse, Two Old Hippies notified the Defendants on November 4, 2010 that their answers and responses would be due November 19, 2010. The Defendants have not answered or responded.

Two Old Hippies moves the Court to compel Catch the Bus[1] to answer and respond to its discovery, for its attorneys' fees and costs related to this Motion, and for such other and further relief as proper. Two Old Hippies has no working telephone number for the Catch the Bus. Two Old Hippies attempted to notify the Defendants about this motion by electronic mail transmission and post on January 19, 2011 in an effort to confer, but the Defendants have not responded. Catch the Bus has not filed opposition briefs or otherwise responded to Two Old Hippies' Motion.

At the hearing, no one appeared for the Catch the Bus.[2] The Court's Courtroom Deputy attempted to reach the Defendants on three telephone numbers it has for the Defendants. When the Courtroom Deputy attempted 575-491-6594, a child answered who did not seem to know who the parties the Court sought. When the Courtroom Deputy attempted 888-428-2892, it reached what appeared to be a facsimile transmission apparatus. When the Courtroom Deputy attempted 575-437-8081, she found the telephone number had been disconnected. Additionally, the Court's mail to Catch the Bus had been returned undeliverable. See Mail sent from the Court to Fallon Mack Returned as Undeliverable, filed February 23, 2011 (Doc. 44); Mail sent from the Court to Catch the Bus, LLC, Returned as Undeliverable, filed February 23, 2011 (Doc. 45); Mail sent from the Court to Gary Mack Returned as Undeliverable, filed February 23, 2011 (Doc. 46).

---

1 Two Old Hippies moved to compel all the Defendants to respond to its discovery. The Court, however, dismissed Two Old Hippies' claims against the individual Defendants on February 11, 2011. See Memorandum Opinion and Order, filed February 11, 2011 (Doc. 37).

2 In the Court's Memorandum Opinion and Order, filed February 24, 2011 (Doc. 38), the Court stated that the Court would grant Plaintiff Two Old Hippies, LLC's Motion to Strike Pleadings of and Enter Default Judgment Against Defendant Catch the Bus, LLC, filed November 2, 2010 (Doc. 27) if Catch the Bus, did not obtain new counsel within ten days of the order. Counsel has not appeared for Catch the Bus, and the Court entered Default Judgment Against Catch the Bus and struck its pleadings on March 11, 2011. See Doc 51.

ANALYSIS

Two Old Hippies served Catch the Bus with discovery. Catch the Bus has failed to respond to the discovery request. Catch the Bus has further failed to respond to Two Old Hippies' Motion. "The failure of a party to file and serve a response in opposition to a motion within the time prescribed for doing so constitutes consent to grant the motion." D.N.M.LR-Civ. 7.1(b). The Court therefore grants the Motion.

The Court also reviewed Two Old Hippies' discovery. It appears reasonable and to be expected in a case of this nature. From the face of the discovery, there does not appear to be a substantial reason, if any, Catch the Bus should not respond.

IT IS ORDERED that the Court grants the Plaintiff's Motion to Compel Discovery Responses, filed January 25, 2011 (Doc. 33). Defendant Catch the Bus, LLC, should respond to Plaintiff Two Old Hippies, LLC's discovery within ten days of the entry of this order. Two Old Hippies should submit an affidavit stating its attorney fees and costs for filing its motion and appearing at the March 11, 2011 hearing, and the Court will enter a separate order granting fees and costs for this motion.

_____
UNITED STATES DISTRICT JUDGE

C

EXPERIENTIAL ASSIGNMENTS

1. In the Frensch case, plaintiff has asked defendant to produce records and summaries of all falls in all stores for the past 10 years. Draft a Motion for a Protective Order on behalf of Nickel 'n Dime.

Assume Nickel 'n Dime simply refuses to produce those requested records and summaries. Draft a Motion to Compel asking the court to order production of as much as you think the court would be willing to compel.

2. In the Cash case, Becky Cash had filed a request for production of documents asking that Cari Pearsall turn over her medical records from the hospital stay that Pearsall claims prevented her from performing the contract. Draft a Motion for a Protective Order on Pearsall's behalf.

3. In the Williams case, Mancini made a Request for Production of Documents asking for Williams to turn over "any and all documents prepared by counsel regarding Williams' calculation of damages." The request also asks for "any and all documents reflecting Williams' association with environmental advocacy entities." Your partner asks you to explain how you would respond to these requests. Write one or two pages responding to your partner's request.

CHAPTER 8

Motions for Summary Judgment

MOTIONS FOR SUMMARY JUDGMENT are devices for resolving civil actions without trial. They are different from Motions to Dismiss for Failure to State a Claim in that they typically follow much or all of the discovery in a case. The bottom-line inquiry is related: if there is nothing to be gained from a trial, then the matter should be concluded and judgment entered.

Because the typical Motion for Summary Judgment follows discovery, much more is known than at the time of the pleadings. Depositions have been taken, interrogatories asked and answered, documents shared. If, after all of this factual exploration has taken place, there are no "genuine issues of material fact," then a trial is unnecessary and a judge can determine which side is entitled to judgment as a matter of law.

Both Motions to Dismiss and Motions for Summary Judgment provide efficiencies by allowing civil actions to be disposed of without trial.

In cases that involve crucial scientific evidence, a Motion for Summary Judgment often follows a successful *Daubert* motion. In *Daubert v. Merrell Dow Pharmaceuticals*, 509 U.S. 579 (1993), the Supreme Court articulated standards for the admissibility of scientific evidence. If one party successfully excludes the other party's scientific evidence, and if without that evidence an element of the claim cannot be proven, a successful Motion for Summary Judgment often follows.

A. Note on Burdens of Proof and Presumptions

To understand what happens when a Motion for Summary Judgment is decided, some basic understanding of burdens of proof and presumptions is needed. This same discussion will also be helpful in understanding Motions for Judgment in chapter 9.

Burdens. The law of procedure imposes many different kinds of burdens on the parties. The most commonly discussed is the burden of proof. There are really two burdens inside the burden of proof: the burden of going forward and the burden of persuasion.

The burden of persuasion is the more familiar one. Typically the party who asks the court to change the status quo bears the burden of persuasion. In most instances this is the plaintiff, the one who has brought the action and has asked the court to do something. Defendants bear the burden of persuasion in certain instances, most notably for this course, on affirmative defenses. When a party has the burden of persuasion, that party loses "ties" on fact questions. It might seem odd that any case would be a tie on a fact question, but it is more common than might first appear. If there is a trial, then there are fact disputes: one side says the light was green for the plaintiff while the other side says the light was red for the plaintiff. There will be evidence on both sides of such a question. Plaintiff testifies, "I saw it clearly—the light was green." Defendant calls a bystander to the witness stand who testifies, "I saw it clearly—the light was red for Plaintiff." The fact finder, whether judge or jury, will weigh the evidence and the credibility of the witnesses and other sources of evidence and try to decide: was the light red or green at that crucial moment? More often than one might think, a fact finder is left saying, "I just don't know." When that happens, we say the fact finder is at *equipoise*, that place where the see-saw is balanced and neither side goes up or down without an additional push. When the fact finder is in this position, the party with the burden of persuasion loses. The typical jury instruction is something like: "If the Plaintiff persuades you by a preponderance of the evidence of the truth of these facts, then find for the Plaintiff; if not, then find for the Defendant." This instruction articulates the burden of persuasion. The typical civil action level of persuasion required is "preponderance," often described as "more likely than not," or more than 50% likely. Some fact issues in civil actions require proof by "clear and convincing evidence," which although not mathematically defined, is more than a preponderance. In criminal cases, the government must prove the defendant's guilt by the familiar "beyond a reasonable doubt" standard.

In the vast majority of instances, whichever party starts a case with the burden of persuasion still has that burden at the end when the fact finder deliberates and decides. (We will leave the few rare exceptions to your Evidence course.)

The other burden within the term "burden of proof" is the burden of production, sometimes called the burden of going forward. This burden typically starts a case on the plaintiff as well, but it may shift back and forth during the course of a trial. Imagine a defamation case in which the elements of the plaintiff's claim are publication of the statement by the defendant (defendant told someone something about the plaintiff), defamatory nature of the statement (the nature of the statement was derogatory to the plaintiff), and damage to the plaintiff. In such a case, the defendant may have an affirmative defense of truth (if the statement is true, defendant has no liability). On the elements of the claim, plaintiff will have the burden of going forward; on the defense, the defendant will have the burden of going forward. This chart will help show how the burden of going forward works.

Figure 8-1 Claim/Defense Chart, Pt.1

	Judgment for D	Jury Land	Judgment for P	
P's Claim	XXX	XXXXXXXXXXXXXXXXXXXX	XXX	Aff. Defense
publication				
defamatory				
damage				
				truth

The first column lists the elements of the plaintiff's claim, on which the plaintiff has the burden of going forward. The furthest column on the right indicates the defendant's affirmative defense, on which the defendant has the burden of going forward.

When the trial begins, the plaintiff will offer evidence that he thinks will persuade the fact finder (let's say a jury for this illustration) of the truth of his elements, publication, defamatory nature and damage. Initially, the defendant need do nothing except try to diminish the believability of the plaintiff's evidence. As the plaintiff puts on evidence, we can imagine the mind of the fact finder being pushed along from left to right, less convinced to more convinced, of the truth of the plaintiff's elements. If the plaintiff's evidence only pushes the fact finder into the first column right of his list of elements, the column marked "Judgment for D(efendant)," we would say that "no reasonable fact finder could find the truth of the plaintiff's element." The plaintiff has failed to meet his burden of going forward. If the plaintiff's evidence pushes the fact finder into the middle column, the one marked "Jury land," then we would say that "a reasonable jury could find the truth of the plaintiff's element," and plaintiff has met his burden of going forward. If the plaintiff's proof is so powerful that it pushes the fact finder all the way to the last column before the list of affirmative defenses, the one marked "Judgment for P(laintiff)," then we would say that reasonable jurors must find that plaintiff's element is true, In such an instance, the plaintiff has not only met his burden of going forward, he has shifted it to the defendant. Let's say the plaintiff puts on his evidence and at the end, the impact of his proof makes the chart look like this.

Figure 8-2 Claim/Defense Chart, Pt. 2

	Judgment for D	Jury Land	Judgment for P	
P's Claim	XXX	XXXXXXXXXXXXXXXXXXXX	XXX	Aff. Defense
publication	⟶			
defamatory		⟶		
damage		⟶		
				truth

Because the plaintiff bears the burden of going forward on his three elements and he has failed to meet the burden of going forward on one of his elements, a Motion for Judgment (Chapter 9) will be granted for the defendant and the case will end.

Now let's say the plaintiff has done better and the chart looks like this.

Figure 8-3 Claim/Defense Chart, Pt. 3

	Judgment for D	Jury Land	Judgment for P	
P's Claim	XXX	XXXXXXXXXXXXXXXXXXXX	XXX	Aff. Defense
publication			→	
defamatory		→		
damage		→		
				truth

Now the plaintiff has met his burden of going forward on all three elements and has shifted the burden of going forward to the defendant on the publication element. When the arrow lands in the middle column as it has on two of plaintiff's elements, a jury question is created. The jury will be asked if it finds defamatory nature and damage. Because the plaintiff also bears the burden of persuasion on all three elements, the jury will be told through an instruction that if they find all three elements by a preponderance, they should find for plaintiff and if not, they should find for defendant. This instruction will mean that the plaintiff loses on any ties left in the minds of the jury.

In this last chart (Pt. 3), it is also true that plaintiff has shifted the burden of going forward on the publication issue (did defendant say the statement to someone) to the defendant. At the stage represented by this chart, we would say that no reasonable juror could fail to find for plaintiff on the publication issue. Because the defendant now has the burden of going forward on that single issue, if the defendant offers no contrary evidence on that issue, a judge would instruct a jury that they must find on that issue for the plaintiff. However, if a defendant offers some contrary evidence on this issue (let's say he calls a witness who says she was present when the statement was supposed to have been made and she never heard the defendant speak), then defendant may be able to satisfy his newly imposed burden of going forward and create a jury question on which reasonable jurors could disagree. (See Pt. 4) If defendant does so, then the case will end with all three elements being jury questions, and the plaintiff continuing to bear the burden of persuasion on all three. The chart below represents that situation.

Figure 8-4 Claim/Defense Chart, Pt. 4

	Judgment for D	Jury Land	Judgment for P	
P's Claim	XXX	XXXXXXXXXXXXXXXXXXXX	XXX	Aff. Defense
publication				
defamatory				
damage				
				truth

If the trial ended now, the jury would decide all three elements and reach a verdict. But there was also the defense of truth. The defendant bears the burden of going forward on the defense and all three of the possible scenarios outlined for plaintiff's elements could also apply to the defense, as indicated by Pt. 5 chart. The results would be the same as outlined with the plaintiff's elements. The short line means the defendant has failed to meet his burden of going forward and he will not even get the jury to consider the truth defense; the middle-length line means he has met his burden of going forward and has created a jury question, on which the judge will instruct the jury when they begin to deliberate; the long line means he has not only met his burden of going forward but has shifted the burden to plaintiff. In this last instance, if plaintiff fails to offer evidence that pushes the line back into the jury land, then this issue will be decided against plaintiff by the judge, and because the truth defense is a complete defense to the defamation claim, the judge will enter judgment for the defendant and the jury will never need to deliberate at all.

Figure 8-5 Claim/Defense Chart, Pt. 5

	Judgment for D	Jury Land	Judgment for P	
P's Claim	XXX	XXXXXXXXXXXXXXXXXXXX	XXX	Aff. Defense
publication			→	
defamatory		→		
damage		→		
	←	←	←	truth

Presumptions. There are three different devices that the law sometimes calls a presumption, only one of which is of interest here. Here we are only interested in presumptions as devices for shifting burdens of going forward, the third of the three kinds listed next. (There is one kind of presumption that also shifts the burden of persuasion, but we will leave that for the Evidence course.)

1. Some so-called presumptions are irrebuttable. These are really rules of law: "A child under 7 years old cannot commit a felony" is a rule that embodies an irrebuttable presumption that a child under 7 cannot have the mental state necessary to commit a felony crime.

2. Some devices called presumptions are just permissive inferences, really meaning nothing more than that the existence of some basic fact (BF) is evidence sufficient to permit a fact finder to find a presumed fact (PF). "If a vehicle says 'Marzo Construction' on the side, it belongs to Marzo Construction." All this means is that when a party introduces evidence of this BF (the sign on the truck saying "Marzo Construction," they will have met their burden of going forward on the PF (ownership of the truck by Marzo Construction).

3. Real presumptions are production burden shifters. This means that if a party shows some BF that the law says is significant, then some PF must be found to be true unless the party against whom the presumption operates puts in evidence sufficient to support a finding of "NOT-PF" (the opposite of the presumed

fact). In this sense, the presumption can be rebutted by evidence sufficient to support a finding of "NOT-PF."

Some examples may help.

- If a party can show that he mailed a letter with the right address and post-age (BF), the presumption is that the addressee received it (PF). A fact finder would be required to find receipt unless the recipient-party put on sufficient evidence of non-receipt. Sufficient evidence on non-receipt might be, for example, the sworn testimony of the addressee saying he checked his mail every day but no such letter ever arrived. Once such contradicting evidence came in, it would be up to the jury to decide, based on all the evidence, whether the letter had been received or not.

- If a party can show that a person has not been heard from for seven years (BF), the presumption is that he's dead (PF). Evidence contradicting PF in this instance might be someone's testimony that they saw the person three years ago, alive and well.

- If a will that was created cannot be found (BF), then it was revoked by the will-maker (PF).

- (A Property law example) If goods are delivered to a bailee in good condition and they are returned from the bailee in bad condition (BF), the bailee was negligent (PF).

- If husband and wife live together when a child is conceived (BF), the child is legitimate (PF).

- Many presumptions exist in the law of many topics. Some are created by legislation and others are created by court decision.

There are multiple reasons why the law creates presumptions: strong inferential connection (avoid mistakes, mailing); convenience (most of the evidence is in the hands of the party against whom presumption works or is altogether unavailable); liability distribution planning; or public policy preferences (the legitimacy presumption). Often a combination of these operate.

We care about presumptions in Civil Procedure because of the role they may play in deciding Motions for Summary Judgment and also Motions for Judgment (Chapter 9). Just as we saw earlier in the discussion of a party's failure to meet a burden of going forward, a party to whom a presumption has operated must meet a burden of going forward on some fact issue that has been shifted by the operation of the presumption.

B. Summary Judgment

Rule Material

Rule 56 Summary Judgment

(a) Motion for Summary Judgment or Partial Summary Judgment. A party may move for summary judgment, identifying each claim or defense — or the part of each claim or defense — on which summary judgment is sought. The court shall grant summary judgment if the movant shows that there is no genuine dispute as to any material fact and the movant is entitled to judgment as a matter of law. The court should state on the record the reasons for granting or denying the motion.

(b) Time to File a Motion. Unless a different time is set by local rule or the court orders otherwise, a party may file a motion for summary judgment at any time until 30 days after the close of all discovery.

(c) Procedures.

(1) *Supporting Factual Positions.* A party asserting that a fact cannot be or is genuinely disputed must support the assertion by:

(A) citing to particular parts of materials in the record, including depositions, documents, electronically stored information, affidavits or declarations, stipulations (including those made for purposes of the motion only), admissions, interrogatory answers, or other materials; or

(B) showing that the materials cited do not establish the absence or presence of a genuine dispute, or that an adverse party cannot produce admissible evidence to support the fact.

(2) *Objection That a Fact Is Not Supported by Admissible Evidence.* A party may object that the material cited to support or dispute a fact cannot be presented in a form that would be admissible in evidence.

(3) *Materials Not Cited.* The court need consider only the cited materials, but it may consider other materials in the record.

(4) *Affidavits or Declarations.* An affidavit or declaration used to support or oppose a motion must be made on personal knowledge, set out facts that would be admissible in evidence, and show that the affiant or declarant is competent to testify on the matters stated.

(d) When Facts Are Unavailable to the Nonmovant. If a nonmovant shows by affidavit or declaration that, for specified reasons, it cannot present facts essential to justify its opposition, the court may:

(1) defer considering the motion or deny it;

(2) allow time to obtain affidavits or declarations or to take discovery; or

(3) issue any other appropriate order.

(e) Failing to Properly Support or Address a Fact. If a party fails to properly support an assertion of fact or fails to properly address another party's assertion of fact as required by Rule 56(c), the court may:

(1) give an opportunity to properly support or address the fact;

(2) consider the fact undisputed for purposes of the motion;

(3) grant summary judgment if the motion and supporting materials — including the facts considered undisputed — show that the movant is entitled to it; or

(4) issue any other appropriate order.

(f) Judgment Independent of the Motion. After giving notice and a reasonable time to respond, the court may:

(1) grant summary judgment for a nonmovant;

(2) grant the motion on grounds not raised by a party; or

(3) consider summary judgment on its own after identifying for the parties material facts that may not be genuinely in dispute.

(g) Failing to Grant All the Requested Relief. If the court does not grant all the relief requested by the motion, it may enter an order stating any material fact — including an item of damages or other relief — that is not genuinely in dispute and treating the fact as established in the case.

(h) Affidavit or Declaration Submitted in Bad Faith. If satisfied that an affidavit or declaration under this rule is submitted in bad faith or solely for delay, the court — after notice and a reasonable time to respond — may order the submitting party to pay the other party the reasonable expenses, including attorney's fees, it incurred as a result. An offending party or attorney may also be held in contempt or subjected to other appropriate sanctions.

Celotex Corporation v. Catrett

477 U.S. 317, 106 S.Ct. 2548 (1986)

REHNQUIST, J., delivered the opinion of the Court, in which WHITE, MARSHALL, POWELL, and O'CONNOR, JJ., joined. WHITE, J., filed a concurring opinion. BRENNAN, J., filed a dissenting opinion, in which BURGER, C.J., and BLACKMUN, J., joined. STEVENS, J., filed a dissenting opinion.

Justice REHNQUIST delivered the opinion of the Court.

The United States District Court for the District of Columbia granted the motion of petitioner Celotex Corporation for summary judgment against respondent Catrett because the latter was unable to produce evidence in support of her allegation in her wrongful-death complaint that the decedent had been exposed to petitioner's asbestos products. A divided panel of the Court of Appeals for the District of Columbia Circuit reversed, however, holding that petitioner's failure to support its motion with evidence tending to negate such exposure precluded the entry of summary judgment in its favor. This view conflicted with that of the Third Circuit. We granted certiorari to resolve the conflict, and now reverse the decision of the District of Columbia Circuit.

Respondent commenced this lawsuit in September 1980, alleging that the death in 1979 of her husband, Louis H. Catrett, resulted from his exposure to products containing asbestos manufactured or distributed by 15 named corporations. Respondent's complaint sounded in negligence, breach of warranty, and strict liability. Petitioner's motion, which was first filed in September 1981, argued that summary judgment was proper because respondent had "failed to produce evidence that any [Celotex] product . . . was the proximate cause of the injuries alleged within the jurisdictional limits of [the District] Court." In particular, petitioner noted that respondent had failed to identify, in answering interrogatories specifically requesting such information, any witnesses who could testify about the decedent's exposure to petitioner's asbestos products. In response to petitioner's summary judgment motion, respondent then produced three documents which she claimed "demonstrate that there is a genuine material factual dispute" as to whether the decedent had ever been exposed to petitioner's asbestos products. The three documents included a transcript of a deposition of the decedent, a letter from an official of one of the decedent's former employers whom petitioner planned to call as a trial witness, and a letter from an insurance company to respondent's attorney, all tending to establish that the decedent had been exposed to petitioner's asbestos products in Chicago during 1970-1971. Petitioner, in turn, argued that the three documents were inadmissible hearsay and thus could not be considered in opposition to the summary judgment motion.

In July 1982, almost two years after the commencement of the lawsuit, the District Court granted all of the motions filed by the various defendants. The court explained that it was granting petitioner's summary judgment motion because "there [was] no showing that the plaintiff was exposed to the defendant Celotex's product in the District of Columbia or elsewhere within the statutory period." Respondent appealed only the grant of summary judgment in favor of petitioner, and a divided panel of the District of Columbia Circuit reversed. The majority of the Court of Appeals held that petitioner's summary judgment motion was rendered "fatally defective" by the fact that petitioner "made no effort to adduce any evidence, in the form of affidavits or otherwise, to support its motion." 244 U.S.App.D.C., at 163, 756 F.2d, at 184 (emphasis in original). According to the majority, Rule 56(e) of the Federal Rules of Civil Procedure, and this Court's decision in *Adickes v. S.H. Kress & Co.*, 398 U.S. 144, 159, 90 S.Ct. 1598, 1609 (1970), establish that "the party opposing the motion for summary judgment bears the burden of responding only after the moving party has met its burden of coming forward with proof of the absence of any genuine issues of material fact." 756 F.2d, at 184 (emphasis in original; footnote omitted). The majority therefore declined to consider petitioner's argument that none of the evidence produced by respondent in opposition to the motion for summary judgment would have been admissible at trial. The dissenting judge argued that "[t]he majority errs in supposing that a party seeking summary judgment must always make an affirmative evidentiary showing, even in cases where there is not a triable, factual dispute." 756 F.2d, at 188 (Bork, J., dissenting). According to the dissenting judge, the majority's decision "undermines the traditional authority of trial judges to grant summary judgment in meritless cases." 756 F.2d, at 187.

We think that the position taken by the majority of the Court of Appeals is inconsistent with the standard for summary judgment set forth in Rule 56(c) of the Federal Rules of Civil Procedure. Under Rule 56(c), summary judgment is proper "if the pleadings, depositions, answers to interrogatories, and admissions on file, together with the affidavits, if any, show that there is no genuine issue as to any material fact and that the moving party is entitled to a judgment as a matter of law." In our view, the plain language of Rule 56(c) mandates the entry of summary judgment, after adequate time for discovery and upon motion, against a party who fails to make a showing sufficient to establish the existence of an element essential to that party's case, and on which that party will bear the burden of proof at trial. In such a situation, there can be "no genuine issue as to any material fact," since a complete failure of proof concerning an essential element of the non-moving party's case necessarily renders all other facts immaterial. The moving party is "entitled to a judgment as a matter of law" because the non-moving party has failed to make a sufficient showing on an essential element of her case with respect to which she has the burden of proof. "[T]h[e] standard [for granting summary judgment] mirrors the standard for a directed verdict under Federal Rule of Civil Procedure 50(a). . . ."

Of course, a party seeking summary judgment always bears the initial responsibility of informing the district court of the basis for its motion, and identifying those portions of "the pleadings, depositions, answers to interrogatories, and admissions on file, together with the affidavits, if any," which it believes demonstrate the absence of a genuine issue of material fact. But unlike the Court of Appeals, we find no express or implied requirement in Rule 56 that the moving party support its motion with affidavits or other similar materials *negating* the opponent's claim. On the contrary, Rule 56(c), which refers to "the affidavits, *if any*" (emphasis added), suggests the absence of such a requirement. And if there were any doubt about the meaning of Rule 56(c) in this regard, such doubt is clearly removed by Rules 56(a) and (b), which provide that claimants and defendants, respectively, may move for summary judgment "*with or without supporting affidavits*" (emphasis added). The import of these subsections is that, regardless of whether the moving party accompanies its summary judgment motion with affidavits, the motion may, and should, be granted so long as whatever is before the district court demonstrates that the standard for the entry of summary judgment, as set forth in Rule 56(c), is satisfied. One of the principal purposes of the summary judgment rule is to isolate and dispose of factually unsupported claims or defenses, and we think it should be interpreted in a way that allows it to accomplish this purpose.

Respondent argues, however, that Rule 56(e), by its terms, places on the non-moving party the burden of coming forward with rebuttal affidavits, or other specified kinds of materials, only in response to a motion for summary judgment "made and supported as provided in this rule." According to respondent's argument, since petitioner did not "support" its motion with affidavits, summary judgment was improper in this case. But as we have already explained, a motion for summary judgment may be made pursuant to Rule 56 "with or without supporting affidavits." In cases like the instant one, where the non-moving party will bear the burden of proof at trial on a dispositive issue, a summary judgment motion may properly be made in reliance solely on the "pleadings, depositions, answers to interrogatories, and admissions on file." Such a motion, whether or not accompanied by affidavits, will be "made and supported as provided in this rule," and Rule 56(e) therefore requires the non-moving party to go beyond the pleadings and by her own affidavits, or by the "depositions, answers to interrogatories, and admissions on file," designate "specific facts showing that there is a genuine issue for trial."

We do not mean that the non-moving party must produce evidence in a form that would be admissible at trial in order to avoid summary judgment. Obviously, Rule 56 does not require the non-moving party to depose her own witnesses. Rule 56(e) permits a proper summary judgment motion to be opposed by any of the kinds of evidentiary materials listed in Rule 56(c), except the mere pleadings themselves, and it is from this list that one would normally expect the non-moving party to make the showing to which we have referred.

The Court of Appeals in this case felt itself constrained, however, by language in our decision in *Adickes v. S.H. Kress & Co.*, 398 U.S. 144, 90 S.Ct. 1598 (1970). There we held that summary judgment had been improperly entered in favor of the defendant restaurant in an action brought under 42 U.S.C. § 1983. In the course of its opinion, the *Adickes* Court said that "both the commentary on and the background of the 1963 amendment conclusively show that it was not intended to modify the burden of the moving party . . . to show initially the absence of a genuine issue concerning any material fact." Id., at 159, 90 S.Ct., at 1609. We think that this statement is accurate in a literal sense, since we fully agree with the *Adickes* Court that the 1963 amendment to Rule 56(e) was not designed to modify the burden of making the showing generally required by Rule 56(c). It also appears to us that, on the basis of the showing before the Court in *Adickes*, the motion for summary judgment in that case should have been denied. But we do not think the *Adickes* language quoted above should be construed to mean that the burden is on the party moving for summary judgment to produce evidence showing the absence of a genuine issue of material fact, even with respect to an issue on which the non-moving party bears the burden of proof. Instead, as we have explained, the burden on the moving party may be discharged by "showing"—that is, pointing out to the district court—that there is an absence of evidence to support the non-moving party's case.

The last two sentences of Rule 56(e) were added, as this Court indicated in *Adickes*, to disapprove a line of cases allowing a party opposing summary judgment to resist a properly made motion by reference only to its pleadings. While the *Adickes* Court was undoubtedly correct in concluding that these two sentences were not intended to reduce the burden of the moving party, it is also obvious that they were not adopted to add to that burden. Yet that is exactly the result which the reasoning of the Court of Appeals would produce; in effect, an amendment to Rule 56(e) designed to facilitate the granting of motions for summary judgment would be interpreted to make it more difficult to grant such motions. Nothing in the two sentences themselves requires this result, for the reasons we have previously indicated, and we now put to rest any inference that they do so.

Our conclusion is bolstered by the fact that district courts are widely acknowledged to possess the power to enter summary judgments *sua sponte*, so long as the losing party was on notice that she had to come forward with all of her evidence. It would surely defy common sense to hold that the District Court could have entered summary judgment *sua sponte* in favor of petitioner in the instant case, but that petitioner's filing of a motion requesting such a disposition precluded the District Court from ordering it.

Respondent commenced this action in September 1980, and petitioner's motion was filed in September 1981. The parties had conducted discovery, and no serious claim can be made that respondent was in any sense "railroaded" by a premature motion for summary judgment. Any potential problem with such premature motions can be adequately dealt with under Rule 56(f), which allows a summary judgment motion to be denied, or the hearing on the motion to be continued, if the non-moving party has not had an opportunity to make full discovery.

In this Court, respondent's brief and oral argument have been devoted as much to the proposition that an adequate showing of exposure to petitioner's asbestos products was made as to the proposition that no such showing should have been required. But the Court of Appeals declined to address either the adequacy of the showing made by respondent in opposition to petitioner's motion for summary judgment, or the question whether such a showing, if reduced to admissible evidence, would be sufficient to carry respondent's burden of proof at trial. We think the Court of Appeals with its superior knowledge of local law is better suited than we are to make these determinations in the first instance.

The Federal Rules of Civil Procedure have for almost 50 years authorized motions for summary judgment upon proper showings of the lack of a genuine, triable issue of material fact. Summary judgment procedure is properly regarded not as a disfavored procedural shortcut, but rather as an integral part of the Federal Rules as a whole, which are designed "to secure the just, speedy and inexpensive determination of every action." Fed.Rule Civ.Proc. 1. Before the shift to "notice pleading" accomplished by the Federal Rules, motions to dismiss a complaint or to strike a defense were the principal tools by which factually insufficient claims or defenses could be isolated and prevented from going to trial with the attendant unwarranted consumption of public and private resources. But with the advent of "notice pleading," the motion to dismiss seldom fulfills this function any more, and its place has been taken by the motion for summary judgment. Rule 56 must be construed with due regard not only for the rights of persons asserting claims and defenses that are adequately based in fact to have those claims and defenses tried to a jury, but also for the rights of persons opposing such claims and defenses to demonstrate in the manner provided by the Rule, prior to trial, that the claims and defenses have no factual basis.

The judgment of the Court of Appeals is accordingly reversed, and the case is remanded for further proceedings consistent with this opinion.

It is so ordered.

Justice WHITE, concurring.

I agree that the Court of Appeals was wrong in holding that the moving defendant must always support his motion with evidence or affidavits showing the absence of a genuine dispute about a material fact. I also agree that the movant may rely on depositions, answers to interrogatories, and the like, to demonstrate that the plaintiff has no evidence to prove his case and hence that there can be no factual dispute. But the movant must discharge the burden the Rules place upon him: It is not enough to move for summary judgment without supporting the motion in any way or with a conclusory assertion that the plaintiff has no evidence to prove his case.

A plaintiff need not initiate any discovery or reveal his witnesses or evidence unless required to do so under the discovery Rules or by court order. Of course, he must respond if required to do so; but he need not also depose his witnesses or obtain their affidavits to defeat a summary judgment motion asserting only that he has failed to produce any support for his case. It is the defendant's task to negate, if he can, the claimed basis for the suit.

Petitioner Celotex does not dispute that if respondent has named a witness to support her claim, summary judgment should not be granted without Celotex somehow showing that the named witness' possible testimony raises no genuine issue of material fact.

Justice BRENNAN, with whom THE CHIEF JUSTICE and Justice BLACKMUN join, dissenting.

This case requires the Court to determine whether Celotex satisfied its initial burden of production in moving for summary judgment on the ground that the plaintiff lacked evidence to establish an essential element of her case at trial. I do not disagree with the Court's legal analysis. The Court clearly rejects the ruling of the Court of Appeals that the defendant must provide affirmative evidence disproving the plaintiff's case. Beyond this, however, the Court has not clearly explained what is required of a moving party seeking summary judgment on the ground that the non-moving party cannot prove its case. This lack of clarity is unfortunate: district courts must routinely decide summary judgment motions, and the Court's opinion will very likely create confusion. For this reason, even if I agreed with the Court's result, I would have written separately to explain more clearly the law in this area. However, because I believe that Celotex did not meet its burden of production under Federal Rule of Civil Procedure 56, I respectfully dissent from the Court's judgment.

I

Summary judgment is appropriate where the Court is satisfied "that there is no genuine issue as to any material fact and that the moving party is entitled to a judgment as a matter of law." Fed.Rule Civ.Proc. 56(c). The burden of establishing the nonexistence of a "genuine issue" is on the party moving for summary judgment. This burden has two distinct components: an initial burden of production, which shifts to the non-moving party if satisfied by the moving party; and an ultimate burden of persuasion, which always remains on the moving party. The court need not decide whether the moving party has satisfied its ultimate burden of persuasion unless and until the Court finds that the moving party has discharged its initial burden of production.

The burden of production imposed by Rule 56 requires the moving party to make a prima facie showing that it is entitled to summary judgment. The manner in which this showing can be made depends upon which party will bear the burden of persuasion on the challenged claim at trial. If the moving party will bear the burden of persuasion at trial, that party must support its motion with credible evidence—using any of the materials specified in Rule 56(c)—that would entitle it to a directed verdict if not controverted at trial. Such an affirmative showing shifts the burden of production to the party opposing the motion and requires that party either to produce evidentiary materials that demonstrate the existence of a "genuine issue" for trial or to submit an affidavit requesting additional time for discovery. Fed.Rules Civ.Proc. 56(e), (f).

If the burden of persuasion at trial would be on the *non-moving* party, the party moving for summary judgment may satisfy Rule 56's burden of production in either of two ways. First, the moving party may submit affirmative evidence that negates an essential element of the non-moving party's claim. Second, the moving party may demonstrate to the Court that the non-moving party's evidence is insufficient to establish an essential element of the non-moving party's claim. If the non-moving party cannot muster sufficient evidence to make out its claim, a trial would be useless and the moving party is entitled to summary judgment as a matter of law.

Where the moving party adopts this second option and seeks summary judgment on the ground that the non-moving party-who will bear the burden of persuasion at trial-has no evidence, the mechanics of discharging Rule 56's burden of production are somewhat trickier. Plainly, a conclusory assertion that the non-moving party has no evidence is insufficient. Such a "burden" of production is no burden at all and would simply permit summary judgment procedure to be converted into a tool for harassment. Rather, as the Court confirms, a party who moves for summary judgment on the ground that the non-moving party has no evidence must affirmatively show the absence of evidence in the record. This may require the moving party to depose the non-moving party's witnesses or to establish the inadequacy of documentary evidence. If there is literally no evidence in the record, the moving party may demonstrate this by reviewing for the court the admissions, interrogatories, and other exchanges between the parties that are in the record. Either way, however, the moving party must affirmatively demonstrate that there is no evidence in the record to support a judgment for the non-moving party.

If the moving party has not fully discharged this initial burden of production, its motion for summary judgment must be denied, and the Court need not consider whether the moving party has met its ultimate burden of persuasion. Accordingly, the non-moving party may defeat a motion for summary judgment that asserts that the non-moving party has no evidence by calling the Court's attention to supporting evidence already in the record that was overlooked or ignored by the moving party. In that event, the moving party must respond by making an attempt to demonstrate the inadequacy of this evidence, for it is only by attacking all the record evidence allegedly supporting the non-moving party that a party seeking summary judgment satisfies Rule 56's burden of production[1] Thus, if the record disclosed that the moving party had overlooked a witness who would provide relevant testimony for the non-moving party at trial, the Court could not find that the moving party had discharged its initial burden of production unless the moving party sought to demonstrate the inadequacy of this witness' testimony. Absent such a demonstration, summary judgment

---

1 Once the moving party has attacked whatever record evidence-if any-the non-moving party purports to rely upon, the burden of production shifts to the non-moving party, who must either (1) rehabilitate the evidence attacked in the moving party's papers, (2) produce additional evidence showing the existence of a genuine issue for trial as provided in Rule 56(e), or (3) submit an affidavit explaining why further discovery is necessary as provided in Rule 56(f). Summary judgment should be granted if the non-moving party fails to respond in one or more of these ways, or if, after the non-moving party responds, the court determines that the moving party has met its ultimate burden of persuading the court that there is no genuine issue of material fact for trial.

would have to be denied on the ground that the moving party had failed to meet its burden of production under Rule 56.

The result in *Adickes v. S.H. Kress & Co.*, supra, is fully consistent with these principles. In that case, petitioner was refused service in respondent's lunchroom and then was arrested for vagrancy by a local policeman as she left. Petitioner brought an action under 42 U.S.C. § 1983 claiming that the refusal of service and subsequent arrest were the product of a conspiracy between respondent and the police; as proof of this conspiracy, petitioner's complaint alleged that the arresting officer was in respondent's store at the time service was refused. Respondent subsequently moved for summary judgment on the ground that there was no actual evidence in the record from which a jury could draw an inference of conspiracy. In response, petitioner pointed to a statement from her own deposition and an unsworn statement by a Kress employee, both already in the record and both ignored by respondent, that the policeman who arrested petitioner was in the store at the time she was refused service. We agreed that "[i]f a policeman were present, . . . it would be open to a jury, in light of the sequence that followed, to infer from the circumstances that the policeman and Kress employee had a 'meeting of the minds' and thus reached an understanding that petitioner should be refused service." 398 U.S., at 158, 90 S.Ct., at 1609. Consequently, we held that it was error to grant summary judgment "on the basis of this record" because respondent had "failed to fulfill its initial burden" of demonstrating that there was no evidence that there was a policeman in the store.

The opinion in *Adickes* has sometimes been read to hold that summary judgment was inappropriate because the respondent had not submitted affirmative evidence to negate the possibility that there was a policeman in the store. The Court of Appeals apparently read *Adickes* this way and therefore required Celotex to submit evidence establishing that plaintiff's decedent had not been exposed to Celotex asbestos. I agree with the Court that this reading of *Adickes* was erroneous and that Celotex could seek summary judgment on the ground that plaintiff could not prove exposure to Celotex asbestos at trial. However, Celotex was still required to satisfy its initial burden of production.

II

I do not read the Court's opinion to say anything inconsistent with or different than the preceding discussion. My disagreement with the Court concerns the application of these principles to the facts of this case.

Defendant Celotex sought summary judgment on the ground that plaintiff had "failed to produce" any evidence that her decedent had ever been exposed to Celotex asbestos. Celotex supported this motion with a two-page "Statement of Material Facts as to Which There is No Genuine Issue" and a three-page "Memorandum of Points and Authorities" which asserted that the plaintiff had failed to identify any evidence in responding to two sets of interrogatories propounded by Celotex and that therefore the record was "totally devoid" of evidence to support plaintiff's claim.

Approximately three months earlier, Celotex had filed an essentially identical motion. Plaintiff responded to this earlier motion by producing three pieces of evidence which she claimed "[a]t the very least . . . demonstrate that there is a genuine factual dispute for trial": (1) a letter from an insurance representative of another defendant describing asbestos products to which plaintiff's decedent had been exposed, id., at 160; (2) a letter from T.R. Hoff, a former supervisor of decedent, describing asbestos products to which decedent had been exposed, id., at 162; and (3) a copy of decedent's deposition from earlier workmen's compensation proceedings, id., at 164. Plaintiff also apparently indicated at that time that she intended to call Mr. Hoff as a witness at trial. Tr. of Oral Arg. 6-7, 27-29.

Celotex subsequently withdrew its first motion for summary judgment. However, as a result of this motion, when Celotex filed its second summary judgment motion, the record did contain evidence-including at least one witness-supporting plaintiff's claim. Indeed, counsel for Celotex admitted to this Court at oral argument that Celotex was aware of this evidence and of plaintiff's intention to call Mr. Hoff as a witness at trial when the second summary judgment motion was filed. Tr. of Oral Arg. 5-7. Moreover, plaintiff's response to Celotex' second motion pointed to this evidence-noting that it had already been provided to counsel for Celotex in connection with the first motion-and argued that Celotex had failed to "meet its burden of proving that there is no genuine factual dispute for trial." App. 188.

On these facts, there is simply no question that Celotex failed to discharge its initial burden of production. Having chosen to base its motion on the argument that there was no evidence in the record to support plaintiff's claim, Celotex was not free to ignore supporting evidence that the record clearly contained. Rather, Celotex was required, as an initial matter, to attack the adequacy of this evidence. Celotex' failure to fulfill this simple requirement constituted a failure to discharge its initial burden of production under Rule 56, and thereby rendered summary judgment improper.

This case is indistinguishable from *Adickes*. Here, as there, the defendant moved for summary judgment on the ground that the record contained no evidence to support an essential element of the plaintiff's claim. Here, as there, the plaintiff responded by drawing the court's attention to evidence that was already in the record and that had been ignored by the moving party. Consequently, here, as there, summary judgment should be denied on the ground that the moving party failed to satisfy its initial burden of production.

[The dissenting opinion of Justice STEVENS is omitted.]

Example Documents

UNITED STATES DISTRICT COURT
FOR THE DISTRICT OF NEW MEXICO

TWO OLD HIPPIES, LLC,
      Plaintiff,
      v.   No: 10-CV-459 JB/RLP
CATCH THE BUS, LLC,
GARY MACK and FALLON MACK,
      Defendants.

PLAINTIFF'S MOTION FOR SUMMARY JUDGMENT TO SET THE AMOUNT OF DAMAGES AND MEMORANDUM IN SUPPORT

Plaintiff moves for summary judgment setting the amount of damages against Two Old Hippies, LLC, and in support states as follows:

A: Introduction

The Court entered a judgment against Catch the Bus, LLC ("CTB") as to liability. Doc.51. This motion seeks entry of a judgment setting damages against CTB. Plaintiff has no known way to contact CTB to ascertain its position on this motion.

B. Statement of Material Facts
as to Which No Genuine Issue Exists

1. In July 2009, TOH purchased a restored VW bus from CTB for $42,645.60 ("Bus #1"). Affidavit of Molly Bedell ("Aff"), attached as Exhibit A, 5.

2. In October 2009, TOH purchased a second restored VW bus from CTB for $34,646.00 ("Bus #2"). Aff, 6.

3. The purchase price of Bus #1 and Bus #2 together totals $77,269.60. Aff, 7.

4. TOH planned to use Bus #1 in its business and incurred $2,779.37 in design and graphics expense for Bus #1, and give away Bus #2 in a business promotion to an entrant who won Bus #2 in the promotion. Aff, 8.

5. TOH informed CTB of the intended uses of the buses prior to the purchases of the buses. Aff, 9.

6. After CTB delivered Bus #1 to TOH, Bus #1 was not safely operable, and TOH discovered that Bus #1 had many serious mechanical and physical defects when TOH had mechanics examine Bus #1. Aff, 10.

7. After CTB delivered Bus #2, TOH conducted the business promotion at an advertising expense of $21,910 and awarded the bus to its winning entrant, a gentlemen from California. Aff, 11.

8. After CTB delivered Bus #2 to TOH's winning entrant, the entrant and subsequently TOH determined that Bus #2 was not operable and had many serious mechanical and physical defects. Aff, 12.

9. Because of the many serious mechanical and physical defects, TOH has never been able to use Bus#1. Aff, 13.

10. Because of the many serious mechanical and physical defects, TOH reacquired Bus #2 from its winning entrant for $34,624.00 cash making the total amount paid for Bus #2 $69,248.00 and the total for both buses $111,893.60. Aff, 14.

11. The cost of transporting Bus #2 to the contest winner was $243. Aff, 15.

12. The cost of transporting Bus #2 back to TOH was $1,384. Aff, 16.

13. Because of the many serious mechanical and physical defects, TOH has spent more than $3,240.68 in repair and towing costs on Bus #1 to attempt to make it safely operable, but despite the repairs, Bus #1 is not safely operable. Aff, 17.

14. Because Bus #1 is not safely operable and Bus #2 is not operable and because of the many mechanical and physical defects, the buses have no value. Aff, 18.

15. TOH has suffered monetary damages at a minimum as follows:

    a. Purchase price of the two buses and reacquisition
       of Bus #2 $111,893.60

    b. Repairs and towing on Bus #1 $3,240.68

    c. Transportation expense on Bus #2 $1,627.00

d. Design and graphic expense on Bus #1 $2,779.34

e. Advertising expense on Bus #2 $21,910.00

f. Total damages $141,450.62. Aff, 19.

16. CTB paid $2,722.48 toward repairs on Bus #1. Offsetting that payment reduces TOH's total damages to $138,728.14. Aff, 20

17. TOH has incurred attorneys' fees and costs and seeks recovery of those items per the contemporaneously submitted affidavit of Thomas P. Gulley, attached as Exhibit B. Aff, 21.

18. TOH has incurred significant additional monetary damages not itemized herein. The cost of disposal of the two buses exceeds any salvage value. Aff, 22.

C. TOH's Damages

TOH's compensatory damages are a minimum of $138,728.14 as established by the Affidavit of Molly Bedell, Exhibit A.

Because the judgment on liability includes a judgment for fraud as defined by NMSA 57-16-31 of the Motor Dealers Franchising Act (Count III) and a judgment on TOH's claim for violation of New Mexico's Unfair Practices Act (Count IV), TOH is entitled to treble damages of $416,184.42, plus reasonable attorneys' fees of $22,843.00 plus tax on those fees of $1,584.90 for a total of $24,427.90 (Affidavit of Thomas P. Gulley, attached.)

Trebled damages of $416,184.42 plus attorneys' fees and tax of $24,427.90 total $440,612.32.

WHEREFORE, Two Old Hippies, LLC prays for entry of a money judgment against Catch the Bus, LLC, of $440,612.32, plus costs of suit and such other and further relief as is just and proper.

Respectfully submitted,
BANNERMAN & JOHNSON, P.A.

By: s/ Thomas P. Gulley
Thomas P. Gulley
Rebecca L. Avitia
2201 San Pedro, NE, Building 2, Suite 207
Albuquerque, New Mexico 87110
(505) 837-1900
Attorneys for Plaintiff

UNITED STATES DISTRICT COURT
FOR THE DISTRICT OF NEW MEXICO

TWO OLD HIPPIES, LLC,
      Plaintiff,

v.

CATCH THE BUS, LLC,
GARY MACK and FALLON MACK,
      Defendants.

No: 10-CV-459 JB/RLP

AFFIDAVIT OF MOLLY BEDELL IN SUPPORT OF
PLAINTIFF'S MOTION FOR SUMMARY JUDGMENT
TO SET THE DOLLAR AMOUNT OF ITS JUDGMENT

Molly Bedell under oath states as follows:

1. My spouse Thomas W. Bedell and I operate a business in Colorado called Two Old Hippies, LLC ("TOH"), Plaintiff in this case.

2. In the course of operation of the business, I dealt directly with Gary Mack, Fallon Mack and their business Catch the Bus, LLC ("CTB") in TOH purchasing two Volkswagen busses as described below.

3. I have been involved in all events described herein and am well familiar with the facts and circumstances set forth in this affidavit.

4. I am an adult and under no disabilities.

5. In July 2009, TOH purchased a restored VW bus from CTB for $42,645.60 ("Bus #1").

6. In October 2009, TOH purchased a second restored VW bus from CTB for $34,646.00 ("Bus #2").

7. The purchase price of Bus #1 and Bus #2 together totals $77;269.60.

8. TOH planned to use Bus #1 in its business and incurred $2,779.37 in design and graphics expense for Bus #1, and give away Bus #2 in a business promotion to an entrant who won Bus #2 in the promotion.

9. TOR informed CTB of the intended uses of the buses prior to the purchases of the buses.

10. After CTB delivered Bus #1 to TOH, Bus #1 was not safely operable, and TOR discovered that Bus #1 had many serious mechanical and physical defects when TOH had mechanics examine Bus #1.

11. After CTB delivered Bus #2, TOH conducted the business promotion at an advertising expense of $21,910 and awarded the bus to its winning entrant, a gentlemen from California.

12. After CTB delivered Bus #2 to TOH's winning entrant, the entrant and subsequently TOR determined that Bus #2 was not operable and had many serious mechanical and physical defects.

13. Because of the many serious mechanical and physical defects, TOR has never been able to use Bus #1.

14. Because of the many serious mechanical and physical defects, TOH reacquired Bus #2 from its winning entrant for $34,624.00 cash making the total amount paid for Bus #2 $69,248.00 and the total for both buses $111,893.60.

15. The cost of transporting Bus #2 to the contest winner was $243.

16. The cost of transporting Bus #2 back to TOH was $1,384.

17. Because of the many serious mechanical and physical defects, TOH has spent more than $3,240.68 in repair and towing costs on Bus #1 to attempt to make it safely operable, but despite the repairs, Bus #1 is not safely operable.

18. Because Bus #1 is not safely operable and Bus #2 is not operable and because of the many mechanical and physical defects, the buses have no value.

19. TOH has suffered monetary damages at a minimum as follows:

a. Purchase price of the two buses and reacquisition of Bus #2 $111,893.60

b. Repairs and towing on Bus #1 $3,240.68

c. Transportation expense on Bus #2 $1,627.00

d. Design and graphic expense on Bus #1 $2,779.34

e. Advertising expense on Bus #2 $21,910.00

Total damages $141,450.62

20. CTB paid $2,722.48 toward repairs on Bus #1. Offsetting that payment reduces TOH's total damages to $138,728.14.

21. TOH has incurred attorneys' fees and costs and seeks recovery of those items per the contemporaneously submitted affidavit of Thomas P. Gulley.

22. TOH has incurred significant additional monetary damages not itemized herein.

The cost of disposal of the two buses exceeds any salvage value.

STATE OF Colorado   )

) ss.

COUNTY OF Pitkin   )

Signed and sworn before me on May 26, 2011 by Molly Bedell.

_____
Notary Public

My Commission Expires:

05/29/2012

NICOLE BROWN
NOTARY PUBLIC
STATE OF COLORADO

My Commission Expires 05/29/2012

**UNITED STATES DISTRICT COURT
FOR THE DISTRICT OF NEW MEXICO**

TWO OLD HIPPIES, LLC,

     Plaintiff,

     v.   No: 10-CV-459 JB/RLP

CATCH THE BUS, LLC,

GARY MACK and FALLON MACK,

     Defendants.

**AFFIDAVIT OF THOMAS P. GULLEY IN SUPPORT OF
PLAINTIFF'S MOTION FOR AN AWARD OF ATTORNEYS' FEES**

Thomas P. Gulley, on oath, states as follows:

1. I am an attorney licensed to practice in New Mexico and admitted to practice in this court. I have practiced law for 37 years in state and federal courts, the last 24 of which have been in New Mexico.

2. I am well-familiar with attorney fee rates customarily charged clients in New Mexico in commercial litigation matters. I have been the lawyer in charge of this matter since inception at the firm of Bannerman & Johnson, P.A.

3. My hourly rate in this case is $275 per hour. I have used an associate, Rebecca L. Avitia to assist me in this case. She has practiced law for 4 years. Her hourly rate is $195. Amanda Ruben and Nicole Larranaga, paralegals, also briefly worked on this file. Their hourly rate is $90.

4. Together, through the filing of this affidavit and the motion it supports, Bannerman & Johnson has billed its client Two Old Hippies $22,843.00 in attorneys' fees (including $330.00 of paralegal fees) to this matter, plus New Mexico gross receipts tax of $1,584.90 for a total of $24,427.90.

EXHIBIT

1B

5. In the course of representing Two Old Hippies, Ms. Avitia and I have conferred with our client to get the facts, examined documents, prepared the complaint, reviewed the court's scheduling order, conferred with opposing counsel, prepared discovery, reviewed responses to discovery, reviewed the motion to dismiss and responded to it, prepared the joint status report, analyzed and researched the law, prepared a motion to strike the pleadings, attended court hearings, prepared a settlement facilitation report, attended a settlement conference, engaged in settlement negations with Catch the Bus, LLC, prepared a settlement agreement, prepared this motion for summary judgment and supporting affidavit, and engaged in related activities.

6. In my opinion, based on my many years of practice and experience in these types of matters in New Mexico and familiarity with rates charged by lawyers with like experience, these activities and the time charged for them were reasonable and necessary toward the successful prosecution of this case, and the rates charged were reasonable and in line with customary rates charged by lawyers in matters of this type in New Mexico. The same is true of the small amount of paralegal time charged to this matter.

_____

THOMAS P. GULLEY

STATE OF NEW MEXICO   )
) ss.

COUNTY OF BERNALILLO   )

Signed and sworn before me on June_1_, 2011 by Thomas P. Gulley.

My Commission Expires:

_____
Notary Public

April 28, 2012

EXPERIENTIAL ASSIGNMENTS

Draft a Motion for Summary Judgment for one party or the other in the Frensch, Cash or Williams cases as assigned. Start by looking at the FRCP Appendix of Forms. Include a brief but well-organized legal argument for your position.

CHAPTER 9

Jury Trial Right

A DISTINGUISHING FEATURE of the American civil justice system is the jury trial. Most European and Asian nations have no jury trials at all. Some have them for criminal but not civil matters.

Jury trials are expensive for many reasons. They consume more court time than bench (judge) trials. The U.S. system of Evidence law is largely driven by the need to be sensitive to what information reaches the jurors.

The framers of the Constitution held the right to jury trial, even in civil cases, dear. One of the major complaints leveled against the Crown in colonial times was the frequent suspension of the right to a jury trial. The Sixth Amendment refers to the right in criminal cases. The Seventh Amendment establishes the right in most civil cases "at law." Originally, of course, the Seventh Amendment created a right to jury trial in federal courts. After the Civil War, when the Fourteenth Amendment was adopted, some thought that all of the Bill of Rights provisions would apply to the states. However, the Court has chosen one at a time which of the Bill of Rights provisions apply to the states. Interestingly, the Seventh Amendment has never been held to apply to the states. The right to jury trial varies from state court system to state court system in its details, but generally, state statutes and constitutions make jury trials available in most state court actions.

A. The Basic Right

Constitutional Material
Seventh Amendment

In Suits at common law, where the value in controversy shall exceed twenty dollars, the right of trial by jury shall be preserved, and no fact tried by a jury, shall be otherwise re-examined in any Court of the United States, than according to the rules of the common law.

Rule Material

Rule 38 Right to Jury Trial; Demand

(a) Right Preserved. The right of trial by jury as declared by the Seventh Amendment to the Constitution—or as provided by a federal statute—is preserved to the parties inviolate.

(b) Demand. On any issue triable of right by a jury, a party may demand a jury trial by:

> (1) serving the other parties with a written demand—which may be included in a pleading—no later than 14 days after the last pleading directed to the issue is served; and

> (2) filing the demand in accordance with Rule 5(d).

(c) Specifying Issues. In its demand, a party may specify the issues that it wishes to have tried by a jury; otherwise, it is considered to have demanded a jury trial on all the issues so triable. If the party has demanded a jury trial on only some issues, any other party may—within 14 days after being served with the demand or within a shorter time ordered by the court— serve a demand for a jury trial on any other or all factual issues triable by jury.

(d) Waiver; Withdrawal. A party waives a jury trial unless its demand is properly served and filed. A proper demand may be withdrawn only if the parties consent.

. . .

Rule 39 Trial by Jury or by the Court

(a) When a Demand Is Made. When a jury trial has been demanded under Rule 38, the action must be designated on the docket as a jury action. The trial on all issues so demanded must be by jury unless:

(1) the parties or their attorneys file a stipulation to a nonjury trial or so stipulate on the record; or

(2) the court, on motion or on its own, finds that on some or all of those issues there is no federal right to a jury trial.

(b) When No Demand Is Made. Issues on which a jury trial is not properly demanded are to be tried by the court. But the court may, on motion, order a jury trial on any issue for which a jury might have been demanded.

(c) Advisory Jury; Jury Trial by Consent. In an action not triable of right by a jury, the court, on motion or on its own:

(1) may try any issue with an advisory jury; or

(2) may, with the parties' consent, try any issue by a jury whose verdict has the same effect as if a jury trial had been a matter of right, unless the action is against the United States and a federal statute provides for a nonjury trial.

Chauffeurs, Teamsters and Helpers, Local No. 391 v. Terry, et al.

494 U.S. 558, 110 S.Ct. 1339 (1990)

Justice MARSHALL delivered the opinion of the Court, except as to Part III-A.

This case presents the question whether an employee who seeks relief in the form of backpay for a union's alleged breach of its duty of fair representation has a right to trial by jury. We hold that the Seventh Amendment entitles such a plaintiff to a jury trial.

I

McLean Trucking Company and the Chauffeurs, Teamsters, and Helpers Local No. 391 (Union) were parties to a collective-bargaining agreement that governed the terms and conditions of employment at McLean's terminals. The 27 respondents were employed by McLean as truck drivers in bargaining units covered by the agreement, and all were members of the Union. In 1982 McLean implemented a change in operations that resulted in the elimination of some of its terminals and the reorganization of others. As part of that change, [Respondents were laid off and lost seniority rights. After filing two unsuccessful grievances through the Union,] Respondents filed a third grievance with the Union, but the Union declined to refer the charges to a grievance committee on the ground that the relevant issues had been determined in the prior proceedings.

In July 1983, respondents filed an action in District Court, alleging that McLean had breached the collective-bargaining agreement in violation of § 301 of the Labor Management Relations Act, and that the Union had violated its duty of fair representation. Respondents requested a permanent injunction requiring the defendants to cease their illegal acts and to reinstate them to their proper seniority status; in addition, they sought, inter alia, compensatory damages for lost wages and health benefits. In 1986 McLean filed for bankruptcy; subsequently, the action against it was voluntarily dismissed, along with all claims for injunctive relief.

Respondents had requested a jury trial in their pleadings. The Union moved to strike the jury demand on the ground that no right to a jury trial exists in a duty of fair representation suit. The District Court denied the motion to strike. After an interlocutory appeal, the Fourth Circuit affirmed the trial court, holding that the Seventh Amendment entitled respondents to a jury trial of their claim for monetary relief. We granted the petition for certiorari to resolve a Circuit conflict on this issue, and now affirm the judgment of the Fourth Circuit.

II

The duty of fair representation is inferred from unions' exclusive authority under the National Labor Relations Act (NLRA) to represent all employees in a bargaining unit. The duty requires a union "to serve the interests of all members without hostility or discrimination toward any, to exercise its discretion with complete good faith and honesty, and to avoid arbitrary conduct." A union must discharge its duty both in bargaining with the employer and in its enforcement of the resulting collective-bargaining agreement. Thus, the Union here was required to pursue respondents' grievances in a manner consistent with the principles of fair representation.

Because most collective-bargaining agreements accord finality to grievance or arbitration procedures established by the collective-bargaining agreement, an employee normally cannot bring a § 301 action against an employer unless he can show that the union breached its duty of fair representation in its handling of his grievance. Whether the employee sues both the labor union and the employer or only one of those entities, he must prove the same two facts to recover money damages: that the employer's action violated the terms of the collective-bargaining agreement and that the union breached its duty of fair representation.

III

We turn now to the constitutional issue presented in this case—whether respondents are entitled to a jury trial. The Seventh Amendment provides that "[i]n Suits at common law, where the value in controversy shall exceed twenty dollars, the right of trial by jury shall be preserved." The right to a jury trial includes more than the common-law forms of action recognized in 1791; the phrase "Suits at common law" refers to "suits in which legal rights [are] to be ascertained and determined, in contradistinction to those where equitable rights alone [are] recognized, and equitable remedies [are] administered." Since the merger of the systems of law and equity, see Fed.Rule Civ.Proc. 2, this Court has carefully preserved the right to trial by jury where legal rights are at stake.

To determine whether a particular action will resolve legal rights, we examine both the nature of the issues involved and the remedy sought. "First, we compare the statutory action to 18th-century actions brought in the courts of England prior to the merger of the courts of law and equity. Second, we examine the remedy sought and determine whether it is legal or equitable in nature." The second inquiry is the more important in our analysis.[1]

A

An action for breach of a union's duty of fair representation was unknown in 18th-century England; in fact, collective bargaining was unlawful. We must therefore look for an analogous cause of action that existed in the 18th century to determine whether the nature of this duty of fair representation suit is legal or equitable.

---

1   Justice STEVENS' analysis emphasizes a third consideration, namely whether "the issues [presented by the claim] are typical grist for the jury's judgment." Post, at 1354. This Court, however, has never relied on this consideration "as an independent basis for extending the right to a jury trial under the Seventh Amendment." *Tull v. United States,* 481 U.S. 412, 418, n. 4, 107 S.Ct. 1831, 1835, n. 4, 95 L.Ed.2d 365 (1987). We recently noted that this consideration is relevant only to the determination "whether Congress has permissibly entrusted the resolution of certain disputes to an administrative agency or specialized court of equity, and whether jury trials would impair the functioning of the legislative scheme." *Granfinanciera, S.A. v. Nordberg,* 492 U.S., at 42, n. 4, 109 S.Ct., at 2790, n. 4. No one disputes that an action for breach of the duty of fair representation may properly be brought in an Article III court; thus, the factor does not affect our analysis.

The Union contends that this duty of fair representation action resembles a suit brought to vacate an arbitration award because respondents seek to set aside the result of the grievance process. In the 18th century, an action to set aside an arbitration award was considered equitable. 2 J. Story, Commentaries on Equity Jurisprudence § 1452, pp. 789-790 (13th ed. 1886) (equity courts had jurisdiction over claims that an award should be set aside on the ground of "mistake of the arbitrators"); see, e.g., *Burchell v. Marsh*, 17 How. 344, 15 L.Ed. 96 (1855) (reviewing bill in equity to vacate an arbitration award). In support of its characterization of the duty of fair representation claim, the Union cites *United Parcel Service, Inc. v. Mitchell*, 451 U.S. 56, 101 S.Ct. 1559, 67 L.Ed.2d 732 (1981), in which we held that, for purposes of selecting from various state statutes an appropriate limitations period for a § 301 suit against an employer, such a suit was more analogous to a suit to vacate an arbitration award than to a breach of contract action.

The arbitration analogy is inapposite, however, to the Seventh Amendment question posed in this case. No grievance committee has considered respondents' claim that the Union violated its duty of fair representation; the grievance process was concerned only with the employer's alleged breach of the collective-bargaining agreement. Thus, respondents' claim against the Union cannot be characterized as an action to vacate an arbitration award because "[t]he arbitration proceeding did not, and indeed, could not, resolve the employee's claim against the union.... Because no arbitrator has decided the primary issue presented by this claim, no arbitration award need be undone, even if the employee ultimately prevails."

The Union next argues that respondents' duty of fair representation action is comparable to an action by a trust beneficiary against a trustee for breach of fiduciary duty. Such actions were within the exclusive jurisdiction of courts of equity. 2 Story,*supra*, § 960, p. 266; Restatement (Second) of Trusts § 199(c) (1959). This analogy is far more persuasive than the arbitration analogy. Just as a trustee must act in the best interests of the beneficiaries, 2A W. Fratcher, Scott on Law of Trusts § 170 (4th ed. 1987), a union, as the exclusive representative of the workers, must exercise its power to act on behalf of the employees in good faith. Moreover, just as a beneficiary does not directly control the actions of a trustee, 3 Fratcher, *supra*, § 187, an individual employee lacks direct control over a union's actions taken on his behalf, see Cox, The Legal Nature of Collective Bargaining Agreements, 57 Mich.L.Rev. 1, 21 (1958).

The trust analogy extends to a union's handling of grievances. In most cases, a trustee has the exclusive authority to sue third parties who injure the beneficiaries' interest in the trust, 4 Fratcher,*supra*, § 282, pp. 25-29, including any legal claim the trustee holds in trust for the beneficiaries, Restatement (Second) of Trusts, *supra*, § 82, comment *a*. The trustee then has the sole responsibility for determining whether to settle, arbitrate, or otherwise dispose of the claim. Restatement (Second) of Trusts, *supra*, § 192. Similarly, the union typically has broad discretion in its decision whether and how to pursue an employee's grievance against an employer. Just as a trust beneficiary can sue to enforce a contract entered into on his behalf by the trustee only if the trustee "improperly refuses or neglects to bring an action against the third person," Restatement (Second) of Trusts, *supra*, § 282(2), so an employee can sue his employer for a breach of the collective-bargaining agreement only if he shows that the union breached its duty of fair representation in its handling of the grievance.

Respondents contend that their duty of fair representation suit is less like a trust action than an attorney malpractice action, which was historically an action at law, see, *e.g.*, *Russell v. Palmer*, 2 Wils.K.B. 325, 95 Eng.Rep. 837 (1767). In determining the appropriate statute of limitations for a hybrid § 301/duty of fair representation action, this Court in *DelCostello* noted in dictum that an attorney malpractice action is "the closest state-law analogy for the claim against the union."

The attorney malpractice analogy is inadequate in several respects. Although an attorney malpractice suit is in some ways similar to a suit alleging a union's breach of its fiduciary duty, the two actions are fundamentally different. The nature of an action is in large part controlled by the nature of the underlying relationship between the parties. Unlike employees represented by a union, a client controls the significant decisions concerning his representation. Moreover, a client can fire his attorney if he is dissatisfied with his attorney's performance. This option is not available to an individual employee who is unhappy with a union's representation, unless a majority of the members of the bargaining unit share his dissatisfaction. Thus, we find the malpractice analogy less convincing than the trust analogy.

Nevertheless, the trust analogy does not persuade us to characterize respondents' claim as wholly equitable. The Union's argument mischaracterizes the nature of our comparison of the action before us to 18th-century forms of action. As we observed in *Ross v. Bernhard*, 396 U.S. 531, 90 S.Ct. 733, 24 L.Ed.2d 729 (1970), "The Seventh Amendment question depends on the nature of the issue to be tried rather than the character of the overall action." Id., at 538, 90 S.Ct., at 738 (emphasis added) (finding a right to jury trial in a shareholder's derivative suit, a type of suit traditionally brought in courts of equity, because plaintiffs' case presented legal issues of breach of contract and negligence). As discussed above, see *supra*, at 1344, to recover from the Union here, respondents must prove both that McLean violated § 301 by breaching the collective-bargaining agreement and that the Union breached its duty of fair representation. When viewed in isolation, the duty of fair representation issue is analogous to a claim against a trustee for breach of fiduciary duty. The § 301 issue, however, is comparable to a breach of contract claim—a legal issue.

Respondents' action against the Union thus encompasses both equitable and legal issues. The first part of our Seventh Amendment inquiry, then, leaves us in equipoise as to whether respondents are entitled to a jury trial.

B

Our determination under the first part of the Seventh Amendment analysis is only preliminary. In this case, the only remedy sought is a request for compensatory damages representing backpay and benefits. Generally, an action for money damages was "the traditional form of relief offered in the courts of law." This Court has not, however, held that "any award of monetary relief must necessarily be 'legal' relief." Nonetheless, because we conclude that the remedy respondents seek has none of the attributes that must be present before we will find an exception to the general rule and characterize damages as equitable, we find that the remedy sought by respondents is legal.

First, we have characterized damages as equitable where they are restitutionary, such as in "action[s] for disgorgement of improper profits." The backpay sought by respondents is not money wrongfully held by the Union, but wages and benefits they would have received from McLean had the Union processed the employees' grievances properly. Such relief is not restitutionary.

Second, a monetary award "incidental to or intertwined with injunctive relief" may be equitable. Because respondents seek only money damages, this characteristic is clearly absent from the case.

We hold, then, that the remedy of backpay sought in this duty of fair representation action is legal in nature. Considering both parts of the Seventh Amendment inquiry, we find that respondents are entitled to a jury trial on all issues presented in their suit.

IV

On balance, our analysis of the nature of respondents' duty of fair representation action and the remedy they seek convinces us that this action is a legal one. Although the search for an adequate 18th-century analog revealed that the claim includes both legal and equitable issues, the money damages respondents seek are the type of relief traditionally awarded by courts of law. Thus, the Seventh Amendment entitles respondents to a jury trial, and we therefore affirm the judgment of the Court of Appeals.

It is so ordered.

Justice BRENNAN, concurring in part and concurring in the judgment.

I agree with the Court that respondents seek a remedy that is legal in nature and that the Seventh Amendment entitles respondents to a jury trial on their duty of fair representation claims. I therefore join Parts I, II, III-B, and IV of the Court's opinion. I do not join that part of the opinion which reprises the particular historical analysis this Court has employed to determine whether a claim is a "Sui[t] at common law" under the Seventh Amendment, because I believe the historical test can and should be simplified.

The current test, first expounded in *Curtis v. Loether,* 415 U.S. 189, 194, 94 S.Ct. 1005, 1008, 39 L.Ed.2d 260 (1974), requires a court to compare the right at issue to 18th-century English forms of action to determine whether the historically analogous right was vindicated in an action at law or in equity, and to examine whether the remedy sought is legal or equitable in nature. However, this Court, in expounding the test, has repeatedly discounted the significance of the analogous form of action for deciding where the Seventh Amendment applies. I think it is time we dispense with it altogether. I would decide Seventh Amendment questions on the basis of the relief sought. If the relief is legal in nature, i.e., if it is the kind of relief that historically was available from courts of law, I would hold that the parties have a constitutional right to a trial by jury—unless Congress has permissibly delegated the particular dispute to a non-Article III decisionmaker and jury trials would frustrate Congress' purposes in enacting a particular statutory scheme.[2]

I believe that our insistence that the jury trial right hinges in part on a comparison of the substantive right at issue to forms of action used in English courts 200 years ago needlessly convolutes our Seventh Amendment jurisprudence. For the past decade and a half, this Court has explained that the two parts of the historical test are not equal in weight, that the nature of the remedy is more important than the nature of the right. Since the existence of a right to jury trial therefore turns on the nature of the remedy, absent congressional delegation to a specialized decisionmaker, there remains little purpose to our rattling through dusty attics of ancient writs. The time has come to borrow William of Occam's razor and sever this portion of our analysis.

---

2   As the majority notes, ante, at 1345, n. 4, where Congress has delegated a particular claim to an administrative agency or specialized court of equity, a court must consider whether the delegation is a permissible one and "whether jury trials would impair the functioning of the legislative scheme." *Granfinanciera, S.A. v. Nordberg,* 492 U.S. 33, 42, n. 4, 109 S.Ct. 2782, 2790, n. 4, 106 L.Ed.2d 26 (1989). These questions are not implicated in this case, as it is undisputed that an action for breach of the duty of fair representation may be brought in an Article III court.

[An opinion by Justice STEVENS, concurring in part and concurring in the judgment, is omitted.]

Justice KENNEDY, with whom Justice O'CONNOR and Justice SCALIA join, dissenting.

This case asks whether the Seventh Amendment guarantees the respondent union members a jury trial in a duty of fair representation action against their labor union. The Court is quite correct, in my view, in its formulation of the initial premises that must govern the case. Under *Curtis v. Loether*, the right to a jury trial in a statutory action depends on the presence of "legal rights and remedies." To determine whether rights and remedies in a duty of fair representation action are legal in character, we must compare the action to the 18th-century cases permitted in the law courts of England, and we must examine the nature of the relief sought.

I disagree with the analytic innovation of the Court that identification of the trust action as a model for modern duty of fair representation actions is insufficient to decide the case. The Seventh Amendment requires us to determine whether the duty of fair representation action "is more similar to cases that were tried in courts of law than to suits tried in courts of equity." *Tull v. United States*, 481 U.S. 412, 417, 107 S.Ct. 1831, 1835, 95 L.Ed.2d 365 (1987). Having made this decision in favor of an equitable action, our inquiry should end. Because the Court disagrees with this proposition, I dissent.

A

In three cases we have found a right to trial by jury where there are legal claims that, for procedural reasons, a plaintiff could have or must have raised in the courts of equity before the systems merged. In *Beacon Theatres, Inc. v. Westover*, 359 U.S. 500, 79 S.Ct. 948, 3 L.Ed.2d 988 (1959), Fox, a potential defendant threatened with legal antitrust claims, brought an action for declaratory and injunctive relief against Beacon, the likely plaintiff. Because only the courts of equity had offered such relief prior to the merger of the two court systems, Fox had thought that it could deprive Beacon of a jury trial. Beacon, however, raised the antitrust issues as counterclaims and sought a jury. We ruled that, because Beacon would have had a right to a jury trial on its antitrust claims, Fox could not deprive it of a jury merely by taking advantage of modern declaratory procedures to sue first. The result was consistent with the spirit of the Federal Rules of Civil Procedure, which allow liberal joinder of legal and equitable actions, and the Declaratory Judgment Act, 28 U.S.C. §§ 2201, 2202 (1982 ed.), which preserves the right to jury trial to both parties.

In *Dairy Queen, Inc. v. Wood*, 369 U.S. 469, 82 S.Ct. 894, 8 L.Ed.2d 44 (1962), we held, in a similar manner, that a plaintiff, by asking in his complaint for an equitable accounting for trademark infringement, could not deprive the defendant of a jury trial on contract claims subsumed within the accounting. Although a court of equity would have heard the contract claims as part of the accounting suit, we found them severable under modern procedure.

In *Ross v. Bernhard*, 396 U.S. 531, 90 S.Ct. 733, 24 L.Ed.2d 729 (1970), a shareholder-plaintiff demanded a jury trial in a derivative action asserting a legal claim on behalf of his corporation. The defendant opposed a jury trial. In deciding the case, we recognized that only the courts of equity had procedural devices allowing shareholders to raise a corporation's claims. We nonetheless again ruled that modern procedure allowed trial of the legal claim to a jury.

These three cases responded to the difficulties created by a merged court system. They stand for the proposition that, because distinct courts of equity no longer exist, the possibility or necessity of using former equitable procedures to press a legal claim no longer will determine the right to a jury. Justice MARSHALL reads these cases to require a jury trial whenever a cause of action contains legal issues and would require a jury trial in this case because the respondents must prove a breach of the collective-bargaining agreement as one element of their claim.

I disagree. The respondents, as shown above, are asserting an equitable claim. Having reached this conclusion, the Beacon, Dairy Queen, and Ross cases are inapplicable. Although we have divided self-standing legal claims from equitable declaratory, accounting, and derivative procedures, we have never parsed legal elements out of equitable claims absent specific procedural justifications. Actions which, beyond all question, are equitable in nature may involve some predicate inquiry that would be submitted to a jury in other contexts. For example, just as the plaintiff in a duty of fair representation action against his union must show breach of the collective-bargaining agreement as an initial matter, in an action against a trustee for failing to pursue a claim the beneficiary must show that the claim had some merit. But the question of the claim's validity, even if the claim raises contract issues, would not bring the jury right into play in a suit against a trustee.

III

The Court must adhere to the historical test in determining the right to a jury because the language of the Constitution requires it. The Seventh Amendment "preserves" the right to jury trial in civil cases. We cannot preserve a right existing in 1791 unless we look to history to identify it. Our precedents are in full agreement with this reasoning and insist on adherence to the historical test. No alternatives short of rewriting the Constitution exist. If we abandon the plain language of the Constitution to expand the jury right, we may expect Courts with opposing views to curtail it in the future.

It is true that a historical inquiry into the distinction between law and equity may require us to enter into a domain becoming less familiar with time. Two centuries have passed since the Seventh Amendment's ratification, and the incompleteness of our historical records makes it difficult to know the nature of certain actions in 1791. The historical test, nonetheless, has received more criticism than it deserves. Although our application of the analysis in some cases may seem biased in favor of jury trials, the test has not become a nullity. We do not require juries in all statutory actions.

If Congress has not provided for a jury trial, we are confined to the Seventh Amendment to determine whether one is required. Our own views respecting the wisdom of using a jury should be put aside. Like Justice BRENNAN, I admire the jury process. Other judges have taken the opposite view. See, e.g., J. Frank, *Law and the Modern Mind* 170-185 (1931). But the judgment of our own times is not always preferable to the lessons of history. Our whole constitutional experience teaches that history must inform the judicial inquiry. Our obligation to the Constitution and its Bill of Rights, no less than the compact we have with the generation that wrote them for us, do not permit us to disregard provisions that some may think to be mere matters of historical form.

Notes

1. On what issues may a party demand a jury trial? The standard answer has been that a jury trial right attaches to cases "at law," as the language of the Seventh Amendment says. That only goes so far to answering the question for all cases. The starting point, however, is the remedy sought and history. If the party is seeking money damages, the traditional "law" remedy, that fact alone lends strong support to the existence of a jury trial right on that issue. By contrast, when a party seeks the traditional equitable remedies, such as specific performance or injunctive relief, the starting point is that there is no jury trial right.

But even when the relief would point to a jury trial right, there are some wrinkles.

First, there is the so-called "complexity exception." In *Markman v. Westview Instruments Inc.*, the Supreme Court held that the very complex fact issue of interpreting a term of art in a patent should be the judge's decision and not a jury's. The concept is that a term of art in a patent is nearly like interpreting law, and thus should be reserved for the judge. There has not been much spread into other areas beyond patent of the "complexity exception." Most conclude that the mere fact of complexity of a fact decision is insufficient to take it from the jury if there would otherwise be a jury trial right.

Second, if Congress creates a scheme for the resolution of "public rights" and specifically assigns the determination of such cases to an administrative tribunal, then the jury trial right may be curtailed. *Granfinanciera, S.A. v. Nordberg*, 492 U.S. 33, 109 S.Ct. 2782 (1989). The Court explained this concept as follows:

In *Atlas Roofing*, we noted that "when Congress creates new statutory 'public rights,' it may assign their adjudication to an administrative agency with which a jury trial would be incompatible, without violating the Seventh Amendment's injunction that jury trial is to be 'preserved' in 'suits at common law.' " 430 U.S., at 455, 97 S.Ct., at 1269. We emphasized, however, that Congress' power to block application of the Seventh Amendment to a cause of action has limits. Congress may only deny trials by jury in actions at law, we said, in cases where "public rights" are litigated: "Our prior cases support administrative factfinding in only those situations involving 'public rights,' e.g., where the Government is involved in its sovereign capacity under an otherwise valid statute creating enforceable public rights. Wholly private tort, contract, and property cases, as well as a vast range of other cases, are not at all implicated."

2. Jury trial right flow-chart

- Has a jury been demanded? If not, no jury. (FRCP 38b)

- Does the statute under which the claim arises create its own jury trial right? If yes, jury. If no, continue. (FRCP 38a)

- Examine the first two prongs (history of the applicable claim and the remedy sought's relationship to law or equity), with prong two being dominant. If that analysis points away from jury, done. If it points to jury, keep going.

- Has Congress mandated judicial or administrative fact-finding for this claim? If yes, is the matter being adjudicated a "public rights" matter? If yes, no jury. (This is the *Granfinanciera* case.) If no, proceed.

- For what appear to be jury-triable claims, examine each fact issue. Consider historical practice, functional abilities of judge and jury, and policy. Determine which issues should be decided by the jury. (This is the *Markman* case.)

- Check fact issues for overlap. Where overlap exists, let the jury say the final fact-finding word.

3. Notice the relationship between preclusion doctrine (chapter 10) and the jury trial right. In some instances, an issue that has previously been resolved in front of a judge or even an administrative agency, may be binding on a later litigation involving the same fact issue even though that subsequent litigation is before a jury. Thus, that particular issue would be taken from the jury as already resolved, even though it had been resolved by a non-jury decision-maker. Notice this when you read the *Parklane Hosiery* case in chapter 10.

EXPERIENTIAL ASSIGNMENTS

You have just received this e-mail from a supervising lawyer in your firm. Answer it.

To:	Associate
From:	Supervisor
Date:	Today
Re:	Jury trial question

Urgent.

Associate,

I am working on a thorny jury trial right issue in the *Guillen* case. One thing: I have never understood why the 7th amendment stands still while interpretation of other constitutional provisions can sometimes adjust to modern times. Anything unique about the text of the amendment that makes it so?

Supervisor

B. Judgment During and After Trial, Despite or Instead of a Jury Verdict

During the litigation, before trial, Motions for Default Judgment, Motions to Dismiss and Motions for Summary Judgment are common devices for asking that the action be concluded in whole or in part. These devices all ask for a judgment in the moving party's favor. Cases that do reach trial may sometimes be disposed of without the jury's verdict or even despite it.

Rule Material

Rule 50 Judgment as a Matter of Law in a Jury Trial; Related Motion for a New Trial; Conditional Ruling

(a) Judgment as a Matter of Law.

(1) *In General.* If a party has been fully heard on an issue during a jury trial and the court finds that a reasonable jury would not have a legally sufficient evidentiary basis to find for the party on that issue, the court may:

(A) resolve the issue against the party; and

(B) grant a motion for judgment as a matter of law against the party on a claim or defense that, under the controlling law, can be maintained or defeated only with a favorable finding on that issue.

(2) *Motion.* A motion for judgment as a matter of law may be made at any time before the case is submitted to the jury. The motion must specify the judgment sought and the law and facts that entitle the movant to the judgment.

(b) Renewing the Motion After Trial; Alternative Motion for a New Trial. If the court does not grant a motion for judgment as a matter of law made under Rule 50(a), the court is considered to have submitted the action to the jury subject to the court's later deciding the legal questions raised by the motion. No later than 28 days after the entry of judgment—or if the motion addresses a jury issue not decided by a verdict, no later than 28 days after the jury was discharged—the movant may file a renewed motion for judgment as a matter of law and may include an alternative or joint request for a new trial under Rule 59. In ruling on the renewed motion, the court may:

(1) allow judgment on the verdict, if the jury returned a verdict;

(2) order a new trial; or

(3) direct the entry of judgment as a matter of law.

(c) Granting the Renewed Motion; Conditional Ruling on a Motion for a New Trial.

(1) *In General.* If the court grants a renewed motion for judgment as a matter of law, it must also conditionally rule on any motion for a new trial by determining whether a new trial should be granted if the judgment is later vacated or reversed. The court must state the grounds for conditionally granting or denying the motion for a new trial.

(2) *Effect of a Conditional Ruling.* Conditionally granting the motion for a new trial does not affect the judgment's finality; if the judgment is reversed, the new trial must proceed unless the appellate court orders otherwise. If the motion for a new trial is conditionally denied, the appellee may assert error in that denial; if the judgment is reversed, the case must proceed as the appellate court orders.

(d) Time for a Losing Party's New-Trial Motion. Any motion for a new trial under Rule 59 by a party against whom judgment as a matter of law is rendered must be filed no later than 28 days after the entry of the judgment.

(e) Denying the Motion for Judgment as a Matter of Law; Reversal on Appeal. If the court denies the motion for judgment as a matter of law, the prevailing party may, as appellee, assert grounds entitling it to a new trial should the appellate court conclude that the trial court erred in denying the motion. If the appellate court reverses the judgment, it may order a new trial, direct the trial court to determine whether a new trial should be granted, or direct the entry of judgment.

Rule 59 New Trial; Altering or Amending a Judgment

(a) In General.

(1) *Grounds for New Trial.* The court may, on motion, grant a new trial on all or some of the issues—and to any party—as follows:

(A) after a jury trial, for any reason for which a new trial has heretofore been granted in an action at law in federal court; or

(B) after a nonjury trial, for any reason for which a rehearing has heretofore been granted in a suit in equity in federal court.

(2) *Further Action After a Nonjury Trial.* After a nonjury trial, the court may, on motion for a new trial, open the judgment if one has been entered, take additional testimony, amend findings of fact and conclusions of law or make new ones, and direct the entry of a new judgment.

(b) Time to File a Motion for a New Trial. A motion for a new trial must be filed no later than 28 days after the entry of judgment.

(c) Time to Serve Affidavits. When a motion for a new trial is based on affidavits, they must be filed with the motion. The opposing party has 14 days after being served to file opposing affidavits. The court may permit reply affidavits.

(d) New Trial on the Court's Initiative or for Reasons Not in the Motion. No later than 28 days after the entry of judgment, the court, on its own, may order a new trial for any reason that would justify granting one on a party's motion. After giving the parties notice and an opportunity to be heard, the court may grant a timely motion for a new trial for a reason not stated in the motion. In either event, the court must specify the reasons in its order.

(e) Motion to Alter or Amend a Judgment. A motion to alter or amend a judgment must be filed no later than 28 days after the entry of the judgment.

Rule 60 Relief from a Judgment or Order

(a) Corrections Based on Clerical Mistakes; Oversights and Omissions. The court may correct a clerical mistake or a mistake arising from oversight or omission whenever one is found in a judgment, order, or other part of the record. The court may do so on motion or on its own, with or without notice. But after an appeal has been docketed in the appellate court and while it is pending, such a mistake may be corrected only with the appellate court's leave.

(b) Grounds for Relief from a Final Judgment, Order, or Proceeding. On motion and just terms, the court may relieve a party or its legal representative from a final judgment, order, or proceeding for the following reasons:

(1) mistake, inadvertence, surprise, or excusable neglect;

(2) newly discovered evidence that, with reasonable diligence, could not have been discovered in time to move for a new trial under Rule 59(b);

(3) fraud (whether previously called intrinsic or extrinsic), misrepresentation, or misconduct by an opposing party;

(4) the judgment is void;

(5) the judgment has been satisfied, released, or discharged; it is based on an earlier judgment that has been reversed or vacated; or applying it prospectively is no longer equitable; or

(6) any other reason that justifies relief.

(c) Timing and Effect of the Motion.

(1) *Timing.* A motion under Rule 60(b) must be made within a reasonable time—and for reasons (1), (2), and (3) no more than a year after the entry of the judgment or order or the date of the proceeding.

(2) *Effect on Finality.* The motion does not affect the judgment's finality or suspend its operation.

(d) Other Powers to Grant Relief. This rule does not limit a court's power to:

(1) entertain an independent action to relieve a party from a judgment, order, or proceeding;

(2) grant relief under 28 U.S.C. §1655 to a defendant who was not personally notified of the action; or

(3) set aside a judgment for fraud on the court.

(e) Bills and Writs Abolished. The following are abolished: bills of review, bills in the nature of bills of review, and writs of *coram nobis*, *coram vobis*, and *audita querela*.

Ackermann v. United States (Two Cases)

340 U.S. 193, 71 S.Ct. 209 (1950)

Mr. Justice MINTON delivered the opinion of the Court.

Petitioner Hans Ackermann filed a motion in the District Court for the Western District of Texas to set aside a judgment entered December 7, 1943, in that court cancelling his certificate of naturalization. The motion was filed March 25, 1948, pursuant to amended Rule 60(b) of the Federal Rules of Civil Procedure, 28 U.S.C.A., which became effective March 19, 1948. The United States filed a motion to dismiss petitioner's motion. The District Court denied petitioner's motion and the Court of Appeals affirmed. We granted certiorari.

The question is whether the District Court erred in denying the motion for relief under Rule 60(b).

Petitioner and his wife Frieda were natives of Germany. They were naturalized in 1938. They resided, as now, at Taylor, Texas, where petitioner and Max Keilbar owned and operated a German language newspaper. Frieda Ackermann wrote for the paper. She was a sister of Keilbar, who was also a native of Germany and who had been naturalized in 1933.

In 1942 complaints were filed against all three to cancel their naturalization on grounds of fraud. Petitioner and Keilbar were represented by counsel and answered the complaints. After an order of consolidation, trial of the three cases began November 1, 1943, and separate judgments were entered December 7, 1943, cancelling and setting aside the orders admitting them to citizenship. Keilbar appealed to the Court of Appeals, and by stipulation with the United States Attorney his case in that court was reversed, and the complaint against him was ordered dismissed. The Ackermanns did not appeal.

Petitioner in his motion here under consideration alleges that his 'failure to appeal from said judgment is excusable' for the reason that he had no money or property other than his home in Taylor, Texas, owned by him and his wife and worth $2,500, 'and the costs of transcribing the evidence and printing the record and brief on appeal were estimated at not less than $5,000.00.' On December 11, 1943, petitioner was detained in an Alien Detention Station at Seagoville, Texas. Before time for appeal had expired, petitioner was advised by his attorney that he and his wife could not appeal on affidavits of inability to pay costs until they had 'appropriated said home to the payment of such costs to the full extent of the proceeds of a sale thereof'; that this information distressed them, and they sought advice from W. F. Kelley, 'Assistant Commissioner for Alien Control,

Immigration and Naturalization Department,' in whose custody petitioner and his wife were being held, 'and he being a person in whom they had great confidence'; that Kelley on being informed of their financial condition and the advice of their attorney that it would be necessary for them to dispose of their home in order to appeal, advised them in substance to 'hang on to their home,' and told them further that they had lost their American citizenship and were stateless, and that they would be released at the end of the war; that relying upon Kelley's advice, they refrained from appealing from said judgments; that on April 29, 1944, after time for appeal had expired, they were interned, and on January 25, 1946, the Attorney General ordered them to depart within thirty days or be deported. They did not depart, and they have not been deported, although the orders of deportation are still outstanding. Petitioner further alleged that he would show that the judgment of December 7, 1943, was unlawful and erroneous by producing the record in the Keilbar case.

The District Court on September 28, 1948, denied petitioner's motion to vacate the judgment of denaturalization, the court stating in the order that 'there is no merit to said motion.'

It will be noted that petitioner alleged in his motion that his failure to appeal was excusable. A motion for relief because of excusable neglect as provided in Rule 60(b)(1) must, by the rule's terms, be made not more than one year after the judgment was entered. The judgment here sought to be relieved from was more than four years old. It is immediately apparent that no relief on account of 'excusable neglect' was available to this petitioner on the motion under consideration.

But petitioner seeks to bring himself within Rule 60(b)(6), which applies if 'any other reason justifying relief' is present, as construed and applied in *Klapprott v. United States*, 335 U.S. 601, 69 S.Ct. 384, 389, 93 L.Ed. 266. The circumstances alleged in the motion which petitioner asserts bring him within Rule 60(b)(6) are that the denaturalization judgment was erroneous; that he did not appeal and raise that question because his attorney advised him he would have to sell his home to pay costs, while Kelley, the Alien Control officer, in whom he alleges he had confidence and upon whose advice he relied, told him 'to hang on to their home' and that he would be released at the end of the war; and that these circumstances justify failure to appeal the denaturalization judgment.

We cannot agree that petitioner has alleged circumstances showing that his failure to appeal was justifiable. It is not enough for petitioner to allege that he had confidence in Kelley. On the allegations of the motion before us, Kelley was a stranger to petitioner. In that state of the pleadings there are two reasons why petitioner cannot be heard to say his neglect to appeal brings him within the rule.

First, anything said by Kelley could not be used to relieve petitioner of his duty to take legal steps to protect his interest in litigation in which the United States was a party adverse to him. Secondly, petitioner had no right to repose confidence in Kelley, a stranger. There is no allegation of any fact or circumstance which shows that Kelley had any undue influence over petitioner or practiced any fraud, deceit, misrepresentation, or duress upon him. There are no allegations of privity or any fiduciary relations existing between them. Indeed, the allegations of the motion all show the contrary. However, petitioner had a confidential adviser in his own counsel. Instead of relying upon that confidential adviser, he freely accepted the advice of a stranger, a source upon which he had no right to rely. Petitioner made a considered choice not to appeal, apparently because he did not feel that an appeal would prove to be worth what he thought was a required sacrifice of his home. His choice was a risk, but calculated and deliberate and such as follows a free choice. Petitioner cannot be relieved of such a choice because hindsight seems to indicate to him that his decision not to appeal was probably wrong, considering the outcome of the Keilbar case. There must be an end to litigation someday, and free, calculated, deliberate choices are not to be relieved from.

As further evidence of the inadequacy of petitioner's motion to bring himself within any division of Rule 60(b) which would excuse him from not having taken an appeal, we call attention to the fact that Keilbar got the record before the Court of Appeals, and it contained all the evidence that was introduced as to petitioner and his wife, who were tried together with Keilbar. The Ackermanns and Keilbar were related, yet no effort was made to get into the Court of Appeals and use the same record as to the evidence that Keilbar used. It certainly would not have taken five thousand dollars or one-tenth thereof for petitioner and his wife to have supplemented the Keilbar record with that pertaining to themselves and to prepare a brief, even if all of it were printed. We are further aware of the practice of the Courts of Appeals permitting litigants who are poor but not paupers to file typewritten records and briefs at a very small cost to them. With the same counsel representing petitioner as represented his kinsman Keilbar, and with Frieda Ackermann having funds sufficient to employ separate counsel, failure to appeal because of the fear of losing his home in defraying the expenses of the brief and record, makes it further evidence that Rule 60(b) has no application to petitioner in this setting.

The Klapprott case was a case of extraordinary circumstances. Mr. Justice Black stated in the following words why the allegations in the Klapprott case, there taken as true, brought it within Rule 60(b)(6): 'But petitioner's allegations set up an extraordinary situation which cannot fairly or logically be classified as mere 'neglect' on his part. The undenied facts set out in the petition reveal far more than a failure to defend the denaturalization charges due to inadvertence, indifference, or careless disregard of consequences. For before, at the time, and after the default judgment was entered, petitioner was held in jail in New York, Michigan, and the District of Columbia by the United States, his adversary in the denaturalization proceedings. Without funds to hire a lawyer, petitioner was defended by appointed counsel in the criminal cases. Thus petitioner's prayer to set aside the default judgment did not rest on mere allegations of 'excusable neglect.' The foregoing allegations and others in the petition tend to support petitioner's argument that he was deprived of any reasonable opportunity to make a defense to the criminal charges instigated by officers of the very United States agency which supplied the secondhand information upon which his citizenship was taken away from him in his absence. The basis of his petition was not that he had neglected to act in his own defense, but that in jail as he was, weakened from illness, without a lawyer in the denaturalization proceedings or funds to hire one, disturbed and fully occupied in efforts to protect himself against the gravest criminal charges, he was no more able to defend himself in the New Jersey court than he would have been had he never received notice of the charges.' *Klapprott v. United States*, 335 U.S. 601, 613-614, 69 S.Ct. 384, 389, 93 L.Ed. 266.

By no stretch of imagination can the voluntary, deliberate, free, untrammeled choice of petitioner not to appeal compare with the Klapprott situation. Mr. Justice Black set forth in order the extraordinary circumstances alleged by Klapprott. We paraphrase them and give the comparable situation of Ackermann.

In the spring of 1942 Klapprott was ill, and the illness left him financially poor and unable to work. On May 12, 1942, proceedings were commenced in a New Jersey District Court to cancel his citizenship. As for Ackermann, when he was sued he was well, and had a home worth $2,500, one-half interest in a newspaper, and the means to employ counsel.

When complaint was served upon Klapprott, he had no money to hire a lawyer, and he wrote an answer to the complaint filed against him and a letter to the American Civil Liberties Union asking it to represent him without fee. Ackermann had the means to hire and did hire able counsel of his own choice who prepared and filed an answer for him.

In less than two months after the complaint was served on the penniless, ill Klapprott, he was arrested for conspiracy to violate the Selective Service Act, 50 U.S.C.A.Appendix s 301 et seq., and taken to New York and jailed in default of bond. His letter to the American Civil Liberties Union was taken by the Federal Bureau of Investigation before time for him to answer had expired, and was not mailed by that Bureau. Ackermann was never indicted or in jail from the time complaint was filed against him until after judgment, during all of which time he had the benefit of counsel and freedom of movement and action.

Within ten days after his arrest, Klapprott was defaulted in the citizenship proceedings in New Jersey. He was still in jail in New York. No evidence was offered to prove the complaint in the denaturalization proceedings, which complaint was verified on information and belief only. In Ackermann's case, no default was entered. He appeared in person and by counsel and had a trial in open court with able counsel to defend him. Much evidence was introduced and a record was made of it.

Klapprott was convicted in New York and sent to a penitentiary in Michigan. He was later transferred to the District of Columbia, where he was lodged in jail and tried on another charge, later dismissed. The New York conviction was reversed, but he had been in jail for about two years. He was then lodged at Ellis Island for deportation because his citizenship had been cancelled in the New Jersey proceedings where he had been defaulted. While at Ellis Island, the motion to relieve from the default judgment cancelling his citizenship was prepared and filed, denied by the District Court and the Court of Appeals and finally sustained by this Court. Ackermann was never under criminal charges or detained while the suit for cancellation of his citizenship was pending. During all of that time he was free, well, and able to defend himself, and in that regard had able counsel representing him in a trial in open court. Even after the judgment cancelling his citizenship, he had counsel and free access to him, although detained by the United States Government.

From a comparison of the situations shown by the allegations of Klapprott and Ackermann, it is readily apparent that the situations of the parties bore only the slightest resemblance to each other. The comparison strikingly points up the difference between no choice and choice; imprisonment and freedom of action; no trial and trial; no counsel and counsel; no chance for negligence and inexcusable negligence. Subsection 6 of Rule 60(b) has no application to the situation of petitioner. Neither the circumstances of petitioner nor his excuse for not appealing is so extraordinary as to bring him within Klapprott or Rule 60(b)(6).

The motion for relief was properly denied, and the judgment is affirmed.

Affirmed.

No. 36, *Frieda Ackermann v. United States*, is a companion case to No. 35, and it was stipulated that the decision in No. 36 should be the same as in No. 35. The judgment in No. 36 therefore is also affirmed.

Affirmed.

Mr. Justice CLARK took no part in the consideration or decision of this case.

Mr. Justice BLACK, with whom Mr. Justice FRANKFURTER and Mr. Justice DOUGLAS concur, dissenting.

The Court's interpretation of amended Rule 60(b) of the Federal Rules of Civil Procedure neutralizes the humane spirit of the Rule and thereby frustrates its purpose. The Rule empowers courts to set aside judgments under five traditional, specified types of circumstances in which it would be inequitable to permit a judgment to stand. But the draftsmen of the Rule did not intend that these specified grounds should prevent the granting of similar relief in other situations where fairness might require it. Accordingly, there was added a broad sixth ground: 'any other reason justifying relief from the operation of the judgment.' The Court nevertheless holds that the allegations of the present motions were not sufficient to justify the District Court in hearing evidence to determine whether justice would best be served by granting relief from the judgments against petitioners. Because I disagree with this interpretation of Rule 60(b), it becomes necessary to summarize the allegations of the motions.

In holding that the allegations of these motions are not even sufficient to justify the District Court in hearing evidence, the Court relies heavily on its assertion that petitioners 'had no right to repose confidence in Kelley' because Kelley was a 'stranger' to them. In the first place, Rule 60(b)'s broad grant of power to the District Court should not be constricted by the importation of the concept of legal 'rights.' Moreover, far from being a stranger, Kelley was the United States official who held petitioners in custody. Any person held by the United States should be able to repose confidence in the Government official entrusted with his custody. There are obvious reasons why this should be true in the case of the foreign born, less familiar with our customs than are our native citizens.

The Court also relies on the fact that the motions to set aside the judgments contain 'no allegations of privity or any fiduciary relations existing' between petitioners and Kelley. Surely the liberalizing provisions of 60(b) should not be emasculated by common-law ideas of 'privity' or 'fiduciary relations.' If relevant, however, I should think that the phrase 'fiduciary relations' given its best meaning encompasses the relationship between petitioners and the official who held them in custody.

Finally, since the Court holds that the allegations of petitioners' motions were insufficient to justify the hearing of evidence by the District Court, I think it inappropriate for the Court to consider what purports to be its judicial knowledge of the cost of transcripts and the ability of litigants to file typewritten records and briefs. The motions refute any such knowledge on the part of these petitioners and I am satisfied that no such knowledge would be established if the District Court were permitted to try these cases.

The result of the Court's illiberal construction of 60(b) is that these foreign-born people, dependent on our laws for their safety and protection, are denied the right to appeal to the very court that held (on the Government's admission) that the judgment against their co-defendant was unsupported by adequate evidence. It does no good to have liberalizing rules like 60(b) if, after they are written, their arteries are hardened by this Court's resort to ancient common-law concepts. I would reverse.

NOTE

Is finality a good enough reason to deny relief to the Ackermanns? What would happen if a case could always be reopened when a party said it had found new evidence or had some other reason? Can you craft a rule that strikes the balance better than does FRCP 60?

EXPERIENTIAL ASSIGNMENTS

The plaintiff's evidence is concluded in the Frensch, Cash and Williams cases. Assume that everything in the Complaints in chapter 5 has been supported by some evidence. As Defendant, make an oral Motion for Judgment as assigned. (Or write the text of what you would say, if so assigned.)

C. Procedures to Facilitate Judgment by a Judge or Jury

When a civil action does reach its conclusion at a trial, devices must allocate the law to the judge and the fact-finding to the jury, or in the case of a bench trial, force the judge to divide her roles between rulings on the law and finding of facts.

Rule Material

Rule 51 Instructions to the Jury; Objections; Preserving a Claim of Error

(a) Requests.

> (1) *Before or at the Close of the Evidence.* At the close of the evidence or at any earlier reasonable time that the court orders, a party may file and furnish to every other party written requests for the jury instructions it wants the court to give.
>
> (2) *After the Close of the Evidence.* After the close of the evidence, a party may:
>
>> (A) file requests for instructions on issues that could not reasonably have been anticipated by an earlier time that the court set for requests; and
>>
>> (B) with the court's permission, file untimely requests for instructions on any issue.

(b) Instructions. The court:

> (1) must inform the parties of its proposed instructions and proposed action on the requests before instructing the jury and before final jury arguments;
>
> (2) must give the parties an opportunity to object on the record and out of the jury's hearing before the instructions and arguments are delivered; and
>
> (3) may instruct the jury at any time before the jury is discharged.

(c) Objections.

> (1) *How to Make.* A party who objects to an instruction or the failure to give an instruction must do so on the record, stating distinctly the matter objected to and the grounds for the objection.
>
> (2) *When to Make.* An objection is timely if:
>
>> (A) a party objects at the opportunity provided under Rule 51(b)(2); or
>>
>> (B) a party was not informed of an instruction or action on a request before that opportunity to object, and the party objects promptly after learning that the instruction or request will be, or has been, given or refused.

(d) Assigning Error; Plain Error.

(1) *Assigning Error.* A party may assign as error:

(A) an error in an instruction actually given, if that party properly objected; or

(B) a failure to give an instruction, if that party properly requested it and—unless the court rejected the request in a definitive ruling on the record—also properly objected.

(2) *Plain Error.* A court may consider a plain error in the instructions that has not been preserved as required by Rule 51(d)(1) if the error affects substantial rights.

Rule 52 Findings and Conclusions by the Court; Judgment on Partial Findings

(a) Findings and Conclusions.

(1) In General. In an action tried on the facts without a jury or with an advisory jury, the court must find the facts specially and state its conclusions of law separately. The findings and conclusions may be stated on the record after the close of the evidence or may appear in an opinion or a memorandum of decision filed by the court. Judgment must be entered under Rule 58

.   .   .

Rule 54 Judgment; Costs

(a) Definition; Form. "Judgment" as used in these rules includes a decree and any order from which an appeal lies. A judgment should not include recitals of pleadings, a master's report, or a record of prior proceedings.

(b) Judgment on Multiple Claims or Involving Multiple Parties. When an action presents more than one claim for relief—whether as a claim, counterclaim, cross-claim, or third-party claim—or when multiple parties are involved, the court may direct entry of a final judgment as to one or more, but fewer than all, claims or parties only if the court expressly determines that there is no just reason for delay. Otherwise, any order or other decision, however designated, that adjudicates fewer than all the claims or the rights and liabilities of fewer than all the parties does not end the action as to any of the claims or parties and may be revised at any time before the entry of a judgment adjudicating all the claims and all the parties' rights and liabilities.

(c) Demand for Judgment; Relief to Be Granted. A default judgment must not differ in kind from, or exceed in amount, what is demanded in the pleadings. Every other final judgment should grant the relief to which each party is entitled, even if the party has not demanded that relief in its pleadings.

(d) Costs; Attorney's Fees.

(1) Costs Other Than Attorney's Fees. Unless a federal statute, these rules, or a court order provides otherwise, costs—other than attorney's fees—should be allowed to the prevailing party. But costs against the United States, its officers, and its agencies may be imposed only to the extent allowed by law. The clerk may tax costs on 14 days' notice. On motion served within the next 7 days, the court may review the clerk's action.

(2) Attorney's Fees.

(A) Claim to Be by Motion. A claim for attorney's fees and related nontaxable expenses must be made by motion unless the substantive law requires those fees to be proved at trial as an element of damages.

(E) Exceptions. Subparagraphs (A)–(D) do not apply to claims for fees and expenses as sanctions for violating these rules or as sanctions under 28 U.S.C. §1927.

. . .

EXPERIENTIAL ASSIGNMENTS

Both plaintiff's and defendant's evidence has been offered in the Frensch, Cash and Williams cases.

a. Assume a bench trial. Draft Proposed Findings of Fact and Conclusions of Law as assigned.

b. Assume a jury trial. Draft a basic set of proposed Jury Instructions.

CHAPTER 10

Preclusion Doctrine

PRECLUSION DOCTRINE is unlike most of the material in the Civil Procedure course. It is not much connected with the FRCPs and is not based on federal statutory or constitutional law. Instead, it is a doctrine of the common law that is necessary to make the civil litigation process function smoothly. There is a subtle connection between the doctrine and the claim joinder rules. For efficiency's sake, closely related claims and theories should be combined into a single civil action when possible. And for finality's sake, once a claim or a discrete issue has been adequately resolved, it should remain resolved and not be re-litigated.

Rush v. City of Maple Heights

167 Ohio St. 221, 147 N.E.2d 599 (1958)

Syllabus by the Court

Where a person suffers both personal injuries and property damage as a result of the same wrongful act, only a single cause of action arises, the different injuries occasioned thereby being separate items of damage from such act. (Paragraph four of the syllabus in the case of *Vasu v. Kohlers, Inc.*, 145 Ohio St. 321, 61 N.E.2d 707, 166 A.L.R. 855, overruled.)

This cause was commenced in the Court of Common Pleas of Cuyahoga County as an action to recover damages for personal injuries resulting from a fall while plaintiff, appellee herein, was riding on a motorcycle over a street in defendant city of Maple Heights, appellant herein.

Plaintiff alleges that [she was riding as a passenger on her husband's motor-cycle] when she was thrown to the ground and injured.

She alleges further that the defendant was negligent in failing to keep Schreiber Road in good repair and free from nuisance, in suffering large holes, 'bumps' and 'dips' to exist in the regularly traveled portion of the street, and in failing to erect warning signs giving notice of the unsafe and dangerous condition of Schreiber Road; that the city had notice; and that her injuries were caused directly and proximately by the negligence of the defendant city.

She then alleges:

'Thereafter the plaintiff herein, Lenore Rush, duly filed an action for damage to personal property in the Municipal Court of Cleveland, Ohio, against the city of Maple Heights. The cause proceeded to trial on or about the 23rd day of March 1954, the Municipal Court of Cleveland rendered its judgment in favor of the plaintiff therein, Lenore Rush, and against the defendant therein, the city of Maple Heights. Thereafter upon the motion of the defendant, the city of Maple Heights, the Municipal Court of Cleveland rendered its findings of fact and conclusions of law as follows:

'The court finds that the city of Maple Heights had actual notice of the condition of Schreiber Road.

'That the city was negligent in not repairing the hole complained of in plaintiff's petition.

'That such negligence on the part of the city was the proximate cause of the damages sustained by plaintiff in the amount of $100.

'Conclusions of law.

'Judgment for plaintiff in the amount of $100.

[The Plaintiff alleged that Defendant unsuccessfully appealed to the appellate and state supreme courts.]

'The plaintiff in [the prior case] is the same Lenore Rush who is the plaintiff herein; the defendant is the same city of Maple Heights, defendant herein. The allegations of negligence in the Municipal Court of Cleveland are the same as the allegations of negligence hereinbefore set forth. The issue of negligence is therefore res judicata between the parties hereto.'

Plaintiff then filed a motion for an order setting the cause for trial 'on the issue of damages alone for the reason that the liability of the defendant has been determined heretofore by the Supreme Court in [the prior case] in the Municipal Court of Cleveland.'

In its answer, defendant denies plaintiff's allegations charging it with negligence.

Relative to the effect of the previous action between the parties in the Cleveland Municipal Court, the defendant answers as follows:

'* * * defendant admits the filing of a lawsuit by plaintiff against defendant in Cleveland Municipal Court and that plaintiff obtained judgment therein, but this defendant denies that said Cleveland Municipal Court judgment is controlling herein.

Defendant's answer admits further that it appealed from the judgment of the Municipal Court to the Court of Appeals and to the Supreme Court as alleged by plaintiff and denies for want of knowledge that plaintiff was injured at the time and place or in the manner and to the extent described in plaintiff's petition.

After a pretrial conference, the motion of plaintiff for an order setting this cause for trial on the issue of damages only was sustained, and the case was assigned for trial. A jury was empanelled, and the case submitted.

The court charged the jury that it was not to be 'concerned with the issues of defendant's negligence, proximate cause or plaintiff's contributory negligence,' because those issues were resolved favorably to the plaintiff and against the defendant in another action between the same parties in the Cleveland Municipal Court, and that the action in that court did not involve a claim for bodily injury, and under the law plaintiff had the right to bring her separate action for personal injuries in the Court of Common Pleas.

The jury returned a verdict for the plaintiff in the amount of $12,000.

An appeal was perfected to the Court of Appeals, which affirmed the judgment.

HERBERT, Judge.

The eighth error assigned by the defendant is that 'the trial and appellate courts committed error in permitting plaintiff to split her cause of action and to file a separate action in the Cleveland Municipal Court for her property damage and reduce same to judgment, and, thereafter, to proceed, in the Cuyahoga County Common Pleas Court, with a separate action for personal injuries, both claims arising out of a single accident.'

In the case of *Vasu v. Kohlers, Inc.*, 145 Ohio St. 321, 61 N.E.2d 707, 709, 166 A.L.R. 855, plaintiff operating an automobile came into collision with defendant's truck, in which collision he suffered personal injuries and also damage to his auto-mobile. At the time of collision, plaintiff had coverage of a $50 deductible collision policy on his automobile. The insurance company paid the plaintiff a sum cover-ing the damage to his automobile, whereupon, in accordance with a provision of the policy, the plaintiff assigned to the insurer his claim for such damage.

In February 1942, the insurance company commenced an action in the Common Pleas Court of Mahoning County against Kohlers, Inc., the defen-dant in the reported case, to recoup the money paid by it to cover the damage to Vasu's automobile.

In August 1942, Vasu commenced an action in the same court against Kohlers, Inc., to recover for personal injuries which he suffered in the same collision.

In March 1943, in the insurance company's action, a verdict was rendered in favor of the defendant, followed by judgment.

Two months later an amended answer was filed in the Vasu case, setting out as a bar to the action for recovery of damages for the personal injuries suf-fered by plaintiff the judgment rendered in favor of defendant in the insurance company case. A motion to strike that defense having been sustained, a second amended answer was filed omitting allegations as to such judgment. A trial of the action resulted in a verdict for plaintiff, upon which judgment was entered.

On appeal to the Court of Appeals the defendant claimed that the Court of Common Pleas erred in sustaining plaintiff's motion to strike from the defen-dant's answer the defense of res judicata claimed to have arisen by reason of the judgment in favor of the defendant in the action by the insurance company.

The Court of Appeals reversed the judgment of the Court of Common Pleas and entered final judgment in favor of defendant.

This court reversed the judgment of the Court of Appeals, holding in the syllabus, in part, as follows:

'4. Injuries to both person and property suffered by the same person as a result of the same wrongful act are infringements of different rights and give rise to distinct causes of action, with the result that the recovery or denial of recovery of compensation for damages to the property is no bar to an action subsequently prosecuted for the personal injury, unless by an adverse judgment in the first action issues are determined against the plaintiff which operate as an estoppel against him in the second action.

[Later Ohio Supreme Court cases], distinguishing and explaining the Vasu case, have not changed the rule established in paragraph four of the syllabus of the latter case, holding that injuries to both person and property suffered by the same person as a result of the same wrongful act are infringements of different rights and give rise to distinct causes of action.

However, it is contended here that that rule is in conflict with the great weight of authority in this country and has caused vexatious litigation. The following quotation from 1 American Jurisprudence, 494, Section 114, states this question well:

> 'It sometimes happens that a single wrongful or negligent act causes damage in respect of both the person and the property of the same individual, as, for instance, where the owner of a vehicle is injured in a collision which also damages the vehicle. In such a case, the question arises as to whether there are two causes of action or only one, and the authorities are in conflict concerning it. The majority rule is that only one cause of action arises, the reason of the rule being that as the defendant's wrongful act is single, the cause of action must be single, and that the different injuries occasioned by it are merely items of damage proceeding from the same wrong. * * *

> 'In other jurisdictions, the rule is that two causes of action result from a negligent act which inflicts injury on a person and his property at the same time. This conclusion has been reached in different jurisdictions by different lines of reasoning.'

Upon examination of decisions of courts of last resort, we find that the majority rule is followed in the following cases in each of which the action was between the person suffering injury and the person committing the tort, and where insurers were not involved, as in the case here.

The minority rule [is] that separate actions may be maintained to recover for personal injuries and for damages to property resulting from the same wrongful act, is set forth in the following cases:

The reasoning behind the majority rule seems to be well stated in the case of *Mobile & Ohio Rd. Co. v. Matthews*, supra, as follows:

> 'The negligent action of the plaintiff in error constituted but one tort. The injuries to the person and property of the defendant in error were the several results and effects of one wrongful act. A single tort can be the basis of but one action. It is not improper to declare in different counts for damages to the person and property when both result from the same tort, and it

is the better practice to do so where there is any difference in the measure of damages, and all the damages sustained must be sued for in one suit. This is necessary to prevent multiplicity of suits, burdensome expense, and delays to plaintiffs, and vexatious litigation against defendants. * * *

> 'Indeed, if the plaintiff fails to sue for the entire damage done him by the tort, a second action for the damages omitted will be precluded by the judgment in the first suit brought and tried.'

The minority rule would seem to stem from the English case of *Brunsden v. Humphrey* (1884), 14 Q.B. 141. The facts in that case are set forth in the opinion in the Vasu case (145 Ohio St. at page 329, 61 N.E.2d at page 713), concluding with the statement:

> 'The Master of the Rolls, in his opinion, stated that the test is 'whether the same sort of evidence would prove the plaintiff's case in the two actions,' and that, in the action relating to the cab, 'it would be necessary to give evidence of the damage done to the plaintiff's vehicle. In the present action it would be necessary to give evidence of the bodily injury occasioned to the plaintiff, and of the sufferings which he has undergone, and for this purpose to call medical witnesses. This one test shows that the causes of action as to the damage done to the plaintiff's cab, and as to the injury occasioned to the plaintiff's person, are distinct."

The fallacy of the reasoning in the English court is best portrayed in the dissenting opinion of Lord Coleridge, as follows:

> 'It appears to me that whether the negligence of the servant, or the impact of the vehicle which the servant drove, be the technical cause of action, equally the cause is one and the same: that the injury done to the plaintiff is injury done to him at one and the same moment by one and the same act in respect of different rights, i.e. his person and his goods, I do not in the least deny; but it seems to me a subtlety not warranted by law to hold that a man cannot bring two actions, if he is injured in his arm and in his leg, but can bring two, if besides his arm and leg being injured, his trousers which contain his leg, and his coat-sleeve which contains his arm, have been torn.'

There appears to be no valid reason in these days of code pleading to adhere to the old English rule as to distinctions between injuries to the person and damages to the person's property resulting from a single tort. It would seem that the minority rule is bottomed on the proposition that the right of bodily security is fundamentally different from the right of security of property and, also, that, in actions predicated upon a negligent act, damages are a necessary element of each independent cause of action and no recovery may be had unless and until actual consequential damages are shown.

The decision of the question actually in issue in the Vasu case is found in paragraphs six, seven and eight of the syllabus, as it is quite apparent from the facts there that the first judgment, claimed to be res judicata in Vasu's action against the defendant, was rendered against Vasu's insurer in an action initiated by it after having paid Vasu for the damages to his automobile.

We, therefore, conclude and hold that, where a person suffers both personal injuries and property damage as a result of the same wrongful act, only a single cause of action arises, the different injuries occasioned thereby being separate items of damage from such act. It follows that paragraph four of the syllabus in the Vasu case must be overruled.

Accordingly, the judgment of the Court of Appeals is reversed, and final judgment is entered for defendant.

WEYGANDT, C. J., and STEWART, TAFT, MATTHIAS and BELL, JJ., concur.

[A concurring opinion of STEWART, Judge is omitted.]

[A dissenting opinion of ZIMMERMAN, Judge is omitted.]

Parklane Hosiery Company, Inc., et al. v. Shore

439 U.S. 322, 99 S.Ct. 645 (1979)

Mr. Justice STEWART delivered the opinion of the Court.

This case presents the question whether a party who has had issues of fact adjudicated adversely to it in an equitable action may be collaterally estopped from relitigating the same issues before a jury in a subsequent legal action brought against it by a new party.

The respondent brought this stockholder's class action against the petitioners in a Federal District Court. The complaint alleged that the petitioners, Parklane Hosiery Co., Inc. (Parklane), and 13 of its officers, directors, and stockholders, had issued a materially false and misleading proxy statement in connection with a merger.[1] The complaint sought damages, rescission of the merger, and recovery of costs.

---

1 The amended complaint alleged that the proxy statement that had been issued to the stockholders was false and misleading because it failed to disclose: (1) that the president of Parklane would financially benefit as a result of the company's going private; (2) certain ongoing negotiations that could have resulted in financial benefit to Parklane; and (3) that the appraisal of the fair value of Parklane stock was based on insufficient information to be accurate.

Before this action came to trial, the SEC filed suit against the same defendants in the Federal District Court, alleging that the proxy statement that had been issued by Parklane was materially false and misleading in essentially the same respects as those that had been alleged in the respondent's complaint. Injunctive relief was requested. After a 4-day trial, the District Court found that the proxy statement was materially false and misleading in the respects alleged, and entered a declaratory judgment to that effect. *SEC v. Parklane Hosiery Co.*, 422 F.Supp. 477. The Court of Appeals for the Second Circuit affirmed this judgment.

The respondent in the present case then moved for partial summary judgment against the petitioners, asserting that the petitioners were collaterally estopped from relitigating the issues that had been resolved against them in the action brought by the SEC. The District Court denied the motion on the ground that such an application of collateral estoppel would deny the petitioners their Seventh Amendment right to a jury trial. The Court of Appeals for the Second Circuit reversed, holding that a party who has had issues of fact determined against him after a full and fair opportunity to litigate in a non-jury trial is collaterally estopped from obtaining a subsequent jury trial of these same issues of fact. The appellate court concluded that "the Seventh Amendment preserves the right to jury trial only with respect to issues of fact, [and] once those issues have been fully and fairly adjudicated in a prior proceeding, nothing remains for trial, either with or without a jury." Because of an inter-circuit conflict, we granted certiorari.

I

The threshold question to be considered is whether, quite apart from the right to a jury trial under the Seventh Amendment, the petitioners can be precluded from relitigating facts resolved adversely to them in a prior equitable proceeding with another party under the general law of collateral estoppel. Specifically, we must determine whether a litigant who was not a party to a prior judgment may nevertheless use that judgment "offensively" to prevent a defendant from relitigating issues resolved in the earlier proceeding.[2]

---

2   In this context, offensive use of collateral estoppel occurs when the plaintiff seeks to foreclose the defendant from litigating an issue the defendant has previously litigated unsuccessfully in an action with another party. Defensive use occurs when a defendant seeks to prevent a plaintiff from asserting a claim the plaintiff has previously litigated and lost against another defendant.

A

Collateral estoppel, like the related doctrine of res judicata,[3] has the dual purpose of protecting litigants from the burden of relitigating an identical issue with the same party or his privy and of promoting judicial economy by preventing needless litigation. Until relatively recently, however, the scope of collateral estoppel was limited by the doctrine of mutuality of parties. Under this mutuality doctrine, neither party could use a prior judgment as an estoppel against the other unless both parties were bound by the judgment. Based on the premise that it is somehow unfair to allow a party to use a prior judgment when he himself would not be so bound, the mutuality requirement provided a party who had litigated and lost in a previous action an opportunity to relitigate identical issues with new parties.

By failing to recognize the obvious difference in position between a party who has never litigated an issue and one who has fully litigated and lost, the mutuality requirement was criticized almost from its inception. Recognizing the validity of this criticism, the Court in *Blonder-Tongue Laboratories, Inc. v. University of Illinois Foundation, supra*, abandoned the mutuality requirement, at least in cases where a patentee seeks to relitigate the validity of a patent after a federal court in a previous lawsuit has already declared it invalid. The "broader question" before the Court, however, was "whether it is any longer tenable to afford a litigant more than one full and fair opportunity for judicial resolution of the same issue." 402 U.S., at 328, 91 S.Ct., at 1442. The Court strongly suggested a negative answer to that question:

> "In any lawsuit where a defendant, because of the mutuality principle, is forced to present a complete defense on the merits to a claim which the plaintiff has fully litigated and lost in a prior action, there is an arguable misallocation of resources. To the extent the defendant in the second suit may not win by asserting, without contradiction, that the plaintiff had fully and fairly, but unsuccessfully, litigated the same claim in the prior suit, the defendant's time and money are diverted from alternative uses—productive or otherwise—to relitigation of a decided issue. And, still assuming that the issue was resolved correctly in the first suit, there is reason to be concerned about the plaintiff's allocation of resources. Permitting

---

3   Under the doctrine of res judicata, a judgment on the merits in a prior suit bars a second suit involving the same parties or their privies based on the same cause of action. Under the doctrine of collateral estoppel, on the other hand, the second action is upon a different cause of action and the judgment in the prior suit precludes relitigation of issues actually litigated and necessary to the outcome of the first action.

repeated litigation of the same issue as long as the supply of unrelated defendants holds out reflects either the aura of the gaming table or 'a lack of discipline and of disinterestedness on the part of the lower courts, hardly a worthy or wise basis for fashioning rules of procedure.' *Kerotest Mfg. Co. v. C-O-Two Co.*, 342 U.S. 180, 185, 72 S.Ct. 219, 222 (1952). Although neither judges, the parties, nor the adversary system performs perfectly in all cases, the requirement of determining whether the party against whom an estoppel is asserted had a full and fair opportunity to litigate is a most significant safeguard." Id., at 329, 91 S.Ct., at 1443.

B

The Blonder-Tongue case involved defensive use of collateral estoppel—a plaintiff was estopped from asserting a claim that the plaintiff had previously litigated and lost against another defendant. The present case, by contrast, involves offensive use of collateral estoppel—a plaintiff is seeking to estop a defendant from relitigating the issues which the defendant previously litigated and lost against another plaintiff. In both the offensive and defensive use situations, the party against whom estoppel is asserted has litigated and lost in an earlier action. Nevertheless, several reasons have been advanced why the two situations should be treated differently.

First, offensive use of collateral estoppel does not promote judicial economy in the same manner as defensive use does. Defensive use of collateral estoppel precludes a plaintiff from relitigating identical issues by merely "switching adversaries." *Bernhard v. Bank of America Nat. Trust & Savings Assn.*, 19 Cal.2d, at 813, 122 P.2d, at 895. Thus defensive collateral estoppel gives a plaintiff a strong incentive to join all potential defendants in the first action if possible. Offensive use of collateral estoppel, on the other hand, creates precisely the opposite incentive. Since a plaintiff will be able to rely on a previous judgment against a defendant but will not be bound by that judgment if the defendant wins, the plaintiff has every incentive to adopt a "wait and see" attitude, in the hope that the first action by another plaintiff will result in a favorable judgment. Thus offensive use of collateral estoppel will likely increase rather than decrease the total amount of litigation, since potential plaintiffs will have everything to gain and nothing to lose by not intervening in the first action.

A second argument against offensive use of collateral estoppel is that it may be unfair to a defendant. If a defendant in the first action is sued for small or nominal damages, he may have little incentive to defend vigorously, particularly if future suits are not foreseeable. The *Evergreens v. Nunan*, 141 F.2d 927, 929

(CA2); cf. *Berner v. British Commonwealth Pac. Airlines,* 346 F.2d 532 (CA2) (application of offensive collateral estoppel denied where defendant did not appeal an adverse judgment awarding damages of $35,000 and defendant was later sued for over $7 million). Allowing offensive collateral estoppel may also be unfair to a defendant if the judgment relied upon as a basis for the estoppel is itself inconsistent with one or more previous judgments in favor of the defendant.[4] Still another situation where it might be unfair to apply offensive estoppel is where the second action affords the defendant procedural opportunities unavailable in the first action that could readily cause a different result.

C

We have concluded that the preferable approach for dealing with these problems in the federal courts is not to preclude the use of offensive collateral estoppel, but to grant trial courts broad discretion to determine when it should be applied. The general rule should be that in cases where a plaintiff could easily have joined in the earlier action or where, either for the reasons discussed above or for other reasons, the application of offensive estoppel would be unfair to a defendant, a trial judge should not allow the use of offensive collateral estoppel.

In the present case, however, none of the circumstances that might justify reluctance to allow the offensive use of collateral estoppel is present. The application of offensive collateral estoppel will not here reward a private plaintiff who could have joined in the previous action, since the respondent probably could not have joined in the injunctive action brought by the SEC even had he so desired. Similarly, there is no unfairness to the petitioners in applying offensive collateral estoppel in this case. First, in light of the serious allegations made in the SEC's complaint against the petitioners, as well as the foreseeability of subsequent private suits that typically follow a successful Government judgment, the petitioners had every incentive to litigate the SEC lawsuit fully and vigorously.[5] Second, the judgment in the SEC action was not inconsistent with any previous

---

4   In Professor Currie's familiar example, a railroad collision injures 50 passengers all of whom bring separate actions against the railroad. After the railroad wins the first 25 suits, a plaintiff wins in suit 26. Professor Currie argues that offensive use of collateral estoppel should not be applied so as to allow plaintiffs 27 through 50 automatically to recover.

5   After a 4-day trial in which the petitioners had every opportunity to present evidence and call witnesses, the District Court held for the SEC. The petitioners then appealed to the Court of Appeals for the Second Circuit, which affirmed the judgment against them. Moreover, the petitioners were already aware of the action brought by the respondent, since it had commenced before the filing of the SEC action.

decision. Finally, there will in the respondent's action be no procedural opportunities available to the petitioners that were unavailable in the first action of a kind that might be likely to cause a different result.[6]

We conclude, therefore, that none of the considerations that would justify a refusal to allow the use of offensive collateral estoppel is present in this case. Since the petitioners received a "full and fair" opportunity to litigate their claims in the SEC action, the contemporary law of collateral estoppel leads inescapably to the conclusion that the petitioners are collaterally estopped from relitigating the question of whether the proxy statement was materially false and misleading.

II

The question that remains is whether, notwithstanding the law of collateral estoppel, the use of offensive collateral estoppel in this case would violate the petitioners' Seventh Amendment right to a jury trial.[7]

A

"[T]he thrust of the [Seventh] Amendment was to preserve the right to jury trial as it existed in 1791." *Curtis v. Loether,* 415 U.S. 189, 193, 94 S.Ct. 1005, 1007. At common law, a litigant was not entitled to have a jury determine issues that had been previously adjudicated by a chancellor in equity.

Recognition that an equitable determination could have collateral-estoppel effect in a subsequent legal action was the major premise of this Court's decision in *Beacon Theatres, Inc. v. Westover,* 359 U.S. 500, 79 S.Ct. 948. In that case the plaintiff sought a declaratory judgment that certain arrangements between it and the defendant were not in violation of the antitrust laws, and asked for an injunction to prevent the defendant from instituting an antitrust action to challenge the arrangements. The defendant denied the allegations and counterclaimed for treble damages under the antitrust laws, requesting a trial by jury of the issues common to both the legal and equitable claims. The Court of Appeals upheld denial of the request, but this Court reversed, stating:

"[T]he effect of the action of the District Court could be, as the Court of Appeals believed, 'to limit the petitioner's opportunity fully to try to a jury every

---

6 It is true, of course, that the petitioners in the present action would be entitled to a jury trial of the issues bearing on whether the proxy statement was materially false and misleading had the SEC action never been brought—a matter to be discussed in Part II of this opinion. But the presence or absence of a jury as factfinder is basically neutral, quite unlike, for example, the necessity of defending the first lawsuit in an inconvenient forum.

7 The Seventh Amendment provides: "In Suits at common law, where the value in controversy shall exceed twenty dollars, the right to jury trial shall be preserved . . . ."

issue which has a bearing upon its treble damage suit,' for determination of the issue of clearances by the judge might 'operate either by way of res judicata or collateral estoppel so as to conclude both parties with respect thereto at the subsequent trial of the treble damage claim.' " Id., at 504, 79 S.Ct., at 953.

It is thus clear that the Court in the Beacon Theatres case thought that if an issue common to both legal and equitable claims was first determined by a judge, relitigation of the issue before a jury might be foreclosed by res judicata or collateral estoppel. To avoid this result, the Court held that when legal and equitable claims are joined in the same action, the trial judge has only limited discretion in determining the sequence of trial and "that discretion . . . must, wherever possible, be exercised to preserve jury trial." Id., at 510, 79 S.Ct., at 956.[8]

Both the premise of *Beacon Theatres*, and the fact that it enunciated no more than a general prudential rule were confirmed by this Court's decision in *Katchen v. Landy*, 382 U.S. 323, 86 S.Ct. 467. In that case the Court held that a bankruptcy court, sitting as a statutory court of equity, is empowered to adjudicate equitable claims prior to legal claims, even though the factual issues decided in the equity action would have been triable by a jury under the Seventh Amendment if the legal claims had been adjudicated first. The Court stated:

"Both *Beacon Theatres* and *Dairy Queen* recognize that there might be situations in which the Court could proceed to resolve the equitable claim first even though the results might be dispositive of the issues involved in the legal claim." Id., at 339, 86 S.Ct., at 478.

Thus the Court in *Katchen v. Landy* recognized that an equitable determination can have collateral-estoppel effect in a subsequent legal action and that this estoppel does not violate the Seventh Amendment.

B

Despite the strong support to be found both in history and in the recent decisional law of this Court for the proposition that an equitable determination can have collateral-estoppel effect in a subsequent legal action, the petitioners argue that application of collateral estoppel in this case would nevertheless violate their Seventh Amendment right to a jury trial. The petitioners contend that since the scope of the Amendment must be determined by reference to the common law as it existed in 1791, and since the common law permitted collateral

---

8 Similarly, in both *Dairy Queen, Inc. v. Wood*, 369 U.S. 469, 82 S.Ct. 894, and *Meeker v. Ambassador Oil Corp.*, 375 U.S. 160, 84 S.Ct. 273, the Court held that legal claims should ordinarily be tried before equitable claims to preserve the right to a jury trial.

estoppel only where there was mutuality of parties, collateral estoppel cannot constitutionally be applied when such mutuality is absent.

The petitioners have advanced no persuasive reason, however, why the meaning of the Seventh Amendment should depend on whether or not mutuality of parties is present. A litigant who has lost because of adverse factual findings in an equity action is equally deprived of a jury trial whether he is estopped from relitigating the factual issues against the same party or a new party. In either case, the party against whom estoppel is asserted has litigated questions of fact, and has had the facts determined against him in an earlier proceeding. In either case there is no further factfinding function for the jury to perform, since the common factual issues have been resolved in the previous action. Cf. Ex parte Peterson, 253 U.S. 300, 310, 40 S.Ct. 543, 547 ("No one is entitled in a civil case to trial by jury, unless and except so far as there are issues of fact to be determined").

The Seventh Amendment has never been interpreted in the rigid manner advocated by the petitioners. On the contrary, many procedural devices developed since 1791 that have diminished the civil jury's historic domain have been found not to be inconsistent with the Seventh Amendment. See *Galloway v. United States*, 319 U.S. 372, 388-393, 63 S.Ct. 1077, 1086-1088 (directed verdict does not violate the Seventh Amendment); *Gasoline Products Co. v. Champlin Refining Co.*, 283 U.S. 494, 497-498, 51 S.Ct. 513-514 (retrial limited to question of damages does not violate the Seventh Amendment even though there was no practice at common law for setting aside a verdict in part); *Fidelity & Deposit Co. v. United States*, 187 U.S. 315, 319-321, 23 S.Ct. 120, 121-122 (summary judgment does not violate the Seventh Amendment).

The Galloway case is particularly instructive. There the party against whom a directed verdict had been entered argued that the procedure was unconstitutional under the Seventh Amendment. In rejecting this claim, the Court said:

"The Amendment did not bind the federal courts to the exact procedural incidents or details of jury trial according to the common law in 1791, any more than it tied them to the common-law system of pleading or the specific rules of evidence then prevailing. Nor were 'the rules of the common law' then prevalent, including those relating to the procedure by which the judge regulated the jury's role on questions of fact, crystalized in a fixed and immutable system. . . .

"The more logical conclusion, we think, and the one which both history and the previous decisions here support, is that the Amendment was designed to preserve the basic institution of jury trial in only its most fundamental elements, not the great mass of procedural forms and details, varying even then so widely among common-law jurisdictions." 319 U.S., at 390, 392, 63 S.Ct., at 1087 (foot-note omitted).

The law of collateral estoppel, like the law in other procedural areas defining the scope of the jury's function, has evolved since 1791. Under the rationale of the Galloway case, these developments are not repugnant to the Seventh Amendment simply for the reason that they did not exist in 1791. Thus if, as we have held, the law of collateral estoppel forecloses the petitioners from relitigating the factual issues determined against them in the SEC action, nothing in the Seventh Amendment dictates a different result, even though because of lack of mutuality there would have been no collateral estoppel in 1791.

The judgment of the Court of Appeals is

Affirmed.

Mr. Justice REHNQUIST, dissenting.

It is admittedly difficult to be outraged about the treatment accorded by the federal judiciary to petitioners' demand for a jury trial in this lawsuit. Outrage is an emotion all but impossible to generate with respect to a corporate defendant in a securities fraud action, and this case is no exception. But the nagging sense of unfairness as to the way petitioners have been treated, engendered by the *imprimatur* placed by the Court of Appeals on respondent's "heads I win, tails you lose" theory of this litigation, is not dispelled by this Court's antiseptic analysis of the issues in the case. It may be that if this Nation were to adopt a new Constitution today, the Seventh Amendment guaranteeing the right of jury trial in civil cases in federal courts would not be included among its provisions. But any present sentiment to that effect cannot obscure or dilute our obligation to enforce the Seventh Amendment, which was included in the Bill of Rights in 1791 and which has not since been repealed in the only manner provided by the Constitution for repeal of its provisions.

I

B

The Seventh Amendment requires that the right of trial by jury be "preserved." Because the Seventh Amendment demands preservation of the jury trial right, our cases have uniformly held that the content of the right must be judged by historical standards. If a jury would have been impaneled in a particular kind of case in 1791, then the Seventh Amendment requires a jury trial today, if either party so desires.

C

Judged by the foregoing principles, I think it is clear that petitioners were denied their Seventh Amendment right to a jury trial in this case. Neither respondent nor the Court doubts that at common law as it existed in 1791, petitioners would have been entitled in the private action to have a jury determine whether the proxy statement was false and misleading in the respects alleged. The reason is that at common law in 1791, collateral estoppel was permitted only where the parties in the first action were identical to, or in privity with, the parties to the subsequent action. It was not until 1971 that the doctrine of mutuality was abrogated by this Court in certain limited circumstances. *Blonder-Tongue Laboratories, Inc. v. University of Illinois Foundation*, 402 U.S. 313, 91 S.Ct. 1434. But developments in the judge-made doctrine of collateral estoppel, however salutary, cannot, consistent with the Seventh Amendment, contract in any material fashion the right to a jury trial that a defendant would have enjoyed in 1791. In the instant case, resort to the doctrine of collateral estoppel does more than merely contract the right to a jury trial: It eliminates the right entirely and therefore contravenes the Seventh Amendment.

The Court responds, however, that at common law "a litigant was not entitled to have a jury [in a subsequent action at law between the same parties] determine issues that had been previously adjudicated by a chancellor in equity," and that "petitioners have advanced no persuasive reason . . . why the meaning of the Seventh Amendment should depend on whether or not mutuality of parties is present." *Ante,* at 652, 654. But that is tantamount to saying that since a party would not be entitled to a jury trial if he brought an equitable action, there is no persuasive reason why he should receive a jury trial on virtually the same issues if instead he chooses to bring his lawsuit in the nature of a legal action. The persuasive reason is that the Seventh Amendment requires that a party's right to jury trial which existed at common law be "preserved" from incursions by the government or the judiciary. Whether this Court believes that use of a jury trial in a particular instance is necessary, or fair or repetitive is simply irrelevant. If that view is "rigid," it is the Constitution which commands that rigidity. To hold otherwise is to rewrite the Seventh Amendment so that a party is guaranteed a jury trial in civil cases unless this Court thinks that a jury trial would be inappropriate.

II

Even accepting, *arguendo*, the majority's position that there is no violation of the Seventh Amendment here, I nonetheless would not sanction the use of collateral estoppel in this case. The Court today holds:

"The general rule should be that in cases where a plaintiff could easily have joined in the earlier action or where, either for the reasons discussed above or for other reasons, the application of offensive estoppel would be unfair to a defendant, a trial judge should not allow the use of offensive collateral estoppel."

In my view, it is "unfair" to apply offensive collateral estoppel where the party who is sought to be estopped has not had an opportunity to have the facts of his case determined by a jury. Since in this case petitioners were not entitled to a jury trial in the Securities and Exchange Commission (SEC) lawsuit. I would not estop them from relitigating the issues determined in the SEC suit before a jury in the private action. I believe that several factors militate in favor of this result.

NOTES

1. What is the relationship between claim and issue preclusion? If claim preclusion did not apply, could Rush have successfully used issue preclusion against the City of Maple Heights?

2. What is the relationship between preclusion doctrine and joinder of claims under FRCP 8, 13, and 18?

3. And between preclusion doctrine and the jury trial right?

4. Might there be times when the process in the initial piece of litigation is so flawed that it should not have its normal, preclusive effect on later litigation?

C

EXPERIENTIAL ASSIGNMENT

1. Normal issue preclusion

- A v. X, (1), A prevails on an issue that was actually litigated and necessary for the decision.

- In A v. X, (2), where the same issue is present, X is precluded from relitigating the issue.

Sarah files a complaint against VeryCorp, claiming that she was injured by exposure to a product made by VeryCorp while at her office. Sarah wins a verdict that could not have been rendered unless the jury found the product "dangerous."

Sarah files a second action against VeryCorp, for wrongful death of her daughter, claiming that the same product is present in her home and that her daughter died as a result of her exposure to it. VeryCorp should be precluded from relitigating the "dangerousness" issue.

2. Non-mutual offensive issue preclusion (Parklane)

- A v. X, A prevails on an issue that was actually litigated and necessary for the decision.

- In B v. X, where the same issue is present, X is precluded from relitigating the issue.

Irakli, a brilliant law student, files a complaint against his law school for inducing his application and attendance with fraudulent employment statistics. Irakli wins a verdict that implies a necessary finding that the law school has engaged in fraud.

Sanya, also a brilliant law student attending the same school as Irakli in the same class as Irakli, files essentially the same complaint against the law school. The law school is precluded from relitigating the fraud-related fact issues.

3. Non-mutual defensive issue preclusion

- A v. X, X prevails on an issue that was actually litigated and necessary for the decision.

- In A v. Y, where the same issue is present, A is precluded from relitigating the issue.

Steve files a complaint against Sears Roebuck claiming that its agent, a salesman in a Kalamazoo Sears store, assaulted him while arresting Steve for allegedly stealing a Craftsman ratchet. The jury returns a verdict for Sears, making a special finding, necessary to the verdict, that the salesman did not use excessive force in restraining Steve.

Steve learns that the salesman has a million dollars from winning the lottery and files a complaint against the salesman for assault in the same incident. Steve should be precluded from relitigating the excessive force issue.

Prepare a Motion to Dismiss or a Motion for Partial Judgment based on Claim or Issue Preclusion in one or more of these three situations, as assigned by your professor.

Example Document

Just to satisfy your curiosity, here is the Final Order in Two Old Hippies. Consider what issues or claims would be precluded in any subsequent actions.

IN THE UNITED STATES DISTRICT COURT
FOR THE DISTRICT OF NEW MEXICO

TWO OLD HIPPIES, LLC,
      Plaintiff,

    vs.   No. CIV 10-0459 JB/RLP

CATCH THE BUS, LLC,
GARY MACK and FALLON MACK,
      Defendants.

FINAL JUDGMENT

THIS MATTER comes before the Court on: (i) the Court's Memorandum Opinion and Order, filed February 11, 2011 (Doc. 37); and (ii) the Court's Memorandum Opinion and Order, filed August 31, 2011 (Doc. 74). The February 11, 2011 Memorandum Opinion and Order dismissed all claims against Defendants Gary Mack and Fallon Mack and Plaintiff Two Old Hippies' claims under the Colorado Consumer Protection Act, C.R.S. §§ 6-1-101 through 6-1-115. The August 31, 2011 Memorandum Opinion and Order granted in part and denied in part the Plaintiff's Motion for Summary Judgment to Set the Amount of Damages, filed June 1, 2011 (Doc. 56), awarding Two Old Hippies $113,596.54 in compensatory damages, $300.00 in statutory damages under the New Mexico Unfair Practices Act, N.M.S.A. 1978, §§ 57-12-1 through 57-12-26, and $19,925.50 in attorneys' fees and $1,367.97 in taxes. Because the Court's Memorandum Opinions and Orders resolve all matters before it, the Court now enters final judgment.

IT IS ORDERED that final judgment is entered against Plaintiff Two Old Hippies, LLC, and for Defendants Gary Mack and Fallon Mack, and final judgment is entered for Two Old Hippies and against Defendant Catch the Bus, LLC, in the amount of $135,190.01.

_____
UNITED STATES DISTRICT JUDGE

Index